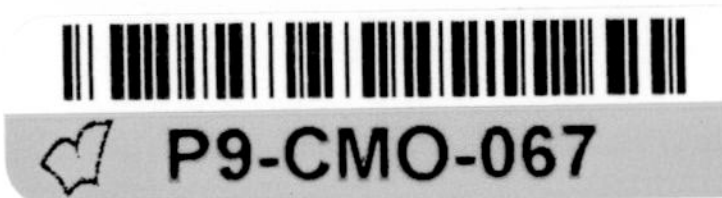

Fodor's

EXPLORING LONDON

Fodor's Travel Publications, Inc.
New York • Toronto • London • Sydney • Auckland

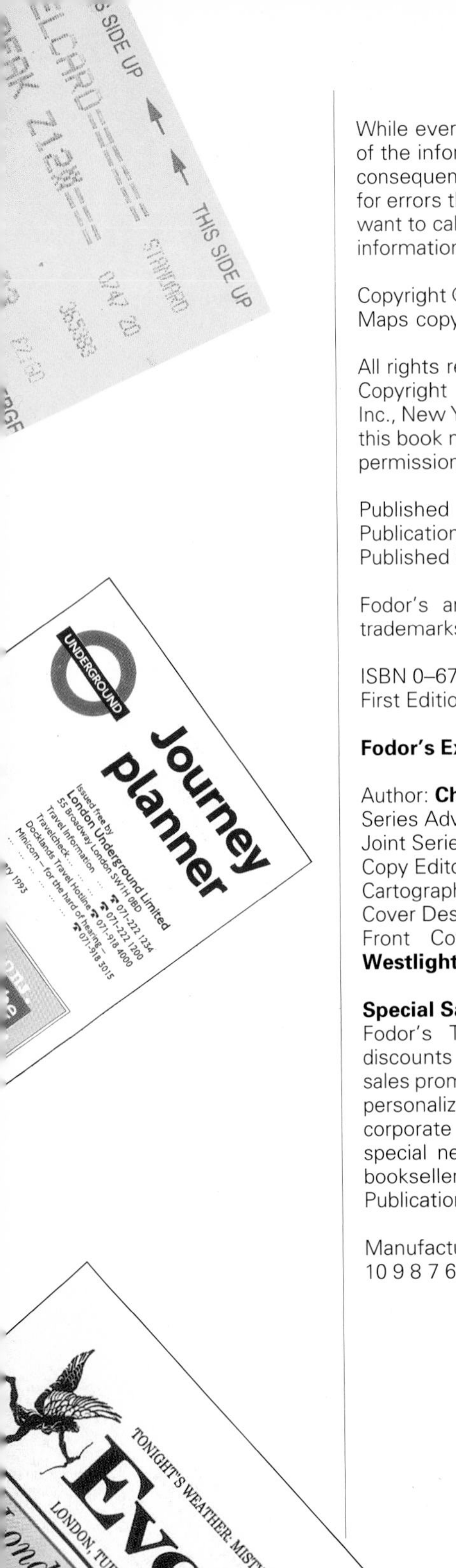

Published in the United States by Fodor's Travel Publications, Inc.
Published in the United Kingdon by AA Publishing.

Fodor's and Fodor's Exploring Guides are registered trademarks of Fodor's Travel Publications, Inc.

ISBN 0–679–02661–4
First Edition

Fodor's Exploring London

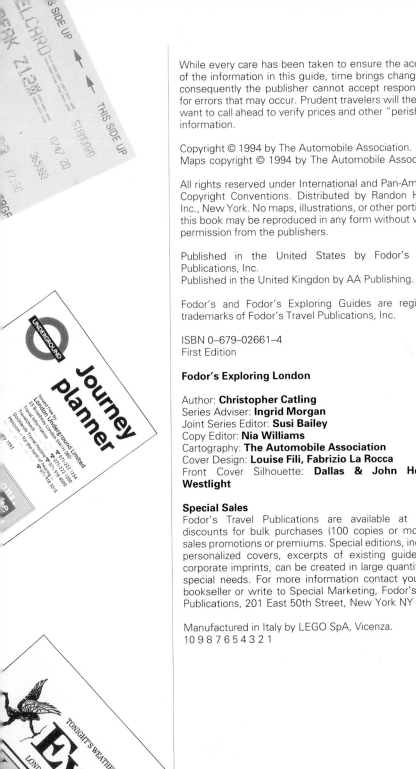

Author: **Christopher Catling**
Series Adviser: **Ingrid Morgan**
Joint Series Editor: **Susi Bailey**
Copy Editor: **Nia Williams**
Cartography: **The Automobile Association**
Cover Design: **Louise Fili, Fabrizio La Rocca**
Front Cover Silhouette: **Dallas & John Heaton/ Westlight**

Special Sales

Fodor's Travel Publications are available at special discounts for bulk purchases (100 copies or more) for sales promotions or premiums. Special editions, including personalized covers, excerpts of existing guides, and corporate imprints, can be created in large quantities for special needs. For more information contact your local bookseller or write to Special Marketing, Fodor's Travel Publications, 201 East 50th Street, New York NY 10022.

Manufactured in Italy by LEGO SpA, Vicenza.
10 9 8 7 6 5 4 3 2 1

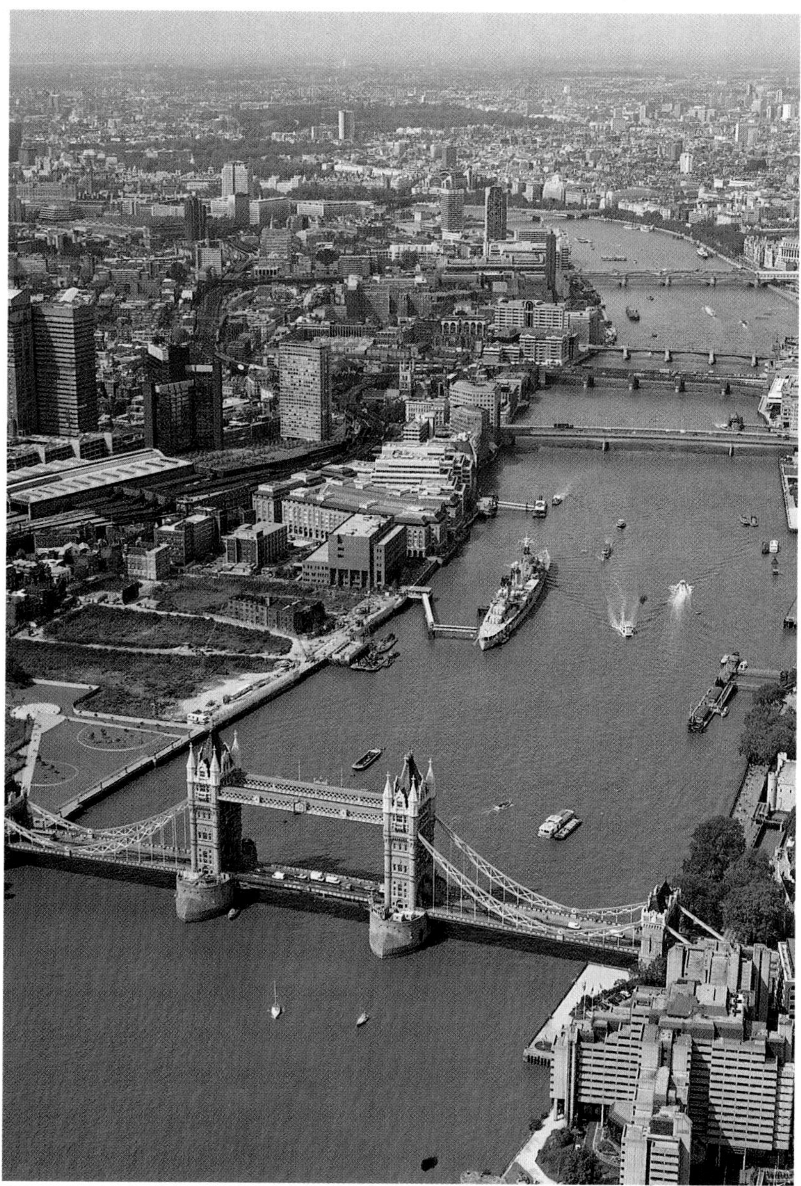

An aerial view of the Thames, looking upstream from Tower Bridge

Christopher Catling is the author of numerous books and articles on travel, including *Singapore* in the AA Essential Travel Guide series, *Tuscany & Umbria* in the AA European Regional Guide series, and *Amsterdam* in the Thomas Cook Travellers series. He lived in London for many years, getting to know the city intimately by walking everywhere in preference to driving or using public transport. He contributes articles to newspapers and magazines, and his recent books have included the *Economist Business Traveller's Guide to China*, the *Shell Guide to East Anglia* and the *Insight Guide to Oxford*.

How to use this book

This book is divided into five main sections:

- ❑ Section 1: ***London Is***
  Discusses aspects of life and living today, from politics to royalty.

- ❑ Section 2: ***London Was***
  Places the city in its historical context and explores those past events whose influences are felt to this day.

- ❑ Section 3: ***A to Z Section***
  Broken down into neighborhood chapters, it covers places to visit and includes walks and excursions. Within this section fall the Focus-on articles, which consider a variety of subjects in greater detail.

- ❑ Section 4: ***Travel Facts***
  Contains the strictly practical information vital for a successful trip.

- ❑ Section 5: ***Hotels and Restaurants***
  Recommended establishments throughout London, with a brief description of each.

How to use the rating system:
Most of the places described in this book have been given a separate rating:

▶▶▶ **Do not miss**

▶▶ **Highly recommended**

▶ **Worth seeing**

Not essential to see

Map references:
To make the location of a particular place easier to find, every main entry in this book has a map reference to the right of its name. This includes a number, followed by a letter, followed by another number, such as 176B3. The first number (176) refers to the page on which the map can be found. The letter (B) and the second number (3) pinpoint the square in which the place is located. The maps on the inside front cover and inside back cover are referred to as IFC and IBC, respectively.

Contents

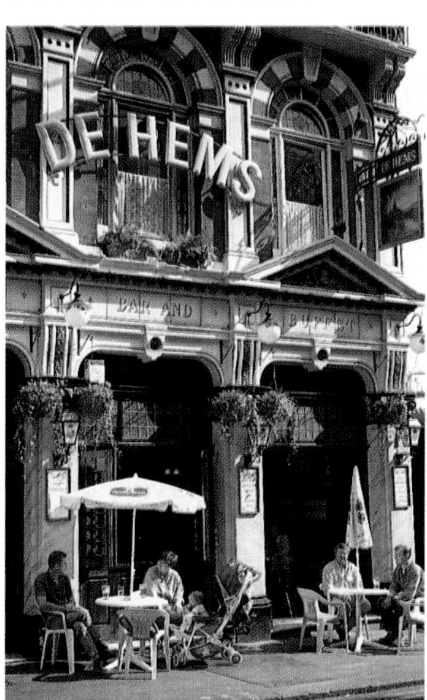

De Hems, a Dutch-style pub in Macclesfield Street

Quick reference

This quick reference guide highlights the features of the book you will use most often: the maps; the introductory features; the Focus-on articles; the walks and the excursions.

Maps

London Is

London Was

Focus on

Quick reference

Walks

Excursions

The Lloyd's Building, Lime Street

James Bishop became editor of the *Illustrated London News* in 1970, and has been Editor-in-Chief of the ILN Group since 1987 and a director of the Illustrated London News and Sketch Ltd since 1973. Married with two children, he lives in London, not far from where he was born in 1929.

by James Bishop

Although I was born in London and have lived most of my life here, I still bump into something new every day; something I had not known before, or something that has happened while I wasn't looking. The river is the key to London's history, the one constant in a city that is forever changing—sometimes successfully, sometimes with disastrous results. What particularly delights me about London is that change does not totally obscure the past. It is still possible to see something of the city's origins. Bits of the Roman wall stand proud and uncovered among the tarmacked city streets, and in Leadenhall Market, which is built on the site of the great Roman basilica, you will find part of its foundation behind racks of suits in the basements of a men's outfitters. And around every corner you will find a sudden oasis of colour and quiet. London is a green city, and where there is not room for a garden then trees are encouraged to burst out of pavements, and flowers to bloom from boxes on flat-dwellers' window-sills.

It is this wonderful diversity that gives London its particular spice. It has more to offer than anyone can hope to absorb, but I believe that even a day's exploration will provide more pleasant surprises than can be found anywhere else.

Janet Street-Porter trained as an architect, but moved into television in 1975. She has produced several series for Channel 4 and ITV, including the BAFTA winning "Network 7". Since joining the BBC in 1988 as Head of Youth Programmes, her department was expanded in May 1991 to take in entertainment features.

My London

by Janet Street-Porter

I was born and grew up in Fulham, then a working-class area excitingly close to the King's Road. In the 1960s I spent many a school lunchtime hanging out around the trendy boutiques, trying to look groovy rather than the gangling six-footer in school uniform I really was. King's Road is no longer my scene, but I do enjoy walking along many of the back streets near by, such as Royal Avenue with its perfect example of a Georgian square. Fulham has now become very middle class, although pockets of the old Fulham I knew still survive. Bishop's Park remains a wonderful place to walk by the river, and the streets around Hurlingham Park are unchanged and full of interesting houses—a mix of Victorian and Edwardian terraces, particularly along Hurlingham Road.

Today I live on the edge of the City of London. During the week it is incredibly noisy, but at six o'clock in the evenings and at weekends it is amazingly tranquil. My favourite walk is from Clerkenwell, through the back of the Barbican (where you can still see remnants of London's Roman wall) and through the heart of the City past the Bank of England and the new Lloyd's Building to Tower Bridge. When you cross the bridge and sit down at Butler's Wharf for a drink, you can look back at your route and at the skyline of the City, one of Europe's historic gems.

LONDON IS

LONDON IS *a melting pot*

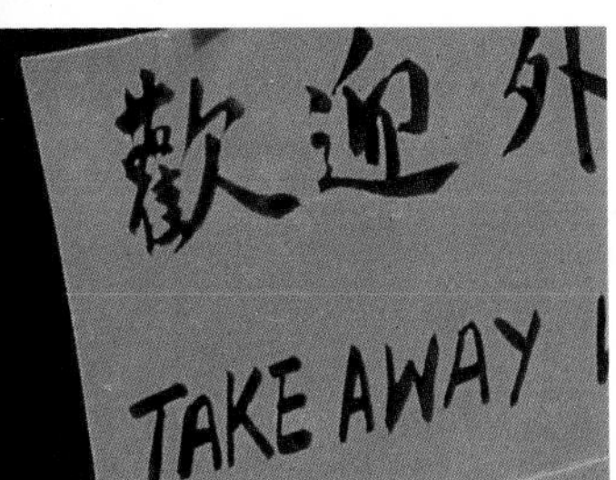

■ The term "Londoner" embraces people of every race and creed. Throughout history, London has served as a magnet to foreign traders, has offered a place of refuge to people fleeing persecution, and, as the capital of an empire which once spanned the globe, has absorbed great numbers of immigrants. The result is a multiethnic city where the worst excesses of racial tension are remarkably rare. .....■

As early as the 7th century, the Venerable Bede called London "a mart of many peoples," and social historians say that the rapid growth in London's population during the Middle Ages can only be explained by large-scale immigration. Among the later migrants were Jews expelled from Portugal and Spain, who arrived via the Netherlands after 1656, when Oliver Cromwell extended an official welcome, and Huguenots from France, who settled in the Soho and Spitalfields areas after 1685, when Louis XIV denied their right to religious freedom by revoking the Edict of Nantes. It was during this period that London became the most populous city in Western Europe, overtaking Paris, Venice, Naples, and Milan as its population grew from around 200,000 in 1600 to 600,000 by 1700.

From the late 18th century onwards mass migration, reflecting the miseries of war, tyranny, and political upheaval, swelled the population of London even further: Refugees from the French Revolution and its aftermath began to arrive from 1794 on, followed by Scottish and Irish settlers during the famine years of the 1840s.

Antisemitic pogroms in Russia and Eastern Europe brought Jewish refugees in the 1880s, and another wave arrived in the 1930s fleeing Fascist persecution. Londoners might have reacted antagonistically to all these newcomers but most did not: When Sir Oswald Mosley, leader of the Fascist Blackshirts, tried to march through the streets of the East End in 1936, 500,000 Londoners turned out to stop him.

Postwar migration In the postwar era, many Londoners, made homeless by the Blitz, were rehoused in new towns (such as Bracknell, Harlow, and Hemel Hempstead); others left the country altogether, seeking a new life in Australia, Canada, or New Zealand. To compensate for the labor shortage, Commonwealth citizens were encouraged to settle in London to work in the transport system or the National Health Service or on construction projects such as Heathrow and Gatwick airports. Greek and Turkish Cypriots,

In London's Chinatown

Vietnamese, Chinese, Bangladeshi, and Ugandan Asian refugees, fleeing from warfare or dictatorship, also joined London's communities, although not all of them managed to find work; unemployment in London is highest among ethnic minorities.

Integration Despite, or perhaps because, of this long history of migration, London is generally free of racial tension. A wide range of ethnic traditions has been absorbed into London life: It has the biggest Caribbean carnival in Europe—the Notting Hill Carnival that takes place during the last weekend in August; the splendid Regent's Park Central Mosque has added to its rich architectural heritage; and London would be a duller place to eat without the range of good, cheap restaurants serving Armenian or Malaysian food, and many regional Chinese and Indian dishes. Thanks to hard-working Asian entrepreneurs, every neighborhood has corner shops that are open all hours, and the drab streets of Brick Lane have been turned into a bust-ling Little India district, full of street stalls, stores selling exotic fabrics, and restaurants.

❑ London's population reached a peak of around 8.6 million in 1939. Since then it has fallen to 6.7 million—the highest of any city in Europe and about 12 percent of the total UK population—but the numbers are still falling, by around 10 percent a year, as people move out to greener suburbs and commute into the city to work. Around 1.25 million commuters travel in and out every day from places as far afield as Oxford, Brighton, or Peterborough. London also receives 23 million visitors a year from all over the globe. Given these figures, it is not surprising to discover that London's bus and subway network carries 5 million passengers a day. ❑

A city of ethnic diversity

Politics and problems

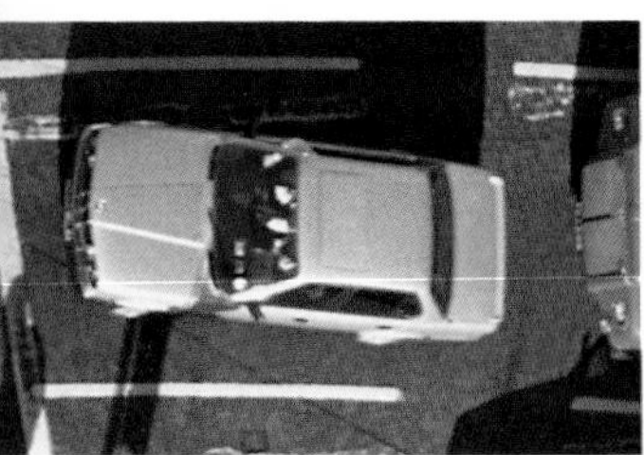

■ London is full of symbolic monuments and buildings, none more potent than the Houses of Parliament, known as 'the mother of Parliaments'. To many Londoners, however, politics is not just something that goes on within the House of Commons: it is part of daily life, from litter to the state of the city's roads and transport. .....■

London is run by a number of local borough governments; it is the only major city in the world that does not have a single elected body responsible for its infrastructure. This state of affairs reflects the power of the national government, which abolished the Greater London Council (GLC) in 1986, regarding it as too left-wing, its policies at odds with those of Margaret Thatcher's party. The GLC had frequently courted controversy by channeling arts funding to left-wing theater groups at the expense of established and so-called élitist bodies, such as the Royal Opera and Royal Shakespeare Company. It also hung a huge banner across the façade of County Hall, its headquarters, proclaiming the number of Londoners who were out of work. The banner was a constant irritant to members of the government having tea on the terrace of the Houses of Parliament opposite and some say this was the last straw.

❑ Visitors sometimes expect to see the city as Dickens described it, its dark medieval alleys made darker still by fog as thick as pea soup. Smog was no joke, however: It killed plants and trees, turned honey-colored buildings black, left encrustations on the varnish covering historic paintings, bleached clothes and ancient fabrics and caused great damage to human health. In the worst winter smogs of the 19th century, theater-goers could not see the actors on stage for smoke, and pedestrians could hardly see their feet. One of the last smogs to hit the city, the "killer smog" of December 1952, caused an estimated 4,000 deaths among bronchial sufferers, and the resulting outcry led to London being declared a smokeless zone under the Clean Air Act of 1956. ❑

Litter and homelessness Political conflict did not end with the GLC's abolition; it simply moved onto a

Sleeping on the streets

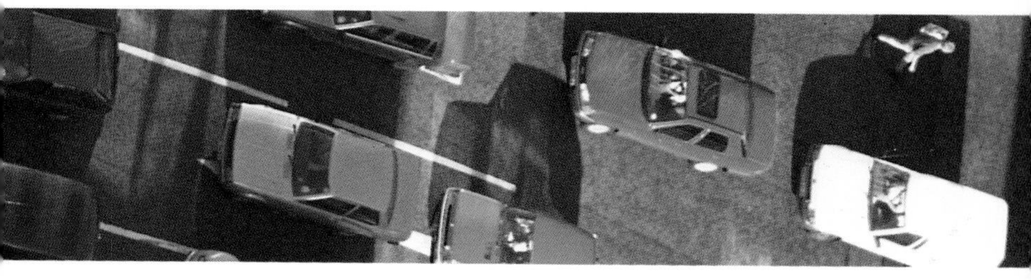

broader stage. The national government has a powerful grip on the budgets of local authorities and often intervenes, through a process known as "capping," if any borough threatens to overspend. Some boroughs have responded by cutting expenditure on street cleaning and other services, arguing that limited funds must be spent on essentials, such as housing and education. Litter has thus been turned into a pawn in the political game and is an all too familiar sight in certain parts of the city. More distressing is the huge number of people who sleep out on London's streets, huddling for shelter in shop doorways because they have nowhere else to go. The sight provokes puzzlement and anger in Londoners, most of whom are unsure of the causes or the solution. It is estimated that about 2,000 people sleep outdoors in London every night, and the increasing visibility of this problem has turned homelessness into a hot political issue.

Transport and pollution Another pressing problem is the sheer quantity of traffic and the resulting pollution. London made great strides to solve its pollution problems following the Clean Air Acts of 1956 and 1968. Smog, a noxious mixture of smoke, chemical fumes and fog that had characterized London for centuries, became a thing of the past when coal burning was banned, and industry and homeowners were encouraged to switch to oil, gas, and electricity for heating and power. Many buildings were cleaned of the sooty encrustations blackening their stonework—the Houses of Parliament and Westminster Abbey are among the most recent to be restored to pristine condition. A new menace, however, is less visible but equally damaging: photochemical smog, resulting from the action of sunlight on vehicle exhaust emissions and causing a condition similar to hay fever. Other vehicle pollutants contribute to acid rain. Several measures are under consideration, from electronic road pricing to high gasoline taxes, all designed to discourage car use. Critics say a better solution would be a much improved and subsidized public transport system. The River Thames could also play an important role in the future: it was a vital transportation artery until this century and could easily become so again.

Combatting vehicle pollution

Many of the 23 million visitors to London come for the same reason as the cat in the nursery rhyme: to look at the Queen, or at least to look at the palaces, jewels, and ceremonies associated with royalty. Ironically, fascination with things royal tends to be strongest among visitors from republican countries, while the Queen's own subjects are increasingly skeptical about the role of the monarchy. ....

The fire that damaged the State Apartments at Windsor Castle in 1992 did not provoke sympathy for the Queen, as might be expected; in fact there was a public outcry against the idea of taxpayers funding the restoration of the royal palace while the Queen, the richest woman in the world, contributed nothing.

The controversy came at the end of a year which the Queen described as an *annus horribilis* (a dreadful year). It had seen the break-up of two royal marriages, including that of Prince Charles to Princess Diana, much hounding of the royal family by the press, and calls for the Queen to pay tax on her vast annual income, "just like any ordinary citizen." This last demand was one to which the Queen did concede, marking an important stage in a long-running saga: the definition of an appropriate role for monarchy in the modern age.

Newspaper polls suggest that half Britain's population would like to see an end to the monarchy, and some say that Britain would long ago have become a republic but for one thing—the thought of who might be elected President.

The succession If the British people were allowed to elect a monarch from the present royal family, the Princess Royal (Princess Anne) would probably romp to victory. She represents the modern face of monarchy better than any of her siblings and is widely admired for her work for the Save the Children Fund. By contrast, Prince Charles is seen as a forlorn figure, still seeking a role. He has espoused many causes, but only with his comments on the excesses of modern architecture has he ever really spoken to the nation's heart.

Trooping the Colour

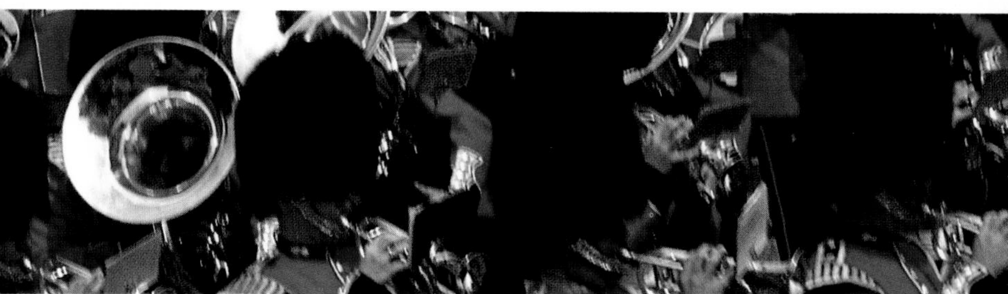

The royal year The Queen's official life follows an established pattern. The New Year is usually spent at Sandringham, in Norfolk, which was bought in 1861 for the Prince of Wales (later Edward VII). February and March often involve overseas tours but she returns to London, dividing her time between Buckingham Palace and Windsor Castle, for the spring and early summer. On the second Saturday in June she travels down the Mall in a horse-drawn carriage for the Trooping the Colour ceremony in Horse Guards, in celebration of her official birthday (her real one is on April 21st). June is also the month when the Queen goes to the races, often to see her own horses compete, for the Derby and for Ascot Week (famous for the showy hats worn by female socialites). In July the Queen hosts garden parties at Buckingham Palace for the great and worthy, before heading north to Scotland, to visit Holyrood House, Edinburgh and then Balmoral Castle for the grouse-shooting season. Foreign tours may take place in September but the Queen is back for the State Opening of Parliament (late October or early November), which takes place in the House of Lords; no monarch has been admitted to the Commons since 1642, when Charles I burst in demanding the arrest of five Members of Parliament. In November the Queen lays a wreath to commemorate the war dead at the Cenotaph in Whitehall on Remembrance Sunday.

❑ The most ancient and romantic symbol of monarchy is a simple block of sandstone set in the base of the Coronation Chair in Westminster Abbey. It came from Ireland, where it was known as *Lia Fail*, Stone of Destiny, and was used to crown the kings at Tara perhaps as early as the 4th or 5th centuries. It then went to Scotland, and its first recorded use was in 1057, when Macbeth's stepson, Lulach, was crowned king of Scotland at Scone, in Perthshire. Edward I carried it off to Westminster in 1296 and it has been used for the coronation of every English monarch since. Some Scots have never forgiven Edward's theft, and the stone was taken from the abbey by Scottish nationalists in 1950 but was recovered by the English in April 1951. ❑

The Queen in bejeweled splendor

Styles and trends

■ London likes to think of itself as one of the world's style capitals, giving birth to new ideas that become world fashions. The last time this happened in any big way was in the mid-1970s, when punk was born in the King's Road in Chelsea, and designers from Tokyo to New York began producing black clothes covered in studs, zippers, and safety pins. It has been a long time since such an idea came out of London—but who knows what lies around the corner? .....■

London stars in the 1950s were singers like Tommy Steele and Joe Brown, with their "Cockney" accents—quite acceptable to most parents. Youngsters dressed like their parents, except for the Teddy Boys, who were generally thought of as a rough crowd.

Suddenly, towards the end of the 1960s, youth began to create its own fashions. The King's Road, along with Carnaby Street, became the center of all that was hip and new in the London of the Swinging Sixties. Boutiques like Mary Quant's Bazaar became the trendsetters for those "dedicated followers of fashion" sung about by the Kinks. London also dominated the music scene, especially after the Beatles made this city their home: They, the Who, and the Rolling Stones dominated the pop charts on both sides of the Atlantic.

Patriotic punk

Thirty years later, the innocent, fun London pictured with its "Bobbies on their bicycles, two by two" in songs such as "England swings like a pendulum do" is just a memory, but anyone nostalgic for the past can join a Rock Tour of London (tel. 071 734 0227), which takes you to places like Abbey Road, where the Beatles album cover was shot, the clubs where they and other groups performed, and the homes (past and present) of famous rock stars such as Mick Jagger.

Punk By contrast, punk has no lasting memorials, unless you count Vivienne Westwood's clothes shop, World's End (No. 430 King's Road), which still sells punk styles. You can also see "punks" hanging around the King's Road on summer weekends, especially on the square opposite Chelsea Town Hall—but these are semiprofessionals: art students, by and large, who have found that they can supplement their grants by dyeing their hair with lurid colors and posing for photographs (they expect a tip, of course). They have little in common with the raw, vicious, anti-establishment music, clothing, and attitudes that were born in London during the long, hot summers of 1975 and 1976, although punk ideas have been absorbed into the amorphous style that characterizes many of today's young Londoners.

Yuppies and the Me generation In the 1980s London took its tune from America, and the streets were crammed with 18-year-old Porsche owners doing global deals over their mobile phones and putting down options on penthouse apartments (yet to be built) in the Docklands. Something of this era still hangs around: Walls in the Docklands bear fading graffiti scrawled with blunt messages by disaffected East Enders, such as "Mug a yuppie" and "Class War." Another relic of the era is the Design Museum at Butler's Wharf, conceived in an era in which it was chic to live in any type of converted industrial space, and equally chic to decorate your home with the kind of hard-edged minimalist objects that the Design Museum displays.

Mary Quant, 1960s fashion queen

Full circle In the 1990s, the style that characterizes young Londoners can best be described as eclectic. There is often talk of global love, a New Age—all faintly reminiscent of the Sixties. Care for the environment is the new issue of the day, and many Londoners have taken to cycling in a big way—not just on any old bike, but on expensive machines on which, dressed in skintight lycra, complete with pollution masks and crash helmets, they cruise past frustrated drivers in traffic jams.

The music that is listened to by young Londoners owes much to styles born on the streets of America, but London has not entirely lost its edge as a breeding ground for new talent. One of the most exciting and original sounds to emerge recently in this multi-ethnic city is traditional Indian sitar and tabla music set to the rhythms of Western pop. This music, which is called Bhangra Rock or Gujarati Rock, has yet to reach mainstream culture, but that may only be a matter of time.

■ From double-decker buses to soldiers in red tunics and bearskin helmets guarding Buckingham Palace, London is a city steeped in tradition and pageantry. No matter what time of year you visit this city, there is bound to be some colorful event going on. .....■

The most famous of London's regular events is the Changing of the Guard. It is worth remembering that this takes place in several different locations: In summer the crowds at Buckingham Palace often block the view, and you may prefer the alternative ceremonies at Whitehall or St. James's Palace, while the hour-long event at Windsor Castle, with its marching bands and music, is the best of all.

January's big event is the Lord Mayor of Westminster's New Year's Day Parade. This only started in 1986 but has become a popular attraction, with floats, bands, and American-style cheerleaders, who march from Piccadilly to Hyde Park starting at 12:30p.m. On the anniversary of Charles I's execution (January 30th) members of the Royal Stuart Society, in appropriate costume, retrace the monarch's route to the scaffold from St. James's Palace and lay a wreath on his statue at the head of Whitehall.

Shrove Tuesday, which usually falls in February, is celebrated with pancake races in Carnaby Street; seven weeks later, on Easter Sunday, there is a carnival in Battersea Park, while on Easter Monday there is a parade of working horses (still used to draw brewers' carts) in Regent's Park at noon.

In May another piece of pageantry takes place in Horse Guards Parade, called Beating the Retreat, when military bands mark the setting of the sun and perform by floodlight (advance reservation essential: details from Premier Box Office, tel. 071 976 7115). Chelsea Pensioners parade in honour of their founder, Charles II, on Oak Apple Day, May 29th (see pages 92–3), and every Wednesday evening in May and June you can see traditional Morris dancers performing outside Westminster Abbey.

There are festivals galore in July (one of the best is the City of London Festival—contact the City Arts Trust, tel. 071 377 0540 for details) but for something more unusual you can watch the start of the Swan Upping

❑ The Trooping the Colour ceremony takes place in June, but it is a matter of pure luck whether you will be able to get a ticket (50,000 people apply for 4,000 seats). To try, write requesting tickets (a maximum of two) with a stamped, addressed envelope to The Brigade Major, Trooping the Colour, Household Division, Horse Guards, Whitehall, between January 1st and March 1st. You can also apply for tickets to the dress rehearsals on the two preceding Saturdays, with a better chance of success. ❑

Bearskins and bayonets

ceremony at Temple Stairs on the Embankment: From here, the Queen's Swan Keeper travels upriver to Henley-on-Thames to mark the cygnets born that year (which enjoy royal protection).

The annual Costermonger's Harvest Festival, held in early October at St. Martin-in-the-Fields, Trafalgar Square, brings together the hardy characters who sell fruit and vegetables from stalls all over London. It is here that you are most likely to see London's famous Pearly Kings and Queens, so called because of their coats covered with buttons made of mother of pearl. They were originally elected by costermongers to act as unofficial community leaders, sorting out disputes between street traders, who were reluctant to involve the police in their affairs. Today most Pearly Kings and Queens devote their spare time to raising money for charity.

On the first Sunday in November you can watch the start of the famous London to Brighton Veteran Car Run; only cars made before 1905 can take part, and their owners dress in period costumes. The rally commemorates the abolition in 1896 of the law requiring all cars to be preceded by someone walking with a red warning flag. The second Saturday in November sees the colorful Lord Mayor's Show (see page 163), and soon afterwards numerous events lead up to Christmas, from the turning on of the lights in Oxford and Regent Streets to carols around the tree in Trafalgar Square (every day at 4p.m. from mid-December on) Even Christmas Day itself, one of the quietest days in the London year, has its traditional outdoor event: the annual Peter Pan Cup swimming race, when competitors brave the bitter cold to swim the Serpentine in Hyde Park.

The Lord Mayor's Show

London is in an almost constant state of flux, as buildings are knocked down and new ones are put up in their place, or historic buildings are restored to pristine splendor. Here is a summary of the main changes that have taken place within the last 10 years and of the major developments that are still on the drawing board. .....

Fleet Street Although Fleet Street still looks the same, the newspaper printworks and the journalists have gone, scattered to various parts of the city, including Marsh Wall (the *Daily Telegraph*) and Wapping (*The Times*, *Sunday Times*, *Sun,* and *News of the World*.) Strikes and violence accompanied the break-up of Fleet Street (and the break-up of the once powerful print unions), as newspaper proprietors embraced new technology and moved into new purpose-designed premises. Some of these are important landmarks of modern architecture: One of the best is the *Observer* building in Queenstown Road, Battersea, opened in 1988. Another fine building associated with the newspaper industry is Bracken House (in Cannon Street), the pink building put up for the *Financial Times* in 1956–59 and recently extended with sympathy and imagination for new owners.

Lloyd's (by Richard Rogers)

The Thames embankments Post-modernism has broken out all over London but is especially striking along the Thames. At Vauxhall Bridge is the conspicuous green and white building, completed in 1992, that houses the headquarters of the secretive MI6, the government organization responsible for "foreign intelligence" (or, in plain terms, spying). Further east, one of the leading proponents of the postmodernist style, the architect Terry Farrell, has built an eight-story office block above Charing Cross Station, which seems to hover like a giant glowering beetle above the water. On the opposite bank, at Waterloo Station, a major extension was completed in 1992 to serve trains and passengers using the Channel Tunnel. This is expected to be the catalyst for a major redevelopment of the whole south bank of the Thames, long the poor relation, lined with dull industrial buildings. Visitors to London in the mid-1990s can expect to see the stretch from County Hall to London Bridge slowly transformed into a pedestrianized area of shops, hotels, offices, gardens, and entertainment centers.

Docklands The availability of so much development land within the core areas of London (including a 50-hectare project for King's Cross, plus the wholesale redevelopment of Spitalfields, London Wall and the area around St. Paul's Cathedral) may mean even slower progress in developing the Docklands, already hit by the

The Nat West Tower

effects of recession. Canary Wharf, the largest commercial development Europe has ever seen, is already a major landmark, but it remains to be seen whether it will ever be completed. The government has announced plans to extend the Underground system to the Docklands (the so-called Jubilee Line extension) on the assumption that improved access will overcome the reluctance of many companies to move here. In reality, the future of the area will depend very much on whether London remains one of the world's most important financial centers, against some very stiff competition from Frankfurt.

The future now Several projects in London show what the city may look like in the near future. The massive Broadgate development, alongside Liverpool Street Station, is a typical example, using steel frames hung with cladding. Critics call it façadism, but the intimacy of this design, with its courtyards and covered walkways, greenery and sculpture, is a huge improvement on the bleak and windswept architecture of the 1960s and 1970s, typified by Paternoster Square, the area around St. Paul's. This area is itself due to be redeveloped, and the featureless 1960s buildings will be replaced with much friendlier buildings in the Italianate style, currently all the rage among classicists in the architectural profession. There are those who would dearly love to turn London into a new Venice, with paved squares, colonnades, and soaring belltowers. For a vision of how that might look, go and see the architect Quinlan Terry's work at Richmond Riverside (see page 231.)

Battersea Power Station

The cradle of the nation London is a city so steeped in history that it sometimes seems as if every building has its own story to tell, from the humblest pub with its low, beamed ceilings to the grandest palaces and cathedrals.

London has played an extraordinarily dominant role in the history both of Britain and of the world: Within living memory London was the biggest city on the earth, the capital of a powerful empire spanning the world,

LONDON WAS

upon which it was said that the sun never set. Since the end of World War II, with the rapid dismantling of the empire, Britain and London have diminished greatly in importance and influence. That process seems set to continue, as closer integration with Europe will inevitably mean that less power is wielded by London-based politicians and a great deal more by institutions based in Brussels or Strasbourg. Even so, London retains many reminders of its past history, in its buildings, its museums, its stately palaces, its statues and works of art. Visiting them reminds us of all the many great events that the city has witnessed in its long history, such as the first performances of Shakespeare's plays or the creation of the first democratic Parliament.

■ Little did the Romans suspect that the city they founded on the north bank of the Thames in A.D.43 would one day eclipse Rome itself and grow to be the biggest city in the world. Surprisingly enough, substantial remains of that first Roman city can still be seen today, despite 2,000 years of rebuilding and development. .....■

London owes its existence to chance and the building of a bridge. The Emperor Claudius had intended that Colchester, in Essex, should be the capital of Roman Britain, and that is where the Roman invasion force headed in A.D.43 after landing near the site of today's Richborough, in Kent. To reach Colchester, the seat of King Cunobelin (Shakespeare's Cymbeline), who ruled all of south-east England, the Romans had to cross the Thames at some point. They constructed a wooden bridge not very far away from the site of today's London Bridge—in fact, though London Bridge has been rebuilt many times since, it has never moved very far from the spot that the Romans originally chose. London's bridge became the focus of the road network that the Romans built to enable troops to be moved quickly around the newly conquered province of Britannia. Market forces began to operate, for where there is a major road junction, with troops stationed and ships calling, merchants will inevitably set up shops. Before very long, *Londinium* was a thriving settlement and port.

Mithras, the Roman army's cult god

The Boudiccan Revolt *Londinium* was strategically important to the Romans and, as a new settlement, was a symbol of Rome's colonial ambitions. As such it was a target for those disaffected Iron Age peoples who had not welcomed the invasion. They formed an alliance under the leadership of Boudicca (Boadicea), leader of the Iceni tribe, whose territory covered much of modern Norfolk. Boudicca chose her time well, waiting until Suetonius Paulinus, the Roman governor, was putting down a revolt in Anglesey, before marching on *Londinium* in A.D.60. The city was burned to the ground and its inhabitants massacred. What happened after that is not entirely known. Flushed with victory, Boudicca's troops pursued the Roman cavalry to a battle site somewhere in the Midlands, where, according to Tacitus, the Romans achieved an easy victory through superior discipline, killing 80,000 British, while only 400 Romans died. Boudicca is said by Tacitus to have poisoned herself, but other contemporary writers suggest that she died of an illness. It is said that the Britons gave her a rich burial, and many people believe that she is buried, complete with chariot and retainers, beneath the round barrow, or burial mound, that sits on Parliament Hill, on Hampstead Heath. Boudicca has

Boudicca, the Celtic warrior queen

become a popular folk figure, a symbol of resistance against tyranny. Ironically, the magnificent bronze statue of her that stands on the Thames at Victoria Embankment was made in the 1850s, at exactly the time when Britain was itself pursuing a policy of imperial expansion.

Roman London London was rapidly rebuilt and, because its location was clearly more convenient than Colchester, it became the official administrative capital of Britannia sometime around A.D.100. As such, London had its full complement of civic buildings, palaces, and temples; the Museum of London (see page 166) has excellent reconstructions showing the appearance and development of the Roman city from this time. Of visible remains, there is the Temple of Mithras (see page 167) and substantial parts of the city wall built around A.D.200; one well-preserved stretch can be seen just north of Tower Hill, by the tube station, and there is another good stretch still serving as the churchyard boundary wall next to the church of All Hallows on the Wall, near the corner of London Wall and Broad Street. You can follow the whole route of the wall (1.7 miles/2.8km) with the aid of the *London Wall Walk* leaflet published by the Museum of London.

■ **Major developments took place in the medieval period that have had lasting effects on the shape of London—most notably, the founding of Westminster Abbey and its adjacent royal palace, which was to become the focus of lawmaking and administration, while the City developed as an important commercial and industrial center. .....■**

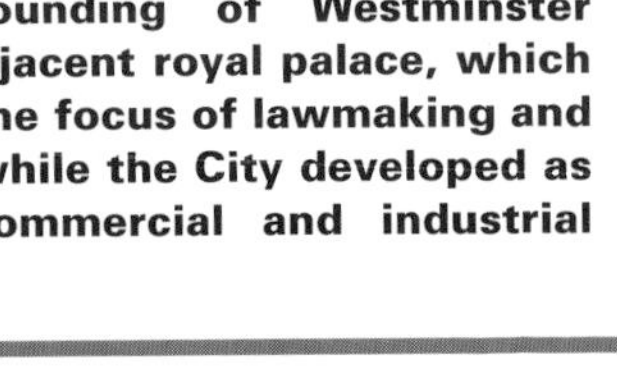

The Dark Ages The period that followed the withdrawal of Roman troops from Britain in A.D.410 is one of the most intriguing in history, precisely because so little is known about it. We do know that the first churches were built in London in the 7th century, if not before, and archaeological finds suggest that the port of London continued to thrive, exporting wool and cloth.

London appears in the historical record again in the 9th century, when chroniclers recorded "great slaughter" resulting from Viking raids. In 994 the city was again attacked by Sweyn Forkbeard, son of the Danish King, who was eventually bought off—London was a major contributor to the *danegeld* tax that the Danes demanded in return for peace. In the end, Sweyn's son, Canute, was accepted as "King of all England" in 1017 and crowned in London.

Glass in the medieval Guildhall

❑ **Monarchs and their reigns**

Normans
William I (the Conqueror) 1066–87
William II 1087–1100
Henry I 1100–35
Stephen 1135–54

Plantagenets
Henry II 1154–89
Richard I 1189–99
John 1199–1216
Henry III 1216–72
Edward I 1272–1307
Edward II 1307–27
Edward III 1327–77
Richard II 1377–99

Lancastrians
Henry IV 1399–1413
Henry V 1413–22
Henry VI 1422–61 (deposed); 1470–1 (restored)

Yorkists
Edward IV 1461–70; 1471–83
Edward V 1483
Richard III 1483–5 ❑

Edward the Confessor London as we know it today began to develop during the reign of Edward the Confessor, who came to the throne in 1042. He devoted his income to a magnificent new abbey church at Westminster, building a royal palace alongside it. This marked a decisive shift away from the old Roman city, and from that time onwards London consisted of two distinct parts: the royal center around Westminster and the commercial center in the City.

The Normans The importance of Westminster was confirmed when William I, the Norman Conqueror, was crowned King of England in the abbey. A huge number of immigrant merchants began to settle in London in the wake of the Conquest, including Jewish bankers, who occupied the area still known as Old Jewry. This street runs down to Cheapside, which was one huge open air market place. Other streets leading off Cheapside were devoted to particular crafts or products, as names such as Bread Street, Poultry Lane, Goldsmiths Row, and Friday Street (the site of the Friday fish market) still recall.

Law and literacy As a system of law and concepts such as trial by jury were established, London developed new institutions, such as the Inns of Court, built midway between the City and Westminster during the 13th century for the training and housing of law students. While the universities of the time trained students to become clergymen, the Inns of Court were more like business schools, turning out advisers to the King, ambassadors and administrators.

❑ One of London's most impressive medieval buildings is the Guildhall, which dates to around 1411 but existed as early as the 12th century. The size and splendor of this hall reflects the strength of London merchants, who were organized into guilds to protect their interests: They regulated prices and, through apprenticeship schemes, effectively controlled who could and who could not enter their lucrative professions. Under the medieval system of government each ward or district of the City appointed an alderman, usually from the elite of the guilds, and together the aldermen ran all the City's affairs, guided by their leader, the mayor. The aldermen and mayor still exist, but with more limited powers. ❑

Geoffrey Chaucer, poet and clerk

One such was Geoffrey Chaucer, whose career included spells as Controller of Customs, ambassador to France, and Clerk of the King's Works. In between he found time to write (but never complete) *The Canterbury Tales* (begun around 1387), a book that helped to establish English as a respectable, poetic language, well able to compete with Latin and French. The widespread availability of Chaucer's work resulted from the activities of William Caxton, who studied printing in Cologne. Edward IV encouraged him to set up a press at Westminster in 1476, and between then and his death in 1491 he published a total of 80 books. Caxton's apprentice, Wynkyn de Worde, took over the business and moved the press to Fleet Street in 1500, thus beginning that street's long association with the printed word.

The Tudor age brought far reaching changes to London, sparked off by Henry VIII's decisive break with the church of Rome and the dismantling of monastic power. The effect was to usher in the more confident and secular age of Elizabeth I and William Shakespeare. .....

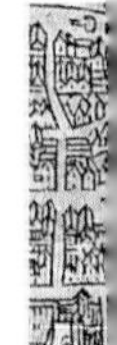

Monarchs and their reigns

Tudors
Henry VII 1485–1509
Henry VIII 1509–47
Edward VI 1547–53
Mary I 1553–8
Elizabeth I 1558–1603

Henry VII The Tudor era began with a great act of piety: the building of a beautiful fan-roofed chapel in Westminster Abbey by Henry VII, a shrewd financier and politician who was determined to strengthen the role of the monarchy. The chapel was still unfinished in 1509, when Henry VII died, and was completed by his son, Henry VIII.

Henry VIII and the Dissolution
Soon Henry VIII was busy with demolition, rather than building. He produced the final answer to a debate that had been raging since early medieval times (and that had resulted in countless wars and the martyrdom of Thomas Beckett); he declared himself, rather than the Pope, to be the absolute head of the church in England. Conveniently this meant that he could appropriate the vast wealth of the church; the church tithe (a tax of one-tenth of all crops and revenues) was diverted to the Crown in 1534, and in 1536 Henry dissolved the monasteries, gaining a vast stockpile of property with which to reward his supporters. Religious houses in and around London were converted to mansions by favored courtiers; Blackfriars, for example, became the estate of the Master of Revels, Thomas Cawarden. A huge amount of property in the City that had previously been owned by the church was sold or given away, so that rents plummeted and houses stood empty.

The Tower of London in 1509

Population growth and planning laws This situation did not last long, however, for the reign of Elizabeth I was marked by a fourfold growth in London's population, resulting in serious overcrowding and the passing of the first ever planning law. This was issued as a royal proclamation in 1580 (and made law in 1592). It prohibited any new building within a 3-mile (4.6km) radius of the city, and any subdivision of existing buildings. This and similar laws issued in the early 17th century were totally ignored, with the effect that the many monastic gardens and fields

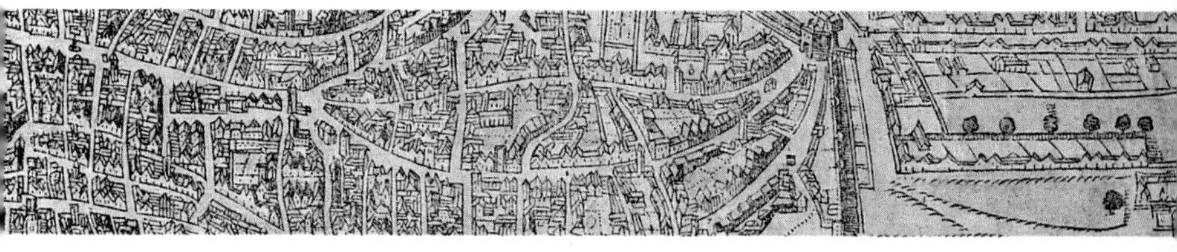

Gross genius: Henry VIII

that had previously existed within the boundaries of the city rapidly became clogged with shoddy timber buildings. Much of the Elizabethan city was destroyed a century later by the Great Fire, but the spirit of the time lives on in Shakespeare's great plays, and in the comedies of his contemporary, Ben Jonson, whose *Bartholomew Fair* gives a pretty clear idea of the rough life of the early 17th century.

Expanding trade No area was rougher than Southwark, where Shakespeare's Globe Theatre was built in 1598–99, alongside the brothels, taverns, bearpits, and cockpits to which apprentices would come for entertainment. This area developed rapidly as London burst beyond its Roman and medieval limits, and the south bank became the place where poorer, semiskilled, or manual laborers lived. They were joined by a growing population of sailors and shipbuilders as London's overseas trade contacts expanded. The Royal Exchange was opened in 1570 by Elizabeth I, designed to compete with increasingly powerful markets in Antwerp and Amsterdam (though, ironically, the original building was built from Dutch and Flemish materials), and British merchants such as Thomas Gresham made vast fortunes from trade with Russia, the Levant and the East Indies.

❑ London Bridge was one of the wonders of Tudor London. Since its completion in 1209 it had acquired some unusual features: One was the sheer number of shops and houses packed onto the bridge, resulting in great congestion. Another was the ornate Nonsuch House, built towards the Southwark end of the bridge in 1577; this folly was so called because there was "none such" like it. The heads of traitors executed in the nearby Tower of London were displayed on poles above the gatehouse of the bridge, having been boiled and dipped in tar to preserve them. This practice ended in 1661, and the bridge itself, having stood for 600 years, was replaced in 1831 by a new bridge designed by Sir John Rennie. In 1972 Rennie's bridge was replaced, only to be sold and re-erected in Lake Havasu City, Arizona. ❑

War, plague and fire

■ The 17th century began with the coronation of James I in 1603; since he was already James VI of Scotland, the two kingdoms were united for the first time and conciliation was the theme of the Jacobean age. But soon Britain would be gripped by civil war and a king would lose his head, while London would be decimated by plague and then destroyed by fire. .....■

The Gunpowder Plot In the early years of James I's reign an event took place that is still commemorated with bonfires and fireworks all over Britain. Catholic conspirators, who looked to Rome and the Pope as head of the church, sought to further their cause by placing explosives in the cellars beneath the House of Lords. The plan, known as the Gunpowder Plot, failed, and Guy Fawkes was caught before lighting the gunpowder fuse on November 5, 1605, with the aim of killing the King and all the assembled peers.

The Civil War Parliament was again the scene of an explosive event on January 4,1642, when Charles I burst into the House of Commons demanding the arrest of five Members. This was the culmination of a bitter power struggle between the King and Parliament, which then erupted into war. London took the side of Parliament in the battles that ensued, and City merchants made a substantial contribution to the cost of the Parliamentary army that finally defeated the Royalists at Naseby. In 1649 the King was beheaded and after a period of confusion and instability, Oliver Cromwell became Lord Protector, imposing a puritanical rule that lasted until his death in 1658 and the restoration of the monarchy in 1660.

❑ **Monarchs and their reigns**
Stuarts
James I 1603–25
Charles I 1625–49
The Commonwealth 1649–53
The Protectorate 1653–59
Charles II 1660–85 ❑

Fires lit to fend off the plague

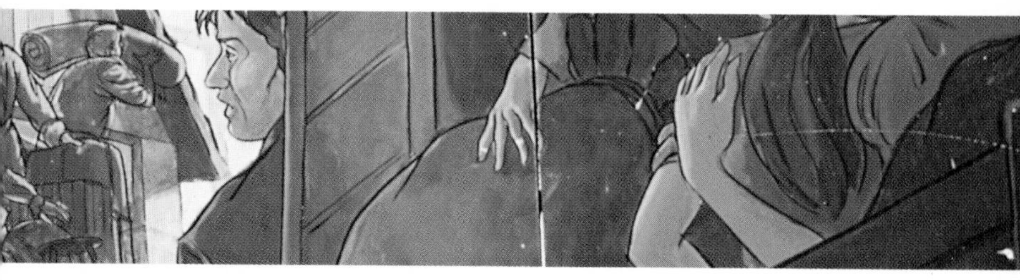

London's burning

The Great Plague Two great disasters were to hit the city in the 1660s. The first signs of the Great Plague were detected at Christmas 1664 and soon all those who could afford it, including most of the city's doctors, had fled. Many theories were propounded about the cause of the plague—dogs and cats were blamed and killed by official exterminators, exacerbating the problem; rats, the true carriers of plague, simply multiplied. At the height of the plague, 14,000 people were dying every week, their corpses dumped into vast plague pits.

The cold winter of 1665 brought a decline in casualties, and by February 1666 the King and court had returned to London. At least 100,000 people had died but the city soon returned to its normal bustle.

The Great Fire A mere six months later, on the night of September 2, 1666, a baker's shop caught fire in Pudding Lane. The Lord Mayor was alerted but is reported to have said that the fire was so trivial that "a woman might piss it out." Samuel Pepys, on arising from his bed the next day, was horrified to learn that 300 houses were already burned by "an infinite great fire," and that nobody was attempting to quench the flames. Remarkably, only nine people lost their lives in the Great Fire, which raged for three days, but the damage to property was immense. Nearly every building within the 160 hectares of the City had been destroyed: 13,200 houses, 44 guildhalls, and 87 churches. St. Paul's Cathedral was so badly damaged that repair was impossible. Those Londoners who had survived the Great Plague were now camped in the fields around the smoldering ruins of their city, wondering what further disaster might occur.

❑ The Great Plague of 1665 was only one of a series to hit the city. The Black Death of 1348–49 carried off at least half of the city's population, and the plague recurred, on and off, for the next 300 years. Ordinances were passed banning the slaughter of animals in the city—the waste was thought to be the source of disease. Burning fires in the streets to purify the air and breathing the scent of nose gays made of herbs were tried as preventative measures, and arsenic was prescribed as a cure. Finally the Great Fire put an end to the epidemics, destroying the rat-infested buildings in which the plague had thrived. ❑

■ Out of the ashes of the Great Fire a new and prosperous city soon arose. In the 150 years following the fire, a huge amount of building took place that totally transformed London's appearance, resulting in the city that we see today. .....■

Sir Christopher Wren The task of rebuilding London after the Great Fire fell to Sir Christopher Wren, Surveyor General to the Crown, but all his initial proposals met with resistance. Wren planned a radical redevelopment of the medieval city, replacing the narrow alleys and jumbled wharfs with a new waterfront and graceful public buildings. His visionary scheme foundered on practicality; comprehensive redevelopment was prevented by the complex pattern of land and property holding in the city, and by the fact that Londoners themselves wanted to rebuild their houses and shops as quickly as possible. The city was rebuilt along the existing street pattern, but using brick, stone, and tile, instead of timber and thatch, as a precaution against fire.

Wren's scheme for St. Paul's was also frustrated. Faced with the challenge of building the world's first Protestant cathedral, he produced a building that broke with the past, as his "Great Model" in the cathedral crypt shows. His clients, however, wanted to cling to their medieval liturgy, which required a processional nave and a chancel, so the design was eventually altered—some would say compromised—in order to meet their wishes.

Wren, the idealistic architect

❑ Monarchs and their reigns

James II 1685–8
William and Mary 1689–1702
Anne 1702–14

Hanoverians
George I 1714–27
George II 1727–60
George III 1760–1820
George IV 1820–30
William IV 1830–7 ❑

The great building boom Over the next decades, the city developed its own character and became a place where people did their work, rather than where they lived. Looking down from the dome of St. Paul's, a mason working on its construction in the last years of the 17th century would have seen large private gardens, fields, orchards, and grazing animals only a short distance away. Soon that view was to change, for a huge building boom began in 1713 that continued at breakneck pace for the next 100 years. The private gardens lining the Strand were the first to be developed, followed by Holborn, Spitalfields and Soho, Mayfair, and St. James's. Many of the residential areas that were developed at this time bear the names of landowners who grew rich on bricks and mortar: families like the Curzons, Portmans,

Cadogans, Camdens, Sloanes, and Grosvenors.

Some of the earliest residential areas, such as Mayfair and St. James's, were built for wealthy aristocrats and courtiers, with elegant houses set around garden squares. The subsequent building boom was, however, fueled by the rise of the professional classes: Doctors, lawyers, underwriters, stockbrokers, and merchants, even actors, artists, and publishers had the means to move out of the cramped and overcrowded city into West End property. London must have resembled a vast building site for much of the period, especially towards the end of the 18th century and the beginning of the 19th, when major public buildings went up, such as the Mansion House, the Bank of England, and the British Museum. Two projects epitomise the buoyancy of this era: The architect John Nash undertook the remodeling of a whole swathe of London, from the Mall northwards to Regent's Park, providing the kind of dramatic vistas that London had so far lacked, while Trafalgar Square was cleared of its royal stables and transformed into a public space leading towards Whitehall, where new buildings, such as the Admiralty, symbolized England's colonial might. One medieval building remained in the midst of all these new monuments: the Palace of Westminster. It had such a long history that nobody dared suggest rebuilding it, though it was an archaic and impractical place. Few were sorry, however, when the palace finally went up in flames in November 1834, marking the end of an era.

❑ Before the Great Fire London was built largely of timber; the city lacks any local source of good building stone. Stone for prestigious churches such as St. Paul's had to be brought by sea from Portland in Dorset or along the Thames from the Cotswolds. During the building boom of the 18th century, bricks became the standard material. At first these were made locally by extracting clay from farmland on the fringes of the city. The pits were then filled in with domestic garbage and the land leased to speculative builders. By the 19th century, bricks were being brought in by rail or canal, principally from the clayfields and brick kilns of Bedford, Fletton, and Peterborough. ❑

Wren's masterpiece, St. Paul's

■ Queen Victoria came to the throne in 1837, aged only 18. During the 63 years of her reign London continued its inexorable growth. It was a city at the heart of a vast empire, the financial capital of the world, a city of magnificent buildings and great institutions; at the same time it had a huge population of extremely poor people living in squalid conditions; the word slum, which had been introduced by Jewish migrants, began to be applied to parts of London at this time. .....■

The Great Exhibition The most spectacular public event of Queen Victoria's reign was "The Great Exhibition of the Works of Industry of All Nations," staged in Hyde Park in 1851. Six million people poured through the turnstiles between May 1st and October 15th to see the exhibits housed in Joseph Paxton's Crystal Palace. The profits were sufficient for a new museum complex to be set up, including the Victoria and Albert, the Science and the Natural History museums, built on the former market gardens of South Kensington.

The Great Exhibition, with its emphasis on technology and industry, set many of the themes of the era—even the Crystal Palace itself, basically a greenhouse or conservatory on a massive scale, inspired scores of similar buildings using iron as the core structural material, rather than wood, brick, or stone. Examples range from the Agricultural Hall in Islington to covered markets such as Leadenhall, Smithfield, and Covent Garden. The same technology was used for railway stations such as the beautifully restored Liverpool Street or Paddington, the terminus of the Great Western Railway.

Queen Victoria

The Transportation Revolution Paddington Station was built in its present form in 1854, but the line itself opened in 1838, offering a service to West Drayton. In 1842, Queen Victoria set the royal seal of approval on this new form of transport by taking her first train journey along the same line, traveling from Slough to Paddington, a distance of 17 miles (27km), in 23 minutes—an average of 44mph (70kph); Prince Albert is reported to have instructed the conductor: "Not so fast next time." By the end of Victoria's reign, 390,000 commuters were being carried in and out of the city every day, traveling a distance of up to 30 miles (18.6km), an indication of just how far London had spread by then.

London's docks expanded rapidly during the same era. Smaller boats, mainly carrying cargoes such as coal and grain from other British ports, still used riverside wharves, but congestion on the Thames was such that purpose-built docks were needed to handle the big oceangoing vessels. Whole new villages and communities grew up to serve the docks, but poverty was endemic because wages were extremely low. London was becoming an increasingly stratified city, with a relatively prosperous West End and a poor East End. Model dwellings to house the poor began to appear—the American philanthropist, George Peabody, left substantial funds for their construction—but never enough to make any serious dent in the growing problem of the slums. The situation gave rise to many philanthropic initiatives, such as the founding in 1878 of William Booth's Salvation Army, which set up soup kitchens and hostels to help the very poor. Ultimately, the extreme poverty in London was to have massive and worldwide repercussions: Karl Marx's observations on its causes and solutions were to become the basis for Communist-inspired revolutions in several parts of the world. ❑

❑ London lacked any kind of system for disposing of waste until the mid-19th century. Garbage and sewage were dumped into its rivers, earning it the names "Venice of drains" and "capital of cholera." The first covered sewers were introduced in 1858, known as "the Year of the Great Stink" because they were completely ineffectual. Nobody went anywhere near the Thames unless they had to and the windows of the newly rebuilt Houses of Parliament were draped with sheets soaked in chloride of lime to keep the smell at bay. The saviour of London, whose name is forgotten but who ought to be regarded as a national hero, was Sir Joseph Bazalgette: his system of brick-lined sewers, linked to treatment plants and pumping stations, came into operation in the 1860s. Bazalgette's 1,300-mile (2,080km) system, carrying 70,200 gallons a day, still forms the basis of London's drainage system. ❑

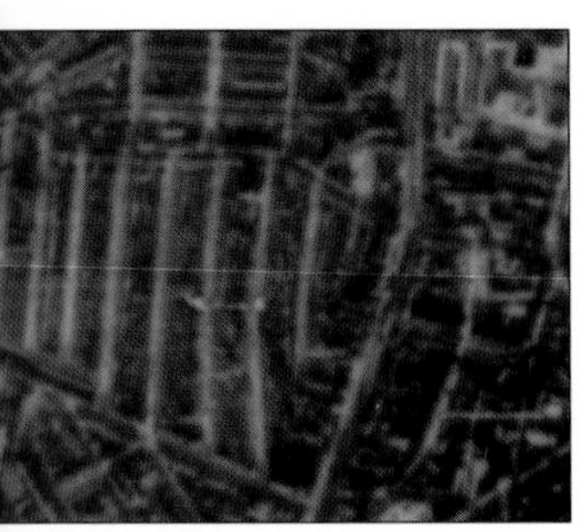

■ Not long after the century turned, Victoria died and modern history began. Cultural values and attitudes began to change, and in place of the *laissez-faire* attitude to development, the London County Council began to impose order. All was to be shattered, however, in the Blitz, when German bombers attacked London repeatedly between September 1940 and May 1941, reducing large parts of the capital to rubble. .....■

The London County Council was officially created in 1888, as a directly elected body with substantial powers. It needed them to tackle the problems of a city that had grown out of control, but it was not until the early 20th century, under Progressive (Liberal) leadership, that it began to show its muscle. Soon the LCC was involved in everything from slum clearance to building houses. It also created many parks and open spaces, including the Green Belt, designed to halt the city's spread. Some of the LCC's housing plans, such as the Boundary Street development in Bethnal Green, became models for developments in other parts of Europe.

The inter-war years The pace of building continued after World War I; in the words of a slogan of the time, Britain needed "homes fit for heroes." Increasingly these were "high-rise" blocks, five storys or so high—called "flats" and regarded with suspicion because residents of flats enjoyed none of the benefits of street-based community life.

The middle-class dream was to escape the city, and the prospect of achieving that dream was offered by the creation of a comprehensive and cheap public transit system, the Underground (a subway system that came to be called "the tube") starting in 1906. As the Underground expanded in the 1920s and 1930s, more people chose to live in new suburban housing developments, where houses had running water and electricity. Soon, however, the Underground would serve another purpose: providing shelter for Londoners during nightly air raids at the height of the Blitz.

❑ **Monarchs and their reigns**

Victoria 1837–1901
Edward VII 1901–10
George V 1910–36
Edward VIII 1936
George VI 1936–52
Elizabeth II 1952–present ❑

The Blitz The *Blitzkrieg* ("lightning war") was Hitler's weapon for beating Britain into submission, although its effect was to strengthen resistance. Recognizing that aerial bombing would play a major role in the war, the authorities had already evacuated 690,000 children to temporary rural homes in September 1939. Many poor evacuees from the East End thereby gained their first glimpse of farm animals, and rural people discovered that the children of the East End were not the degenerates, the "people of the abyss," that they were often portrayed.

Meanwhile, German bombs began to rain down, and a nightly pattern was established: A two minute siren wail would warn Londoners of approaching aircraft, giving them time to take cover in basements, in "Anderson" shelters dug at the back of private yards or in the Underground. Even Churchill, the wartime leader, had an underground bunker, now an intriguining museum, in the Cabinet War Rooms in Whitehall.

Throughout the Blitz, everyone tried to live life as normal, although bus and train services were constantly disrupted, along with gas, electricity, and water supplies. Even so, nightclubs and theaters remained open. The Café de Paris, which optimistically called itself "the safest nightclub in town" and had mirrored walls copied from the ballroom of the *Titanic*, received a direct hit in March 1941. It was just one event in the raids that left 29,890 dead and 3.5 million buildings in London severely damaged or destroyed.

The worst of the Blitz was over by May 1941. Towards the end of the war, however, a new bombing campaign began: In reprisal for British air raids on German cities, Hitler unleashed his new "wonder weapons," the V1 flying bomb and the V2 rocket, from June 1944. These created havoc, landing indiscriminately and causing great loss of life in the last months of the war.

St. Paul's Throughout the Blitz, a special effort was made to protect St. Paul's, which survived intact, even when every building around it was flattened. Prompt action enabled potentially dangerous fires to be put out, but sheer good fortune played a part as well; the cathedral received a direct hit on September 12, 1940, but the bomb failed to explode and was extracted from the foundations three days later. It was then driven to Hackney Marsh and set off. The resulting explosion created a crater more than 115 ft. across.

Life goes on, despite the war

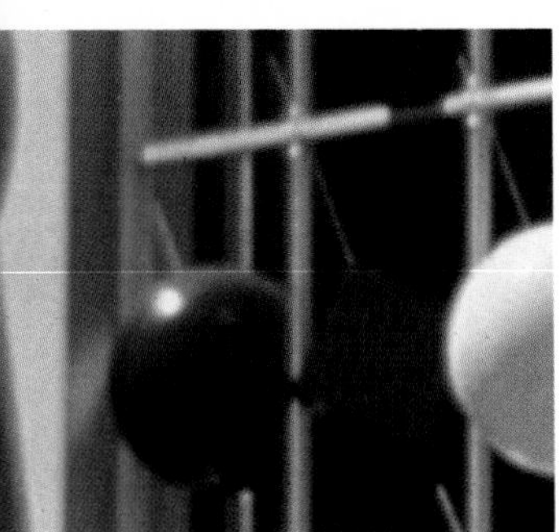

■ Nikolaus Pevsner, founder of the *Buildings of England* series of books, observed that postwar planners and architects caused greater damage to England's historic cities than the Luftwaffe ever did during the Blitz. More recently the sentiment has been repeated by Prince Charles, an outspoken critic of modern architecture. The postwar rebuilding of London certainly transformed the city, but it has, until recently, given Londoners few buildings to be proud of. .....■

Planning laws In the period immediately following the war two key pieces of planning legislation were passed that would be beneficial to the appearance of London. Under the Town and Country Planning Act of 1947, protection was given to historic buildings, which could no longer be demolished or altered at will. The Civic Amenities Act of 1967 extended this concept to whole areas of London, thus creating the notion of "conservation areas" within which development was severely restricted. The other great step forward was the 1956 Clean Air Act, which successfully brought an end to London's smog.

Buildings of the age Set against these triumphs, London acquired a large body of mediocre and alienating buildings, some of which have since been demolished while others face an uncertain future. One example is the South Bank complex, a legacy of the 1951 Festival of Britain. The Royal Festival Hall was put up in a great hurry when this celebration was first conceived as a way of cheering up the nation after the rationing and austerity that followed the war. As a symbol of the bright new world, the Festival Hall is singularly uninspiring; it is, nevertheless, regarded with some affection by Londoners for the simple reason that it is not as ugly as the bunker-like structures that surround it, such as the Hayward Gallery and the National Theatre. A new facing has been proposed as a way of improving their appearance, but this has not yet been undertaken despite years of complaints.

London's airport Another symbol of the postwar city is one that many visitors encounter first: Heathrow Airport. This was transferred from military to civil use in 1946. In 1955 the first of its major passenger-terminals was completed; this, like much of the airport, was built by Sikh laborers from the Punjab (a region of India and Pakistan), encouraged to move to London to fill labor shortages. Heathrow quickly became one of the world's busiest freight and passenger airports, with a huge impact on the west of London and its economy.

Makeshift antismog masks

The docks By contrast, east London went into dramatic decline as manufacturing industries began to relocate out of London, and the docks began to close down with astonishing speed. Many blamed the dockworkers themselves, notoriously prone to going on strike, for the death of London's docklands, but just as relevant was the rise of Rotterdam and the difficulty of navigating huge vessels up the Thames.

Brave new world The politicians of the 1980s tried hard to turn the decline of the docks into an opportunity; they talked optimistically of complete regeneration, of a new and futuristic city rising in the east as a center for the financial and service industries on which London would flourish well into the 21st century. These same politicians were confident that private enterprise would fund the transformation and were determined that no taxpayers' money would go into this, or towards the construction of a new rail link between London and the rest of Europe via the Channel Tunnel.

Many of these decisions have since been reversed. Some critics claim that more public money must be spent on improving London's infrastructure, or else the city will face a slow decline; better managed cities such as Paris or Frankfurt will attract the private investors, and even London's supremacy as a major international center for finance can no longer be taken for granted within a unified European community.

Whatever the truth of these arguments, London remains a compelling city. It has its rough edges and faults, but it also has an underlying vitality, which, in the final analysis, is its greatest strength.

Visiting the Festival of Britain

Sightseeing tours by bus
One of the best ways to get your bearings in London is to join one of London Transport's Official Sightseeing Tours and see the city from a double-decker bus (or open top in summer). Tours depart every 30 minutes from 10 to 5 daily (except Christmas Day) from Victoria Station, Baker Street Station, Marble Arch (by Speakers' Corner), and Piccadilly Circus (by Haymarket). The guided tours last one and a half hours and tickets can be bought on the bus, or from Victoria, Piccadilly Circus, Oxford Circus, Euston, and King's Cross Underground stations.

London area by area London resembles a giant patchwork quilt, made up of many different districts and communities. In between lie vast areas of public park, as well as monumental palaces, museums, and churches. Taken together, this rich and intricate tapestry can seem dauntingly complex. Fortunately, the historic core of London can be divided into districts, reflecting the city's amalgamation over the centuries of villages and parishes. Each area has its own character, which is summarized below.

Whitehall and Westminster This historic district has long been the center of government, and its main thoroughfares are lined with the offices of ministries and departments of state. The highlights include the Houses of Parliament and Westminster Abbey—as well as the art collections of the National Gallery, the National Portrait Gallery, and the Tate.

St. James's and the Mall Leading westwards out of Trafalgar Square, the noble, tree-lined Mall leads to Buckingham Palace, the official residence of the Queen. To the north, St. James's contains exclusive clubs and some of London's most elegant shops.

Mayfair and Piccadilly This district is partly enclosed by famous shopping streets—Piccadilly, Regent Street, and Oxford Street—while Park Lane, with its luxurious hotels, makes up its fourth side. Within these borders, Mayfair encompasses a fascinating mixture of art galleries and exclusive shops.

LONDON BY AREA

Chelsea and Knightsbridge Chelsea's King's Road has been at the cutting edge of fashion since the Swinging '60s, although today the center of chic has shifted northwards to Brompton Road. On the northern borders are the vast Science, Geological, Natural History, and Victoria and Albert museums.

Kensington and Hyde Park Kensington, with markets, antiques shops, and a royal palace, is separated from the West End by the former monastic lands of Hyde Park, now an expanse of woodland, lawns, and water, where you can listen to soapbox debates at Speakers' Corner.

Marylebone and Regent's Park Marylebone Road features Madame Tussaud's Waxworks, one of London's most popular attractions. The area is rich in fine Regency architecture, and Regent's Park, with its gardens and canalside walks, offers another haven of tranquillity.

Bloomsbury and Fitzrovia This district's wealth of literary associations include Dickens' House and the haunts of the Bloomsbury Group, who set the intellectual tone in the 1920s and 1930s. Here, too, are the British Museum and the University of London.

Covent Garden and Soho This vibrant district encapsulates all that is most fascinating about London: Bookstores, museums and theaters jostle for space in the warren of streets that surround Covent Garden's craft shops and street performers. Adding spice to the mixture

Walking tours
Tour Guides International offer, several theme walks, including Royal London, Government and Democracy, and Upstairs, Downstairs; details from 2 Bridge Street, SW1 (tel. 071 839 2498). Guided walks are also offered by London Walking Tours (tel. 081 460 4532) and by The Original London Walks (tel. 071 624 3978).

are the shops and restaurants of Chinatown and the more questionable pleasures of Soho's sex shops and shows.

Holborn and the Strand Linking the City to the West End, this district contains the heart of legal London and the Courtauld Institute's superb collection of Impressionist art.

The City Best known for its banks and financial institutions, the City has scores of attractions, from St. Paul's Cathedral to the modern architecture of the Lloyd's building.

Clerkenwell, Islington and the East End The Blitz brought havoc to the working class East End of London,

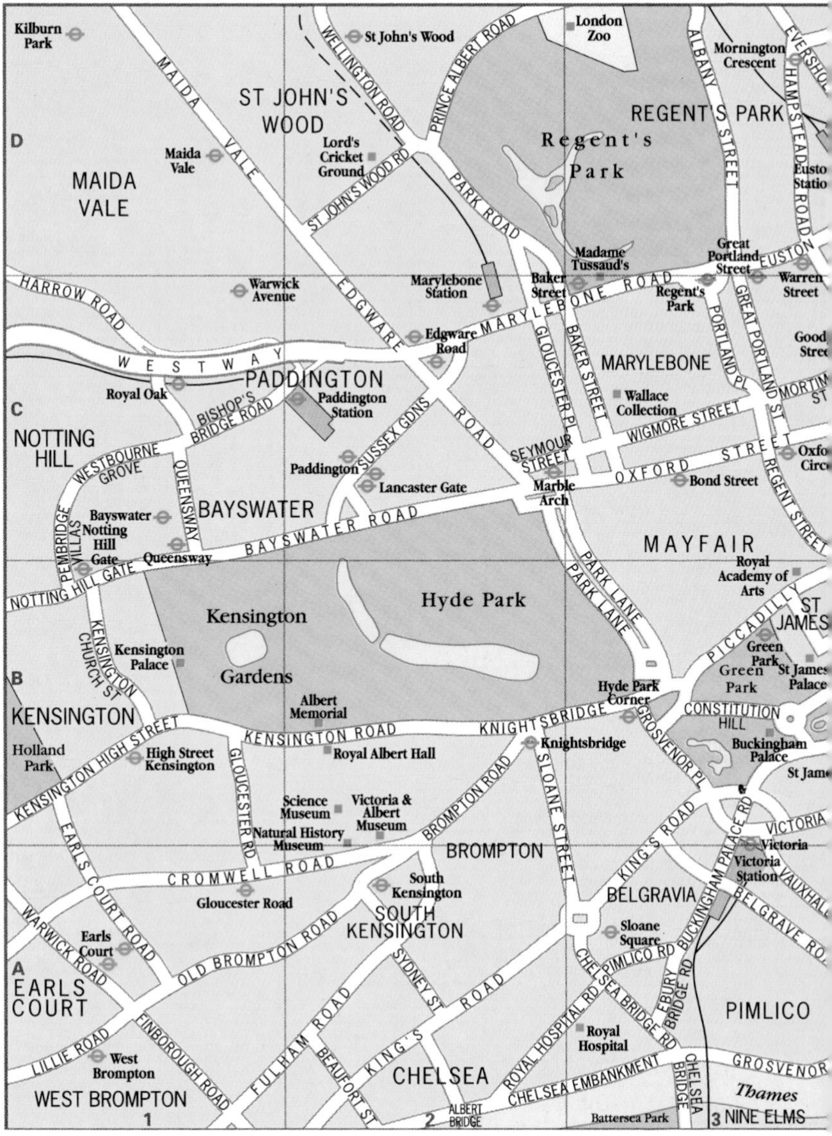

but its robust character survives in the colorful street markets. Further north, Islington's 18th-century terraces form a genteel backdrop to antiques and crafts markets.

Docklands This regenerated area offers a new focus to the city's east. Warehouses by the Thames now house shops and apartments, and marinas and offices have transformed Wapping, Limehouse, and the Isle of Dogs.

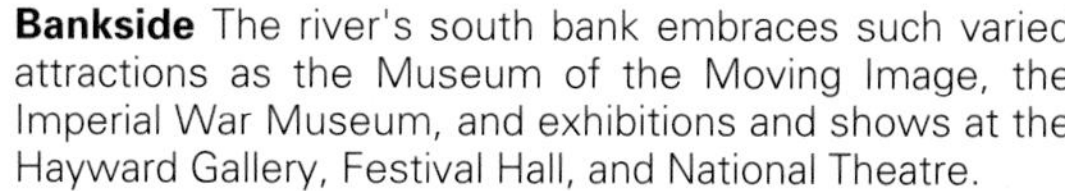

Bankside The river's south bank embraces such varied attractions as the Museum of the Moving Image, the Imperial War Museum, and exhibitions and shows at the Hayward Gallery, Festival Hall, and National Theatre.

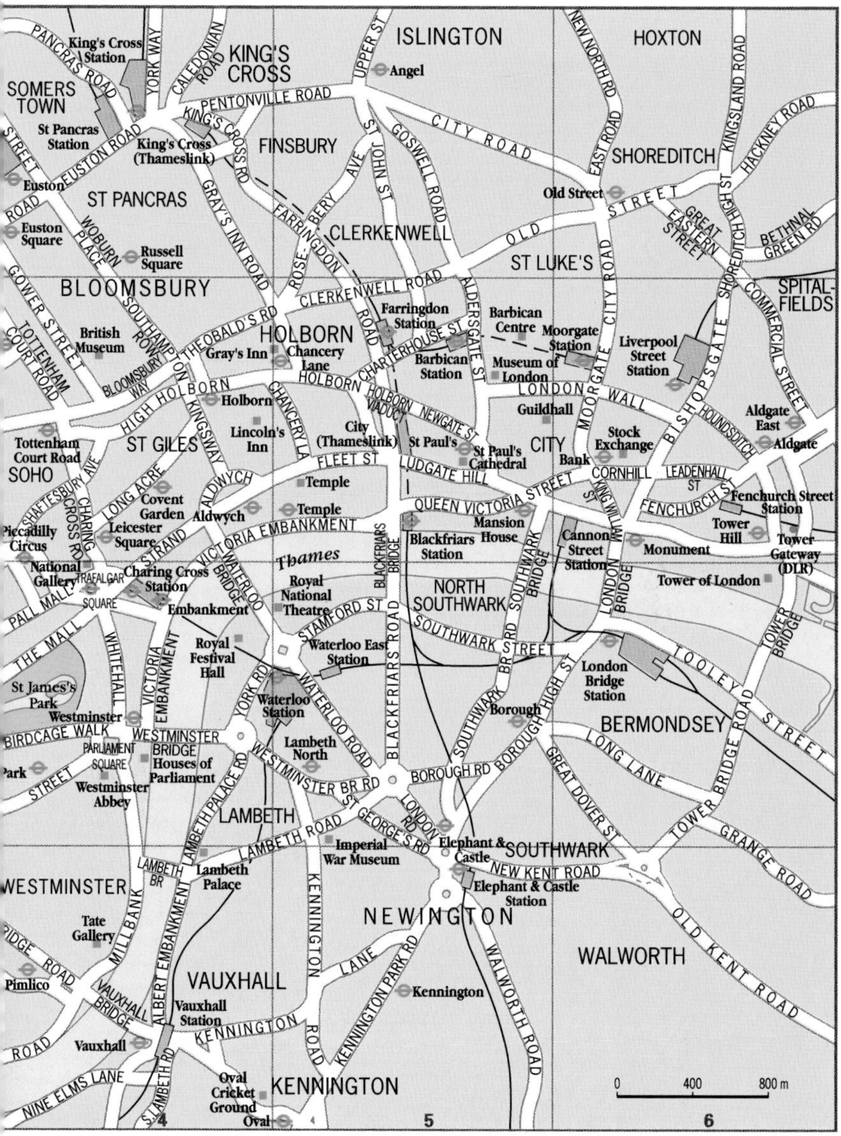

WHITEHALL AND WESTMINSTER

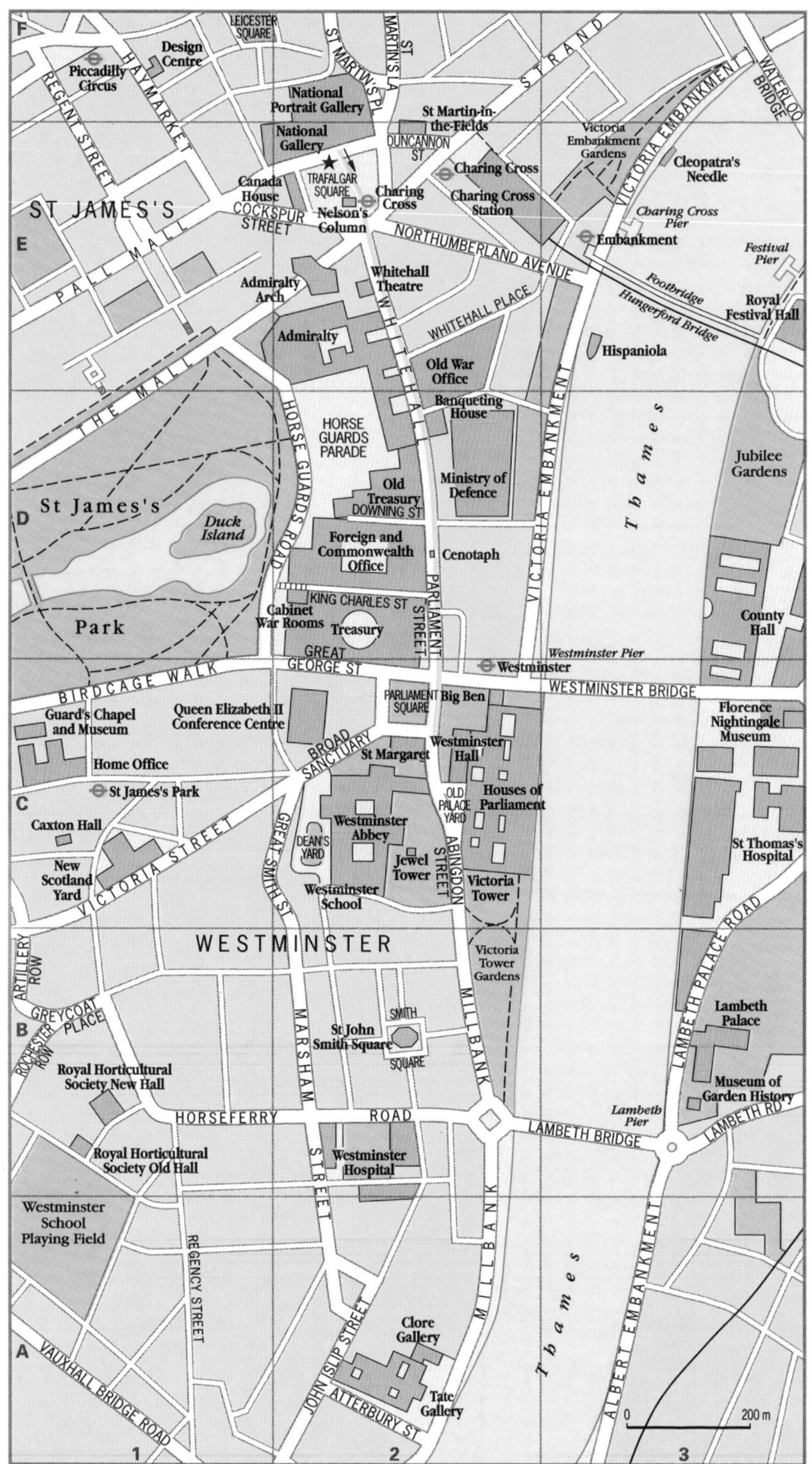

WHITEHALL AND WESTMINSTER

Whitehall and Westminster The name Westminster was first used in the 8th century, when it referred to the minster that stood to the west of the City of London. Today this site is occupied by Westminster Abbey. The original church was begun by Edward the Confessor after he moved the royal court out of the City in 1042, beginning London's westward expansion. Since then, Westminster has been synonymous with government. Its major buildings, along with those on Whitehall, house the main departments of state: the Treasury, the Ministry of Defence, the Foreign and Commonwealth Office. At its heart stand the abbey and the Houses of Parliament.

Whitehall and Westminster walk Start in Trafalgar Square, on the steps of the National Gallery.

Trafalgar Square is the center of the city—a bronze plaque in the pavement behind Charles II's statue marks the spot. The square was laid out in 1829 in honor of Lord Nelson's naval victory against Napoleon in 1805. Its centerpiece is a statue of Nelson on top of a Corinthian column, 175 ft. tall. Flocks of pigeons settle here or fly down to be photographed and fed (birdseed is available for a price). Beyond is a fine view down Whitehall and to the left is the church of St. Martin-in-the-Fields.

Crossing the square, pause to admire Sir Edward Landseer's four bronze lions (1867) and then walk towards Whitehall. Stranded on an island at the head of the broad avenue, is Hubert le Sueur's animated statue of Charles I on horseback (1633) looking towards Banqueting House, the scene of his execution in 1649. The first building on the right, the Admiralty, is fronted by Robert Adam's stone screen (1759) adorned with two sea horses. The country's naval affairs were run from this building when the British fleet was considered the most powerful in the world. Next comes Horse Guards, where two members of the Household Cavalry mount guard on horseback daily between 10 and 4—a tradition that survives even though all that remains of the former royal palace is the Banqueting House opposite. Beyond Horse Guards is Downing Street, the official residence of the Prime Minister (No. 10) and the Chancellor of the Exchequer (No. 11). There is no longer public access, but you may see government members arriving by car. Further down Whitehall, in the middle of the road, is the Cenotaph, designed by the architect Sir Edwin Lutyens (1920) to commemorate the dead of World War I. Whitehall ends at Parliament Square, with the Houses of Parliament to the left and Westminster Abbey to the right.

The execution of Charles I
Charles I is said to have faced death with exemplary courage. He is reputed to have worn two shirts so that he would not shiver in the January cold and give the impression that he was afraid. Andrew Marvell, the poet who witnessed the execution, wrote of the king that "He nothing common did or mean/Upon that memorable scene." Many went to the scaffold both before and after Charles I, but never an anointed monarch, and many considered his execution an unforgivable act of regicide. To this day, Charles I continues to have his admirers, who place wreaths on his statue, at the head of Whitehall, on January 30th, the anniversary of his death.

▶▶ Banqueting House 44D2

Whitehall
Underground: Charing Cross

The Banqueting House (closed Sunday) is one of Britain's most important architectural monuments. It was built between 1619 and 1622 by Inigo Jones, who had trained in Livorno, (Tuscany) Italy, and absorbed the influence of the architect Palladio. He introduced the purity of classical design to London, first with the Queen's House, Greenwich (now part of the National Maritime Museum complex, see page 218), then with this sophisticated and seminal building.

The Banqueting House is now so hemmed in by other classical buildings that it is difficult to imagine how exotic and different it would once have appeared, crisply faced in white Portland stone, and surrounded by the ramshackle brick and timber buildings that were typical of Tudor London.

The Banqueting House occupies part of the site of the former Whitehall Palace, acquired (or rather seized) by Henry VIII from Cardinal Wolsey, and used for courtly entertainment. When fire destroyed part of the palace, James I employed Inigo Jones to rebuild it on a massive scale (modeled on the Tuileries Palace in Paris), but only the Banqueting House was ever completed.

The exterior is relatively restrained, except for the festive frieze of garlands running beneath the parapet. The colorful ceiling paintings inside provide a powerful contrast. They were commissioned by Charles I and designed by Peter Paul Rubens, who was knighted for this work. Painted in Antwerp and installed in 1635, the nine pictures are intended to emphasise the divine authority of the monarch (a contentious political issue at the time): James I (Charles' father) is shown being received into heaven while other scenes depict the claimed benefits of his rule: peace, prosperity, and the Union of England and Scotland.

Rubens' ceiling paintings in the Banqueting House

Churchill's office and bedroom in the Cabinet War Rooms

Rubens' ceiling paintings are quite ironic in the light of subsequent events, for Charles I went to his execution from this room on January 30, 1649, having fought and lost the seven-year Civil War against Oliver Cromwell and the Parliamentarians. A scaffold was erected outside the north annex (since demolished) of the Banqueting House, and it was from here, through a window, that Charles I stepped out onto the scaffold to meet his death. A bust of Charles I over the staircase entrance marks the probable site of that window.

► Cabinet War Rooms *44D2*

Clive Steps, King Charles Street
Underground: Westminster
This labyrinth of underground rooms provides an intriguing glimpse of the spartan conditions under which Sir Winston Churchill, the War Cabinet, and the Chiefs of Staff operated during World War II; from the cramped confines of this dark basement, they directed the strategies and forces of a global war. Being below ground, the suite of 17 rooms offered a degree of protection against aerial bombardment, and it was here that many important decisions concerning the conduct of the war were taken between 1939 and the Japanese surrender of 1945.

The rooms are equipped exactly as they were during this traumatic period. Six rooms are open, including the Cabinet Room, arranged as if for a meeting. The Prime Minister's room served as a combined office and bedroom for Churchill; here is the desk from which he made some of his most famous and morale-boosting radio broadcasts to the nation and the British Empire. The Map Room contains a map of the world, on which the Allied campaign was charted, and the Telephone Room contains the hot-line telephone on which Churchill discussed his plans of strategy with the U.S. President, Franklin D. Roosevelt.

Henry VIII's wine cellar
Behind the Banqueting House, in Horse Guards Avenue, is the Ministry of Defence head office, its entrance flanked by huge sculptures representing Earth and Water. In the basement of this building is the only surviving part of the original royal palace of Whitehall; known as Henry VIII's Wine Cellar, it consists of a simple vaulted brick chamber. This was considered such an important monument that it was moved over 39 ft. from its original site when the foundations of the Ministry of Defence building were built in the 1940s. Despite the money spent on its preservation it remains a little-visited monument, because you must obtain a written appointment to enter the building.

Parliament

The Gunpowder Plot
One of the most celebrated dates in British history is November 5, 1605, when Guy Fawkes and a number of other Roman Catholic conspirators attempted to blow up Parliament, along with James I and his ministers. Effigies of Guy Fawkes (and other unpopular figures) are burned on bonfires at firework parties all over the country on this date, and the cellars of the House are still checked to this day by the Yeomen of the Guard before the ceremonial State Opening of Parliament. The Queen presides over the State Opening from the House of Lords; no monarch has ever been admitted to the Commons since 1642, when Charles I forced his way in and tried to arrest five Members of Parliament, an event that sparked off the seven-year Civil War between Royalists and Parliamentarians.

▶▶▶ Houses of Parliament *44C2*

St Margaret Street
Underground: Westminster
The general public may attend debates when Parliament is in session; admission is gained by standing in line at the St. Stephen's porch entrance, which is clearly signposted. At other times, however, the Houses of Parliament are closed to the public for security reasons, though visits can be arranged—tel. 071 219 4272 for details.

Although access to this monumental building complex is restricted, the exterior alone is a splendid sight, especially now that the stonework has been cleaned. The best views are to be had from the far side of Westminster Bridge, looking across the Thames to the 270 yd. frontage, with its symmetrically placed towers and pinnacles. The Parliament Square façade is much more varied, stretching from the Clock Tower (popularly known as Big Ben) to the Victoria Tower. In between lies the low roof of Westminster Hall, the oldest surviving building on the site. Inside it has a magnificent hammerbeam roof dating to 1399, but the Hall itself is much older, having been completed in 1099 (there is talk of opening the Hall to the public in the near future).

Edward the Confessor built the Palace of Westminster on this site in 1049, and successive monarchs used it as their main London residence until 1529, when Henry VIII decided to move northwards to the Palace of Whitehall. Parliament (from the Old French *parlement*, a discussion or debate) first met in the Chapter House of Westminster Abbey, but transferred its sessions to the vacated Palace of Westminster in 1547, where it has met ever since.

Fire destroyed most of the old Palace of Westminster in 1834, and a public competition was held to choose an architect for the new buildings. From 97 entries, Charles Barry's design was chosen as the winner and he brought in A. W. Pugin, the expert on authentic Gothic detailing, to assist him. The result is a palatial building in the Tudor Perpendicular style, which perfectly fulfils its symbolic role as the building from which the nation is governed.

The interior of "The House," as it is known to those who work in it, is a cramped warren containing 1,100 rooms, 100 staircases, and almost two miles of corridor. The public areas are magnificently decorated in neo-Gothic and Arts and Crafts style. The actual debating chambers are so small that seating in the House of Commons can only accommodate 346 of the 650 elected Members of Parliament (the rest have to stand). This intimacy lends the House a club-like atmosphere and encourages the noisy barracking that some regard as undignified, others as an essential feature of parliamentary debate. The layout of the Commons, and of the second chamber, the House of Lords, reflects the fact that parliament formerly met in a chapel: The seating is ranged, like choir stalls, in parallel rows with the Speaker's chair where the altar would have stood.

The House of Lords has been televised since 1985, and the House of Commons introduced the cameras, with trepidation, in November 1989. Some M.P.s reacted by employing "personality stylists" to improve their TV images; and screen-conscious Members have been quick to introduce the "doughnutting" technique during less popular debates, hurrying to fill the empty seats around whichever lonely M.P. is in shot, to give the impression of a full House.

► Jewel Tower *44C2*

Old Palace Yard
Underground: Westminster
The Jewel Tower, which was built in 1366, stands opposite the Houses of Parliament, and once formed part of the original Palace of Westminster. The name refers to the fact that it was built as a strongroom to store the royal jewels and other valuables during Edward III's reign. It was carefully restored in 1956, after suffering bomb damage, and is now used to display an exhibition tracing the history of English parliaments up to the present day. Look out for the hefty 1621 iron door, complete with its original lock, which is located on the first floor; this was made at a time when the Jewel Tower was still being used for the storage of all parliamentary records.

Big Ben
Big Ben is the bell that tolls out the hours from the clock tower alongside the Houses of Parliament—a sound that is broadcast live at the beginning of television and radio news programs. The first bell cracked in 1857, after it was cast, and had to be replaced with a new one, made in 1858. Nobody knows how the bell got its name. Some say it was named after "Big Ben" Caunt, a heavyweight boxer of the day, while others suggest it was named after Sir Benjamin Hall, the rotund man who was in charge of building works at Westminster. The tower has four massive clock faces; the minute hands are nearly 16½ ft. long and made of hollow copper. Gunmetal was originally used, but proved to be too heavy. Each minute space is 12 inches across. Old pennies are used whenever any slight adjustments are needed to the weight of the clock's pendulum—but only very rarely has the time been out by more than a fraction of a second.

Left: the king of clocks, high above the Houses of Parliament

Fine views are to be had from the entrance terrace of the National Gallery

National Gallery Top Ten
Ten pictures in the National Gallery that should not be missed:
1 *The Wilton Diptych*
2 *The Battle of San Romano* by Paolo Uccello
3 *The Baptism of Christ* by Piero della Francesca
4 *The Virgin and Child with Saint Anne and Saint John the Baptist* by Leonardo da Vinci
5 *Bacchus and Ariadne* by Titian
6 *Giovanni Arnolfini and his Wife* by Jan van Eyck
7 *Self Portrait* (1669) by Rembrandt
8 *The Haywain* by John Constable
9 *Rain, Steam and Speed* by J M W Turner
10 *Une Baignade, Asnières* (also called *Bathers at Asnières*) by Georges Seurat

▶▶▶ National Gallery *44E2*

Trafalgar Square
Underground: Charing Cross
The National Gallery fills the whole of the north side of Trafalgar Square. Few people notice that the building itself is a rather uninspired piece of classical design because there are so many competing attractions in the square, and the view from the entrance terrace is superb. Beyond the fountains, the pigeons, and the crowds there is a view of Whitehall and the Houses of Parliament; to the right is Canada House (1824), the headquarters of the High Commissioner for Canada; to the left, the church of St. Martin-in-the-Fields is partnered by South Africa House (1935), the London headquarters of the Republic of South Africa, a building often picketted by anti-apartheid demonstrators. Its façade has lively carvings of South African flora and fauna.

Two bronze statues stand on the lawns on either side of the Gallery entrance: one of James II dressed like a Roman, by Grinling Gibbons (1686), and one of George Washington, presented by the American people in 1921. The National Gallery itself was begun in 1824 when the government of the day decided that London needed a national art collection to compete with famous European galleries, such as the Uffizi in Florence, and the Louvre in Paris. It just happened that the Pall Mall house of John Julius Angerstein was for sale at the time, along with his collection of 38 paintings, including works by Raphael, Rembrandt, and Van Dyck. These were purchased for £57,000 and Angerstein's house was used as the first gallery, until the present building was completed in 1838. In the meantime, a number of important pictures were added to the collection through gifts and bequests, but many of the most famous works were acquired by shrewd gallery directors scouring Europe for masterpieces that could be bought cheaply because the artists were temporarily "out of fashion."

National Gallery mosaics Do not miss the floor mosaics of the National Gallery's main staircase and vestibules, designed by the Russian-born artist Boris Anrep between 1928 and 1952. Those in the west vestibule illustrate the *Labours of Life.* Those in the north vestibule include portraits of Winston Churchill and T. S. Eliot, exemplifying Defiance and Leisure respectively, in a series entitled *The Modern Virtues.* Best of all, the *Awakening of the Muses* on the half-landing includes portraits of the most beautiful women of the 1930s: Greta Garbo as Melpemone (Muse of Tragedy), Virginia Woolf as Clio (Muse of History), and Diana Mitford as Polyhymnia (Muse of Song).

Because space in the gallery was limited (originally it was only one room deep), the directors pursued a policy of quality rather than quantity. The result is one of the world's richest art collections, covering most schools and periods of painting up to the 20th century (the national collection of modern art, along with British works of all periods, is now housed in the Tate Gallery; see pages 56–57). The gallery provides a leaflet explaining where to see the 20 most popular masterpieces. It also highlights a particular painting each day, providing notes on the subject, context, and artistic achievement. If you intend to spend all day at the gallery, enter at the new Sainsbury Wing annex, at the extreme left of the main entrance. Here you can check on the day's free lectures and guided tours at the information desk and obtain a room-by-room guide to the gallery.

The Sainsbury Wing has a controversial history. Earlier plans for the site, incorporating an office building, were abandoned after Prince Charles described the proposed building as "a carbuncle on the well-loved face of Trafalgar Square." The Sainsbury family, owners of the Sainsbury supermarket chain, then donated the funds for today's building, designed by Robert Venturi—another source of controversy, since an American architect was chosen in preference to a British one. Since the annex houses Renaissance works, the architect incorporated motifs inspired by 16th-century Italian *palazzi*. Brilliantly colored paintings are dramatically framed by doorway arches carved in gray *pietra serena*, the stone that lends such grace to many of the best Italian Renaissance buildings. Thus the annex makes a fitting and complementary setting for the varied works of Jan van Eyck, Botticelli, Uccello, and for Leonardo da Vinci's entrancing cartoon (restored after shotgun damage) of the *Virgin and Child.* A bridge leads to the main gallery, where the full riches of European art are displayed, including works by Rembrandt and well-loved paintings such as Constable's *The Haywain* and Seurat's *Une Baignade, Asnières.*

Giovanni Arnolfini and his Wife *by Jan van Eyck*

Gallery of the great and good

National Portrait Gallery Top Ten
1 *Richard II*
2 *Henry VIII* by Hans Holbein
3 *Elizabeth I* by Marcus Gheeraerts
4 *Sir Francis Drake* by Nicholas Hilliard
5 *Oliver Cromwell* by Samuel Cooper
6 *Emma, Lady Hamilton,* Nelson's mistress, by George Romney
7 *Lord Byron* by Thomas Phillips
8 *Jane Austen* by her sister Cassandra
9 *The Brontë Sisters* by their brother Branwell
10 *Virginia Woolf* by Duncan Grant

▶▶▶ National Portrait Gallery *44F2*

2 St. Martin's Place
Underground: Charing Cross

Tucked away at the back of the National Gallery, the National Portrait Gallery is a virtual "Who's Who" of all the famous names in British history, science, and the arts. The collection consists of some 7,000 paintings, drawings, sculptures, and photographs, collected because of the eminence of the subject, regardless of the merits of the artist; even so, many important artists are represented, from Hans Holbein to David Hockney, and the collection as a whole provides an intriguing overview of the development of portraiture from the stylized iconograph representation of early monarchs to the psychological expressiveness of later works.

The portraits are displayed chronologically, with the earliest on the top floor. Here, among the medieval portraits, you will find the poet Geoffrey Chaucer and his patron, Richard II, portrayed as a sensitive and beautiful young man (this is a copy of the original portrait hanging in Westminster Abbey).

Two towering monarchs dominate the Tudor Rooms: Henry VIII, portrayed by Holbein and surrounded by several wives and advisers who fell from grace and lost their handsome heads, and Elizabeth I, partnered by such favorites of hers as the Earls of Leicester and Essex. The portraits of Elizabeth I are a *tour de force* of political propaganda: Marcus Gheeraerts's work shows her triumphantly standing on a map of Britain with storm clouds behind (representing the defeated Spanish Armada) and bright skies ahead.

Although monarchs, politicians, and soldiers dominate the early part of the collection, later rooms have a fair share of writers, artists, and scientists: There are portraits of Shakespeare, Donne, Milton, Pepys, Sir Christopher Wren, and Sir Isaac Newton. Among the most popular pictures are the romantic portrait of the young Lord Byron, the only known portrait of Jane Austen (by her sister Cassandra), and a tender portrait of the Brontë sisters by their brother Branwell.

The late Victorian and 20th-century displays are among the most striking, especially since they show artists seeking new ways to get beneath the skin of their subject and say something about their essential characters. Interestingly, a number of the pictures are self-portraits (Sir Stanley Spencer, Graham Sutherland, David Hockney, Dame Laura Knight) or depictions of one artist by another (Vanessa Bell by Duncan Grant, Henry Moore by Marino Marini). Needless to say, the recent royal portraits of the young Princess Diana, of Prince Charles in polo gear (both painted by Bryan Organ) and of Queen Elizabeth II (by Pietro Annigoni) all attract a great deal of discussion and interest.

► St. Martin-in-the-Fields *44E2*

Trafalgar Square
Underground: Charing Cross
Although dwarfed by its neighbors, this lovely church is by far the best building in Trafalgar Square. It was built by James Gibbs between 1721 and 1726, and resembles a classical temple, except for the fine spire that rises to 185 ft., just a fraction taller than Nelson's Column. If the arrangement of portico and steeple seems familiar, it is because this architectural masterpiece inspired many a church in early colonial America. Inside, either side of the chancel, are boxes for members of the royal family (on the left) and the staff of the Admiralty, whose office is nearby in Whitehall. This was the original home of the Academy of St. Martin-in-the-Fields, the well-known orchestra, and the free lunchtime concerts here, given by a variety of musical groups, are very popular with music lovers (Monday, Tuesday, and Friday at 1:05). The church (closed Sundays except for services) has long been known as a refuge for the homeless; nowadays it also houses a bookshop, brass rubbing center, art gallery, and restaurant (in the crypt), while a craft market is located at the rear. St. Martin-in-the-Fields is often referred to as the "church of the homeless." This is because Dick Sheppard, vicar from 1914 to 1927, opened a shelter in the crypt just after World War I to help unemployed and destitute ex-soldiers. Today the work is continued with soup kitchens and with general assistance for the homeless in the parish rooms' basement.

Famous parishioners
Many famous people are associated with the church of St. Martin-in-the-Fields. George I was the first churchwarden here, and his coat of arms appears on the pediment and above the chancel arch. Charles II was christened in an earlier church on this site in 1630 and his mistress, Nell Gwyn, was buried in the churchyard, as was Chippendale. The original burial ground is gone, however, cleared away in 1829 to make room for Duncannon Street, which runs to the south.

St Martin-in-the-Fields

St. Margaret Westminster — 44C2

Parliament Square
Underground: Westminster

This fine 16th-century church is often overlooked because it stands in the shadow of Westminster Abbey. The stained-glass windows alone make it worth a visit. The east Crucifixion window was commissioned by Ferdinand and Isabella of Spain and made in the Netherlands around A.D.1500 for the marriage of their daughter, Catherine of Aragon, to Prince Arthur. Arthur died in 1502 and Catherine became the wife of his brother, Henry VIII. After nearly 20 years of marriage had failed to produce a male heir, Henry sued for divorce (and broke away from the Catholic church in the process), on the grounds that it was not legal to marry your brother's widow. The south aisle windows contain abstract glass by John Piper (1966), while the north aisle window commemorates John Milton, who was married in this church in 1656, as were Samuel Pepys in 1655 and Winston Churchill in 1908.

The monuments of St. Margaret Church
St. Margaret Westminster contains memorials to many eminent people. A tablet near the altar marks the spot where Sir Walter Ralegh, the explorer and writer, who was beheaded for treason outside the Palace of Westminster in 1618, is said to be buried. Another tablet commemorates William Caxton, the printing pioneer, who was buried here in 1491. James Rumsey, buried here in 1792, has a memorial recalling his role as a pioneer of American steam navigation. There is also a remarkable number of Elizabethan and Jacobean monuments, of which the best is the alabaster effigy of Mary, Lady Dudley (died 1660) in the south aisle.

St. John Smith Square — 44B2

Smith Square
Underground: Westminster

This church is hidden away in the residential streets south of the Houses of Parliament, where many Members of Parliament have flats; the area is known as the "Division Bell" district because many of its pubs and restaurants are wired up to the division bell that rings to summon M.P.s to vote on issues under debate in the House of Commons. M.P.s then have exactly eight minutes in which to rush back to the chamber.

The church itself is sometimes called "Queen Anne's footstool" because of its squat appearance, and the fact that Queen Anne set up a fund to pay for this and other London churches. Built in 1728, this is in fact a bold example of English baroque. Having been bombed during World War II, it was carefully restored, and today is famous as a concert hall: Recitals given here are broadcast live by the B.B.C.

Open for concerts on Mondays at 1p.m. and usually in the evenings at 7:30.

Westminster choristers

■ Westminster Pier, which extends alongside Westminster Bridge on Victoria Embankment, is a popular departure point for trips up and down the River Thames. A wide variety of river tours is offered, including daily lunch and supper cruises and late-night disco cruises on the weekends. Most of the boats have a bar or cafe restaurant and the tours are narrated. You can just turn up and buy a ticket, but it is best to reserve in advance through a travel agent. .....■

Upriver cruises These run from April to early October and go all the way to Hampton Court (you need to set aside a whole day for this trip) and pass through some of the most beautiful and rural scenery that London has to offer, with numerous parks (such as Kew, Syon, and Richmond) coming down to the water's edge. In between are graceful Victorian suspension bridges (notably Chelsea, Albert, and Battersea Bridges) and fine views of the riverside houses and pubs of Chelsea, Chiswick, and Richmond (tel. 071 930 4721 for further information) .

Downriver cruises By contrast, these offer fine views of the City skyline, before stopping at the Tower of London. They then continue through the rejuvenated Docklands district—passing some fairly run-down areas now due for facelifts—on the way to Greenwich, home of the National Maritime Museum, with views of Canary Wharf and its massive 805 ft. tower. Longer cruises continue beyond Greenwich to the Thames Flood Barrier at Woolwich, a remarkable piece of engineering designed to prevent London from being flooded at times of exceptionally high tides or rainfall. Ten moveable gates, straddling the river, can be raised to hold the water back or lowered to let ships through. The lifting machinery for the gates is housed under sail-shaped hoods of steel (tel. 071 930 4097 for further details about downriver cruises).

The Thames Flood Barrier
Each of the Thames Flood Barrier's gates weighs 3,000 tons and is 50 ft. high. Together they constitute the world's biggest moveable flood barrier. A visitor center on Unity Way explains the barrier's workings, and you can tour round the structure by boat.

Thames Flood Barrier

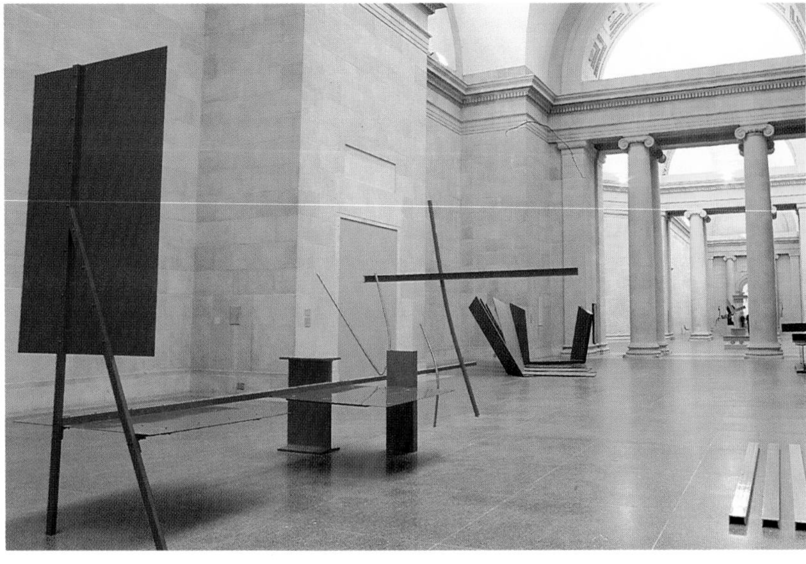

Metallic yet enigmatic —a sculpture by Anthony Caro in the Tate Gallery

The art of controversy
The Tate Gallery will be forever remembered for its purchase of a very expensive pile of bricks. "This is not art," thundered the conservative press, "any child could do it." Undeterred, the Tate recently displayed a piece entitled *Weight and Measure 1992* by the American artist Richard Serra, consisting of nothing but two huge rectangular blocks of steel, forged at great cost in Germany. It almost seems as if the Tate goes out of its way to court controversy, but the fact that it remains immensely popular, especially among art students and practising artists, says something for the gallery's policy of providing a display case for even the most outrageous works.

▶▶▶ Tate Gallery *44A2*

Millbank

Underground: Pimlico

The Tate Gallery houses two great national collections: of British art from the 16th century to the present day, and of modern (late 19th- and 20th-century) international art. Visitors who come for one often find themselves fascinated by the other, and it is the gallery's policy to juxtapose works of widely different periods and artists in such a way as to provoke and challenge the viewer into thinking about the echoes and resonances.

Under the directorship of Nick Serota, the Tate has decided to put a great deal more of its vast collection (the Turner Bequest alone consists of more than 20,000 works) on show to the public. In line with this policy a new regional Tate Gallery has opened in Liverpool, and another in St. Ives, Cornwall. The search is also on for a site in London where a new gallery could house the modern art collection. In the main Tate Gallery the works on display are changed once a year in order to highlight different artists, schools, and themes. Even so, the most popular and celebrated works are shown permanently, and the free maps, obtainable at the entrance, will help you locate them.

It is also worth remembering that the Tate has a very good gift shop and a restaurant that is highly regarded, not least because it serves distinguished wines at very reasonable prices; for that reason you will need to reserve a table in advance (lunch only, closed Sunday, tel. 071 834 6754). The excellent food in the Coffee Shop also makes this a popular spot, ranked in a recent newspaper survey as a good place for unattached art lovers to meet soul mates and potential marriage partners!

The fact that the Tate has a reputation for sociability as well as art reflects both the refreshingly informal atmosphere of the gallery, and the fact that many of the works stimulate discussion by their enigmatic or controversial nature. Everything about the building itself suggests conservatism and high seriousness; it was completed in 1897 (funded by and named after Henry Tate of the Tate & Lyle sugar company) in the high Victorian classical manner, with a giant Corinthian portico surmounted by the figure of Britannia. Yet many works inside express a challenge to convention, from William Blake's visionary illustrations for Dante's *The Divine Comedy* to Stanley Spencer's iconoclastic interpretations of *The Resurrection,* and the work of Abstract Expressionists such as Jackson Pollock.

The collection does also contain more comforting works. There is a series of pictures by John Constable, including the much-loved *Flatford Mill.* The Pre-Raphaelites are well represented by pictures such as Burne-Jones's *King Cophetua and the Beggar Maid* and Rossetti's *Beata Beatrix* (a portrait of his wife, Elizabeth Siddal). There are important works by 20th-century British artists, including Stanley Spencer, Patrick Heron, Francis Bacon, John Piper, and Graham Sutherland, and many familiar works by foreign artists, from Van Gogh to Picasso and Matisse.

Artists who have pushed forward the frontiers of perception are displayed prominently, and none more deservedly so than J.M.W. Turner, whose paintings are among the first truly modern (i.e. not strictly representational) works of art. Turner left his personal collection to the nation at his death in 1851, stipulating that the finished works should be displayed together. It took 136 years for that wish to be fulfilled, as it was not until 1987 that the Clore Gallery extension (entered to the right of the main gallery) was opened to house the Turner Bequest. Perhaps it was worth the wait, because the Clore Gallery, designed by the late James Stirling, is itself an important architectural achievement and one that displays Turner's work to best advantage—lit by natural light which does justice to his subtle palette, and offering through the windows intriguing glimpses of the Thames, beside which Turner painted in his Chelsea home and which features in many of his works.

Tate Gallery Top Ten
Ten works of art in the Tate Gallery that should not be missed:
1 *Le Baiser* (*The Kiss*) by Rodin
2 *Sir Benjamin Truman* by Thomas Gainsborough
3 *Flatford Mill* by John Constable
4 *Snowstorm: Hannibal Crossing the Alps* by J M W Turner
5 *Haymakers* by George Stubbs
6 *The Annunciation* by Dante Gabriel Rossetti
7 *The Sick Child* by Edward Munch
8 *Double Nude Portrait* by Stanley Spencer
9 *The Snail* by Henri Matisse
10 *A Bigger Splash* by David Hockney

Mark Gertler's Merry-Go-Round *(1916) in the Tate Gallery*

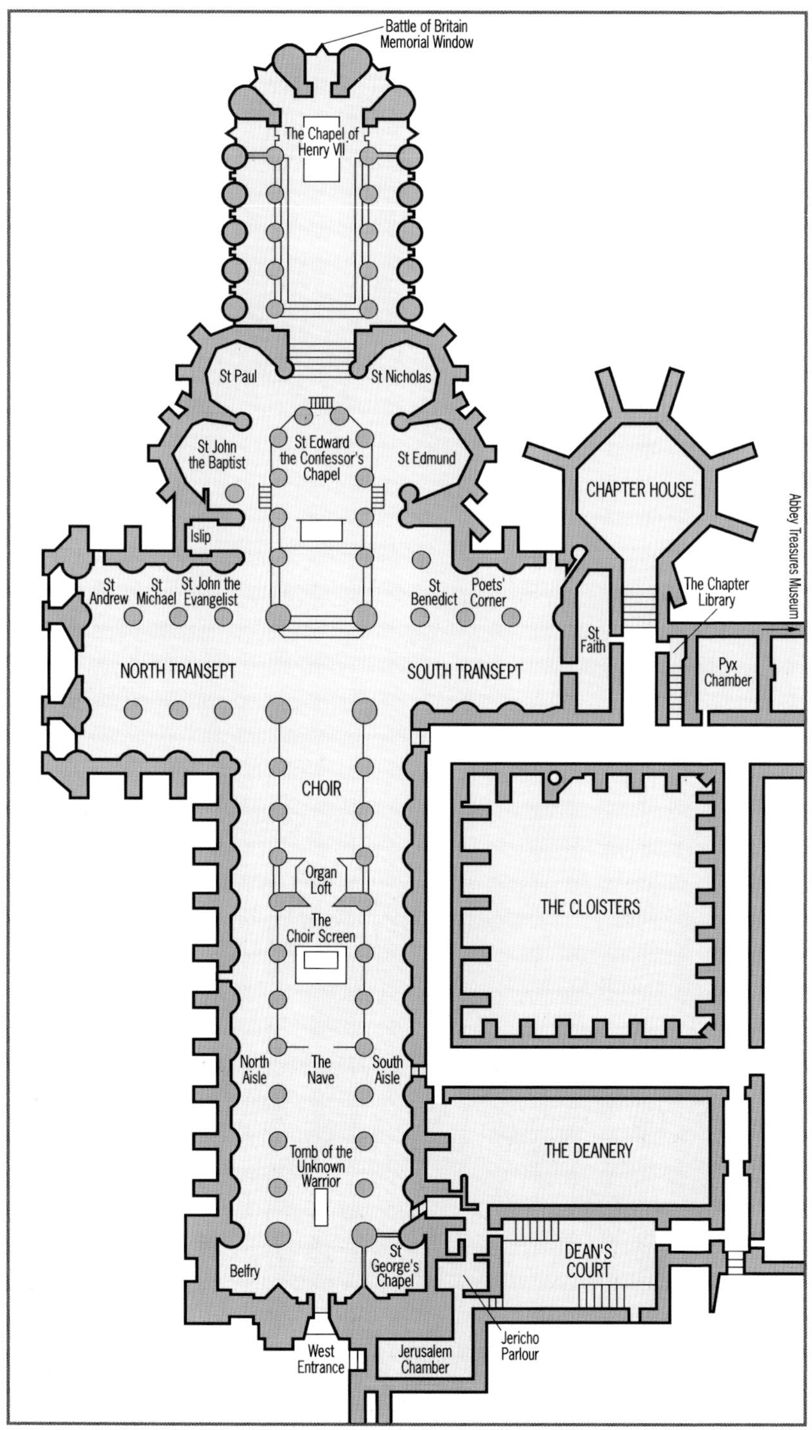

Battle of Britain Memorial Window
The Chapel of Henry VII
St Paul
St Nicholas
St John the Baptist
St Edward the Confessor's Chapel
St Edmund
CHAPTER HOUSE
Abbey Treasures Museum
Islip
St Andrew
St Michael
St John the Evangelist
St Benedict
Poets' Corner
The Chapter Library
St Faith
Pyx Chamber
NORTH TRANSEPT
SOUTH TRANSEPT
CHOIR
THE CLOISTERS
Organ Loft
The Choir Screen
North Aisle
The Nave
South Aisle
THE DEANERY
Tomb of the Unknown Warrior
DEAN'S COURT
Belfry
St George's Chapel
Jericho Parlour
West Entrance
Jerusalem Chamber

Floorplan of Westminster Abbey

The fan-vaulted Henry VII Chapel

▶▶▶ Westminster Abbey *44C2*

Broad Sanctuary
Underground: Westminster

Westminster Abbey is a huge monument, which is crowded at all times but more so in the mornings when coach tours arrive together. To experience the full serenity of the building, it is worth attending a service (8a.m. and 5p.m. Monday to Friday; 8a.m. and 3p.m. Saturday and Sunday), not least to hear the choir boys of Westminster School, accompanied by the abbey organ on which Henry Purcell once played. Parts of the abbey are closed on Sunday except to those attending services.

History The abbey that gave its name to Westminster stood here in the 8th century, but the present building was begun by Edward the Confessor around 1050. He died a week after its consecration, on January 6, 1066 and was the first monarch to be buried here. A year later, William the Conqueror was crowned here, confirming the royal status of the church, which has seen the coronation of every subsequent English monarch.

Edward the Confessor was later canonised, and Henry III embarked on large-scale rebuilding in 1245 to make a shrine fit for the veneration of the sainted king. Today's church, greatly influenced by the French Gothic cathedrals of Amiens and Reims, was the result. In 1503, the Lady Chapel at the east end was replaced by the Henry VII Chapel, the architectural high point of the church. The

The Tomb of the Unknown Warrior

Of the many monuments in Westminster Abbey, the Tomb of the Unknown Warrior, located just in front of the west door, is perhaps the most moving. The simple grave, covered with a black marble slab, contains one anonymous soldier, symbolizing more than a million on the British side alone who gave their lives in World War I. He was buried here on November 11, 1920 in soil brought from the battlefields of France and Belgium. In front is another simple memorial, to Winston Churchill, who died in 1965 and lies buried at Bladon in Oxfordshire, near his birthplace.

More monuments
The north transept contains monuments to many eminent statesmen, including Peel, Gladstone, Palmerston, and Pitt the Elder, while the north choir aisle near the organ is dedicated to musicians, including Purcell, Elgar, Vaughan Williams, and Britten. One of the best monuments here is to the relatively unknown Lady Elizabeth Nightingale. She died in 1731 (the monument erroneously says 1734) of a miscarriage, having been frightened by lightning. A dramatic monument by the French sculptor Roubiliac (in the St. Michael Chapel) depicts her lying in her husband's arms as Death aims his spear at her heart.

west front was not completed until 1745, when the two towers were built to Nicholas Hawksmoor's design. It is there that a tour should begin.

The Nave Entering the west door, look upwards to the majestic nave roof. An astonishing feature of the church is its great height (105 ft.) in relation to its width. The complex patterning of the vault carries the eye eastwards; only by looking up can you appreciate the enormous length of the building, since at ground level the view is stopped by the 19th-century screen that separates the nave from the choir and crossing. Before moving on, note the Tomb of the Unknown Warrior straight ahead and St. George's Chapel to the right, now dedicated to the dead of two World Wars. Just outside the chapel, on a pillar to the left, is a portrait of Richard II (1377–99), the oldest known true portrait of an English monarch.

The Choir and Sanctuary Having paid an admission fee to penetrate beyond the choir screen, you enter the ceremonial heart of the church where services—and royal coronations—take place. There are good views to left and right of the huge and intricate rose windows of the transept. The sanctuary itself is railed off: The floor has a very rare cosmati work pavement, a form of mosaic made of glass and precious stones, dated 1268, but this is usually covered by a carpet.

Hawksmoor's towers

Henry VII Chapel Continuing round the north side of the sanctuary, you are led first into the north aisle of the Henry VII Chapel to view the white-marble effigy of Elizabeth I (died 1603), who shares a tomb with her half-sister, Mary I (died 1558). From the aisle you enter the main part of the Henry VII Chapel. This is the most exciting part of the abbey, with its exquisite fan-vaulted ceiling, and makes an impressive setting for the royal tombs that are arranged around the altar and aisles. Among the finest of these is the tomb of Henry VII, in front of the altar, and of his mother, Lady Margaret Beaufort, near the south aisle altar. Mother and son both died in the same year (1509), and both tombs are the work of the Florentine sculptor, Pietro Torrigiani (who, as a boy, was often involved in fights with Michelangelo). The tombs were the first examples of Renaissance carving to be seen in Britain; there is a certain irony in the fact that the king who built this chapel, the final flowering of Perpendicular Gothic architecture, should be buried in a tomb whose Renaissance style was to eclipse the Gothic.

The chapel is used for installing Knights of the Bath, an order founded by Henry IV in 1399, and their banners hang above the flamboyant canopies of the wooden stalls. More down to earth are the stall misericords, carved with depictions of mermaids, monsters, and a wife beating her husband.

Poets' Corner
Among the best monuments in Poets' Corner are the busts of Dryden, Jonson, Milton, and Blake—the latter sculpted in bronze by Sir Jacob Epstein in 1957. There is also a fine statue of Shakespeare, paid for by public subscription and made in 1740. Two non-poets, though, have the finest monuments of all, both carved by Roubiliac: the composer Handel, on the west wall, holding pages from his oratorio *Messiah*, and the soldier-statesman John, Duke of Argyll and Greenwich, to the left of Handel, surrounded by figures symbolizing Liberty, Eloquence, and Wisdom.

The Confessor's Chapel A bridge leads from the Henry VII Chapel to the Confessor's Chapel, where the king who founded the abbey is buried, along with Henry III, who rebuilt it. Their tombs are plain by comparison with that of Queen Eleanor (died 1290), portrayed in an effigy of bronze. Here too is the wooden Coronation Chair made in 1300, on which all British monarchs are crowned. It incorporates the ancient Scottish throne, the Stone of Scone, which dates back to at least the 9th century and was captured by Edward I in 1297. Scottish nationalists have often tried to reclaim the Stone, so far without success.

Poets' Corner The south side of the sanctuary leads back to the south transept, which, since the 16th century, has been the place where great poets and authors are honored with memorials (though not all are buried here).

The Cloister, Chapter House, and Abbey Treasures Museum A door in the south choir aisle leads to the cloister, with its fine, flowing tracery and superb views of the flying buttresses that support the nave. The Chapter House is an octagonal building of 1253, whose floor is covered in its original tiles. It was here that parliament met between 1257 and 1547, before moving to the Palace of Westminster. For children, the Abbey's highlight is the Norman undercroft, one of the few remaining parts of Edward the Confessor's original church, which houses the Abbey Treasures Museum. Here the macabre wax effigies of Queen Elizabeth I, Charles II, and Lord Nelson are displayed, made using death masks and the real clothes of the people: Nelson's hat and eye-patch are those he wore in life. Some effigies were used to substitute the body for lyings-in-state; others were made in the 18th century to attract visitors to the Abbey.

ST. JAMES'S AND THE MALL

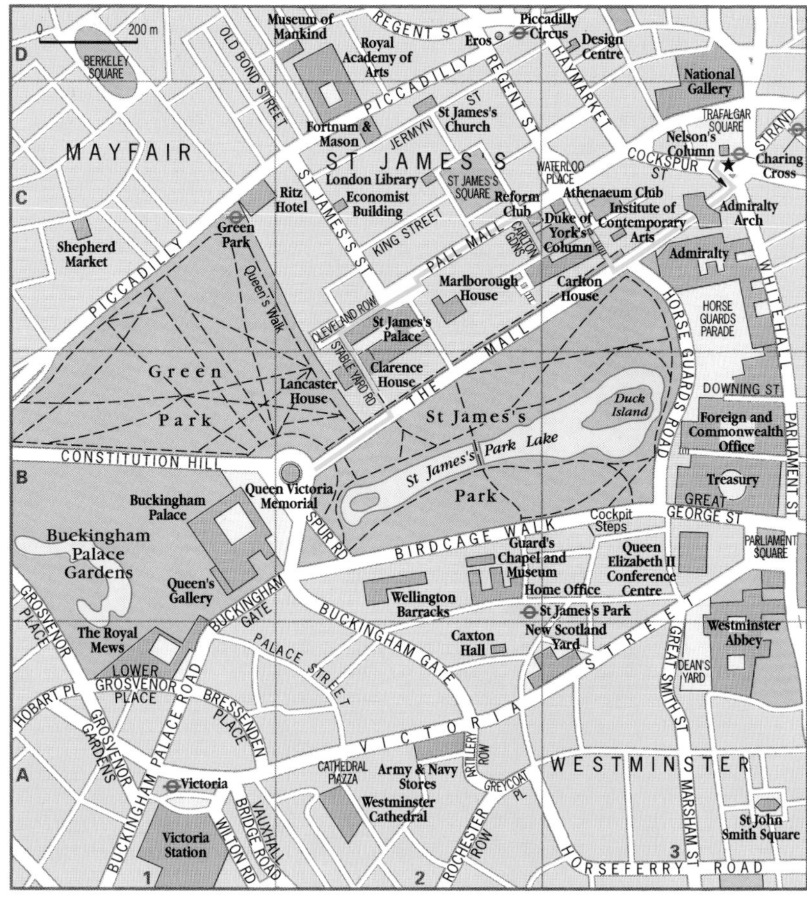

The game of "pell mell"
The Mall and Pall Mall, which runs parallel to the north, are both named after the game of *paille maille* (French for "ball mallet"), or "pell mell" in English. This was a sort of cross between golf and croquet, very popular in the time of Charles II, when London had several such alleys laid out for the game. The aim was to hit the wooden ball through an iron hoop suspended above the alley. No doubt its popularity was partly due to the money that changed hands in the bets accompanying the game.

St. James's and the Mall If Westminster is the center of government, then its neighbor, St. James's, is the seat of royalty. Buckingham Palace, the Queen's official London residence, sits at one end of the Mall, a wide avenue laid out in 1660 that forms the ceremonial route taken by the royal family on great state occasions, such as Trooping the Colour and the State Opening of Parliament.

Not far away is the much older St. James's Palace, surrounded by buildings of aristocratic elegance that house such institutions as the Royal Society, the Royal Fine Art Commission and the Institute of Directors. Famous "gentlemen's" clubs, such as the Athenaeum and the Reform, dominate the Pall Mall area, and the exclusive tone of the whole district is confirmed by the expensive shops of Jermyn Street.

St. James's and the Mall walk If you begin this walk around 10a.m. you should reach Buckingham Palace in time for the Changing of the Guard ceremony (11:20a.m.–12:05p.m. daily from April to August, every other day for the rest of the year).

Starting from Trafalgar Square, walk to the southwest to reach Admiralty Arch. Built in 1910 as a memorial to

Lock & Co, the hat maker, sets St. James's stylish tone

Queen Victoria, the arch separates the chaotic traffic of Trafalgar Square from the relative calm of the Mall. To the left is the grim and windowless **Citadel**, built as a bomb shelter for Admiralty staff in 1940, and ahead is Buckingham Palace. On the right is the front of **Carlton House Terrace**, built in 1832 to the designs of John Nash; at No. 12 is the entrance to the **Institute of Contemporary Arts**, an unlikely-looking site presenting innovative art, drama, film, and video.

The first turning right leads up the Duke of York Steps. Here the **Duke of York's column**, erected in 1833, commemorates the son of George III, who commanded the British army during the Napoleonic Wars. Beyond lies **Waterloo Place**, with more memorials, notably an equestrian statue of Edward VII; another, to the right, of Captain Scott, the Antarctic explorer; and, ahead, the Guards' Crimean Memorial, with a statue of Florence Nightingale.

Turn left into Carlton House Terrace, take the first right into Carlton Gardens, then turn left into Pall Mall, before carrying on into Cleveland Row to get to **St. James's Palace**, a surprisingly homey brick mansion built during the reign of Henry VIII. It was the chief royal residence until Queen Victoria moved to Buckingham Palace in 1837. **Clarence House**, to the west of the palace, is the home of the Queen Mother; there is no public access, but you can see the sentries on duty outside the gatehouse.

Walk past the gatehouse and turn left into Stable Yard Road, passing **Lancaster House**, on the right. This was the venue for the Lancaster House Conference of 1978, when Lord David Owen, then Foreign Secretary, presided over talks that led to the end of white rule in Rhodesia (now Zimbabwe). The building is now used by the government to entertain important foreign visitors.

Having returned to the Mall, turn to the right and walk up towards Buckingham Palace.

Buckingham Palace and the Queen Victoria Memorial

The court and the season
When the Queen is in residence at Buckingham Palace, the Royal Standard is flown from the flagpole above the central pediment. You are most likely to see the flag between April and mid-August, the period when the Queen holds court in London, still known as "the season." Among aristocratic circles the season is marked by numerous social, sporting and fund-raising events, though young ladies making their first official appearances in public ("debutantes" or "debs") are no longer "presented" at court. Come mid-August, the gentry heads for the country for the shooting season, and the Queen circulates between her other residences at Windsor, Sandringham, and Balmoral.

▶▶▶ Buckingham Palace 62B1

Buckingham Gate
Underground: Victoria
The royal court has moved several times in the last 900 years: first from the City to the Palace of Westminster under Edward the Confessor, then to Whitehall Palace under Henry VIII, then to St. James's Palace under Charles II. St. James's remained the official residence of the sovereign throughout the 17th and 18th centuries, and it was here that the big state functions took place. (Foreign ambassadors are still officially accredited to "the Court of St. James's.") Even so, the cramped and ancient Tudor buildings of St. James's could hardly be called palatial, and many a monarch would retire at night to the more opulent rooms of Kensington Palace (see pages 112–13).

It was at Kensington that Queen Victoria lived from her birth in 1819 until her accession to the throne in 1837. She then chose to make Buckingham Palace the official London residence of the court, and thus it has remained to the present day.

The palace is named after Buckingham House, built for the Duke of Buckingham in 1705. It was purchased by George III in 1761 and subsequently remodeled and extended several times, most recently in 1913, when the 363 ft. façade was reworked by Sir Aston Webb. Against this classical backdrop one of London's most popular events takes place daily at 11:20a.m.–12:05p.m. (every other day from August to the end of March), when sentries of the Guards Division in full dress uniform perform the Changing of the Guard. Spectators watch from the palace railings with their five wrought-iron and bronze gates, decorated with cherubs and erected in 1906. An alternative vantage point is the Queen Victoria Memorial, which stands in the traffic island in front of the palace (though climbing it is discouraged). This marble column, erected in 1911, is topped by the gilded figure of Victory, while Queen Victoria sits facing down the Mall, accompanied by the figures of Charity, Truth, and Justice. Surrounding this is a balustrade decorated with mermaids and bronze groups representing Peace, Prosperity, Manufacturing, Agriculture, Painting, Architecture, Shipbuilding, and Mining.

The Queen's Gallery Although Buckingham Palace is only open in August and September, you can visit the Queen's Gallery at the rear of the building all year. This is housed in a temple-like structure that was originally built as a garden conservatory, then converted to the palace chapel in 1893 and finally turned into an art gallery in 1962. Here you can see exhibitions of paintings, drawings, and furniture drawn from the vast royal collections, including works by Rubens, Rembrandt, and Canaletto, as well as watercolors painted by Queen Victoria. The material on display is changed every six months or so.

The Royal Mews More interesting for children is the Royal Mews, built in 1824–25 to house the royal household's horses and coaches. Here are displayed the splendid state carriages that are used on major state occasions. They include the richly carved and gilded Gold Carriage, made for George III in 1762 and used for coronations; the Irish State Coach, bought by Queen Victoria in 1852 and used for the State Opening of Parliament; the so-called Glass State Coach, bought in 1910 and used to convey visiting dignitaries and overseas ambassadors; and the open-top landau used for the weddings of the Prince and Princess of Wales in 1981 and the Duke and Duchess of York in 1986.

Visiting the palace
In 1993 the Queen announced that Buckingham Palace would open to the public for the first time in its long history—but only for six weeks a year, from mid-August to the end of September. The funds raised from admission charges will contribute to the cost of restoring Windsor Castle (see page 236). Despite the very high entrance fee, you should expect long lines, full of people hoping for an intimate insight into the royal lifestyle. The State Apartments are, indeed, very impressive, decorated in the neoclassical style of the mid-19th century.

Mounted officers leaving Buckingham Palace

These two streets are packed with shops that are worth seeing whether you intend to buy anything or not (and many of the goods bear a very high price tag). Some shops have been trading here since the 1760s and several retain their 18th-century frontages and fittings. In keeping with the "gentlemanly" tone of the whole area, these shops cater largely to the tastes of wealthy Englishmen, although it is possible to buy women's clothes, food, antiques, or jewelry. .....

By Royal Appointment
Several shops in the Jermyn Street area display a royal coat of arms, indicating that they have been granted a coveted Royal Warrant of Appointment. Royal Warrants can be granted by The Queen, The Queen Mother, the Prince of Wales, and the Duke of Edinburgh. To qualify, the shop must have been patronized by one of them for at least three years. A handful (including Harrods of Knightsbridge, Piccadilly booksellers Hatchards, and the General Trading Company of Sloane Street) hold all four.

A good place to start is the **Design Centre,** 28 Haymarket. This is run by the government sponsored Design Council and exhibits the best examples of British design, ranging from furniture to industrial tools. There are also gifts and books and magazines on design, art, and architecture on sale.

Jermyn Street proper begins on the opposite side of Haymarket: Once you cross over Regent Street the temptations (for male shoppers) come thick and fast. On the right, **Herbie Frogg** (No. 18) sells men's clothes of modern cut. Next door is **Geo F. Trumper**, hairdresser to some of the most eminent heads in London, followed by **Bates the Hatter**, selling deerstalkers and Panama hats. The masculine tone continues on the opposite side of the road with **Astley's** (No. 109A), selling briar pipes. Next comes **Russell & Bromley**'s shoe shop (No. 95) and **Robin Symes** (No. 94), an antiques dealer specializing in Greek and Roman sculpture. Next door is a highly regarded food establishment, **Paxton & Whitfield** (No. 93). The shop front is mid-Victorian and the company, founded in 1740, stocks a huge array of cheeses, game pies, hams, pâtés, and wines. The Queen Mother buys her provisions

Clothes for the fastidious at Turnbull & Asser

here, while both the Queen and the Prince of Wales patronize **Floris** the perfumier (No. 89). These shops all stand opposite the back entrance to St. James's Church (see page 79). Further down on the right is the short Princes Arcade, built in the 1880s, while further up is the Piccadilly Arcade with its gleaming bow windows, built in Georgian style in 1910.

Passing several more clothing and antiques shops you will come to **Wiltons** restaurant (No. 55), known for its oysters and traditional English cooking (game is a speciality). **Turnbull & Asser** (No. 71), nearly opposite, is a custom tailor specializing in silk and cotton shirts, famous for attention to clients' often idiosyncratic tastes. For made-to-measure shirts you must allow time for fittings and order a minimum of six; ready-made shirts are also available for the less fastidious. At the end of Jermyn Street, turn left into St. James's Street for yet another shop with a pronounced masculine flavor—**Davidoff** (No. 35), full of the aroma of leather, old wood, pipe tobaccos, and cigars.

Further down St. James's Street, you will pass the **Economist Building** (No. 25), an example of modern architecture (1964) that fits in well with the surrounding 18th-century premises of leading clubs (see pages 68–69). The second turning left, King Street, leads to **Christie's,** the auctioneers established in 1766 (No. 8), where new heights were scaled in 1989 when Van Gogh's *Sunflowers* sold for £25 million. **Spink & Son** (No. 7) is perhaps best-known as a dealer in coins, medals, and paper money, but the museum-like rooms of the gallery also display English and Oriental art.

Back on St. James's Street, you will find **John Lobb** (No. 9) the shoemaker, where the staff makes models of patrons' feet in wood for shoes that are a uniquely perfect fit. **Lock & Co** (No. 6) does the same thing for heads (established in 1700; it made Lord Nelson's famous cocked hats). Two doors down is an alley leading to Pickering Place, a paved courtyard typical of many that once existed in 18th-century London. **Berry Bros & Rudd** (No. 3) is early Georgian and hardly changed: Customers scrutinize the wine list, and staff fetch up bottles of rare wines and liquors from the cellars below. There is a huge pair of 18th-century scales to the left of the entrance, designed for weighing humans who are concerned about the effects of too much after-dinner port and brandy.

The pick of pipes

The Economist Building
The Economist Building in St. James's Street is one of a very small number of modern buildings that has been listed Grade II, meaning that it is considered such an important example of architecture that it may not be altered or demolished without government approval. The complex, designed by Alison and Peter Smithson and built between 1962 and 1964, is grouped around a quiet plaza containing Henry Moore's *Reclining Figure* (1969) and other modern sculptures. The buildings house the offices of *The Economist* magazine, a bank, and apartments. They are faced in Portland stone and seem to have a sculptured quality all of their own. The careful siting of the different offices within the complex allows framed glimpses of the Georgian and Victorian buildings that surround it.

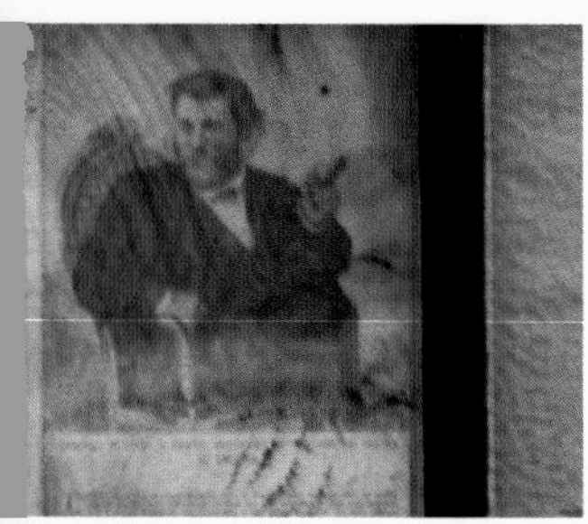

"Clubland" is the name given to St. James's by the popular press because it contains many of London's most exclusive gentlemen's clubs. Most were founded in the 18th century and flourished in an age when men and women led separate social lives, the woman's domain being confined to the home. Some clubs also served as gambling dens, where many an aristocratic fortune was thrown away over an evening's game of cards. .....

Pubs and restaurants
Though you are not allowed within the hallowed walls of London's exclusive clubs, you can at least try one of the nearby restaurants that have a clublike atmosphere. One of the best is Greens (35–6 Duke Street, tel. 071 930 4566), where they serve the same sort of traditional food as club members enjoy: steak and kidney pie, followed by jam roly-poly pudding, for example. Wiltons (55 Jermyn Street, tel. 071 629 9955) is renowned for game, seafood, oysters, and fine port wines. Less expensive is the Red Lion (2 Duke of York Street), a very well preserved Victorian pub full of mahogany paneling and cut glass.

As men began to spend more time at home with their families, the appeal of clubs began to decline, and by the 1930s they were known as the last bastion of crusty, reclusive, and conservative bachelordom. In recent years, though, clubs have undergone something of a revival, partly because some provide excellent sports facilities and an overnight place to stay. Even so, the main attraction remains the same as ever: the snob appeal of belonging to an exclusive circle (mostly of men, since few clubs admit women as members even today).

Pall Mall, leading westwards from Trafalgar Square, is Clubland's main artery. Here, standing on opposite sides of Waterloo Place, you will find the **Institute of Directors**, a club for business leaders, and the **Athenaeum**. If the buildings seem to echo each other, it is because both are the work of Decimus Burton. The Athenaeum is named after Athena, Goddess of Wisdom; her statue stands on the porch, and a frieze, based on the sculptures of the Parthenon, runs beneath the cornice. Founded in 1824 as a club for writers and artists, the Athenaeum's members today include bishops, scientists, and civil servants.

The Athenaeum's neighbors are the **Travellers' Club** and the **Reform**. When the former was founded in 1819, members had to prove that they had traveled more than 500 miles from London—not so easy in the pre-railway age. The Reform, as its name suggests, was formed by supporters of the 1832 Reform Act, which paved the way for an electoral system based on one person, one vote. James Barry was the architect for both buildings; despite their measured Renaissance-style exteriors, the interiors are sumptuous.

The same is true of **The Royal Automobile Club** (No. 89), where members enjoy the use of a marble-lined swimming pool. The RAC stands opposite St. James's Square, first laid out in 1663. The houses around the perimeter were intended for members of the nobility who wanted to live close to St. James's Palace, which was then the official residence of the monarch. **No. 5** was the Libyan People's Bureau; the flowers in the gardens opposite mark a memorial to Yvonne Fletcher, the policewoman who was killed by a Libyan gunman during the siege of April 1984. **No. 10** (Chatham House) is the former residence of three Prime Ministers, William Pitt, the Earl of Derby, and William Gladstone. At **No. 14** is the London Library—which is not a club, though you do have to be

elected to membership and pay a fee. It was founded in 1841 by the historian and polemicist, Thomas Carlyle, and the book collections include many rare and out-of-print volumes. It is much used today by academics, journalists, and writers.

Continuing up Pall Mall, you will pass the **Oxford and Cambridge Club** before turning right into St. James's Street. This street has several of London's oldest clubs, as well as numerous buildings that were built as clubs but have since been turned to other uses. Many are built in Palladian style with fine Venetian windows, columns, and balustrades. At Nos. 69–70 is the **Carlton Club**, whose members include many Conservative Party M.P.s. The Carlton Club is a relative newcomer on the scene, having been founded in 1832. By contrast, **Brooks's Club** (No. 61), started up in 1764; **Boodles** (No. 28), started in 1762; and **White's** (No. 37) is the oldest institution of them all, having evolved from White's Chocolate and Gaming House in 1693.

The Athenaeum, on Pall Mall, was founded in 1824

The arts and sciences
Besides its clubs, St. James's houses the premises of several prestigious bodies. The Royal Society, at No. 6 Carlton House Terrace, was founded by Charles II in 1660 as a scientific society with Samuel Pepys, Christopher Wren, and Isaac Newton among its early Presidents. Today it numbers many Nobel Prize winners among its members. Near by, at No. 17 Carlton House Terrace, you will find the Mall Galleries (open daily 10–5), which display landscapes, portraits, and watercolor paintings by members of the Federation of British Artists; most are for sale. This work tends to be traditional, in contrast with experimental works exhibited at the Institute of Contemporary Arts (Nash House, The Mall, open daily, noon–8 or later).

Scott's Government Offices above the trees of St. James's Park

The landscaping of St. James's Park
Under Henry VIII, St. James's Park was a deer park reserved for royal use. Charles I turned it into a formal garden, and it must have been a matter of great anguish to him that he walked to his death on the scaffold through its leafy avenues. Charles II introduced the wildfowl and opened the park to the public, employing the French landscape gardener, Le Nôtre, to turn it into a pleasure ground. Le Nôtre's work was swept away under George IV, who employed John Nash to give the park a more naturalistic look. Nash reshaped Le Nôtre's canal to create the fine meandering lake, with its central bridge, that still lends so much charm to the park today.

St. James's Park

62B2

St. James's Park is the most attractive of all London's green spaces, principally because of its lovely views. From the footbridge that crosses the lake at the heart of the park there are uninterrupted views westwards to the classical façade of Buckingham Palace, while to the east you see the rear of Sir George Gilbert Scott's glorious Government Offices, all turrets and onion domes, framed by the weeping willows whose branches cascade down to the fringes of the lake. Several varieties of wildfowl add to the lake's attractions; many of the birds are quite tame. You can either take a stroll all the way around the perimeter of the lake, or concentrate on the views from the bridge and then head south to Birdcage Walk, the road that forms the southern park boundary (there were aviaries here in the time of James II).

On the opposite side of the road, Cockpit Steps (a reminder that the birds were also used for sport) lead up to Queen Anne's Gate, a charming enclave of early 18th-century houses, several of them with very ornate wooden canopies over their front doors. There is a statue of Queen Anne in front of No. 15 and blue plaques abound, recording the famous people who were born here or who lived here in the past. No. 36 is the home of the National Trust, England's foremost historic preservation body, which owns and manages many of the country's finest houses and gardens.

At the southern junction of Queen Anne's Gate with Broadway you will find the London Transport Headquarters, above St. James's Park underground station, noted for its façade sculptures: Jacob Epstein's bold figures of *Day and Night* flank the entrance, and higher up are reliefs symbolizing the winds and carved by five artists, including Eric Gill and Henry Moore.

▶ Wellington Barracks 62B2

Birdcage Walk
Underground: Victoria
This building serves as the headquarters of the Guards Division, the soldiers, resplendent in scarlet dress uniforms and bearskin hats, who perform the Changing of the Guard ceremony at Buckingham Palace. Visitors can see the Guards' Chapel (open Monday to Friday, 10–3:30; Sunday service 11a.m.), whose war memorial cloister brings home the grimmer side of the Guards' work. The chapel itself was hit by a bomb in 1944, killing 121 people who were attending a service. It was rebuilt in 1963, incorporating the remains of the 19th-century apse.

The Guards' Museum (open Monday to Thursday, 10–4) is worth a visit if you are interested in military history. It explains the history of the regiments that make up the Household Division and the duties they perform as the official bodyguard to the Queen.

▶ Westminster Cathedral 62A2

Ashley Place
Underground: Victoria
This exuberant Byzantine-style building, with its echoes of the great Basilica of St. Mark in Venice, is the principal Roman Catholic church in England, the seat of the Archbishop of Westminster. It was begun in 1895 but remains unfinished: It was intended that the whole interior be lined with marble and mosaics but the funds were sufficient only to complete the facing of the lower surfaces, leaving the upper surfaces impressively bare. The nave piers feature the 14 Stations of the Cross, crisply carved by the young Eric Gill in his distinctive style. For most visitors, the other main attraction is the superb campanile, built, like the rest of the church, of brick alternating with bands of Portland stone, very similar to Siena Cathedral's belltower. It is 273 ft. in height and there are outstanding views from the summit of all the main buildings of central London and far beyond to the surrounding countryside: What's more, you don't have to be in good physical shape to enjoy the view, since there is an elevator to take you to the top. (Campanile open every day from mid-March to end October, 9–5.)

The stones of Westminster Cathedral
The variegated marbles that cover the walls of Westminster Cathedral came from some of the most ancient and renowned quarries in Europe. Two columns at the west end are of red Norwegian granite, symbolizing the blood of Christ. The green columns came from Thessaly, the same source as the marble used to build Haghia Sophia in Istanbul, to which this church bears a strong resemblance. The white capitals are of Carrara marble, the stone favored by Renaissance sculptors such as Michelangelo. The high altar is a massive block of Cornish granite and the canopy, or baldachino, is supported on columns of yellow Verona marble.

Westminster Cathedral, Britain's premier Catholic church

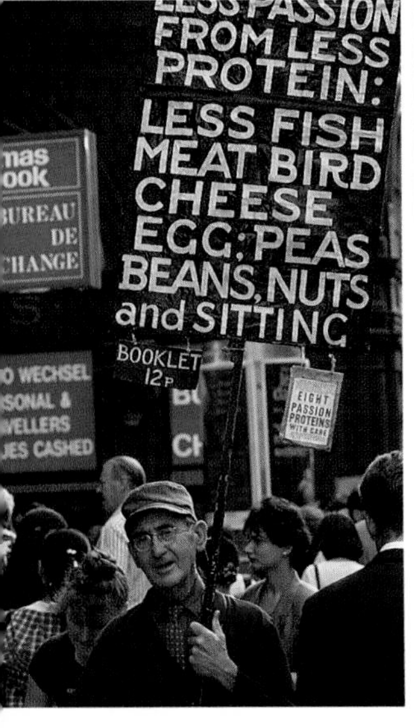

Oxford Street protest

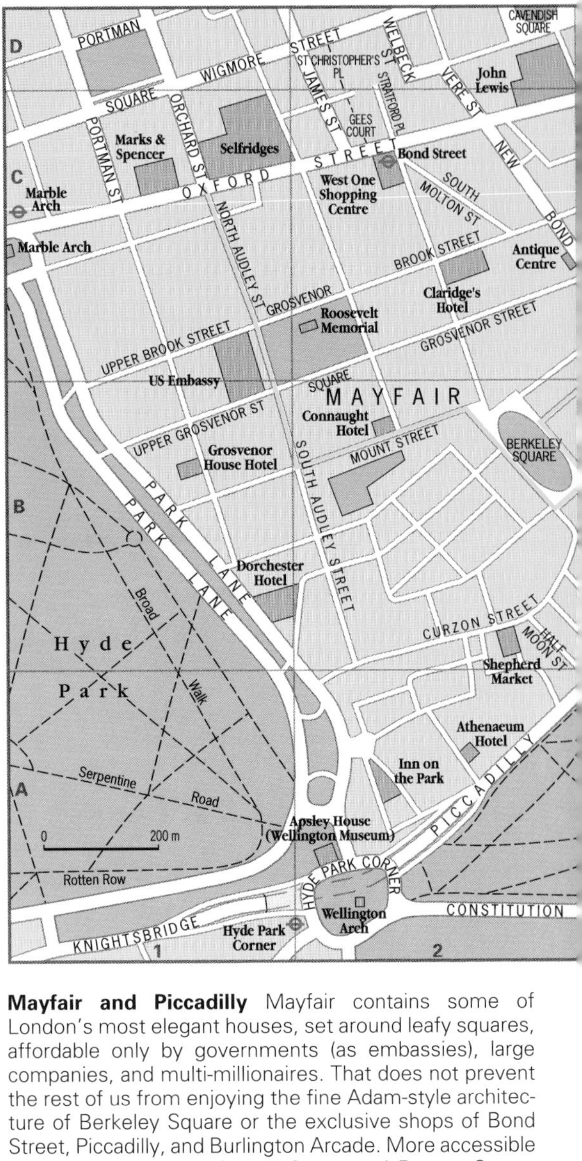

Mayfair and Piccadilly Mayfair contains some of London's most elegant houses, set around leafy squares, affordable only by governments (as embassies), large companies, and multi-millionaires. That does not prevent the rest of us from enjoying the fine Adam-style architecture of Berkeley Square or the exclusive shops of Bond Street, Piccadilly, and Burlington Arcade. More accessible to most budgets are Oxford Street and Regent Street, lined with well-known shops and department stores.

Mayfair and Piccadilly walk Starting at Green Park Underground station, walk east down Piccadilly to reach **Burlington Arcade**, the fifth turning on the left. Burlington Arcade is a covered promenade, built in 1819—one of England's first "shopping precincts." The arcade is Regency in style and atmosphere. Exclusive shops selling antiques, pewter, and clothing line either side, and rules of propriety are enforced by the Beadles, in their top hats and great coats (these retired members of the 10th Hussars regiment are actually very approachable if you need help).

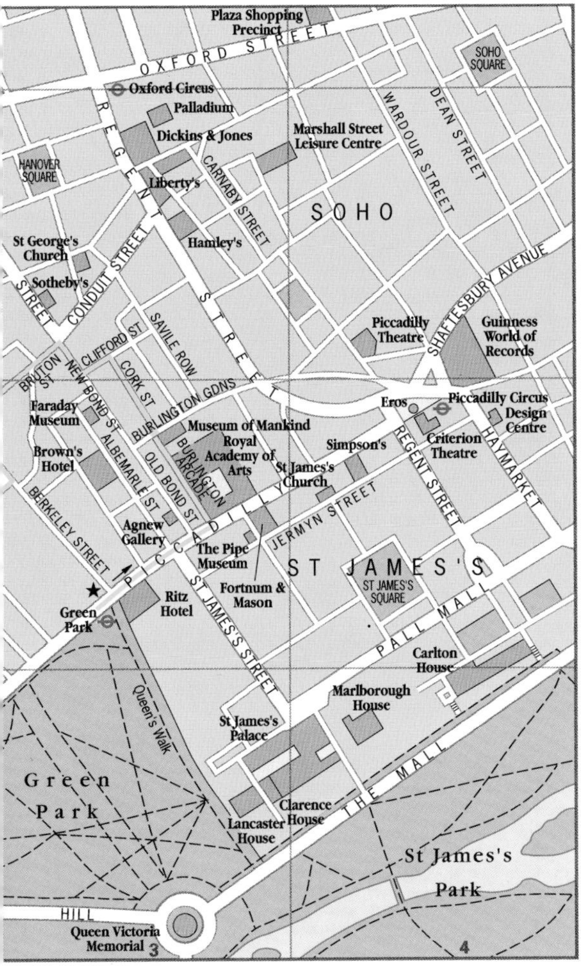

At the opposite end of the arcade, cross Burlington Gardens and walk up Cork Street before turning left into Clifford Street, past well-known art dealers displaying everything from contemporary art to Old Masters.

Turning right into Bond Street brings you to Bruton Street, on the left; on the corner is the Time-Life Building (1952), with panels carved by Henry Moore set in the terrace parapet. Turn left down Bruton Street to **Berkeley Square**. The west side is lined with Georgian houses; you may glimpse through the windows, lavishly plastered interiors and grand staircases.

The top left-hand exit out of Berkeley Square leads left into **Mount Street**. The **Connaught Hotel**, on the right, has one of London's best restaurants.

Turn right at The Audley pub into South Audley Street to reach **Grosvenor Square**, the scene of anti-Vietnam war rallies in the 1960s, the target being the fortress-like American Embassy on the left.

North Audley Street leads from the top left-hand corner of Grosvenor Square to Oxford Street.

■ **Old and New Bond streets together form a continuous thoroughfare cutting through the heart of Mayfair and lined with fashionable shops. Starting at the Piccadilly end, there is a succession of picture dealers selling museum-quality works: On the left is Thos. Agnew and Marlborough Fine Arts, and on the right is the Leger Gallery (No. 13), specializing in British art of the 18th and 19th centuries, and Colnaghi (No. 14), selling European paintings and sculpture. Opposite, Gianni Versace's elegant shop, with marble floors and stucco ceilings, sells the best of Italian couture. .....■**

Savile Row
Parallel with New Bond Street, three blocks east, is Savile Row, a byword for gentlemen's tailoring. Tommy Nutter (No. 19) designs Elton John's way-out clothes; his impeccably tailored suits are worn by many women. Savile Row was where the Beatles made their last public appearance, an impromptu performance on the roof of the Apple Building in 1969.

Bond Street prices are high, but window shoppers can have a field day. Beyond Stafford Street, on the left, is **Gucci**, followed by the cheerful orange-and-white façade of the **Royal Arcade**, where **Charbonnel et Walker** (No. 1) sell their exquisite chocolates, and other shops specialize in silver, paintings, and antiques. The Arcade leads to **Albemarle Street** with more art galleries, plus **Brown's Hotel** (No. 23)—one of London's best, and the **Royal Institution** (Nos. 20–1). The latter, with its temple-like façade, was founded in 1799 for the promotion of scientific knowledge. A small museum in the basement is devoted to the pioneering electro-magnetic experiments of Michael Faraday (open Tuesday to Thursday, 1–4).

Bond Street means silver, paintings, and antiques

Back on Old Bond Street, the **Ferragamo** boutique stands on the right, and if you turn down **Burlington Gardens**, then left into **Cork Street**, you will find several galleries specializing in the works of modern artists.

Asprey & Co (Nos. 165–9 New Bond Street) stands at the junction of Old Bond Street (laid out in 1686) and New Bond Street (extended in 1721). Asprey's itself has big windows of plate glass and iron, considered revolutionary when they were installed around 1848, and is the shop where members of the royal family buy jewelry (Princess Diana's engagement ring was bought here).

Further up, on the corner of New Bond Street and Bruton Street, is **Hermes**, best known for its silk scarves. Beyond Bruton Street, on the left, **The Fine Art Society** (No. 148) has a deep-set shop front dating from 1876 and sells works by 19th- and 20th-century British artists at surprisingly reasonable prices.

Sotheby's (No. 35), on the right, has a modest entrance for such a well-known auctioneers' house. There are viewings and sales here most days: details at the information desk (or tel. 071 493 8080). Rare antiques can also be found at the **Bond Street Antiques Centre** (No. 124) and the **Bond Street Silver Galleries** (Nos. 111–12).

Designer-label clothing and shoe shops predominate in the upper stretch of New Bond Street, but if their prices are beyond your means, try **Fenwicks**, the stylish department store to be found on your right at the Brook Street intersection.

Turning right down Brook Street you will enter **Hanover Square**, laid out in 1717 and named after the Elector of Hanover who took the throne as King George I in 1714. The Hanover Square Rooms (since demolished) were famous for annual performances of Handel's *Messiah* (the composer lived at No. 25 Brook Street). **Brook Street** continues past **Claridge's Hotel**, where frock-coated doormen admit the elite to its opulent interior. Before you reach Claridge's, take a detour right down the pedestrian area of **South Molton Street**. Here, boutiques and antiques shops belie the street's old nickname, Poverty Lane, and in summer there is a festive atmosphere as shoppers enjoy the sunshine from its pavement cafes.

St. George's Church

At the southern end of Hanover Square, in St. George Street, is the church of St. George, built in 1724 by John James and fronted by massive Corinthian columns. The baroque interior retains its 18th-century layout with galleries in the aisles. The Venetian east window is filled with 16th-century stained glass, moved here from a church in Antwerp, showing a Tree of Jesse. St. George was, and remains, a fashionable place for weddings. Among those married here were Benjamin Disraeli, Mary Anne Evans (better known as the novelist George Eliot), Theodore Roosevelt, and the poet Percy Shelley.

■ From Marble Arch in the west to High Holborn in the east, Oxford Street stretches for 1.5 miles to form one of London's busiest shopping streets. In the build-up to Christmas, when festive lights and decorations are strung across the street, it can seem like one of the most crowded places on earth, with police called in to control not the traffic, which has largely been excluded, but the sheer volume of shoppers. .....■

The road to Tyburn
Oxford Street does lead towards Oxford but actually got its name from the Earl of Oxford, who owned much of the surrounding land. Previously it had been known as Tyburn Way because it led to the gallows at Tyburn (located at the intersection of Edgware Road and Marble Arch), where public executions took place until 1783. Public hanging was intended to act as a deterrent to the watching crowds, a warning against crime, but it turned into popular entertainment, with high prices being paid for ringside seats.

Selfridges, one of Oxford Street's star attractions

Selfridges' clock

Most of Oxford Street's shops are ordinary chain outlets, but a few have retained their individuality. One of the most famous chain stores here is **Marks & Spencer**, whose flagship at the Marble Arch end (No. 458) stocks items you may not find in any other branch: New lines are introduced here first and, if they prove popular, are then sold nationwide. Another magnet is **Selfridges** (No. 400), which competes with Harrods (see page 87) as the largest and best-stocked London department store. The building is an impressive Edwardian pile fronted by Ionic columns. If the architecture reminds you of America, it is no accident: The founder, Harry Gordon Selfridge, came from Chicago and borrowed good ideas from his home country. The giant Art Deco clock over the main entrance (by Gilbert Bayes) features the regal figure of *The Queen of Time*, standing on a

prow that represents the ship of commerce. On a completely different scale are **Gees Court** and **St. Christopher's Place**, a narrow pedestrian alley that is easily missed (entered through a tiny archway between James Street and Stratford Place on the north side of Oxford Street). The precinct is lined with small shops and pavement cafes, a different and more intimate world than the big modern **West One Shopping Centre** above Bond Street underground station opposite.

Stratford Place, the next left, is another surprising interruption to Oxford Street's almost continuous line of shop fronts. Set back at the end of this 18th-century cul-de-sac is the elegant and untouched Stratford House of 1723, built in Adam style and housing the Oriental Club, founded in 1824 for colonial civil servants.

Next comes **John Lewis** (Nos. 278-306), another of the street's big stores. Its motto is "We are never knowingly undersold" and the store will refund the difference if you can buy identical goods more cheaply elsewhere.

Oxford Circus forms the busy intersection of Regent Street and Oxford Street. Find a spot, if you can, away from the tide of flowing pedestrians to note the northwards view of **All Souls Church**, Langham Place (see page 118), with its circular portico and spire, built by John Nash to form the focal point of the view up Regent Street, though today it is rather dwarfed by tall office towers and shop signs. Curving façades also give distinction to the buildings of Oxford Circus, but the architecture becomes less distinctive as you continue east. In this stretch you will find two well-known music megastores, **HMV** (No. 150) and **Virgin** (Nos. 14–30).

The eastern end of Oxford Street is dominated by the **Centre Point** building, a rather gloomy structure too tall for its site (400 ft.) and set in a windswept plaza. It remained empty for many years after its completion in 1967 but now houses the offices of the Confederation of British Industry. From here, New Oxford Street continues east, having sliced through the notorious slums of St. Giles (where the Great Plague of London started in 1665) in 1847 to join up with High Holborn.

The pretty church of **St. Giles-in-the-Fields** still stands to the south. David Garrick, the Shakespearian actor, was married here, the children of the poets Shelley and Byron were christened here, and the satirist and poet Andrew Marvell lies buried in the churchyard.

Marble Arch

Marble Arch, designed by Nash in 1827 and inspired by the Arch of Constantine in Rome, was originally intended to form a triumphant gateway to Buckingham Palace. Popular myth says it was moved here in 1851 because it was too narrow for the royal coach to pass through; in fact, it was moved to make way for a new range of buildings. Now it stands in sad isolation at the center of a busy traffic circle, and the central gates remain firmly closed most of the time: To this day only members of the royal family are allowed to drive through.

St Christopher's Place

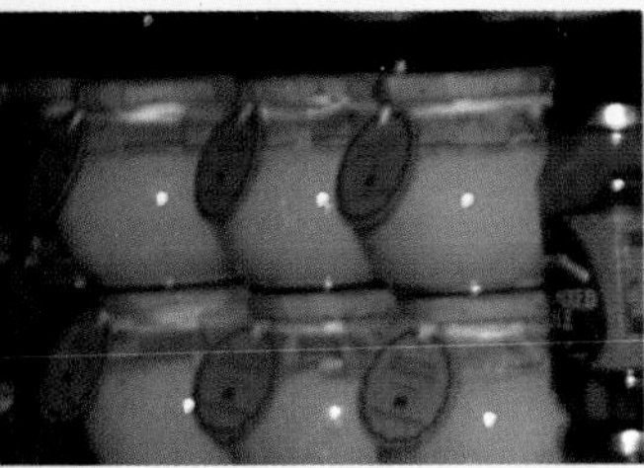

■ Piccadilly's name has its origins in a mansion built here in 1612 for one Robert Baker. He had made his fortune selling "picadils," a type of stiff collar fashionable with the 17th-century court, and his house (and the area surrounding it) became known as Piccadilly. Today, Piccadilly is an intriguing mix of gaudy neon signs, gentlemen's clubs, and splendid old shops. .....■

The Museum of Mankind
The Museum of Mankind lies just north of Piccadilly (at 6 Burlington Gardens) and is one of London's liveliest museums. It displays materials from the British Museum's vast ethnographic collection, not always in boring glass cases but by means of vivid reconstructions of daily life among peoples and cultures of the world. Here you actually wander through the exhibits, examining in detail the construction of a Borneo longhouse or the weaving looms of the Iban people. The exhibitions change regularly and are always worth seeing.

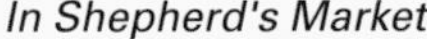

In Shepherd's Market

Piccadilly begins at **Hyde Park Corner**, a spot where cars do battle above while pedestrians get lost in the labyrinthine underpass below. One exit from the underpass leads to the traffic island containing **Constitution** (or Wellington) **Arch**, designed in 1828 by Decimus Burton and intended as a ceremonial gate linking Hyde Park with Buckingham Palace via Constitution Hill. It is topped by animated horses pulling Victory's chariot, a superb bronze sculpture by Adrian Jones (1912). Near by is a statue of the Duke of Wellington (1888) facing his residence, Apsley House (see page 83). To the north are the luxury hotels of Park Lane; the south side of Piccadilly runs alongside **Green Park**, laid out in the 17th century.

Walking up Piccadilly on the north side, you can detour left up White Horse Street to find the shops, pubs, and restaurants around **Shepherd Market**. These narrow streets and alleys were built in 1735 by Edward Shepherd on the site of the ancient May Fair that gave its name to the district. Here you will find **The Bunch of Grapes** (No. 16 Shepherd Market), a Victorian pub, and **Tiddy Dol's** (No. 55), a restaurant set in an 18th-century house.

Continuing up Piccadilly, **Half Moon Street**, the next on the left, is famous as the address of Bertie Wooster, P. G. Wodehouse's comic creation, as well as of Dr. Johnson's real-life friend and biographer, James Boswell.

Beyond Green Park is the Parisian-style **Ritz Hotel** (1906), once a haunt of the fashionable set and still a glamorous (but expensive) place in which to have tea (reservations advised). Further along on the left are Old Bond Street and Burlington Arcade, opposite which is the lesser-known Piccadilly Arcade: Although built as recently as 1910, it too has bow-fronted shops, specializing in china, rare books, and clothing. Next on the right comes **Fortnum & Mason**, the famous grocery store founded in 1707, lit by chandeliers and lined with mahogany paneling. Its shelves are piled high with displays of the goodies that go into Fortnum & Mason hampers, essential among wealthy patrons of the Henley Regatta or the Royal Ascot races. Look out for the clock above the entrance: On the hour, Mr Fortnum and Mr Mason pop out of their niches and bow to each other. **Hatchards** bookstore, next door, has an 18th-century shop front and a comprehensive stock. Opposite is the Royal Academy (see page 82) and further down on the right, slightly set back, is Sir Christopher Wren's church of **St. James's. Simpson,** the outfitters, stands on the corner, known for the store building's progressive 1930s design.

Piccadilly Circus itself is a somewhat confusing sight, which planners have remodeled again and again since 1905. The circus marks the junction of five major streets but lacks the coherence of design to make this clear or provide any focal point. These days it is a rather shabby, over-commercialized place, famous for its enormous, illuminated advertising signs and for Alfred Gilbert's tiny figure of a winged archer, popularly known as Eros, the god of Love, but actually designed as the *Angel of Christian Charity*. This was erected in 1893 as a memorial to the philanthropic Earl of Shaftesbury, who did much to improve the lot of factory and colliery workers (especially children) in the mid-19th century. Today's children, however,are more likely to flock to the **Guinness World of Records exhibition**, on the north side of Piccadilly Circus (open daily 10–10; Sunday 10–9:30), where you can see what the tallest and fattest people in the world really looked like.

Eros, the presiding genius of Piccadilly Circus

St. James's Church
St. James's Church was the last of some 55 churches that Sir Christopher Wren designed for London and the one that he himself liked best. Bombed in 1940, it has been superbly restored (you would not know that the spire of 1968 is made of fiberglass). Its gallery-lined interior contains work by the great carver, Grinling Gibbons, including the angels of the organ case, the Garden of Eden font, and the altar piece. St. James's today is more than a church: There is a natural foods cafe (The Wren at St. James's) to the rear (35 Jermyn Street) with works of art for sale on the walls; its courtyard is the venue for a crafts market on Fridays and Saturdays, and there is a brass-rubbing center in the church hall. Music lovers should look out for lunchtime recitals, especially of baroque music, on Thursdays and Fridays, and the annual music festival in May and June.

Regent Street

■ **Regent Street, named after the Prince Regent, later George IV, was laid out by John Nash between 1813 and 1816 to form a grand boulevard linking Regent's Park with the royal palaces and aristocratic mansions of Carlton House and Pall Mall. Though most of the original buildings have been replaced, Regent Street retains its grandeur, especially at the Piccadilly Circus end. Here, it bends dramatically to the left, obscuring the buildings that lie beyond but promising much; in the weeks preceding Christmas the sense of theater is enhanced by colorful lights soaring above the avenue. .....■**

Above: mural in Carnaby Street
Right: stylish Dickins & Jones

Carnaby Street
Running parallel with Regent Street, two blocks to the east, is Carnaby Street, a byword for trendiness in the Swinging '60s, when Mary Quant was the fashion queen and everyone came here to buy paisley flower-power shirts and bell-bottomed trousers. As fashions changed, so Carnaby Street declined to the point where it became a seedy eyesore. Today it has been spiffed up: It still sells trendy clothes but is perhaps best visited for the Shakespeare's Head pub (No. 29) and the pavement cafes dotted around the traffic-free sidestreets.

The eastern side of Regent Street has many of the best buildings. The **Café Royal** (No. 68) opened in 1865 and was the haunt of Aubrey Beardsley and Oscar Wilde; the Brasserie retains something of its sumptuous *beau monde* atmosphere. **Mappin & Webb** (No. 170) and **Garrard & Co** (No. 112) sell antique and modern jewelry to the wealthy, including the royal family. Between these two, on both sides of the street, are well-known clothes shops including **Aquascutum** (No. 100), **Austin Reed** (No. 103), and **Burberrys** (No. 161), makers of distinctive (and expensive) raincoats, hats, and scarves. Further up, **Hamley's** (Nos. 200–2), established in 1760, is thought to be the largest toy shop in the world; despite its size, expect it to be packed, with lines at the door before Christmas. **Liberty's** comes next with its famous fabrics (the store front is, in fact, on Great Marlborough Street, not Regent Street itself). The range of tempting shops continues with **Laura Ashley** (No. 256), a prime source for clothes, fabrics, and furnishings in contemporary and Victorian-like prints. **Dickins & Jones**, in between (No. 224), is a very stylish department store selling everything from designer-label clothes to glass and china, and the **Wedgwood Gift Centre**, on Oxford Circus, which sells the company's famous Grecian-style pastel ceramics.

■ Liberty's (Nos. 210–220 Regent Street) is a department store unlike any other in London: an Aladdin's Cave housed in a building that is a gem of Arts and Crafts design. A wide and varied range of goods can be bought here, but the distinctive Liberty print fabric is still the main attraction—and carries with it an image of upscale style. .....■

Downstairs, in the packed Liberty's basement, you can still buy the Japanese ceramics, textiles, and prints that were Arthur Lasenby Liberty's trade mark when he opened the store in 1875. The floors above are packed with goods from around the world, from African tribal jewelry to brightly patterned fabrics, all arranged to re-create the atmosphere of a bazaar.

The top floor, by contrast, resembles an informal museum. On one side you can browse among Arts and Crafts furniture, known for the beautiful patina of its wood and its straightforward, clean design. On the other, glass cases line the walls, filled with antique silver and pewter pieces specially commissioned from artists such as Archibald Knox; his flowing, Celtic-inspired designs were so popular that "Liberty style" became synonymous with art nouveau. In between is the central stairwell, where you can peer over the banister and look down on oriental carpets and Liberty's own range of fabrics.

Liberty's Tudor-style wing dates from 1924 and is built of timbers salvaged from HMS *Impregnable* and HMS *Hindustan*. A bridge across Kingly Street, linking the store's two parts, features a clock where St. George and the Dragon do battle every hour. Above the Great Marlborough Street entrance is a gilded caravel, the sailing ship that once carried cargoes of silks, porcelain, and spices; over the Regent Street entrance a frieze shows Britannia receiving goods from the nations of the world.

Liberty's weather-vane depicts a caravel, the ship that once sailed the oceans in search of spices and silk

Liberty's stock, laid out like an eastern bazaar

The Royal Academy Summer Exhibition
The Royal Academy Summer Exhibition is one of the high points of the London Season: Tickets to the fashionable and exclusive private preview are much sought after. The exhibition (which usually opens in June and lasts until mid-August) displays the paintings, sculpture, and architectural drawings of living artists, and much of the work is for sale. Of the 10,000 or so works submitted, the Academicians select just over 1,000 for public display: They have, in the past, been criticized for conservatism and for preferring representational works, while ignoring the abstract. Today, the choice tends to be more adventurous and wide-ranging.

▶▶ Royal Academy of Arts 73B3

Piccadilly
Underground: Green Park or Piccadilly Circus

Burlington House, Piccadilly's most imposing building, was built as a Palladian-style *palazzo* (palace) for the Earl of Burlington around 1720. Today it is the home of the prestigious Royal Academy of Arts, whose members include many well-known British artists and architects. The building is used for major art exhibitions, which change regularly but are always deservedly popular, since they feature masterpieces of art on loan from museums and collections around the world.

Burlington House is set back from the street, and the courtyard in front has a statue of Sir Joshua Reynolds. He was elected first President of the Royal Academy when it was founded in 1768, under the patronage of George III, with the aim of raising the prestige of the arts and of teaching promising painters (Constable and Turner were among the first students). The two wings on either side house the offices, libraries, and meeting rooms of other learned bodies, such as the Society of Antiquaries. The main entrance is straight ahead and the entrance hall, with its grand ceremonial staircase, features ceiling paintings by former Academicians—notably Benjamin West's *The Graces* and *The Four Elements*.

The main exhibition rooms are on the first floor; many of them have splendid doorframes, ceiling decorations, and fireplaces. The top floor of the building (the Sackler Galleries, reached by glass elevator) has recently been remodelled by Sir Norman Foster, himself an Academician, and is used for smaller exhibitions, including shows by living artists. Here, and not to be missed, is Michelangelo's *Madonna and Child with the infant St John*, a circular relief carved in marble in 1504–05 and generally considered to be one of his most beautiful works.

The statues that adorn the Royal Academy's façade were carved by various hands and represent Raphaël, Titian, Wren, and Leonardo da Vinci, among many other eminent figures.

The Royal Academy also has one of London's best museum shops: Apart from a comprehensive range of art books, it sells greetings cards, posters and postcards, artists' materials, and gift items.

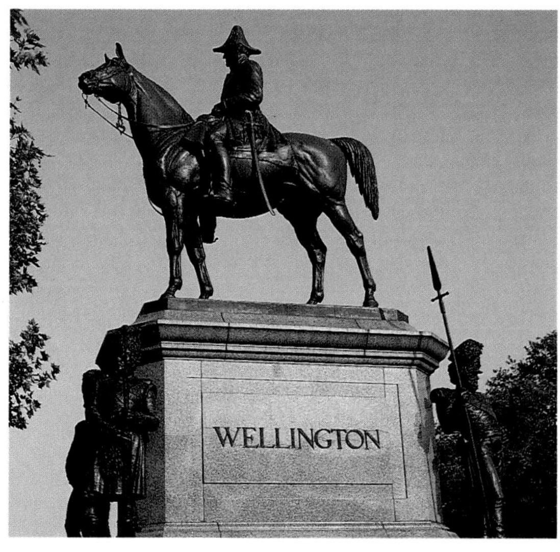

The Iron Duke, a national hero after his defeat of Napoleon Bonaparte

▶▶ Wellington Museum *72A2*

149 Piccadilly

Underground: Hyde Park Corner

When the Duke of Wellington (1769–1852) finally defeated Napoleon at the Battle of Waterloo in 1815, he became the nation's hero. Parliament, in gratitude, voted to give Wellington £200,000 (then a very substantial sum), which he lavished on alterations to his home, Apsley House. The original house was built of brick by Robert Adam in 1778. Wellington's architects (Benjamin and Philip Wyatt) wrapped it in Bath stone, added the giant Corinthian portico and pediment, and designed the vast Waterloo Gallery—where the Duke gave an annual banquet to celebrate his triumph at Waterloo.

Apsley House is today a museum (closed on Mondays) that combines two pleasures: the opportunity (surprisingly rare in London) to see inside an aristocratic 18th-century home; and the chance to admire the Duke's art collection (some of it looted as the spoils of war, some of it bought legitimately, some of it given to Wellington by grateful allies freed from Napoleon's yoke). Yet, in the midst of all this splendor and opulence, it is still Napoleon himself who manages to steal the show: Canova's heroic almost 11 ft. marble statue of the French emperor, nude except for a figleaf, stands at the base of the staircase. Napoleon himself commissioned the work but did not like it because the figure of Victory, in the statue's right hand, appears to be flying away. The statue remained in storage in the Louvre until the British government bought it in 1816 and presented it to Wellington.

Equally intriguing is Goya's *Equestrian Portrait of Wellington,* hung in the Waterloo Gallery: X-rays have shown that this originally depicted Joseph Bonaparte, Napoleon's brother; he was made king of Spain in 1808 but defeated by Wellington at the battle of Vittoria in 1813, and Goya hastily painted Wellington's head over the original in the light of the changed situation!

The Iron Duke

The Duke of Wellington is popularly known as the "Iron Duke" but not, as is often supposed, because of his military achievements. Instead the name dates to the later period in his life when, having served as Prime Minister from 1828 to 1830, he resigned in opposition to parliamentary reform and the extension of democracy. This refusal to support the Reform Bill made him so unpopular that rioters broke the windows of Apsley House. Iron shutters were then put up to prevent a reoccurrence—hence the somewhat sarcastic nickname.

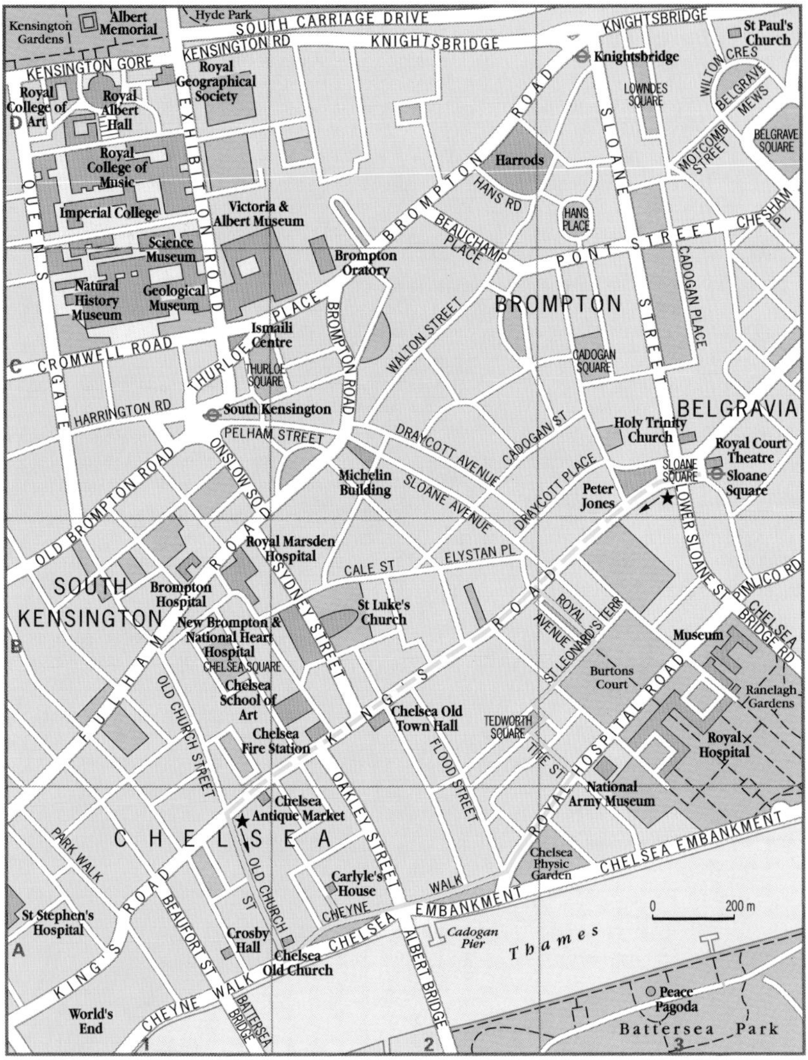

Chelsea and Knightsbridge Although these are primarily residential areas, you have to be extremely wealthy to live here. Elegant houses and gardens convey its image of class and gentility, but Chelsea's King's Road, by a twist of irony, has long stood for youthful rebellion: Its boutiques were the first to sell miniskirts and hippie gear in the '60s, and punk was born here a decade or so later. Another magnet for visitors is the museums complex on Cromwell Road, just a short step away from London's best-known department store, Harrods.

Chelsea and Knightsbridge walk This walk starts and ends at the King's Road, taking in a range of buildings spanning nearly 500 years of Chelsea's past.

Take Bus No. 22 from Sloane Square Underground

station down the King's Road, getting off near the Cannon Cinema, on the corner of Old Church Street. Walking south down Old Church Street, you will pass two important examples of Modern Movement architecture set among pretty Georgian brick houses: **No. 64** (by Mendelssohn and Chermayeff) and **No. 66** (by Gropius and Fry) were both built in 1936.

Turn left at the bottom of the street to reach **Chelsea Old Church**, which has a memorial to Sir Thomas More, Henry VIII's Chancellor, who lived near here from 1524 until he was executed in 1535. It is said that Henry VIII secretly married his third wife, Jane Seymour, in this church in 1536. There are many other important monuments, including an unusual shrouded effigy of Sara Colville (1631).

Turn left from the church into Cheyne Walk; to the right there is a good view of the Albert Bridge (built 1873).

Cheyne (pronounced "Chainy") **Walk** is lined by early Georgian houses, many with elegant railings and balconies. The second street on the left (Cheyne Row) has more modest houses but of the same early 18th-century date, including **Carlyle's House** (see page 90). Cheyne

The elegant Albert Bridge, built in 1873

Walk continues on the other side of Oakley Street. The most splendid of the houses (**No. 16**) was once the home of Dante Gabriel Rossetti. Near by, on Chelsea Embankment, **Swan House** (No. 17), built in 1875, and its neighbor, **Cheyne House** (1876), are pioneering examples of Norman Shaw's "Queen Anne" style of architecture, with characteristic oriel windows.

Continue up Royal Hospital Road and take the third left, **Tite Street**, whose playful houses and studios were once popular with artists. Oscar Wilde wrote several of his best-known plays at **No. 34**, Whistler lived at **No. 46**, John Singer Sargent at **No. 31,** and Augustus John at **No. 33**.

Turn right onto Tedworth Square (Mark Twain lived at No. 23) and right onto St. Leonards Terrace, with its fine 18th-century houses (Nos. 14–32). Turn left onto Royal Avenue to return to the King's Road.

Brompton Road has a clutch of chic shops and restaurants and is where some of the world's best-known designers have their boutiques. As a shopping area, this may be beyond most people's budgets, but there is plenty of window-shopping potential; and some of the buildings themselves warrant a closer look. .....

If you start at South Kensington tube station, it is a short walk down Pelham Street to Fulham Road and the **Michelin Building** (No. 81), a striking Art Deco building of 1911, decorated with ceramic-tile panels of racing cars. It was built for the French tire company and rescued from the threat of demolition in 1985; now it houses the **Conran Shop**, specializing in imaginative furnishings, and **Bibendum**, a highly regarded French restaurant.

To the south, down Fulham Road, there are other interior furnishings shops. To the north, Brompton Road leads towards Harrods, passing stylish boutiques such as **Joseph** (No. 317), **Jasper Conran** (No. 303), **Issey Miyake** (No. 270), and **Emporio Armani** (No. 191).

The huge Italianate baroque church of St Philip Neri—better known as the Brompton Oratory—stands at the busy intersection of Thurloe Place and Brompton Road. This is a fashionable church among intellectual and upper-crust Roman Catholics. Choral mass is held every Sunday at 11a.m., and the sermons are often highly theatrical and very entertaining.

The fourth right turn, beyond this church leads to another enclave of chicdom: Beauchamp Place. **Caroline Charles** (No. 56-57) is a very "in" designer with a feminine touch; opposite, **Janet Reger** (No. 2) sells fine lingerie, and **Kanga** (No. 8) carries exotic evening wear. Back on the right-hand side, more affordable Indian cottons in bold colors and patterns based on traditional Mogul designs are the speciality of **Monsoon** (No. 52), while **Annabel Jones**, next door, sells chunky jewelry. If your tastes in fashion are more conservative, try **Michelle Holden** (No. 42) for classic couture (for men, women, and children). On the left, **Bruce Oldfield** (No. 27), one of the biggest stars of modern British fashion, will create something original—at a price.

Brompton Oratory
Brompton Oratory is the work of Herbert Gribble, a young and almost unknown architect who designed this large and flamboyant baroque building in 1876. The huge Carrara marble statues of the Twelve Apostles in the nave, carved in the 1680s by Giuseppe Mazzuoli, originally stood in Siena Cathedral. On a more intimate scale is the Chapel of St. Wilfrid, with its triptych by Rex Whistler of the *Martyrdom of St. Thomas More and St. John Fisher* (1938).

Bibendum, now a gourmet restaurant

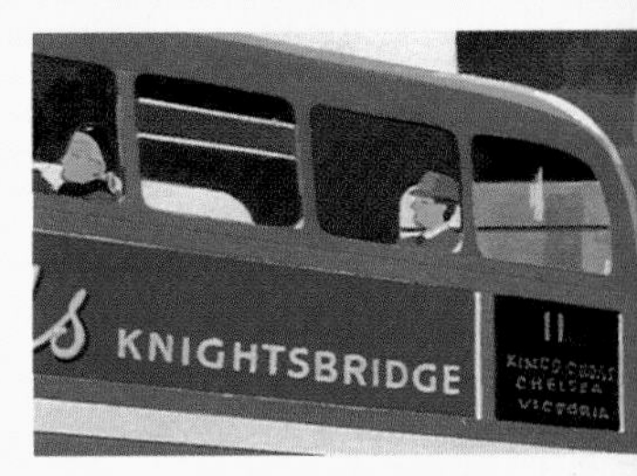

■ Harrods (at 87–135 Brompton Road; closed Sunday) is more than a store: it is a miniature kingdom, over which the princes of high finance have fought bitter battles. Its vast, terracotta building (illuminated at night) has grown to occupy 6 hectares—a far cry from its origins as a small grocer's store founded by Charles Henry Harrod in 1849. .....■

Harrods has 230-plus departments, more than 4,000 staff, and has been known to take in £6 million in a single day (in 1986), though normal turnover is a more modest £1.1 million a day. Harrods' Latin motto (*Omnia, omnibus, ubique* —everything, for everyone, everywhere) sums up the philosophy of a store that attracts visitors from around the world and sells almost everything the world produces.

You would be well advised to use a map to find your way around (pick up the *Store Guide* from information desks at the entrance and ask about the day's exhibitions, author signings, and product demonstrations).

The hallowed food halls of Harrods

For many the highlight will be the splendid food halls on the ground floor, partly for the unbelievable range of good foods on display, but also for W.J. Neatley's tiled ceilings above the fish, meat, and poultry halls, illustrating *The Hunt* and dating from 1902. Equally lavish Art Deco ceramics decorate both the men's hairdressing rooms and the women's restroom. Children should not miss the pet shop or the Toy Kingdom on the upper floors.

Of course, there is a price to pay for so much free entertainment—the crowds can be unbearable, and the store is best visited early in the day. If you want tea at Harrods, in the plush Georgian Room, be prepared for long lines; avoid the store altogether in December and January if you don't like crowds.

Harrods sales
At the famous January sale, reductions are huge, but so are the crowds, and some people are so eager to secure a bargain that they will camp outside the entrance over Christmas. Once inside the store, even dignified and aristocratic ladies lose all sense of decorum—elbows and fists fly in this test of consumer tenacity that can sometimes resemble a game of rugby.

HARROD'S STORES, LIM
The Cheapest Stores in London for Every
OPEN FREE TO ALL.
INSPECTION INVITED.
SPECIAL ATTENTION GIVEN TO EXPORT ORDERS.
LIST OF DEPARTMENTS.
AS OTHERS SEE US

London, a city once scorned by gourmets, is now one of the great culinary capitals of the world. This is partly thanks to a new generation of innovative chefs, who have transformed traditional British recipes, once regarded as heavy and bland, into dishes that restaurant reviewers rave about......

Soho
Soho has a cosmopolitan range of restaurants. Try Hungarian dishes at the **Gay Hussar**, 2 Greek Street (tel. 071 437 0973); French meals at **Au Jardin des Gourmets**, 5 Greek Street (tel. 071 437 1816); Cypriot food at **Jimmy's**, 23 Frith Street (tel. 071 437 9521) or Oriental cuisine at **Vietnamese Saigon**, 45 Frith Street (tel. 071 437 7109); **Thai Sri Siam**, 14 Old Compton Street (tel. 071 434 3544); or the **Indonesian Desaru**, 60–2 Old Compton Street (tel. 071 734 4379).

Oysters and fresh fish are the speciality of Rudland & Stubbs

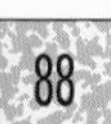

Here are some of the very best restaurants in town. Most are expensive; advance reservations are advised, and you should dress up (men are expected to wear jackets and ties).

British Modern British cooking at its best can be sampled at **Alastair Little**, 49 Frith Street (tel. 071 734 5183) and the **Quality Chop House**, 94 Farringdon Road (tel. 071 837 5093); the latter does not accept credit cards. Alternatively, try **Simpson's-in-the-Strand**, 100 Strand (tel. 071 836 9112), where the Edwardian dining room is renowned for its roast beef, or **Rules**, 35 Maiden Lane (071 836 5314), where you can sample game dishes in a restaurant that has scarcely changed since Dickens dined there. For oysters and huge plates of fresh seafood, **Rudland & Stubbs**, 35–7 Greenhill Rents, Cowcross Street (071 253 0148), is a good, informal choice.

French Some of the top chefs in London owe their allegiance to French cuisine. The doyen is Michel Bourdin at

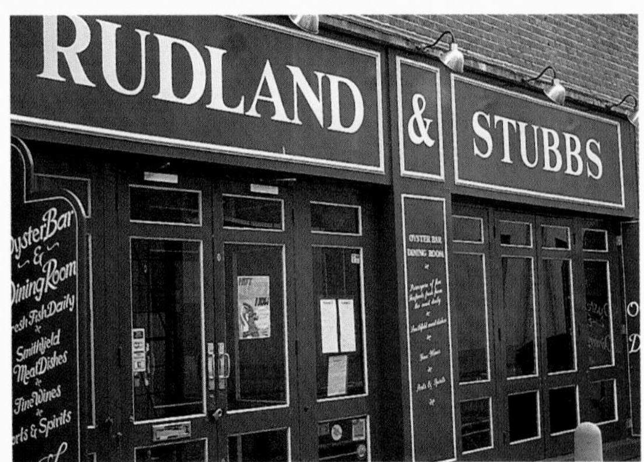

the **Connaught Grill**, 16 Carlos Place (tel. 071 499 7070), one of London's most exclusive restaurants. Modern French cooking has earned Pierre Koffmann, at **La Tante Claire**, 68 Royal Hospital Road (tel. 071 352 6045), two Michelin stars. Perhaps the best known French chef of all is Albert Roux, based at **Le Gavroche**, 43 Upper Brook Street (tel. 071 408 0881), whose evening *Menu Exceptionel* is a feast for gourmets. A relative newcomer is Simon Hopkinson at **Bibendum**, 81 Fulham Road (tel. 071 581 5817), whose regional dishes are so popular that advance reservations are essential. The downstairs oyster bar, with a cheaper menu, is a good second best.

The Quality Chop House: the best of British cooking

Ethnic The choice of so-called "ethnic" food is vast. In Chinatown, you'll join Chinese families enjoying the authentic, top-quality food at **New Loon Fung**, 42–4 Gerrard Street (tel. 071 439 0458). **Bombay Brasserie**, Courtfield Close (tel. 071 370 4040) serves fish and other dishes from southern India. For northern Indian cuisine, the **Red Fort**, 77 Dean Street (tel. 071 437 2410), is an excellent choice, while **Chutney Mary**, 535 King's Road (tel. 071 351 3113), specializes in Anglo-Indian dishes.

For Thai food, **The Blue Elephant**, 4 Fulham Broadway (tel. 071 385 6595), is regarded as one of London's best. The **Thai Garden**, 249 Globe Road (081 981 5748), has won many accolades for its vegetarian cuisine.

Miscellaneous The best chefs defy categorization. Leading the field is Marco Pierre White at **Harvey's**, 2 Bellevue Road (tel. 071 672 0114), *enfant terrible* of the restaurant scene, whose inventive dishes have won him one Michelin star. Another great chef, renowned for his temperament as well as his cooking, is Nico Ladenis. His main restaurant, **Nico at Ninety**, is located in the Grosvenor House Hotel, 90 Park Lane (tel. 071 409 1290). Standing in line out front is part of the attraction of the **Hard Rock Cafe**, 150 Old Park Lane (tel: 071 629 0382), which serves some of the best burgers in town. **Joe Allen**, 13 Exeter Street (tel. 071 836 0651), also specializes in American-style cuisine, but the food is secondary to the fun of watching self-consciously chic diners and the antics of the staff.

Jazz-loving visitors should try **Pizza Express**, which rises above the standards of most chains. The branches at 10 Dean Street (tel. 071 437 9595) and at 11 Knightsbridge (**Pizza on the Park**—tel. 071 235 5273) offer authentic pizzas, good wines, and live music every night.

See also **Food and Drink**, pages 240–1.

Breakfast and afternoon tea
The English are renowned for eating hearty breakfasts and equally gargantuan teas. The best place for a traditional breakfast is the **Fox & Anchor**, 115 Charterhouse Street (tel. 071 253 4838), where you will be served a huge plate of steak, sausage, kidneys, bacon and so on—useful if you have been up all night, which is why the meat-market traders come here from nearby Smithfield. Tea is a far more genteel experience: Try it at **Brown's Hotel**, 19–24 Dover Street (tel. 071 493 6020), where impeccably tailored waiters will serve you with a selection of pretty sandwiches or cakes on silver plates. Alternatively, the **Pâtisserie Valerie**, 44 Old Compton Street (tel. 071 437 3466) will appeal to those who prefer to drink coffee and eat authentic French pastries.

Chelsea salon; here the Carlyles entertained Dickens

The French Revolution
Carlyle's most famous work, entitled *The French Revolution* (1837), is a massive tome and a towering achievement, especially since a major part of the book had to be written twice. Carlyle left the manuscript at the house of his friend, the philosopher John Stuart Mill, who lived at No. 17 Kensington Square. To his horror, Mill discovered that his housemaid, thinking that the pile of paper was discarded, was using it to light fires. As a result, Carlyle had no alternative but to sit down and write the whole of the first volume all over again.

► **Carlyle's House** *84A2*

24 Cheyne Row
Underground: Sloane Square; bus: 22

Few people today read Thomas Carlyle's thunderously oratorical works, such as his history of the French Revolution, but in his day he was regarded with almost religious reverence: Admirers would come from afar to visit the great man, who was renowned for the high moral tone of his work. His wife, the witty Jane Carlyle, poet and letter writer, attracted an equally eminent bevy of admirers: Dickens, Tennyson, Browning and Thackeray among them. This stream of visitors met for conversation in the first floor drawing room of Carlyle's house, where he lived from 1834 until his death in 1881.

Visiting the house today, you gain a very real sense of that mid-Victorian era. The house (built in 1703) was described by Carlyle himself as "old-fashioned, eminent, antique," and some of the rooms, to this day, have no electricity. Heavy furnishings and rose-colored wallpapers add to the dark but dignified atmosphere. The walls are hung with portraits of the Carlyles (including a fine early picture by the pioneer of British photography, Julia Margaret Cameron) and of the men about whom Carlyle wrote in his epic books, notably Frederick the Great of Prussia.

The top-floor attic was specially built for Carlyle in 1853 and was intended to be a soundproof study, though in fact it had the effect of amplifying the sounds of street and river traffic. A touching reminder of domestic life is Carlyle's hat, hung by the back garden door: Thomas was fond of his pipe but had to go into the garden for a smoke, since Jane could not stand the smell. Open April 1 to end October, Wednesday to Sunday 11–5.

►► Chelsea Physic Garden 84A3

66 Royal Hospital Road
Underground: Sloane Square

Founded in 1673, the Chelsea Physic Garden is a haven of privacy and tranquillity in the heart of busy London. As the name suggests, it began as a place of scientific research, planted with species valued for their medicinal properties, under the auspices of the Worshipful Company of Apothecaries. That work continues to this day: The use of feverfew for the relief of migraine is just one of the research projects currently underway.

Within its high sheltering brick walls, the simple rectilinear beds are planted systematically—that is, by genus, according to the system of plant classification established by Linnaeus in the 18th century. Any suggestion of dull formality is banished, however, by the wild and willful way in which these plants, many of them highly fragrant, thrust their colorful blooms outwards and upwards, spilling out over the paths so that progress round this crowded and eventful garden is necessarily slow.

Adding to the sense of informal profusion are the many rare trees that grow here, some of considerable age, such as the striking golden rain tree (*Kolreuteria paniculata*), with its twisted branches. The woodland areas come into their own at the end of the winter, when the ground beneath is carpeted in snowdrops, cyclamen and hellebores. The garden also features the first ever-rock garden constructed in England—more a curiosity than a pleasure to the eye. It dates from 1772 and is made from basaltic lava blocks brought from Iceland and old masonry from the Tower of London.

Open: mid-March to mid-October, Wednesday and Sunday, 2–5, plus daily during Chelsea Flower Show week (usually May 21 to 24), noon–5.

Informal beds at the Chelsea Physic Garden

Sir Hans Sloane
A statue of Sir Hans Sloane in wig and gown stands at the center of the Chelsea Physic Garden. London owes much to this extraordinary man, who was physician to Queen Anne and George II, President of the Royal College of Physicians and immensely wealthy. The British Museum was founded from the collection he bequeathed at his death in 1753. In 1712 he purchased the manor of Chelsea, which included the Physic Garden. Sloane ensured the garden's survival by paying for its restoration (at a time when it was in serious decline), and he made financial arrangements to ensure that the site would never be built upon but would always remain a garden.

Oak Apple Day
Oak Apple Day (May 29) at Chelsea Royal Hospital is one of London's more colorful pageants. The resident veterans parade in their three-cornered hats to honour the birthday of Charles II, their founder. The parade takes place round Grinling Gibbons' statue of Charles II in the Figure Court. The statue is ritually decorated with oak leaves, to commemorate the king's escape from the battle of Worcester (1651) after defeat at the hands of the Parliamentarians. After hiding in a hollow oak tree, the king was able to escape to France, from where he eventually returned, after the death of Cromwell, to be restored to the throne in 1660.

The splendid Great Hall, with Charles II looking on from a distance

▶▶ Chelsea Royal Hospital 84B3

Royal Hospital Road
Tube: Sloane Square

Legend has it that Charles II's mistress, the actress Eleanor Gwyn (also known as Nell Gwyn), persuaded the king to found this hospital because she was moved to tears by the sight of a wounded soldier begging for alms. A more realistic version may be that, with the bitter experiences of the Civil War behind him, Charles II realized the importance of maintaining a standing army that would stay loyal to the Crown and of winning the army's loyalty by providing for aged and injured soldiers, rather than simply throwing them onto the streets without so much as a pension.

The Chelsea Royal Hospital was set up in 1682, an institution modeled on Louis XIV's Hôtel des Invalides in Paris (founded in 1670) to provide food, lodging, and medical care for infirm veterans. The architect was Sir Christopher Wren, who, up to now, had concentrated almost exclusively on designing churches for the reconstruction of the City of London after the Great Fire. This was his first full-scale secular work, and he produced a building of almost barrack-like simplicity but of great dignity, which was subsequently extended (between 1809 and 1817) by Sir John Soane.

The central courtyard is known as the Figure Court because of the figure of Charles II standing at the center; this bronze statue, by Grinling Gibbons, was brought here in 1692 and depicts the king as a Roman soldier. The central block of the hospital building has an imposing octagonal lobby, with the Great Hall and chapel either side. The Great Hall, where the residents take their meals, is noted for its huge painting of Charles II on horseback by Antonio

Chelsea Pensioners in resplendent uniform

Verrio, while the chapel is a typical Wren design with choirstalls by Grinling Gibbons and a huge painting—the *Resurrection*—in the vault by Sebastiano Ricci.

At the river end of the eastern range is the Governor's House, its Council Chamber decorated with sumptuous carving and hung with portraits of Charles I and his family (by Van Dyck), Charles II (by Lely), and William III (by Kneller). Lawns sweep down to the Thames and the terrace displays a cannon captured at Waterloo. To the east, the tree-filled Ranelagh Gardens used to be a vast pleasure garden where, in the words of the 18th-century writer Oliver Goldsmith, the public would flock for "fêtes, frolics, fireworks and fashionable frivolity". To the west, the more formal gardens serve as the site for the famous Chelsea Flower Show and provide good views across the river to Battersea Park.

Today, Chelsea Royal Hospital is home to about 500 pensioners (veterans), who wear a distinctive uniform—a dark blue overcoat in winter and a scarlet frock coat in summer—dating back to the time of the Duke of Marlborough (1650–1722). Pensioners must be ex-soldiers of "good character" and are usually at least 65 years of age, though younger men who suffer disablement in the course of their service are also admitted. The pensioners' duties include attending church and occasional parades, in return for which they receive food, lodging, clothing, and a daily ration of beer and tobacco. Chelsea Pensioners sometimes volunteer to show visitors around the Hospital or to pose for photographs, in which case it is customary to give them a tip.

Open: Monday to Saturday 10–noon and 2–4, Sunday 2–4.

Chelsea Flower Show
The Chelsea Flower Show is one of the great events of the summer season. Established in 1913, it is held in late May and provides a showcase for all that is novel in the gardening world, from the newest rose varieties to the latest in lawnmower technology. Every devoted gardener attends, from the Queen downwards. The horticulturalists who display their stock here spend all year preparing and, by playing tricks with nature, succeed in presenting all the riches of the four seasons in a single week: Snowdrops and sweet-smelling narcissi bloom alongside summer-flowering delphiniums and autumnal chrysanthemums. Often, though, the simplest ideas steal the show—window-box displays or meadow gardens of British native wildflowers. Garden snobs claim the Chelsea Flower Show is now too popular, and too dominated by the big commercial growers. They prefer to attend the other shows organized by the Royal Horticultural Society at their exhibition hall in Vincent Square (for details of these, contact the Royal Horticultural Society, 80 Vincent Square, London SW1P 2PE, tel. 071 834 4333).

Chelsea Flower Show

The Crystal Palace
The Crystal Palace, which housed the Great Exhibition of 1851, stood on the south side of Hyde Park, near the Royal Albert Hall. It was a stupendous building, three times longer than St. Paul's Cathedral (1858 ft.) and tall enough (at 109 ft.) to contain three elm trees that were already growing on the site. Designed by the great landscape gardener, Joseph Paxton, it was a prefabricated greenhouse on a gigantic scale. Skeptics predicted it would crash to the ground in the first strong gale. In fact, six million visitors passed through before the exhibition closed. The Crystal Palace was then dismantled and moved to Sydenham where, unfortunately, it burned down in 1936. Little now remains (see page 215), though the great glasshouses at Kew Gardens (see pages 226–7) convey an idea of what this splendid Victorian building looked like.

►► Geological Museum 84C1

Exhibition Road
Underground: South Kensington
Aware that displays of rock specimens do not have mass appeal, the Geological Museum has recently mounted new displays, which are both enjoyable and informative. One of these is an audio-visual program, *The Story of the Earth*, which explains current thinking on how the earth was and how its major geological features evolved. Others include an earthquake simulator, which gives some idea of what it feels like to experience quakes at different intensities on the Richter scale, and a recreation of an erupting volcano.

For those with a thirst for more detailed knowledge, the second-floor displays provide a comprehensive account of the geology of the British Isles, through models, dioramas, fossils, and rock specimens. The third floor is devoted to the economic uses of minerals, from gold and coal to radioactive materials such as uranium, a sample of which is housed in a sealed container, while a Geiger counter clicks ominously.

Although it has a separate entrance, the Geological Museum is actually a part of the Natural History Museum (see pages 98–9), and the same ticket gets you into either or both.

► National Army Museum 84B3

Royal Hospital Road
Underground: Sloane Square
This museum covers the history of the British Army from 1485 (when the Yeomen of the Guard, the first professional army, was formed) to the present day. Audio-visual presentations and dioramas bring the subject to life, and rather than glorifying war, the museum brings home a sense of the hardships experienced by ordinary and very vulnerable soldiers.

Weapons are displayed in the basement, where the exhibits include a longbow from the *Mary Rose*, the ship that sank in 1554 and that has been raised for restoration (it is now on show in Portsmouth). Upstairs, exhibits illustrate Britain's role in the Napoleonic Wars, and then tell the story of the army in action this century—in two World Wars, and in the Falklands campaign in the South Atlantic. The remaining exhibits, of uniforms, medals, battle paintings, and portraits, are mainly of specialist interest.

Relics of the Battle of Waterloo

■ The Royal Albert Hall (South Kensington Underground) and the buildings that surround it commemorate the vision of Prince Albert, Queen Victoria's husband. It is one of the most prominent of many grandiose buildings added to the cityscape during Victoria's reign and has become a familiar landmark. .....■

The Royal Albert Hall, home of the Proms and rock concert venue

The substantial profits generated by the Great Exhibition of 1851 (an idea conceived by Henry Cole) were used to purchase land for some of London's most important museums. Presiding over this grand scheme was a Royal Commission, headed by Prince Albert. When Albert died in 1861, the public was asked to donate funds to finance the building of the Albert Memorial (see page 111) and the Royal Albert Hall. In the event, the costs of building the Memorial escalated, and plans for the Hall were shelved until 1863, when Henry Cole, in charge of raising funds, hit on the idea of selling 1,300 seats at £100 each, entitling the owners to attend every event staged over the next 999 years! (This arrangement still stands, although the descendants of the original owners often waive their right to attend.)

Finally completed in 1871, the immense domed building, 274 ft. in diameter and 155 ft. high, is capable of seating 8,000. All kinds of cultural and sporting events are held here, but to many the Hall is inextricably linked with the Henry Wood Promenade Concerts, better known simply as the Proms, which take place here every evening between mid-July and mid-September, culminating in the emotion and patriotism of the Last Night of the Proms. Essential to the whole concept of the Proms is the availability of cheap tickets, sold on a first-come, first-served basis; the first few hundred people at the head of the line can stand in the arena, right behind the conductor.

In the vicinity
There are several fine buildings near the Albert Hall. Behind it is the Royal College of Music, where a collection of musical instruments is on public display from October to June, Monday and Wednesday 11–4; look out, too, for the exciting range of concerts given by students. To the west of the Hall, the Royal College of Organists has a façade decorated with a frieze of musicians—but no organist! On Kensington Gore, the Royal Geographical Society (1875), and Albert Hall Mansions (1886) together form a good example of Norman Shaw's Queen Anne–style of architecture.

FOCUS ON

The King's Road

■ The King's Road, as its name indicates, was once a private royal road, providing the route that led from St. James's Palace to Hampton Court and was used only by the monarch and courtiers. Humbler folk took a boat along the Thames if they wanted to visit what was then the small fishing village of Chelsea. .....■

World's End
The main concentration of shops in the King's Road comes to an end at a kink in the road known as World's End, named after the pub of the same name (No. 459). The origin of the name is obscure but, no doubt, the residents of Chelsea feel that the world does end here, on the borders with the less chic Fulham district. Another fine pub here is the Man in the Moon (No. 392), distinguished not only by its engraved glass fittings but also as a theater pub, mounting productions (usually modern drama) most evenings (tel. 071 351 2876).

A pot shop in the King's Road

In 1830 the King's Road was opened to the public, and from that time onwards Chelsea began to expand, becoming something of an artist's colony, whose residents ranged from the eminently respectable to the downright eccentric. This mixture survives to the present day and gives the King's Road much of its character: Shops selling fine antiques or antiquarian books stand cheek by jowl with avant-garde boutiques; punks with weird clothes and outrageous hairstyles parade alongside immaculately tailored *grandes dames* taking their coiffeured poodles for a stroll.

The first stretch of the King's Road, leading westwards from Sloane Square, is lined with the display windows of **Peter Jones** department store (see page 102). Opposite are the early 19th-century barrack buildings of the **Duke of York's Headquarters**. The second street on the right, Blacklands Terrace, leads to **John Sandoe Books** (No. 10), one of the best of the many small bookshops in London.

Further down on the left, there are glimpses towards Chelsea Royal Hospital down Royal Avenue, a leafy boulevard laid out in 1689, and intended as a route connecting Wren's Royal Hospital with Kensington Palace. This short stretch is all that was built of the route, and it was here that, in Ian Fleming's novels, James Bond had his home. At this end of the street, look out for the **Designers Sale**

Keeping the Easy Rider *era alive*

Studio (No. 24), where leading fashion designers dispose of their end-of-line items at discount prices.

Beyond the entrance to Markham Square lies the **Pheasantry** (No. 152), an odd building with Grecian-style caryatids. Built for the breeding of pheasants in the late 19th century, it is now a late-night bar, club, and restaurant. Beginning in 1916, for several years the Pheasantry housed a ballet school run by the Princess Serafine Astafieva, where future stars such as Margot Fonteyn and Alicia Markova took their first steps. Beyond the Pheasantry are some of the King's Road's most interesting shops: **Antiquarius** (Nos. 135–41) is an antiques market where some 70 stallholders sell everything from postcards to Georgian silver. More up-scale items, with an emphasis on art nouveau and Art Deco, are sold at **Chenil Galleries** (Nos. 181–3), and at **Chelsea Antique Market** (Nos. 245–53) you will find books, maps, and prints. Opposite, there is a taste of the country at the **Chelsea Farmers' Market**, with its small foodstalls, and the **Chelsea Garden Centre**, a tiny spot crammed with (very expensive) plants, flowers and pots, on the corner of Sydney Street. Further up Sydney Street is **St. Luke's Church**, all neoGothic frills, where Charles Dickens was married to Catherine Hogarth in 1836. Nowadays fashionable weddings are more likely to take place at the Register Office alongside **Chelsea Old Town Hall**, across the street from the Sidney Street turning.

Continuing up the King's Road, **Green and Stone** (No 259), the artists' supplies shop, is handy for students at the nearby Chelsea College of Art, founded in 1891. Beyond are two interior design premises with contrasting styles: florid fabrics at the **Designers' Guild** (No. 271) and classic wallpapers and fabrics at **Osborne & Little**.

The main part of King's Road ends with two innovative shops: **Rococo** (No. 321) sells way-out confectionery (try Venus's Nipples) as well as eccentric furniture, and **World's End** (No. 430) is Vivienne Westwood's outlet for her humorous and unconventional fashions.

The Cadogan Estate
If architecture interests you more than shops, you should explore the maze of streets that lies to the north of the King's Road, especially the Cadogan Estate, which has some of London's most interesting Queen Anne–style buildings. The style developed in the 1870s in rejection of the flat-brick or stucco-fronted façades of the Georgian and Regency era. Suddenly, Dutch gables, projecting windows, balconies, and all sorts of ornament came into fashion. For typical examples, see the west side of Cadogan Square, particularly the buildings designed by Norman Shaw (Nos. 62, 68, and 72).

The Natural History Museum

Natural History Museum highlights
The Natural History Museum has more than 67 million items in its collection, an indication of the sheer diversity of the natural world. Among the most intriguing exhibits, look out for the skeleton and reconstruction of the extinct dodo in the Bird Gallery, the weird and spiny coelacanth in the Central Hall, and the giant flesh-eating monster, *Tyrannosaurus rex*, in the section devoted to dinosaurs.

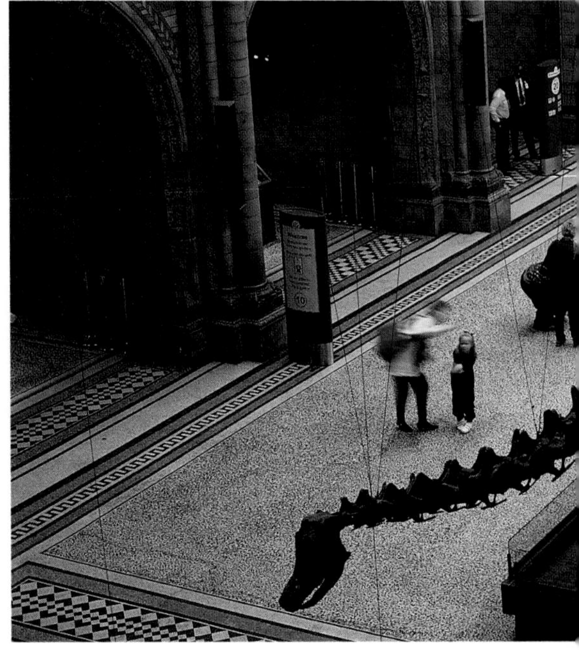

The beast from Wyoming: Diplodocus carnegii

▶▶▶ Natural History Museum *84C1*

Cromwell Road

Underground: South Kensington

The Natural History Museum celebrates the rich variety of life on earth and is housed in a suitably splendid building of cathedral-like proportions. The idea of creating a museum devoted to natural science was first discussed at a controversial time; plans were drawn up in 1862, only three years after Darwin had published *The Origin of the Species*, sparking off a fierce debate between scientists who supported evolutionary theory, and those who insisted on the Biblical version of the Creation. The debate even influenced the style of the building: Purists maintained that the neoGothic style, then in vogue, should be reserved for places of worship and not employed for secular buildings. The architect, Alfred Waterhouse, sidestepped the problem by looking to French Romanesque architecture for his inspiration, choosing a style that was less familiar to the British and less loaded with religious connotations. The building is clad in a bravura display of colored terracotta, with relief panels depicting animals, fossils, plants, and insects running the whole length of the 680-ft. façade; living species are depicted to the left of the entrance, extinct ones to the right.

Stepping through the main entrance, with its twin towers, the sense of entering a cathedral is reinforced by the nave-like form of the Central Hall, though the voices of hundreds of excited children exploring the dinosaurs on display is a far cry from the hushed tranquillity of a church. Soaring staircases provide a viewpoint for admiring the profusion of decoration (note especially the monkeys

The Giant Sequoia tree
Not all the items in the Natural History Museum are animals. One of the most intriguing exhibits is a section through a Giant Sequoia tree (*Sequoiadendron giganteum*) displayed on the stairs to the second floor. This was cut down in 1892, by which time it was 277 ft. tall and measured 49½ ft. round the girth. A tree ring count indicates that it was 1,335 years old when felled, having started its life in California in A.D.557.

scampering up and down the arches) and for looking down on the plaster-cast skeleton of *Diplodocus carnegii* (who comes from Wyoming), 150 million years old, 86 ft. long, and one of the largest land animals ever to have roamed the earth.

Plans displayed in the Central Hall will help you decide what to see, and there is plenty of choice. Many of the most recent displays were designed specifically with children in mind. An exhibition laid out in the east wing is entitled "Creepy Crawlies" and includes models of various insects and spiders and a scorpion enlarged to nightmarish proportions.

In the west wing, the Hall of Human Biology is entered through a darkened room that simulates the interior of a womb; this is followed by blinding lights in an attempt to re-create a newborn baby's first view of the world. The rest of this hall explains human reproduction, development, and perception using imaginative models, push-button displays and sound effects. In the Whale Gallery beyond, a life-size model of a 92½-ft.-long blue whale, suspended from the ceiling, gives a sense of the awesome size of these marine mammals.

On the second floor, beautiful dioramas illustrate the concept of ecology and the interdependence of species, and other imaginative displays bring to life complex ideas such as evolution and genetics. Do not miss the fascinating account of Man's Place in Evolution.

The Natural History Museum attracts large numbers of children and families, and the three eating areas serve snacks. The ground-floor shop sells everything from posters and postcards and do-it-yourself dinosaur construction kits to a comprehensive range of natural-history reference books.

Scientific art
Some of the Science Museum's exhibits bridge the gulf between art and technology. One of them is a work of art, the dramatically lit painting of *Coalbrookdale by Night* by P. J. de Loutherbourg (1801) in the Iron and Steel Gallery. Another is the intricate Orrery of 1716, a working model of the solar system, demonstrating the movement of the planets, made for and named after the Earl of Orrery. Nature's artistry is also demonstrated by the model of the DNA spiral to be found on the second floor, while displays on the same floor show the futuristic possibilities of computer-generated graphics.

▶▶▶ Science Museum *84D1*

Exhibition Road
Underground: South Kensington
Even the most technophobic visitors to London will find something to interest them in this fascinating museum, since many of the displays are as entertaining as they are educational. For that reason, the museum is very popular with children and can sometimes resemble a vast, noisy playground. This is all part of a deliberate policy on the part of the director, Neil Cossons, who rather shocked his purist colleagues in the scientific world by announcing that "we are in the leisure industry" and must "look after our customers as well as our collections." Such an attitude is entirely consistent with the ethos of the founders, whose original museum celebrated the commercial applications of science and technology that gave rise to the Industrial Revolution. Even the building that houses the museum (dating from 1913) borrows from commerce: The architect, Sir Robert Allison, used huge plate-glass windows and department-store construction techniques in order to provide adequate lighting and space for the massive exhibits.

These include, on the ground floor, the tip of the immensely long Foucault Pendulum, whose movement demonstrates the rotation of the earth. On the same floor there are engines of all kinds, elegant iron structures driven by steam, wind and atmospheric pressure, and a section devoted to transportation. Here you can see some of the world's earliest motor cars, such as an 1888 Benz three-wheeler and a 1904 Rolls Royce. The pioneering days of railroads are represented by *Puffing Billy* (1813), the oldest locomotive in the world, and George Stephenson's *Rocket*, which won the Rainhill Trials of 1829. How far railways developed over the next 100 years can be seen in the magnificent *Caerphilly Castle* express locomotive of 1923, a far more beautiful beast than its diesel-electric successor, the *Deltic*, of 1955.

Man and flight at the Science Museum

Space exploration is one of the themes of this floor, featuring the Apollo 10 capsule that took astronauts round the moon for the first time in May 1969, and a recreation of a futuristic moonbase. The lower ground floor features reconstructions of a Victorian bathroom and kitchen, a collection of domestic appliances, and the Bryant & May collection of matches.

On the second floor is the Launch Pad gallery, where a

The brief history of space exploration

Science and history
Among its displays of the cutting edge of technology, the Science Museum also has some ancient exhibits. The oldest of these is the clock mechanism from Wells Cathedral, displayed in the Time Measurement Gallery and still working some 600 years after its construction. An important piece of industrial history is represented by Arkwright's original spinning machine of 1769, one of the pioneering inventions that sparked off the whole Industrial Revolution, with its far-reaching implications for the way we live today.

series of interactive experiments is designed to exercise inquiring minds. The Food for Thought exhibition, sponsored by the Sainsbury supermarket company, also uses interactive displays to explain modern food technology. It struggles, however, to compete with the museum's most popular exhibition, laid out on the third floor, where the displays are devoted to computers and silicon-chip technology.

The computer-generated graphics demonstrated here make the very first photographs, taken by W. H. Fox Talbot in 1835, look primitive—but his cameras, displayed on the fourth floor, are beautiful examples of craftsmanship, as is the microscope near by, made by George Adams around 1770 for George III. Along the corridor, exhibits from the national Aeronautic Collection include early aircraft, such as Alcock and Brown's Vickers-Vimy (1919), the first to cross the Atlantic, and the *Gipsy Moth*, in which Amy Johnson flew to Australia in 1930.

The two remaining floors house the Wellcome Museum of the History of Medicine, with displays of early medical instruments resembling instruments of torture, and interesting historic items, such as Napoleon's toothbrush and Florence Nightingale's moccasins.

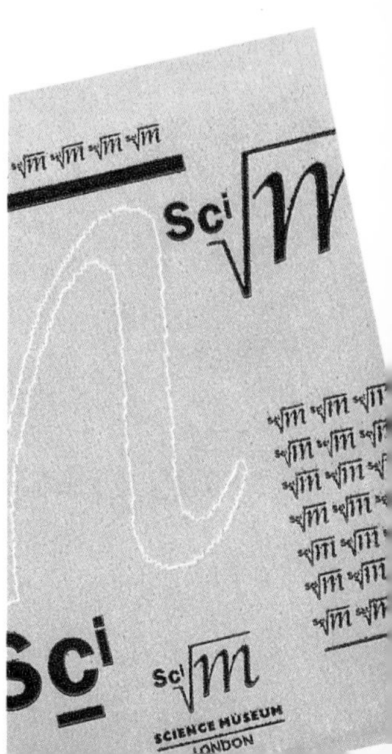

■ The Sloane Street area offers good shops and interesting architecture, as well as being the haunt of the Sloane Rangers, upper-crust girls of good breeding, whose lifestyles were comically described in the *Sloane Ranger Handbook* (by Ann Barr and Peter York). .....■

Pont Street

The mews pubs of Belgravia
Some of London's most interesting pubs are located in the mews of Belgravia, where they were built to serve the coachmen, grooms, and butlers employed by the big houses, and soldiers from the nearby Wellington Barracks. One such is the Grenadier (18 Wilton Row), full of military mementoes and said to be haunted by the ghost of an officer flogged to death for cheating at cards. Another is the Star Tavern (6 Belgrave Mews), the very model of a perfect traditional tavern, with open fires in winter and antique furnishings.

Sloanes, who are very conventional, shop at **Peter Jones** department store, on the west side of Sloane Square, where you can buy everything necessary for decorating and furnishing your home. They are not likely to patronize the **Royal Court Theatre**, on the opposite side of the square; it is famed for radical drama that often satirizes the values they hold dear (John Osborne's play *Look Back in Anger* received its first performance here in 1956). In between, at the heart of the square, plane trees shelter a fountain, which features the figure of Venus (1953, by Gilbert Ledward).

As you head up Sloane Street, one of the first shops you encounter is the **General Trading Company** (No. 144)—definitely part of the Sloane world—selling gifts, toys, china, and furnishings. The fact that the store is one of a tiny handful in London to hold all four royal warrants indicates how upscale it is, but it also sells many affordable items, including crafts from the Far East and Africa.

Across the street from the General Trading Company is **Holy Trinity Church**, a masterpiece of English Arts and Crafts design, completed in 1890. The huge east window contains 48 panels depicting saints and was designed by Edward Burne-Jones (check the notice board for lunchtime concerts here). Further up on the right are the gardens of **Cadogan Place**: Access is limited to residents of nearby apartments, but you can see over the railings. The view is particularly cheering when the winter-flowering shrubs and bulbs are in bloom.

From Cadogan Place northwards, both sides of Sloane Street are lined with shops bearing famous names, **Valentino**, **Kenzo**, **Joseph** and **Katharine Hamnett** among them, plus less expensive fashions at **Laura Ashley** and **Esprit**.

It is tempting to dip into the sidestreets for their characterful buildings. To the west you can walk through Pont Street, Hans Place, and Hans Road to Harrods. **Pont Street** has plenty of fine Queen Anne-style houses with Dutch gables and terracotta decorations. At the far end of the street is St. Columba's Church, built in 1955, with a striking helm roof. **Hans Place** has houses surviving from the time when Henry Holland first laid out his "Hans Town" development in 1777, building in an area that then consisted of open fields. **Hans Road** has pioneering examples of Arts and Crafts architecture by Mackmurdo (No. 12) and Voysey (Nos. 14 and 16). Jane Austen lived briefly at No. 23 in the year 1815 when she was entertained by the Prince Regent, to whom she dedicated her finest novel, *Emma*.

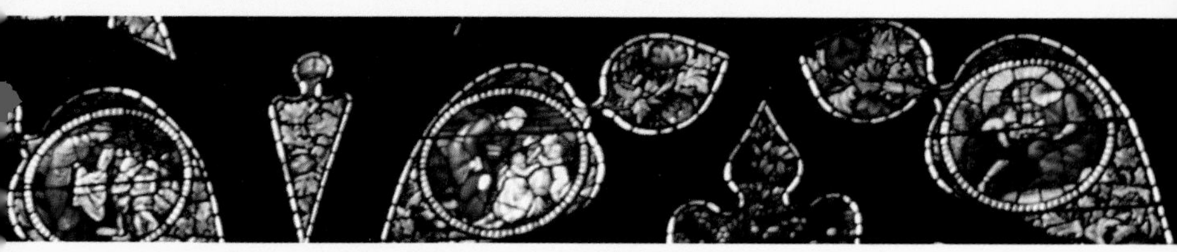

In the opposite direction, the hotel on the corner of Sloane Street and the north end of Cadogan Place is where Oscar Wilde was arrested for homosexual practices in 1895. Beyond lies **Belgrave Square**, at the heart of exclusive Belgravia; many of the huge Regency houses now serve as embassies or ambassadorial residences. The area was developed between 1825 and 1835 by Thomas Cubitt and is characterized by monumental stucco-fronted mansions, backed by cobblestone mews where horses were once stabled and servants lived (today even a simple mews cottage or converted stable is likely to be inhabited by a millionaire). To see the best of this district, visit **Motcomb Street**, with its antiques shops; **Kinnerton Street**, with its pretty courtyards leading off to the left; curving **Wilton Crescent,** and **St. Paul's Church**, in Wilton Place. This last is a Victorian neoGothic church, popular for high-society weddings, with a fine timber roof and rich decorations.

Belgrave Square
Belgrave Square's sunken garden is surrounded by houses designed by George Basevi. For all their monumental proportions, the blank fronts and huge porches have provoked dismissive comments from architectural critics, although the three grand villas at the square's corners (by Kemp, Smirke, and Hardwick) do provide some variety.

A stage for satire

The Great Bed of Ware
The Great Bed of Ware is one of the V & A's most celebrated exhibits, partly because of its prodigious size (10 ft. wide and nearly 13 ft. long) but also because of its great age (made around 1590) and its extravagant carved, painted, and inlaid decoration. Another celebrated curiosity is the large model tiger in the Nehru Gallery, which is shown in the act of eating a British army officer. Made in 1790, for the Tipoo Sahib of Mysore, the model incorporates a small organ that imitates the groans of the tiger's victim.

The V & A entrance, modeled on Victoria's crown

▶▶▶ Victoria and Albert Museum *84C1*

Cromwell Road

Underground: South Kensington

The V & A, as it is affectionately known, is a storehouse of treasures so diverse in their nature as to defy general description. Where else under one roof would you find superb examples of textiles from around the world, architectural fragments from French châteaux, Indian chess sets, medieval reliquaries, and a bed so famous that it featured in the plays of Shakespeare and Ben Jonson? In broad terms, the collection covers "applied art" from every age and nation, but this description does not do any justice to the immense diversity, eclecticism, and idiosyncracy of its material.

This has also been one of London's most controversial museums in recent years. Under the former director, Sir Roy Strong, the V & A was one of the first to introduce

Renaissance masterpieces in replica in the V & A's Italian Cast Court

admission charges (though these are described as voluntary). The museum then ran an advertising campaign to promote its new restaurant with the punchline: "An ace cafe with a museum attached"—considered by some to be demeaning to the academic excellence of the institution and its staff. The current director, Elizabeth Estève-Coll, laid off many of the staff as part of a cost-cutting exercise, sparking off a furious debate about whether museums should have researchers and experts on their staff or whether they should exist purely for entertainment.

The origin of the museum can be traced back to the Great Exhibition of 1851, a celebration of the arts, crafts, and industrial products of the British Empire. Prince Albert, the driving force behind the exhibition, wanted this to be a permanent collection displaying the best examples of commercial art and design as a source of inspiration to future generations. The first museum on the site was a utilitarian structure of iron and glass, nicknamed the Brompton Boilers. As the collection grew, the building expanded to its present size (it covers 5.2 hectares and has over 6 miles of gallery space). The main entrance and Cromwell Road façade were among the last to be built: Queen Victoria laid the foundation stone in 1899 (her last public engagement in London), and the building was completed in 1909. The entrance is topped by a great cupola, whose lantern is shaped like the Queen's imperial crown. The museum within is so vast that you cannot possibly see everything. You can either wander through the maze of galleries or pick out a room or two to study in detail; or you can buy one of the museum's guides and be led by the experts.

Some of the galleries have been remodeled recently, with the help of commercial sponsorship, and you can gain a taste of the museum by concentrating on these. From the main hall, the central corridor houses medieval art, one of the best collections of its kind in the world, ranging from 5th-century ivories to Saxon goldwork and Carolingian gospel bindings. This leads to the Pirelli Garden, a good place to rest weary feet. The garden is overlooked by the Renaissance galleries, while straight ahead you will find the Morris, Gamble, and Poynter rooms. These were, originally, the museum tea rooms and restaurant, and they retain their Minton tilework, William Morris furnishings, and Edward Burne-Jones stained glass. Running to the right of the entrance hall are the newly designed galleries displaying Art and Design in Europe and America from 1800 to 1890. Twentieth-Century Galleries, on the second floor, bring the story of design right up to date (the last section of the galleries, the "Now Room," will have changing exhibits of recent material). Do not miss the Toshiba Gallery of Japanese art, the Nehru Gallery of Indian Art, or the T. T. Tsui Gallery of Chinese Art, all on the ground floor.

When hunger sets in, head for the restaurant, one of the best of any London museum. Save some time for the excellent shop, which sells jewelry, ceramics, and crafts by some of the most innovative designers working in Britain today.

Open Tuesday to Saturday, 10–5:50 (Monday from noon), and Sunday, 10–5:50. See also the Bethnal Green Museum of Childhood, page 179.

Sights close to the V & A
To the south of the Victoria and Albert Museum, a garden in Thurloe Square contains a moving memorial (1982, by Angela Conner) to the Yalta Victims, the many thousands of people who were forcibly repatriated to the Soviet Union and Eastern Europe between 1944 and 1947, only to face imprisonment and death.

Morris wallpaper

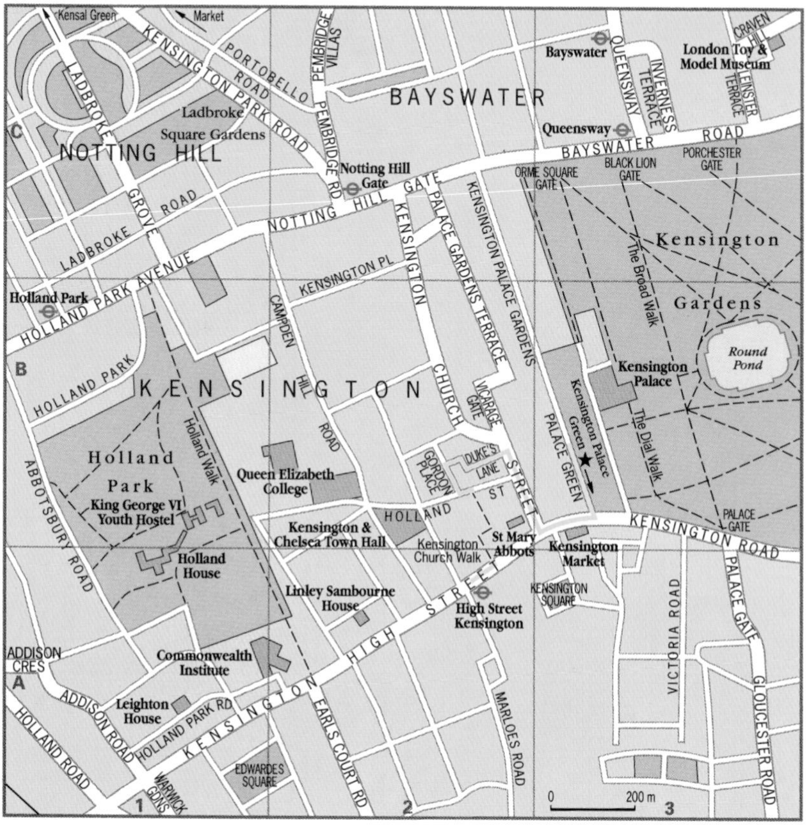

Kensington Square
Kensington Square was one of the first developments in the former village after William III moved to Kensington Palace. Nos. 11 and 12, originally one house, are the best preserved and date from 1693. Among the square's early residents was Richard Steele, founder of *The Spectator*. Hubert Parry, composer of *Jerusalem*, lived at No. 17. Edward Burne-Jones, the artist, lived at No. 41 and John Stuart Mill, the political philosopher, lived at No. 18: It was here that Thomas Carlyle's first manuscript of *The French Revolution* was accidentally burned (see page 90).

Kensington and Hyde Park The great tract of Hyde Park separates the West End from Kensington, which maintains an air of being apart from the rest of central London. Until the 17th century Kensington really was just a small rural village. Its transformation began in 1689 when William III, who suffered from asthma, came to live at Kensington Palace in the hope that the purer air of this country retreat would be beneficial to his health. New buildings were soon built by courtiers, and the district still has a distinctively exclusive atmosphere, even if many of the fine houses, too large for modern styles of living, have been converted to flats, hotels, or offices.

Singing in the park

Kensington walk This route leads from Kensington Palace Gardens, which provide a glimpse of some of the most aristocratic dwellings surviving in the royal borough, to the present-day focus of Kensington life: the High Street shops.

Start in **Kensington Palace Gardens**, a leafy avenue laid out in 1843 on the site of the kitchen gardens of Kensington Palace. It is closed by entrance lodges at either end to reinforce the sense of privacy and exclusivity. In the 19th century its opulent houses, several of which are now embassies, earned it the nickname "Millionaires' Row."

Smart shops in Kensington Church Street

Head south towards Kensington High Street. At the southern end of Kensington Palace Gardens (Palace Green) look for **No. 1**, designed by Philip Webb in 1863 as an experiment in Arts and Crafts style; and **No. 2**, built for the novelist William Makepeace Thackeray in 1860.

Turn right on to Kensington High Street; then right again for Kensington Church Street. On Kensington High Street, **St. Mary Abbots Church** stands on the site of Kensington's original village church. It was rebuilt by George Gilbert Scott in the 1870s in a style intended to reflect the area's wealth and has a fine spire.

Take the second left, Duke's Lane, which still has some cottage-style houses reminiscent of the old Kensington. Turn left again onto picturesque Gordon Place, which has houses originally built for coachmen serving Kensington Palace. Gordon Place quickly leads you into Holland Street, where you turn right. Holland Street retains some unspoiled 18th-century houses (**Nos. 10, 12, 13, and 18–26**) and, at its far end, a left turn down the delightful Kensington Church Walk leads back to the bustle of Kensington High Street. Here, above the tube station, is **Barker's** department store, with its splendid Art Deco façade (built 1937–38) and domed atrium. The store, which was once as famous as Harrods, is now mainly occupied by British Home Stores, and its Roof Garden, entered from Derry Street, is open to shoppers during the day and serves as a nightclub and disco (members only) twice a week.

Nigerian fashions at the Commonwealth Institute

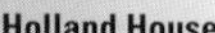

Holland House
Until it was blitzed in World War II, Holland House was one of the finest Jacobean mansions in London and the glittering center of political and literary society. During the Commonwealth, when Cromwell ruled the land, plays were performed here privately in defiance of the Puritan ban on all forms of theatrical activity. In the early 18th century it was home to Joseph Addison, one of the founders of *The Spectator*, who composed his articles for the magazine while strolling up and down the 116-ft.-Long Gallery, taking a sip of wine for inspiration from the glasses he kept at each end. During the first decades of the 19th century it was famous for the salons hosted by Lady Holland and attended by the leading intellectuals of the day, including Byron, Talleyrand, Prince Metternich, and Macaulay. Lady Holland was a passionate supporter of Napoleon. During his brief exile on Elba, she sent him jars of plum jam, books, and a refrigerator as tokens of her belief in his cause.

► Commonwealth Institute *106A1*

230 Kensington High Street
Underground: High Street Kensington
Displays at the Commonwealth Institute change regularly, but they usually consist of three-dimensional tableaux illustrating the peoples of the Commonwealth, their way of life, arts, religion, housing, climate, food, resources, and industries. These lively exhibits are especially appealing to children and are supplemented by film and slide shows. There is also an Activities Room, where children can take part in cooking demonstrations, dress up in costumes, or get involved in music, dance, and drama. The building that houses the Commonwealth Institute is a typical example of 1960s architecture, with its striking green paraboloid roof covered in copper, its opaque glass walls, and its jumble of split-level floors. The Institute itself is a much older organization, having been founded in 1893.

► Holland Park *106B1*

Holland Walk (off Kensington High Street)
Underground: High Street Kensington
Flower-filled formal gardens and wilder woodland areas can both be enjoyed in this varied 22-hectare park. It used to be the private garden of Holland House, built in 1606–07, which was bombed during World War II. All that remains of the house today is the ground floor and the orangery, which contains a tea room and has art exhibitions in summer. The restored east wing is now a youth hostel, and the terrace in front of the house, known as the Holland Park Theatre, is used in June and August for open-air plays, ballets, operas, and concerts (details from the box office, open from mid-April, tel. 071 602 7856). Immediately around the house are a rose garden, a Dutch garden—laid out in 1812 with flower beds bordered by box hedges, and an iris garden, where in the 1790s Lady Holland is said to have grown the first dahlias ever seen in England. Peacocks and other ornamental birds wander freely about the park, adding their color to the scene, and there is a small zoo. The woodland areas to the north are best in May, when the rhododendrons and azaleas are in full bloom, complemented by the pink and creamy spires of horse-chestnut blossom.

▶▶ Leighton House 106A1

12 Holland Park Road
Underground: High Street Kensington
Leighton House (closed Sunday) was built by Frederic Leighton, painter, sculptor, and President of the Royal Academy, whose work found favor with Queen Victoria, ensuring a profitable career. He was the only artist ever to be made a peer, enjoying the title of Baron Leighton of Stretton for only a month before he died in 1896.

During the 1860s Leighton traveled widely in the Near East, painting many pictures on an Oriental theme. His fondness for things Oriental is immediately apparent. Despite the plain brick exterior, the interior features a wonderful Arab Hall, designed by George Aitchison and based on the Moorish buildings of Spain. The hall is lined with tiles, dating from the 13th to 17th centuries, which Leighton collected on his travels in Damascus, Cairo, and Rhodes; these are supplemented with equally exotic tiles designed by William de Morgan. The domed hall has a fountain at its center, a Persian-style mosaic frieze by Walter Crane, and marble columns with capitals carved by Edgar Boehm. Many of the other rooms are cluttered and stuffy but are hung with interesting paintings by Leighton himself, Millais, Watts, Burne-Jones, Alma-Tadema, and Evelyn de Morgan, all leading Pre-Raphaelite artists.

The huge studio where Leighton worked is used for temporary exhibitions. A large garden features Leighton's sculpture, *Athlete struggling with a python* (1877).

Artistic Kensington
Kensington—Melbury Road, in particular—was once a colony of artiness. George Frederick Watts lived at No. 6, where he made the equestrian figure, *Physical Energy*, now in Kensington Gardens (see page 111). No. 8 was built for Marcus Stone, the illustrator of Dickens, in 1876; No. 9 (now No. 29) was built by William Burges for himself in 1875–80 and reveals his preoccupation with Gothic detailing. William Holman Hunt, whose painting *The Light of the World* hangs in St. Paul's Cathedral, lived at No. 18. Nearby, No. 8 Addison Road was built in 1906–07 for Sir Ernest Debenham, founder of the department store, and covered in colorful William de Morgan tiles, earning it the nickname Peacock House.

Leighton House—the Arab Hall

■ Hyde Park and Kensington Gardens together form one huge expanse of trees, flowers, and greenery covering 248 hectares. The dividing line between them is the road that runs from Alexandra Gate in the south, over the Serpentine Bridge, built in 1826, and up to the Victoria Gate in the north. To the west of this line is Kensington Gardens; to the east is Hyde Park. .....■

Speaker's Corner
Speaker's Corner is at the northeastern edge of Hyde Park, near Marble Arch. Here, on Sundays, soapbox orators harangue the crowds on issues ranging from politics and religion to vegetarianism or the evils of smoking. The tradition of free speech and assembly dates from the mid-19th century. There have been huge gatherings here in the past, including demonstrations against nuclear armaments. According to law, anyone can speak on any topic, as long as they do not blaspheme, use obscene language, incite racial hatred, or breach the peace.

Kensington Gardens is a relatively quiet area, with a surprisingly rich wildlife: Herons and grebes can be seen on the willow-fringed Long Water, to the north of the Serpentine Bridge. Hyde Park is more a place of recreation and entertainment, with boats for rent on the Serpentine in summer; bandstand music at lunchtime in June, July and August; and occasionally fairs, concerts, or fireworks parties.

The parks escaped being built upon during the great expansion of London in the 18th century because the land belonged to the Crown. Henry VIII had seized it from the monks of Westminster Abbey at the Dissolution of the Monasteries and had turned it into a huge royal hunting ground. Later it was opened to "respectably dressed people" and became a favorite resort of Samuel Pepys, among others.

A stroll around Hyde Park should begin at Hyde Park Corner. Here, behind Apsley House (see page 83), a triple-arched screen (1828, by Decimus Burton) marks the main entrance. To the south is Rotten Row—the name is a corruption of *route du roi* (King's Road)—down which monarchs once rode on their way to hunt deer in the park. It is now used by the Household Cavalry Brigade for

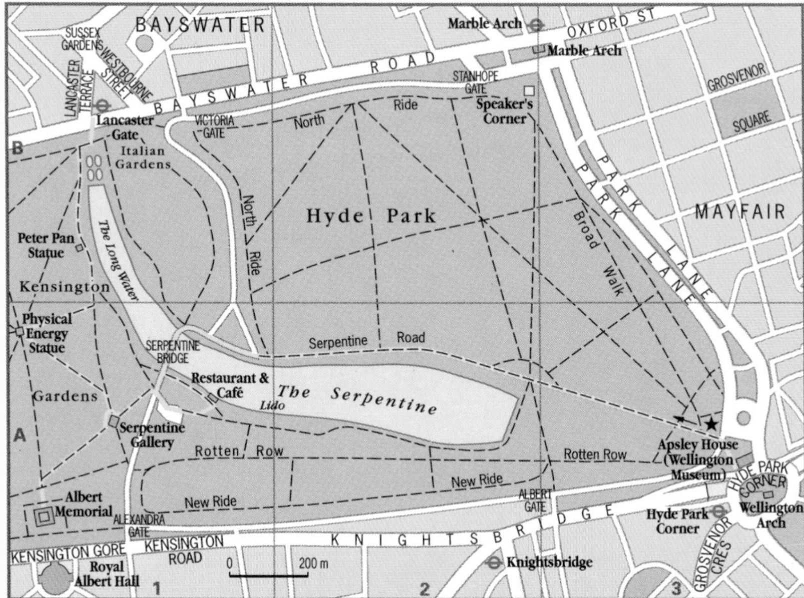

Audience participation at Speaker's Corner, Hyde Park

exercising their horses; at around 10:30 and noon, members of the Brigade ride to and from the Changing of the Guard ceremonies, which take place at Buckingham Palace and Horseguards.

Serpentine Road leads straight ahead to the northern shore of the Serpentine. This lake was created at the instruction of Queen Caroline, wife of George II, by damming the River Westbourne in 1730. A beautiful bridge, built in 1826 by George Rennie, spans the water. Swimming in the Serpentine is allowed at the Lido, on the opposite bank, from 9a.m. to 6p.m. in summer. There is also a hardy band of people, members of the Serpentine Swimming Club, who come here every day for a dip between 6 and 9a.m.—even in the depths of winter.

Nearby is the Serpentine Gallery, which hosts exhibitions of 20th-century art in the summer months. From here there is a choice of routes. You can walk north to see two sculptures: *Physical Energy* (1904) by George Frederick Watts is a powerful equestrian figure, while *Peter Pan* (1912) by George Frampton commemorates the hero of J. M. Barrie's play for children, written in 1904. A short way further north is the Lancaster Gate exit and tube station.

Another option is to walk southwest from the Serpentine Gallery to visit the Albert Memorial (currently hidden by scaffolding—see panel); or you can go west to the Round Pond, where children and adults come to sail model boats at weekends, and from there to the more formal gardens of Kensington Palace.

The Albert Memorial
George Gilbert Scott's flamboyant monument to Prince Albert, husband of Queen Victoria, is a reminder of the values of the Victorian age. In the center is Albert himself, holding the catalog for the 1851 Great Exhibition, which he organized (see page 95). Completed in 1876, the memorial is crowded with 169 portraits of painters, poets, and architects. Its corners illustrate the peoples of Asia, America, Europe, and Africa, while allegorical figures represent Albert's interests: Commerce, Manufacture, Engineering, and Agriculture. Weather and pollution have caused serious deterioration, and protective sheeting now keeps the frost and rain at bay. Some fear that it may remain like this for years to come, because of the huge cost involved in making essential repairs.

A 1930s tea gown from the Court Dress Collection

Kensington Palace; modest without but sumptuous within

▶▶▶ Kensington Palace *106B3*

Kensington Gardens
Underground: High Street Kensington

Until recently, Kensington Palace was the only royal palace in London open to the public. Queen Victoria, who was born here in 1819, decided that the State Apartments should be opened to view in 1889, on her 70th birthday.

Several members of the present royal family still have apartments here, including Princess Margaret, Prince and Princess Michael of Kent, and the Duke and Duchess of Gloucester—you may catch a fleeting glimpse as they depart in their limousines to attend various public engagements in London.

It was the asthmatic William III who first set up home here, in 1689, escaping from the damp and smoke of St. James's to the cleaner air and rural environment of Hyde Park. He purchased the existing house, built in 1605, and had it enlarged by Sir Christopher Wren in the 1690s. It was further extended, under George I, by William Kent in the 1720s. The result is a roughly rectangular brick building, which is arranged around three courtyards; architecturally it is surprisingly modest, more like a country house than a palace in scale and appearance, although the interiors are more sumptuous, and the surrounding gardens are a great delight.

Visitors enter the palace through the garden door, to be greeted by the simple Queen's Staircase, in mellow oak, leading to Queen Mary's Gallery. This paneled room is hung with royal portraits and Kneller's forceful picture of Peter the Great of Russia, painted when the Tsar visited England to study London's naval dockyards in 1698. From here, there is a series of smaller private apartments, decorated with 17th-century furnishings and pictures, including the State Bed, in Queen Mary's Bedchamber, with its original hangings.

The suite of State Apartments is far more striking, though, naturally, less intimate. Italianate in style, the rooms feature magnificent ceiling paintings by William

Kent. The first room, the Privy Chamber, is painted with the figure of Mars (wearing the Order of the Garter) symbolizing the military prowess of George I, and of Minerva, goddess of wisdom, accompanied by figures representing the Sciences and the Arts. The central roundel in the Presence Chamber shows Apollo in his chariot. A door leads off this room to the King's Grand Staircase, with its scrolly wrought ironwork by Jean Tijou, and Kent's *trompe l'œil* wall painting of a gallery crowded with figures, many of them actual portraits of George I's courtiers and servants. One of them, known as Peter the Wild Boy, was discovered living like a wild animal in a forest near Hanover, Germany and brought to England as a freak curiosity, though he rapidly adapted to the ways of the royal court.

The next room is the King's Gallery, with its ceiling paintings of the adventures of Ulysses; this room is used to hang works of art, changed from time to time, from the Royal Collection. A curiosity is the wind-direction dial above the fireplace, turned by a weathervane on the roof. Next comes an anteroom, and then Queen Victoria's bedroom, where a painting illustrates the Queen's marriage to Prince Albert in 1840.

The King's Drawing Room, beyond, enjoys superb views over Kensington Gardens and is followed by the Council Chamber, which exhibits pictures and objects associated with Prince Albert's great project, the Great Exhibition of 1851.

Last comes the most magnificent of all the state apartments, the Cupola Room, with its pillars, figures of Greek and Roman deities, and busts of Roman emperors and ancient philosophers. Downstairs is the excellent Court Dress Collection, with a series of tableaux showing the type of clothing that soldiers, diplomats, and colonial and civil servants would have been expected to wear at official court receptions right up to recent times. By contrast, the wedding dress worn by the Princess of Wales is a delightfully frothy creation.

Kensington Palace Gardens
William III was a keen gardener and lavished much affection on the 10-hectare garden he had laid out, in Dutch style, immediately around Kensington Palace. This has now gone, and in its place is the pretty sunken garden, made in 1909, surrounded by an alley of pleached lime trees on three sides, and with flower beds framing the central lily pond. The fourth side of the garden is closed by the red-brick orangery of 1704. Facing south to catch the sun, this is where Queen Anne used to take tea, as visitors still can—part of the orangery serves as a restaurant. Beyond lies Kensington Gardens (see page 110). An attractive walk from the palace leads up the Broad Walk to Black Lion Gate and Queensway tube station, passing the playground, site of the Elfin Oak, a tree trunk carved by Ivor Innes in 1928 with elves, foxes, frogs, rabbits, and secret doorways.

A glimpse through the gilded gates of Kensington Gardens

Notting Hill Carnival
The Notting Hill Carnival was founded in 1966 as a local neighborhood festival but has since grown to be the biggest Caribbean-style carnival in Britain—perhaps in all Europe. In deference to the English climate it is held over the August Bank Holiday weekend (usually the last weekend in the month), rather than the traditional carnival date of Mardi Gras (Shrove Tuesday), which falls in chilly, wet February. The carnival has been marred in the past by serious crime, racial tension, and violent clashes between revelers and police. Deliberate and successful efforts to clean the carnival up mean that it is now a peaceful event (except for the deafening noise of portable tape players), with processions of colorful floats, street stalls, steel band music, and nonstop dancing.

►► Linley Sambourne House *106A2*

18 Stafford Terrace
Underground: High Street Kensington
Anyone interested in the Victorian era should make an effort to see this excellent museum if at all possible; alternatively, hire the videos or see the Merchant-Ivory films based on E. M. Forster's novels, *A Room with a View* and *Maurice*, for many scenes in both were shot in this house. It is named after Edward Linley Sambourne, the chief political cartoonist for *Punch* magazine who also produced the illustrations for Charles Kingsley's *The Water Babies*, published in 1885. Sambourne bought the house in 1874, soon after it was built, and lived here until his death in 1910. His family continued to use it until 1980, when it was opened as a museum, and throughout the intervening years the house and its furnishings remained almost totally unaltered. The museum is a time capsule, preserving the appearance and atmosphere of the late Victorian and Edwardian eras. The rooms still have their original William Morris wallpapers, and the walls are hung with a mass of paintings, cartoons, and photographs. These contribute a sense of cluttered richness, so beloved by the Victorians, and further enhanced by Oriental rugs, stained glass windows, and heavy, Gothic-inspired furniture.

Among much that is undistinguished in the house, there are some gems on the walls, including paintings by Sambourne's friends—such as Watts, Millais, and Alma-Tadema—and drawings by other well-known book illustrators, such as Kate Greenaway and Sir John Tenniel. Vintage fixtures can be seen in the bathroom and lavatories, and one of the most charming rooms is that of "Roy" Sambourne, the artist's son, complete with its pin-up pictures of popular Edwardian actresses and former girlfriends. (Open: March to October, Wednesday 10–4 and Sunday 2–5.)

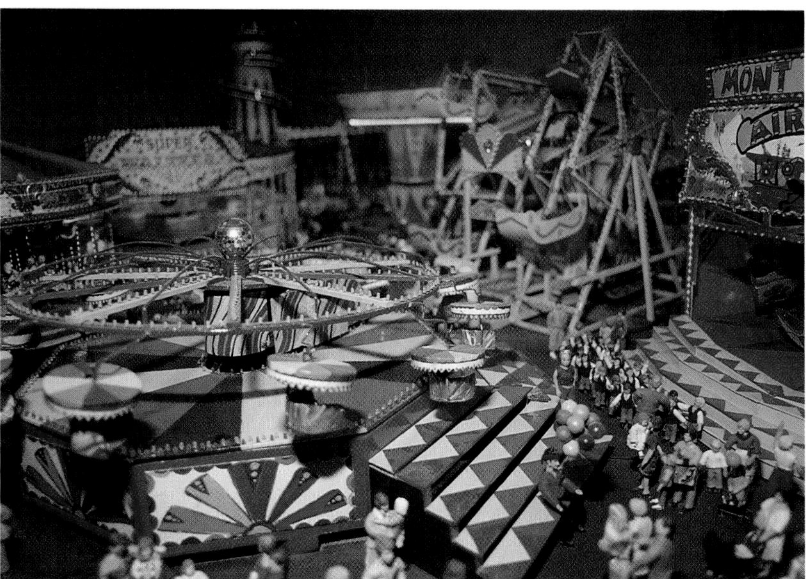

London Toy and Model Museum

► London Toy and Model Museum 106C3

October House, 23 Craven Hill
Underground: Bayswater or Lancaster Gate
Due to reopen in 1995 after reorganization (tel. 071 262 9450 to check the current situation), this deservedly popular museum is crammed with toys that appeal to children and induce nostalgia in adults. Its collection includes a working miniature railway, a late Victorian nursery, soldiers, dolls, teddy bears, and clockwork automata, some over 100 years old. The garden has a carousel and a steam railway, where younger children can take rides. Special events and exhibitions are held throughout the year and in the cafe you will often find excited children consuming home-baked cakes to celebrate a birthday.

Art meets junk in Portobello Road

► Portobello Road Market 106C1

Portobello Road
Underground: Notting Hill Gate
Portobello Road's market changes character according to which day you come. From Monday to Thursday it sells fruit, vegetables, and clothing; on Friday you can find second-hand junk and general bric-à-brac; and Saturday is the day of the famous antiques market (8–5). The prices here are far better than you will find in the plush arcades and shops of Mayfair or St. James's, and there are collectibles that the snootier establishments disdain: antique toys, clothing and records, for example, or vases, pictures, and costume jewelry. Good-natured banter fills the market on any day, and in full swing on Saturday its claim to be the longest streetmarket in Britain is justified. It also has a long history, having started as a gypsy horsemarket in the 1870s, although an official licence wasn't granted until 1929, after years of fierce argument between the stallholders and local shopkeepers, whose prices were being undermined.

Today the market is such a magnet for tourists and bargain hunters that many shops have deliberately moved here to benefit from the passing trade, including some rather upscale antiques shops and art galleries in the area around Golborne Road and Oxford Gardens.

Kensal Green Cemetery
Kensal Green Cemetery, right on the northern borders of Kensington (on Harrow Road, reached from Kensal Green tube station), is, like better-known Highgate Cemetery, full of interesting tombs beside tree-lined avenues. This was the first private cemetery in London (1833) and became fashionable after two of George III's children, Princess Sophia and the Duke of Sussex, were buried here. Other notable tombs are those of Thackeray and Trollope, the novelists; Isambard Kingdom Brunel, the engineer; and the tightrope-walker, Blondin. Here too is the grave of James Barry who, after a successful career as an army surgeon, was made Inspector General of the Army Medical Department; only after "his" death in 1865 was it discovered that James Barry was actually a woman.

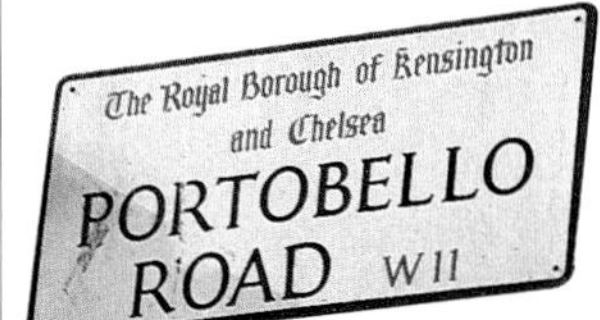

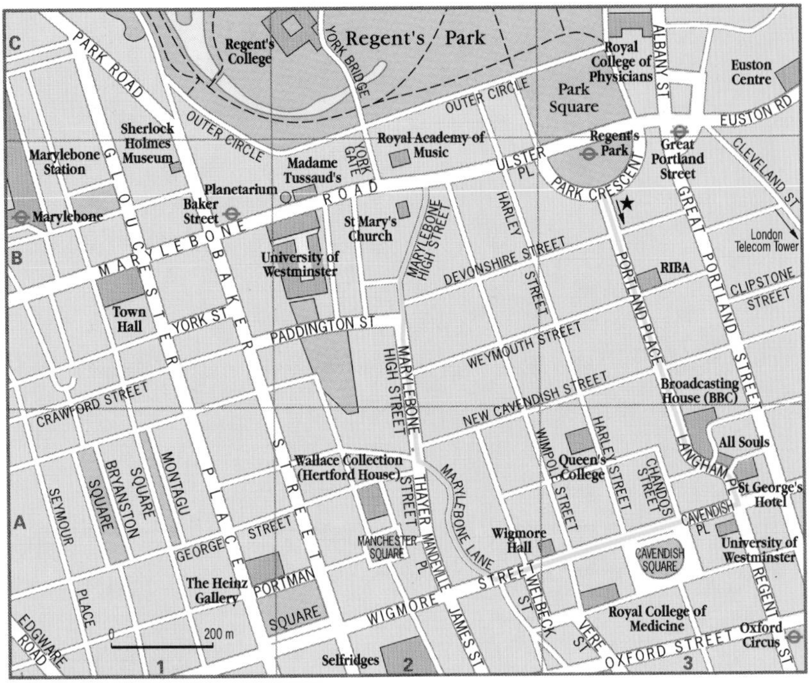

Elizabeth Barrett
No. 50 Wimpole Street (parallel to Portland Place) was the home of Elizabeth Barrett, whose *Poems* (1844) attracted the attention of the younger poet, Robert Browning. A correspondence and a meeting followed, and the two fell in love. Elizabeth's tyrannical father disapproved, so she married Robert secretly in St. Marylebone Church, and the pair later escaped to Italy in one of literary history's most romantic elopements.

Marylebone and Regent's Park In 1812 work began on a bold scheme to transform the West End of London and remodel the Crown-owned lands of Marylebone Park. John Nash, the Prince Regent's architect, cut a swathe through the heart of the metropolis, from Carlton House Terrace north via Regent Street and Portland Place, to Park Crescent. Beyond, he laid out the huge Regent's Park and intended to build a whole garden city of Italianate villas and grand terraces. The scheme was to make London a more beautiful city than Paris, in part a gesture of triumph following the defeat of Napoleon at Waterloo in 1815. The project was never completed in its entirety, but it left London with a new focus, a fine park, and some of its best classical architecture.

Marylebone walk The contrasts of Marylebone are sampled on this tour, which starts with Georgian elegance and ends with shops and cafes.

Take the tube to Regent's Park station, near **Park Crescent**, a daring 1821 design by John Nash, who intended it to be completely circular, in contrast to the squares that characterize Georgian London. Only half of the circle was built, but the curving terrace, with its colonnade of Ionic columns, hints at what Nash intended: a formal but theatrical entrance to Regent's Park, which is now cut off from the Crescent by one of London's busiest roads.

Head south, down **Portland Place**, a wide and handsome street, laid out by Robert Adam (1776–80). The best of the original houses, several serving as embassies, lie between Weymouth and New Cavendish Streets.

The elegant semi-circular sweep of Park Crescent, laid out to a design by Nash in 1821

Beyond are **Broadcasting House** and **All Souls Church** (see page 118), then **St. George's Hotel**, whose rooftop restaurant offers extensive views over London.

Turn right into Cavendish Place, which leads to Cavendish Square. Lord Nelson lived for a time at No. 5 Cavendish Square, but the best buildings are on the north side (**Nos. 11–14**), built in 1770 and originally designed as part of a mansion for the Duke of Chandos. The archway between the two has a large bronze *Madonna* by Jacob Epstein. In Chandos Street, running north from the square, **Chandos House** (1771) is one of Adam's best designs. **Harley Street**, which also leads off Cavendish Square, has been synonymous with medicine since the mid-19th century. Medical practitioners, dentists, psychiatrists, and plastic surgeons have their prestigious consulting rooms here, for the reception of wealthy private clients. On the same street (No. 64) the artist Turner lived from 1804 to 1808, and Queen's College (No. 43) was founded in 1848 as the first college of higher education for women in England.

Leave the square via Wigmore Street, which has interesting shops, as well as **Wigmore Hall** (1901), originally built by the piano maker Friedrich Bechstein next to his showrooms and noted for recitals that are broadcast by the BBC. Further on, on the right, the rigid grid pattern of Marylebone's streets is broken by the serpentine shape of **Marylebone Lane**. This once threaded through the heart of the original medieval village of St. Mary by the Bourne (the River Tyburn). The lane leads to Marylebone High Street, lined with shops and galleries. Try **Pâtisserie Valerie et Sagne** (No. 105), a cafe that has changed little since it opened in the 1920s.

Telecom Tower
Of all the spires and towers that pierce the London skyline, the Telecom Tower is one of the least elegant and most dominant. Many Londoners still refer to it as the Post Office Tower—its name changed when the telephone system, once run by the Post Office, was spun off as British Telecom. The tower was completed in 1964, attracting crowds of tourists who came to enjoy superb views from the revolving restaurant near its 580-ft.-high summit. After a terrorist bomb exploded in the restaurant in 1975, public access was prohibited; too much is at stake to risk another such incident, as the tower is used to transmit and receive satellite phone calls between the City and other financial markets, as well as handling London's radio and TV signals.

The Telecom Tower

► All Souls

116A3

Langham Place
Underground: Oxford Circus
All Souls Church was built in 1822–24 by John Nash—his only church—as an "eye stopper;" that is, to provide a focal point for the view up Regent Street. This is a job it has done supremely well: The curving portico both arrests the eye and takes it around to the left, where Regent Street bends to join Portland Place. The church was ridiculed in its time because Nash mixed together a classical portico with a Gothic spire and was therefore accused of breaking all the rules of architectural propriety, despite the fact that the combination works so well. The silhouette of the spire once dominated the skyline, but bigger buildings, notably Broadcasting House, have since diminished its impact. The interior has been beautifully restored after suffering war damage and is now used by the BBC for broadcasting live lunchtime and evening concerts, as well as religious services.

► Broadcasting House

116A3

Portland Place
Underground: Oxford Circus
Broadcasting House, built in 1931, echoes the shape of All Souls Church, although its curving façade is topped not by a spire but by a radio mast. The building's dominant feature is the sculpture by Eric Gill over the main door, which shows Shakesperare's Prospero sending his ethereal creation Ariel out into the world. Ariel was chosen in the early days of the BBC as an appropriate symbol for the new medium of radio broadcasting. The original 22 studios, from which the BBC began broadcasting in May 1932, are housed within the core of the building so as to be insulated from noise, while the outer shell consists of offices where the Director General and the governors of the BBC meets. The public is admitted to the entrance hall, where there is a bookshop that sells BBC publications.

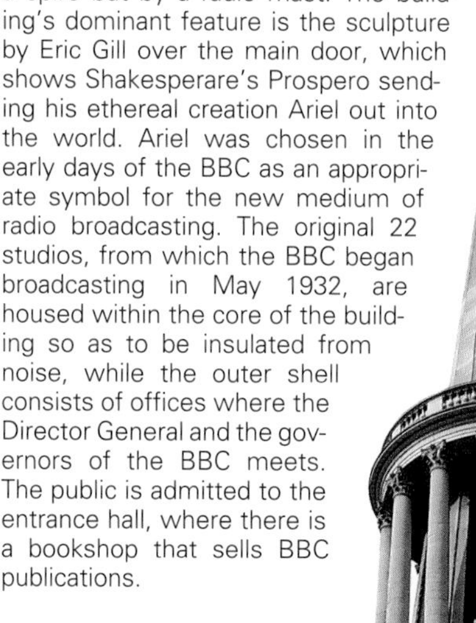

The spire of All Souls, the church used by the BBC for many of its religious broadcasts

The British Broadcasting Corporation (BBC) is one of Britain's best-loved institutions and, at the same time, one that is much criticized. It is known affectionately as "Auntie Beeb" because of its tendency to take a high moral tone and dish up what is best for the audience, rather than what the audience wants. This high-handed manner is very much in the tradition of its founders. .....

The BBC was set up in 1927 in a deliberate government plan to prevent radio broadcasting in Britain from developing along commercial lines, as it had in the USA. The BBC's first Director General, Lord Reith, was a dour figure with strong views about the BBC's missionary role; Christian morality and serious culture were the keynotes. As the "voice of the nation," BBC announcers and presenters were trained to speak "proper" English and regional accents were looked down upon as the products of simple-mindedness. High seriousness was pushed to ridiculous extremes: In the early days of the BBC, radio announcers and newsreaders were expected to wear full evening dress when in front of the microphone.

Despite this, the BBC won the heart of the nation and continues to set high standards of journalistic integrity. Until the coming of television, almost everybody in Britain listened to the BBC, was entertained and educated by it, and many had their lives, ideas, and thoughts shaped by it.

Today the BBC no longer has a monopoly over broadcasting, and British audiences can choose from several TV and radio channels, as well as the BBC's own regional networks. Even so, its financial structure allows the BBC to do things that no other organization can do: The BBC is currently funded by the revenue from selling TV licenses to every television owner in the country, rather than by advertising revenue, and is thus, in theory, free to produce programs "in the public interest." This principle rouses passionate debate, but as long as it lasts, the BBC will broadcast programs that provide some interesting insights into the nuances of the British character.

Prospero and Ariel

When Eric Gill was commissioned to carve Prospero and Ariel over the entrance to Broadcasting House he decided to have a joke or two at the BBC's expense. He did not really think that Prospero and Ariel were appropriate symbols at all, writing sarcastically: "Very clever of the BBC to hit on the idea, Ariel and aerial. Ha! Ha!" He then proceeded to carve huge genitals on the figure of the ethereal youth. Before the carving was unveiled to public view, the BBC governors were invited to a preview and were startled by what they saw. One governor reported somewhat laconically: "I can only say from personal observation that the lad is uncommonly well hung." Gill was asked to cut the statue down to size, which he did, though not to everyone's satisfaction; when it was finally unveiled, the statue caused a scandal. The matter was even raised in Parliament, and there were demands for the carving, described as an offense to public morals and decency, to be torn down. Fortunately, common sense prevailed and Gill's carving has survived as an example of his off-beat sense of humor.

The figures of Prospero and Ariel, from The Tempest, *by Shakespeare, adorn Broadcasting House*

Heroes of every age
One of the secrets of Madame Tussaud's success is keeping up to date with changing fashions: People come to see today's heroes and stars, not yesterday's. In this respect, public personalities can gauge their popularity by the length of time their waxwork figure remains on display. It is a mark of fame to be modeled by Madame Tussaud's at all, and most celebrities so honored cooperate fully, allowing themselves to be photographed or modeled from life, donating clothes, jewelry, or other personal effects to lend authenticity and posing for photographs with the resulting model when it is finally revealed to the public. In this way, Madame Tussaud's has built up an important collection of historic costumes and other objects over the years, ranging from George IV's coronation robes to suits worn by the Beatles and one of Margaret Thatcher's handbags.

► Heinz Gallery 116A1

21 Portman Square
Underground: Marble Arch
Anyone with an interest in architecture should check newspapers or listings magazines to see what's showing at this small gallery. Exhibitions change regularly and draw on the vast collection of drawings and photographs held by the Royal Institute of British Architects (RIBA). These include original drawings by such eminent architects as Andrea Palladio, Inigo Jones, and Edwin Lutyens, and such pioneers of modern building styles as Frank Lloyd Wright, Mies van der Rohe, and Le Corbusier. The gallery, named after its corporate sponsors, opened in 1972 and is housed on the ground floor of an elegant house designed by James Adam in 1772.

Dark deeds in Madame Tussaud's Chamber of Horrors

►►► Madame Tussaud's 116B2

Marylebone Road
Tube: Baker Street
Be prepared to stand in line if you intend to visit Madame Tussaud's, especially in the height of summer, because this is one of London's most popular tourist attractions, receiving well over a million visitors a year. It is also the first and original Madame Tussaud's; the company has now opened similar waxworks displays in capital cities all over the world, but none is quite as fascinating as this

one, because of its range of historical exhibits. One of them is the genuine blade from the Paris guillotine—a grisly reminder of how this celebrated museum of wax figures began. Madame Tussaud (1761–1850) perfected her craft during the French Revolution by taking death masks of guillotine victims, including Louis XVI and Marie Antoinette. In 1802 she fled Paris and arrived in Britain with her macabre collection, first touring the country, then setting up an exhibition of historic figures, living and dead, in London in 1835. In 1884 the collection moved to Marylebone Road, where it has remained to this day. The collection is continually extended to encompass famous figures from every age, but they are made using techniques that have changed little in 200 years.

A £21 million "transformation" of Madame Tussaud's has introduced new features such as the "audio-animatronic" figures in the "Spirit of London" experience, which re-creates the sights, sounds, and smells of the city. The oldest figure on display is Sleeping Beauty, made in 1765, a portrait of Louis XV's mistress, Madame du Barry. Overall, Madame Tussaud's is great fun—a chance to meet and be photographed with your own personal hero, whether that be Michael Jackson, Joan Collins, or even Madame Tussaud herself, whose self-portrait, modeled in 1842, can be seen in the Great Hall.

Planetarium *116B2*

Marylebone Road
Underground: Baker Street
The Planetarium, with its green copper dome, stands alongside Madame Tussaud's; a combined admission ticket is available to both attractions. It uses an extraordinarily complex Zeiss projector to beam a vision of the night sky onto the underside of the dome. Now that street lighting and atmospheric pollution have all but obscured the night sky, this artificial version comes as a revelation to most visitors and is accompanied by an excellent commentary. The adjacent Astronomer's Gallery uses audio-visual techniques to tell the story of scientists such as Galileo and Einstein and their contribution to our knowledge of the universe. In the evenings, the Planetarium is transformed into the Laserium and the same dome gyrates to a light and laser show.

The Chamber of Horrors
Human fascination with death and criminality makes the Chamber of Horrors at Madame Tussaud's one of the most popular attractions, despite the gory nature of its subject matter. Exhibits include a working model of the guillotine, an electric chair, and the gallows from Hertford Gaol, as well as the figures of notorious murderers; one such, George Smith, is shown in the act of drowning one of his unfortunate victims. A taste for the distasteful is nothing new—the Duke of Wellington was a regular visitor to Madame Tussaud's, and he particularly asked to be informed whenever any new exhibit was acquired by the Chamber of Horrors.

The Astronomer's Gallery at the Planetarium

"More like a work of general destruction than anything else." This was how one newspaper described the scene in 1817 as Regent's Park was being laid out. Soon, however, it was being described as "among the magnificent ornaments of our metropolis," and so it remains to this day: a beautiful park of 188 hectares, a fine place for a stroll at any time of year, but especially in summer, when the roses and flower beds are at their best. ....

Camden Lock
Camden Lock lies just to the north of Camden Town tube station, off Chalk Farm Road, and is famous for its lively and atmospheric market (Saturday and Sunday). Here you can browse among stalls selling crafts, hand-knitted and period clothes, antiques, and secondhand books. The lock was built as a branch off the Regent's Park Canal, where barge owners could unload and store their cargoes of lumber, brick, and coal. Many of the original Victorian warehouses have been turned into crafts studios, cafes, and shops, while another has been converted into Dingwalls nightclub, offering live jazz and rock. Just to the east are the studios originally designed for Britain's first commercial breakfast-time TV station, TV-am, by architect Terry Farrell (the station has since lost its broadcasting franchise). Built in 1983, the post-modernist building features giant egg cups along its parapet.

The York Gate entrance, which is served by Baker Street station, lies just beyond **Madame Tussaud's** and the **Planetarium**. As you walk up you will notice, on the right, the **Royal Academy of Music**, founded in 1822, where some of Britain's top performers perfected their art.

On York Bridge, look back to see **St. Mary's Church**, on Marylebone High Street: When Nash laid out Regent's Park he deliberately aligned the York Gate axis to take in a view of the church, with its majestic Corinthian portico and circular tower. York Bridge continues past **Regent's College**, on the left, now a center for European studies and part of Rockford College, Illinois, but formerly part of Bedford College, founded 1849 and a pioneer of the women's education movement. Beyond lies **Queen Mary's Garden**. Here, Nash had intended a temple dedicated to the memory of all who had contributed to British history and culture. Instead, the 7-hectare circle is filled with a rose garden planted to honor Queen Mary, wife of George V. Here, too, is the **Open Air Theatre**, founded in 1932 and famous for its Shakespeare productions (June to August; tel. 071 486 2431 for information).

To the west is the Y-shaped boating lake, and if you walk around the upper part of the lake you will come to the **Hanover Gate**. Here is some of London's most exciting modern architecture. The **London Central Mosque**, to the north, with its splendid dome and minaret, was designed by Sir Frederick Gibberd and opened in 1978 as the principal Islamic mosque in Britain. To the south, fronting the Outer Circle, you can see Quinlan Terry's new villas (completed in 1992), called the **Ionic**, the **Veneto**, and the **Gothick**, an example of the best of architectural craftsmanship. The

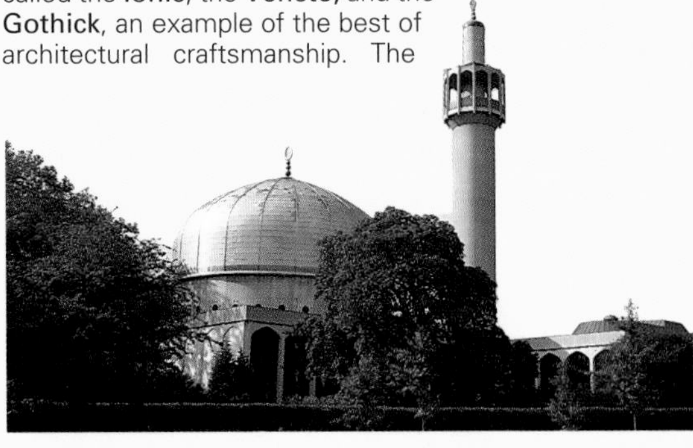

The minaret and golden dome of the London Central Mosque

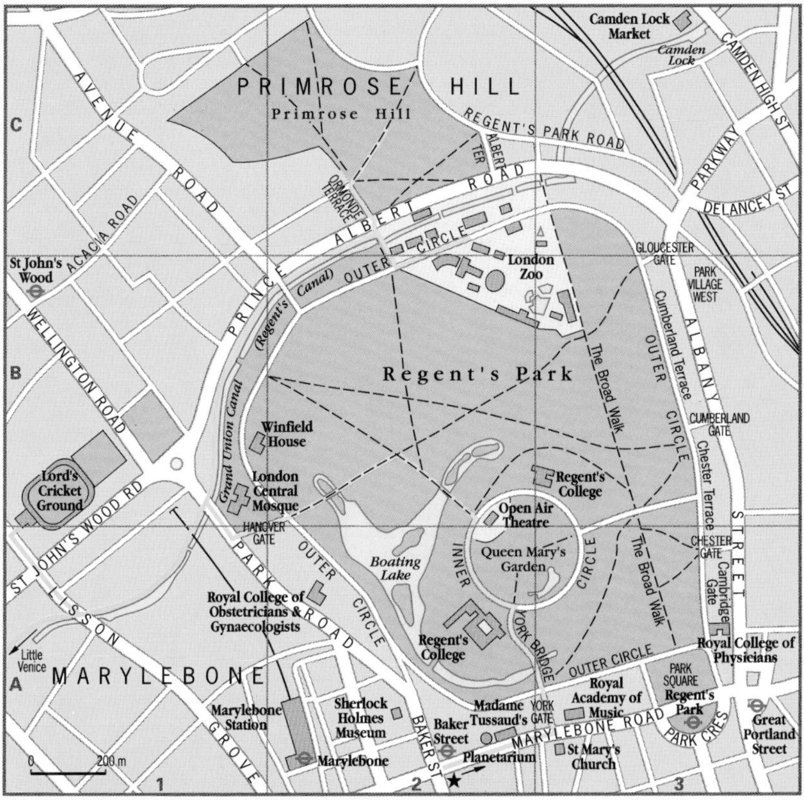

Regent's Park

Summer dreams, Regent's Park

towpath of **Regent's Canal** (a branch of the Grand Union Canal) leads around the northern perimeter of the Park to **London Zoo** (see page 125). From there you can cross over Prince Albert Road to the Primrose Hill extension to Regent's Park; the summit of the hill offers superb views.

Alternatively, follow the canal westwards to the suburbs of St. John's Wood. Star attractions are **Lord's Cricket Ground**, St. John's Wood Road, with a gallery of cricketing memorabilia and tours all year (tel. 071 266 3825); and **"Little Venice"**, around Blomfield Road and Maida Avenue, with its waterside pubs, villas, and narrowboats.

Regent's Canal
The Regent's Canal is a branch of the Grand Union Canal, cut between 1812 and 1820 through the north of London from the Paddington Basin to Limehouse, in the Docklands. Narrowboat cruises with commentaries are run by the London Waterbus Company (summer only, tel. 071 482 2550). The Regent's Canal Information Center (289 Camden High Street), in an old lock-keeper's cottage, describes the canal's history and route and sells excellent guides to its walks and wildlife.

■ **John Nash planned a utopian city for Regent's Park, with houses for the wealthy and for the working classes set in landscaped gardens around a lake. Of that city, only the aristocratic villas and terraces were built, and they can be seen on a stroll around the park's eastern fringes. ...■**

Regency fanlight

The Diorama
The Diorama, which opened in 1823, was the brainchild of Louis Jacques Daguerre, one of the early pioneers of photography. He was also a painter, skilled in creating vast *trompe l'œil* canvases, whose three-dimensional realism was enhanced by lighting and smoke effects, and by solid objects placed in the foreground. The Regent's Park Diorama showed the interior of Canterbury Cathedral: The audience would watch the scene change from daylight to candlelight to the accompaniment of ethereal music. Remarkably, the Diorama has survived, though it closed in 1854. A restoration appeal was launched in 1990, and modern audiences may soon be able to enjoy this curious entertainment.

Great Portland Street and Regent's Park tube stations are both close to Park Crescent, built between 1812 and 1818 (see page 116). Opposite is Park Square, with two long terraces by Nash (1823–25). Three houses on the eastern side of the terrace were built to house the Diorama, once a popular attraction (see side panel).

Just beyond, on the right, is the Royal College of Physicians, in St. Andrew's Place, completed in 1964 to the designs of Sir Denys Lasdun. To the north is Cambridge Gate, built in 1876–80 on the site of the famous Colosseum. This temple-like structure displayed a circular view of London, painted by a Mr. Horner from the top of St. Paul's. It was hugely popular at first, but Londoners soon lost interest, and it was demolished in 1875.

Continue north to Chester Gate; look for the bust of John Nash mounted on the left-hand wall. His Chester Terrace (1825) comes next, a handsome row of houses fronted by great Corinthian pillars, all in gleaming stucco. Nash intended the façade to be decorated by 52 statues but then decided that this would look too fussy. Cumberland Terrace (1826–28) is slightly shorter but much more dramatic, and here Nash did place statues over the pediment of the central block.

Beyond Gloucester Gate you can leave the park, cross Albany Street, and turn right to look at Park Village West. Here, Nash embarked on his scheme for a series of villas set in gardens—notably Tower House, No. 12, once home to Dr. Johnson, physician to William IV.

Corinthian capitals and gleaming white stucco

London Zoo

■ The London Zoological Gardens opened in 1828, the first institution in the world dedicated to the study and display of animals. In its heyday in the 1950s, it received more than 3 million visitors a year. More recently, however, visitor numbers had fallen so far that the zoo could no longer meet its costs. ...■

The zoo announced that it would have to close, but the public reaction to this news was so strong that the decision has now been reversed. Funds have been raised through public donations to the *Save Our Zoo* campaign and through commercial sponsorship to ensure that the zoo can both stay open and modernize its facilities. The zoo's role is also to be redefined, with a far greater emphasis on conservation, education, and the breeding of species that are endangered in the wild—gorillas, Sumatran tigers, and Asian lions, for example.

New displays have been created to explain this work, including the Elephant Tracking Station, which shows how satellites are being used to study the behavior of wild herds and to give early warning of threats from ivory poachers. In another display, in the Sobell Pavilions, a new cage has been added containing a model of a human being. The label on the cage reads: "London Zoo presents the most destructive animal in the world."

Apart from its wide variety of natural life, the zoo has remarkable architectural diversity. The Penguin Pool (1936) is one of the most famous buildings, a pioneering example of modernist design, with an elegant interlocking spiral ramp. The Elephant and Rhino Pavilion (1963–65) is a rare example of Brutalist architecture that works; providing a theatrical backdrop for the animals, its concrete surface reflects their bulky form and skin texture. The Snowdon Aviary (1962–64) allows birds to fly freely and in its own shape suggests a bird in flight. In the Michael Sobell Pavilion for Apes and Monkeys (1970–72) tubular steel space-frame roofs act as a substitute for a forest canopy.

The Elephant and Rhino Pavilion

▶ Sherlock Holmes Museum 116B1

239 Baker Street
Underground: Baker Street
This small museum, lovingly created by the Sherlock Holmes International Society, is dedicated to Sir Arthur Conan Doyle's famous sleuth, one of the first fictional detectives. A re-creation of the detective's home is furnished with his personal possessions and memorabilia from his most important cases. Fans of the Sherlock Holmes stories will remember that the address of his house was 221B Baker Street. The address was pure invention—no such house ever existed—but the site where it would have stood is marked by a plaque on the façade of the Abbey National bank. The Abbey National employs a full-time staff member just to deal with the extraordinary number of letters that arrive from all over the world addressed to Holmes.

The famous fictional detective at home

In the footsteps of Sherlock Holmes
Anyone hooked on *The Adventures of Sherlock Holmes* can eat and sleep with the ghost of their hero. The Sherlock Holmes pub, 10 Northumberland Avenue, is a shrine to the detective. Its walls are covered with Holmes memorabilia, and its upstairs room, next to the restaurant, has a re-creation of Holmes' study, with a model of the man himself seated in front of the fire studying a copy of *The Times*. Sir Arthur Conan Doyle used to drink here himself, and the pub features in *The Hound of the Baskervilles* (Chapter 4) under its old name, the Northumberland Hotel. The restaurant serves food with a Holmesian theme. After dinner here you could retire to the Sherlock Holmes Hotel, 108 Baker Street, part of the Hilton International chain, with plenty of decoration based on the Holmes stories.

▶▶▶ Wallace Collection 116A2

Hertford House, Manchester Square
Tube: Marble Arch
The Wallace Collection, located in the heart of London, just north of Oxford Street, has a world-class collection of art and yet remains little visited. This is a plus for art-lovers, who can enjoy the intimacy of a building that seems more like a private house than a museum; often the only sounds to be heard in the carpeted rooms are the tick-tock and tinkling chimes of the fine French clocks.

The collection was largely put together by the 4th Marquess of Hertford, who lived the life of a recluse in his château in the Bois de Boulogne in Paris. Helped by his illegitimate son, Richard Wallace, the Marquess was an avid collector of 18th-century French paintings and furniture, which he was able to buy cheaply in post Revolutionary France because of its unfashionable (indeed, politically dangerous) associations with the *Ancien Régime*. The Wallace Collection is especially rich in works by Fragonard, Boucher, Watteau, Lancret, and Poussin.

Richard Wallace inherited the collection at his father's death in 1870 and decided to bring it to England because of the unstable political situation in France. He added

Sèvres porcelain in the Wallace Collection

The Laughing Cavalier *(1624), by Frans Hals*

many fine examples of Renaissance ceramics, bronzes, armor, and jewelry, and his widow left the house and the collection to the nation in 1897, on condition that it remain intact. The rooms are packed with objects—not just paintings but everything from wall lights and firescreens, originally made for the palaces of Fontainebleau and Versailles, to the 18th-century saucepans and cabinets packed with guns, porcelain, or bejeweled baubles.

For the general visitor, the paintings make the most impact, the most famous being *The Laughing Cavalier* (1624), displayed upstairs in Room 19, the Big Gallery. Frans Hals's subject, whose identity remains unknown, wears an almost arrogant smirk beneath his carefully combed moustache, the sense of swagger emphasized by the hand on the hip and the rich lace collar. In the same room there is a touching portrait by Rembrandt of his son Titus (*c.*1657), the beautiful *Lady with a Fan* (1638–39) by Velázquez, and Rubens' *Rainbow Landscape* (*c.*1636). Here too is the Poussin painting, *Dance to the Music of Time* (1639–40), that inspired Anthony Powell's novel sequence of the same name. It shows an allegory in which dancers represent Pleasure, Poverty, Riches, and Work, while the two-headed column on the left represents past and future; in the sky, Aurora (dawn) draws the chariot of Apollo (the sun), followed by the Hours.

Among the many other highlights, the festive paintings by Fragonard, Lancret, and Watteau in Room 21 are full of strange, almost other-worldly charm, and there are strong portraits by Gainsborough, Romney, and Reynolds.

Hertford House
The house that holds the Wallace Collection deserves as much study as the paintings. It was built in 1777 for the Duke of Manchester and acquired by the 2nd Marquess of Hertford in 1797. His flamboyant son, the 3rd Marquess, collected many of the 17th-century Dutch paintings in the collection and was able to do so because of his wife's wealth. She was illegitimate—more often than not a barrier to fortune, but in this case two very rich men claimed to be her father (the Duke of Queensberry and George Selwyn) and both left her vast sums of money. The house was refurnished when Richard Wallace moved the collection here. An important feature is the opulent white-marble staircase. This is flanked by a magnificent balustrade, made of wrought iron and bronze in 1723–41 for Louis XV. It was originally installed in the Palais Mazarin (now the Bibliothèque Nationale) in Paris and was acquired by Wallace when it was sold for scrap in the chaotic world of mid-19th century Paris.

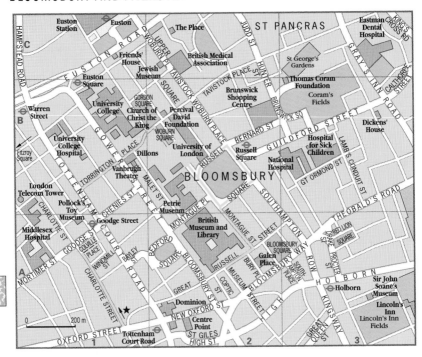

Street entertainer

Bloomsbury and Fitzrovia Bloomsbury is a district of leafy squares, dominated by buildings that house the various departments of the University of London and by the British Museum. It is also associated with a circle of writers who set the pace for artistic and intellectual life in the early decades of this century and who were known collectively as the Bloomsbury Group, because some of their members (including Virginia Woolf, Vanessa Bell, Lytton Strachey, and John Maynard Keynes) lived in the district. Bloomsbury lies to the east of Tottenham Court Road; Fitzrovia, to the west, was the haunt of hard-drinking Bohemian writers, journalists, and artists in the 1940s and '50s (including Dylan Thomas, George Orwell, Cyril Connolly, and Anthony Burgess); these writers were the first to coin the name Fitzrovia to suggest the antithesis of genteel Belgravia.

Bloomsbury and Fitzrovia walk Charlotte Street, where this walk begins, is full of Bohemian atmosphere, with its pubs and inexpensive restaurants serving Greek, Turkish, Indian, and Italian food, and its pavement tables lending something of a Mediterranean air to the area on sunny days.

Turn into Colville Place, a Georgian alley that leads off Charlotte Street just south of Goodge Street; this threads through to **Tottenham Court Road**. To the right, leading south, Tottenham Court Road is lined with brash stores specializing in everything electronic. To the north is the more upscale **Heal's** department store (No. 196), with its big, curved windows (built in 1916). True to the philosophy of its founder, Ambrose Heal, the store specializes in top quality furnishings, including reproductions of its original Arts and Crafts designs.

Charlotte Street bistro

Walk up Torrington Place, to the right beyond Heal's. This leads to **Dillons** bookshop (82 Gower Street), with a vast and comprehensive stock. Beyond Dillons, the tree-filled **Gordon Square** opens up on the left. Its garden is a favorite for students of the nearby Institute of Archaeology. Some of the square's rather dour houses were once centers of Bloomsbury intellectual life: No. 46, the home of Virginia Woolf, Vanessa Bell, and Clive Bell, was the meeting place of a circle that embraced Roger Fry, Duncan Grant, and E. M. Forster, among others. On the opposite, western side of the square is the Dr. Williams Library, where documents relating to the history of Nonconformity are preserved. On the south-western corner, the University Church of Christ the King (1853) is a huge building with an ornate interior, whose intended spire was never built. Immediately south of Gordon Square is **Woburn Square**, lined with restrained Georgian-style terraces. Walking through Woburn Square, you will pass the more aggressively modern buildings of the **School of Oriental and African Studies**.

Continue into **Russell Square**, which was laid out in 1800 and is one of the largest in London. The east side has two hotels: **The Russell Hotel**, of 1898, is modeled on a French château, and the **Imperial**, the modern building that replaced the old Tudor Gothic-style hotel in 1966. The west side of the square has some of its original houses, designed by James Burton, and an entrance to the **Senate House** (begun in 1932), with its massive stone tower. The Senate is the governing body of the 50 or so colleges and faculties that together make up the University of London, Britain's largest university, with more than 64,000 students.

From the southwest corner of Russell Square, Montagu Street leads to Great Russell Street, where you will find the front entrance to the British Museum (see pages 130–1).

The streets south of the museum (Coptic Street, Museum Street, Bury Place, and Galen Place) are worth exploring for their good bookshops, art galleries, pavement cafes, and pubs.

The museum's back door
Some of the British Museum's best galleries, covering prints, drawings, maps, and Oriental art, are among the quietest and least visited, because they lie furthest from the main entrance. If you want to concentrate on these you should slip into the museum by the back door, on Montague Place. From here you enter Room 33, part of which is devoted to a chronological account of Chinese art, the rest to a striking collection of sculpture from temples all over India and Southeast Asia, some gently erotic, some serenely mystic. Below is Room 34, the newly organized collection of Islamic art. Here a variety of miniatures depicts garden scenes, hunting, and courting couples in exquisite color along with displays on scientific ideas that the West absorbed from the Islamic world via Moorish Spain.

Nereid Monument

▶▶▶ **British Museum** *128A2*

Great Russell Street

Underground: Holborn or Tottenham Court Road

This splendid museum, as its Grecian-style façade declares, is a temple to the arts and achievements of the world's civilizations. The British have always been avid collectors and this museum is the result of over 200 years of kleptomania, excavation, or downright looting. It is unrivaled in the world for its variety and richness.

The museum's origins go back to the "curiosities" that were bequeathed to the nation in 1753 by the wealthy physician, Sir Hans Sloane (see page 91), consisting largely of natural history specimens. The collection grew rapidly as a result of the Napoleonic Wars: the victorious British seized many antiquities, including the Rosetta Stone, that the French had looted in Egypt. At the same time, the celebrated sculptures of the Parthenon and other important Greek works were "collected" by the 7th Earl of Elgin (a matter that remains highly controversial, since Greece wants them back) and sold to the British government in 1816. A suitably monumental building was designed for their display in classical style by Sir Robert Smirke and completed in 1848.

The main entrance hall is the place to take your bearings and study plans of the museum. The museum covers an area of 5.4 hectares, but some of the top attractions lie close at hand. To the left, through the bookshop, you can head for Room 8 to see if the Elgin Marbles are still in place. The probability is that they are, even though the room in which they are displayed looks bleak and somewhat temporary. The most important of these sculptures is the so-called Parthenon Frieze, carved between 447 and 432B.C. for the Temple of Athena, patroness of Athens. It originally ran around the interior wall of the temple colonnade, and it illustrates the procession that took place in the city every four years as part of a great festival

The Progress of Civilisation *on the museum's façade*

in Athena's honor. Lord Elgin rescued about half of the original frieze—over 247 ft. in length—from the Parthenon ruins. Other parts had been shattered in 1687 when the Parthenon, used as an ammunitions store by occupying Turks, was hit by a shell and all but destroyed. Two other rooms are worth seeking out near by. Room 9 is known as the Room of the Caryatid, after the figure of a 5th-century B.C. maiden, one of a series of columns from the Erectheion in Athens (a shrine to the mythical king Erectheus). Room 12 contains what little survives of one of the Seven Wonders of the Ancient World, brought from Turkey: sculptural fragments from the Mausoleum of Halicarnassus, the great tomb built for Mausolus, Prince of Caria, by his wife in the 4th century B.C. Mausolus himself is depicted, and possibly his wife, as well as a battle between the Greeks and Amazons.

Celtic jewelry, made in the 1st century B.C.

Assyrian Art
The rooms in the British Museum devoted to Assyrian art are less well known than the Greek antiquities but no less striking. Room 26 has a huge winged lion that once guarded the palace and temple complex at Nimrud, built around 880B.C., and the theme of the lion hunt features in several narrative friezes. These can be seen in Room 19, featuring sculptures from the throne room at Nimrud, and in Room 17, displaying magnificent carvings from the palace at Nineveh (7th century B.C.). These latter scenes seem almost modern in their clean, fluid lines, and the naturalistic portrayal of wounded lions writhing in agony.

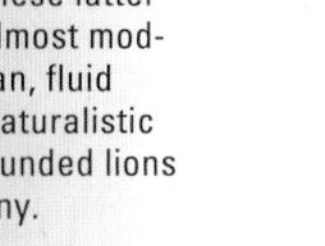

Curiosities
Room 35, on the upper floor, holds the perfectly preserved 2,000-year-old body of Lindow Man, nicknamed "Pete Marsh" by the archaeologists who found him in a waterlogged peat bog in Cheshire. Rooms 60 and 61 are filled with ancient Egyptian coffins and their contents: not just human mummies but also those of sacred animals—crocodiles, cats, dogs, fish, an ape, an ibex, and even a bull. You can compare the dice, mosaic gaming board, and counters in Room 56 (from ancient Babylon, made around 2,600B.C.) with the mid-12th-century Lewis chessmen, carved in ivory, in Room 42. Clocks, watches, and musical timepieces are shown in Room 44. Many are still working, and all chime together on the hour.

The British Museum has one of the richest collections of ancient Egyptian art to be seen anywhere in the world, and some of the best objects are displayed in Room 25. At the southern end is the celebrated Rosetta Stone, named after the town near the mouth of the Nile where it was found in 1799. The insignificant-looking slab unlocked the secret of ancient Egyptian hieroglyphs: Its inscription has a Greek translation alongside, allowing scholars to work from the known to the unknown. Not to be missed among all the other very fine tombs and statues is a naturalistic cat in bronze (wearing nose and ear rings) displayed in one of the central cases.

On the upper floor of the museum, a series of rooms tells the story of Europe and the British Isles from early prehistory to the end of the Middle Ages. Nearly all the most important archaeological treasures unearthed in Britain are displayed here, including some that throw light on London's early history. One such is the superb Battersea Shield (Room 39), a fine example of Celtic Art (mid-1st century B.C.). Another is the tombstone of Julius Classicianus, the Roman official who governed London from A.D.61 to 65 (Room 40). Nearby is the Mildenhall Treasure, a complete set of silver embossed tableware dating from the 4th century, so magnificent that it must have belonged to a Roman governor or another high official. Best of all is the Sutton Hoo Treasure (Room 41), consisting of bejeweled swords, helmets, buckles, bowls, drinking horns, and a bronze cauldron. They all come from a 7th-century ship burial, probably that of Redwald, King of the East Angles, and provide ample evidence that the raiders who settled in England during the so-called Dark Ages were not the uncouth barbarians of popular imagination, but highly skilled craftsmen.

The Elgin marbles

■ The British Museum was originally built around an open courtyard. Not long after the building was finished, it was decided to make better use of this space by roofing it over to create the famous round Reading Room. Since it opened in 1857 many precious books have been consulted here and several important books written—including *Das Kapital*, the political and economic manifesto of Karl Marx (his usual seat in the Reading Room was No. G7). A new set of books is due to fill its shelves, for the museum's library is to move to a new building (see panel), and the space may then be used for the Museum of Mankind's books on travel, anthropology, and ethnology.....■

Members of the public are not normally admitted to the Reading Room (for details of occasional guided tours check at the information desk in the main entrance). Visitors can, however, admire the outstanding collection of historic and literary manuscripts displayed in Rooms 30 and 31 of the British Museum. Anyone who is familiar with the works of Jane Austen, for example, or William Wordsworth is likely to enjoy a special kind of thrill from deciphering their handwriting and reading the manuscript pages, complete with crossings out and amendments, from famous novels or poems. Other cases display the handwritten manuscripts of musical scores, such as that of Handel's *Messiah*, and there is an impressive collection of letters, bills, and notes bearing the signatures of kings and queens, artists such as Michelangelo and playwrights such as George Bernard Shaw. Shaw continues to be a very important patron of the British Museum, and he bequeathed the royalties from his most popular play, *Pygmalion*, to the museum in perpetuity. Since it was generally believed that this gift stemmed from Shaw's frequent use of the British Library, there was a certain amount of controversy when the library separated from the museum as to which institution should keep a hold on the bequest. In the event, the British Museum has retained the Shavian Fund, as it is called, but the British Library still benefits from its earnings.

Other precious items on display include the richly illuminated Lindisfarne Gospels of around 698A.D., two of the earliest surviving copies of the New Testament (dating from the 4th and 5th centuries), and two of the four surviving copies of the *Magna Carta*, the charter sealed by King John at Runnymede in 1215, setting out some of the basic tenets of English law.

Further treats lie in store in Room 32, The King's Library, so named because its walls are lined with shelves of books that once belonged to George III. The cases below them contain children's books, fine bindings, an exhaustive range of postage stamps collected from countries all over the world, and various changing exhibitions.

The British Library
The Library at the British Museum is one of four copyright libraries in the UK to which all the publishers in the country are obliged by law to send a copy of every book, periodical, newspaper, or map they publish. Space to store such a vast reference collection (needing almost 2 miles of additional shelving annually) ran out a long time ago. The solution was the creation of a new organization, the British Library, in 1973. A new British Library building, near Euston station, should have opened in 1991 but has been dogged by delays, cost overruns, and problems with faulty shelving. No one is now prepared to say when the building will be finished. To some scholars, this is good news: They have so far won a reprieve and continue to study beneath the noble dome of the Museum's historic round Reading Room. It is only a matter of time, though, before the books and readers will have to move.

Bust of Charles Dickens

The history of Nonconformity

Two small museums in the Euston Road provide an insight into the history of religious Nonconformity. Friends' House stands opposite Euston Square and is the headquarters of the Religious Society of Friends (better known as the Quakers). The house looks convincingly Georgian, but was built in 1925–27 to the designs of Hubert Lidbetter. Inside the library, founded in 1673, there are displays of Quaker literature, including the journal of George Fox and documents relating to William Penn and the foundation of Pennsylvania. A little further east, at 117–21 Judd Street, the premises of the Salvationist Publishing & Supplies company has a small museum covering the origins of the Salvation Army, founded in 1878 by the Reverend William Booth to help the poor of London's East End.

▶ Dickens' House

128B3

48 Doughty Street

Underground: Russell Square

Charles Dickens, the great 19th-century novelist, is one of that handful of writers who have shaped and molded our vision of London. His descriptions of the fog-bound haunts of torpid lawyers, of the criminal underworld of Fagin and his thieves, or the cramped and crooked home of Little Nell, the Old Curiosity Shop (see page 155), are as vivid now as they were 150 years ago. It only takes a little imagination to conjure up visions of Dickensian London as you wander the city's streets, and a visit to Dickens' house allows you to pursue the illusion further.

The house is the only surviving London home out of several in which Dickens lived and worked. He moved here in 1837, a year after his marriage to Catherine Hogarth. By 1839, Dickens's growing wealth allowed the family to move on to 1 Devonshire Terrace (since demolished), a more impressive house overlooking Regent's Park. In the time that Dickens lived here he was characteristically prolific: He completed the *Pickwick Papers*, wrote *Oliver Twist* and *Nicholas Nickleby,* and began *Barnaby Rudge* all in under three years.

His house, which was bought by the Dickens Fellowship in 1924, retains the heavy Victorian color scheme and the desk and chair where Dickens wrote surrounded by the hustle and bustle of family life (he possessed the remarkable gift of being able to write even with the distractions of noise, visitors, and conversation all around him). Other

The house where Dickens wrote Oliver Twist

Dickens memorabilia on display include first editions of his work, the copies he used for his public readings, marked with cues for gestures and intonation, and Lionel Bart's score for his musical version of *Oliver Twist*. A good shop sells Dickens's work. (Closed Sunday.)

► **Jewish Museum** *128C2*

Woburn House, Tavistock Square
Underground: Euston or Russell Square
This one-room museum (closed Saturday and Monday) covers the fascinating history of Anglo Judaism. An audio-visual program explains how long Jews have lived in England (since Norman times, if not before) though treated with suspicion and subject to persecution. It also explains the two main strands of Judaism. Many of the Jews who settled in England from the 15th century onwards were Sephardic Jews from Spain and Portugal, a large number of whom subjected themselves to Christian baptism, while continuing to practice their religion in secret. Some became wealthy as wool merchants and one, Rodrigo Lopez, became Queen Elizabeth I's physician. Later on, Ashkenazic Jews, victims of persecution in central and eastern Europe, came to England in large numbers, setting up in the cloth, fur, leather, and jewelry trades in London's East End.

The museum's exhibits mainly cover the period from the end of the 17th century (when Cromwell removed the prohibitive laws on Jewish settlement) though there are earlier objects, such as the 13th-century bankers' tallies. Portraits of prominent members of the Anglo-Jewish community hang around the walls, and there is a fine silver salver, dating from 1702, on which Portuguese Jews made an annual presentation of sweetmeats to the Lord Mayor. Other items include 18th-century Staffordshire figures of Jewish peddlers and a 16th-century Synagogue Ark, richly carved and painted, used for storing the Scrolls of the Law. (Anyone interested in learning more should visit the Museum of the Jewish East End, 80 East End Road, which covers the history of the Jewish community in London. This museum is due to move to new premises—tel. 071 388 4525 for information.) As you leave, look out for Edwin Lutyens' building on the east side of Tavistock Square, built in 1911–13 for the Theosophical Society and now housing the British Medical Association. Note, too, the statue of Gandhi in the square's garden, by Fredda Brilliant (1968).

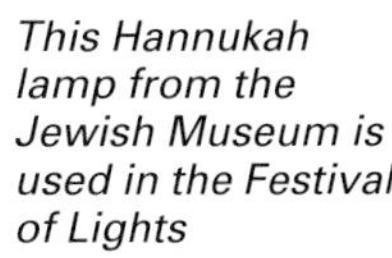

This Hannukah lamp from the Jewish Museum is used in the Festival of Lights

Railway stations
Euston, St. Pancras, and King's Cross stations stand almost side by side along the northern edge of Euston Road, each built in the 19th century by the independent railway companies that competed with each other until they were brought together to form British Rail. (The government now plans to reverse history by privatizing parts of the rail network and splitting it into a number of franchises—despite immense opposition from rail users, who fear a major deterioration in service.) Euston was wholly rebuilt in the 1960s; all that survives of the terminus are two lodge houses, part of the original formal entrance to the station. St. Pancras, by contrast, survives in its original form and is fronted by the Grand Midland Hotel, a magnificent monument of neo-Gothic architecture bristling with towers and spires, built in 1868–72 by George Gilbert Scott. Long empty and disused, it is now under restoration. King's Cross is a much more utilitarian building, designed by Lewis Cubbitt and built in 1851–52. To the rear of the station is a vast area of disused land, once used as a goods yard but now reclaimed by nature; there are now controversial plans to develop a model city of the future on the site, set around parkland.

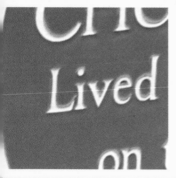

■ Sometimes it seems that there is no building or stretch of street in London that has not witnessed some historic event or been the home of an eminent person. Statues abound and hundreds of buildings bear blue commemorative plaques. Tracking these down can reveal a few interesting surprises—people you never knew lived in the city at all, for example—such as the Italian artist Canaletto (at 41 Beak Street) or the U.S. President John F. Kennedy (at 14 Prince's Gate)....■

Blue plaques
The idea of placing plaques on the houses or sites where distinguished people once lived was devised in 1866 by William Ewart; the scheme was originally run by the Royal Society of Arts, then by the Greater London Council. The first was placed on the birthplace of Lord Byron in Holles Street. There are now over 400 plaques. The person commemorated must have been dead for over 20 years and born more than 100 years ago. He or she must also have made "some important contribution to human welfare or happiness."

In total, London has more than 1,700 statues and 400 blue plaques, originally chocolate-brown but now standardized to a present-day Wedgwood blue with white lettering (see side panel). Here is a selection of the most interesting.

Alfred the Great In front of Holy Trinity Church (now the Henry Wood Hall) in Trinity Church Square (SE1) is a 14th-century statue of Alfred the Great, the 9th-century King of England; this is the oldest commemorative statue that exists in London.

David Ben-Gurion Israel's first prime minister lived at 75 Warrington Crescent, Maida Vale (W9).

Simon Bolivar The Latin-American revolutionary is commemorated by a statue in Belgrave Square, carved by Hugo Daini (1974).

Boudicca The rebellious queen of the Iceni tribe, who led the revolt against the Roman conquest of Britain and burned down London in A.D.60, is depicted in a stirring bronze statue by Thomas Thorneycroft on Victoria Embankment, just by the Houses of Parliament. Prince Albert lent his own horses to be used as the models for those pulling Boudicca's chariot.

Sir Charles Spencer Chaplin Better known as Charlie Chaplin, the comic star of the silent screen lived at 287 Kennington Road, Lambeth (SE11) and has a statue in Leicester Square by John Doubleday (1987), appropriately surrounded by movie theaters.

Frédéric Chopin The Polish-born composer gave his last ever public concert at London's Guildhall and is commemorated by a statue alongside the Festival Hall.

General Charles de Gaulle A plaque at 4

Charlie Chaplin in Leicester Square

Captain Robert Scott, Antarctic explorer

Carlton Gardens shows this was the headquarters of the Free French Forces, led by de Gaulle, beginning in June 1940.

Elizabeth Garrett Anderson The first woman ever to qualify as a doctor in Britain had her home at 20 Upper Berkeley Street.

Wolfgang Amadeus Mozart The child prodigy composed his first symphony at 180 Ebury Street.

Florence Nightingale A statue of the pioneer of nursing, who was christened "the lady with the lamp" by her soldier patients, is part of the Crimean Memorial on Waterloo Place; the house in which she lived and died is at 10 South Street (off Park Lane).

Captain Robert Scott Scott of the Antarctic set off for his last fateful expedition from his house at 56 Oakley Street, Chelsea. Scott is portrayed, wearing the clothes he wore for the trip, in a bronze statue made by his widow, Lady Scott, in Waterloo Place.

Princess Pocahontas The Algonquin Indian princess, who saved the life of Captain John Smith in 1602, is portrayed in a bronze statue in Red Lion Square (off Holborn). She married John Rolfe, came to England in 1614, and was a great success at the Jacobean Court but lacked immunity to western diseases and died in 1617, aged 22.

Bertrand Russell Also in Red Lion Square is a bust of the philosopher, who lectured in nearby Conway Hall.

Sun Yat Sen The father of Chinese republicanism, who led the Kuomintang to overthrow the Ch'ing dynasty in 1911, spent his time in exile at a house on the site of 4 Gray's Inn Place.

Voltaire A plaque recalls the fact that the philosopher whose ideas inspired the Enlightenment once lodged at a house on the site of 10 Maiden Lane, Covent Garden.

Postman's Park
The churchyard of St. Botolph's Church, Aldersgate, is locally known as Postman's Park, since this is where workers from the nearby Postal Sorting Office come to enjoy their lunchtime sandwiches. The park was laid out in 1900 as a national memorial to ordinary men and women whose heroic deeds might otherwise have been forgotten. A long wall contains memorial plaques telling the stories of just a few of those people. One records that Alice Ayres, a laborer's daughter, gave her own life to save three children from a burning house; another commemorates Thomas Simpson, who died of exhaustion in January 1885, having rescued scores of skaters from drowning when the ice broke at Highgate Ponds. Michael Ayrton's powerfully symbolic sculpture, the *Minotaur*, has recently been acquired for the park.

Coram's Fields
The Thomas Coram Foundation fronts onto Coram's Fields, a 3-hectare garden full of trees where the children of the Foundling Hospital used to play until the institution moved to more rural premises in Berkhamsted in the 1920s. The garden is entered by the original entrance gates of 1752, and a sign warns that no adult may visit the gardens unless accompanied by a child. Immediately south is the delightful Lamb's Conduit Street, a traffic-free precinct with many shops, pubs, and restaurants. The Lamb (No. 94) is an unspoiled Victorian pub with original woodwork and glass screens and photographs of music-hall stars on the walls, and the Sun (No. 63) is a beer lover's paradise, stocking a great range of products from small independent breweries.

► Percival David Foundation 128B2

53 Gordon Square
Underground: Russell Square
This small museum is devoted to an exhibition of Chinese ceramics collected by Sir Percival David and donated to London University in 1950. Pieces on display range in date from the Sung (10th century) to the Qing (19th) dynasties. The overwhelming impression they leave is of consummate craftsmanship; some of the most modern looking, in their clear lines and rich color, turn out to be among the most ancient. Closed Saturday and Sunday.

► Petrie Museum 128B2

Department of Egyptology, Malet Place
Underground: Goodge Street or Russell Square
This is another university study collection, consisting of Egyptian antiquities collected by Amelia Edwards and Sir Flinders Petrie (1853–1942). Its sequence of Predynastic pottery provided the means of dating Egyptian ceramic styles. There are charming displays of cat figures, notable relief carvings and a child's linen dress dating, incredibly, from around 2800B.C. Closed Saturday and Sunday.

►► Pollock's Toy Museum 128A1

1 Scala Street
Underground: Goodge Street
Robert Louis Stevenson wrote: "If you love art, folly, or the bright eyes of children, speed to Pollock's." He was referring to the shop (since gone) where Benjamin Pollock sold printed sheets that Victorian and Edwardian children stuck to wood or cardboard to create miniature theaters. This small museum (upstairs), with a shop below, is crammed with Pollock's theaters, as well as other toys, some from the 18th century. The museum is designed for children, with eye-level displays, and there are occasional Punch and Judy shows. Reproductions of toys from around the world are sold in the shop. Closed Sunday.

Pollock's toy theaters

▶▶ Thomas Coram Foundation 128B3

40 Brunswick Square

Underground: Russell Square

The Thomas Coram Foundation (once known as the Foundling Hospital) was set up to provide shelter and an education for orphaned and abandoned children. Its founder was the remarkable Captain Thomas Coram, shipbuilder and master mariner, who played an important role in the colonization of Massachusetts, Georgia, and Nova Scotia. Returning to London in 1732, he was appalled by the sight of abandoned children and infants "left to die on dung hills." He devoted the remainder of his life to working on their behalf, establishing the Foundling Hospital, with George II and many other eminent figures of the age as patrons. The present building, on the same site, dates from 1937. Its walls are hung with paintings given by well wishers, most notably those of artist William Hogarth (who was one of the first governors). Many of the works are on charitable themes or depict Biblical subjects related to the hospital's work. The highlight of the collection, however, is Hogarth's masterful portrait of the founder *Captain Thomas Coram* (1740). The Courtroom, where the present governors still hold their meetings, is a reproduction of the original, with an ornate plaster ceiling and cases containing good-luck tokens and charms left by impoverished mothers with the illegitimate babies they abandoned on London's streets. Handel was another strong supporter of the hospital's work in the courtroom, and you can see the score of the *Messiah* that he donated and the keyboard of the organ on which he gave fund-raising recitals. Closed Saturday and Sunday.

Captain Coram, founder of the Foundling Hospital

Great Ormond Street Hospital

In 1851, a century after Thomas Coram set up the Foundling Hospital, another philanthropist, Dr Charles West, established London's first Hospital for Sick Children in Great Ormond Street. He was, quite rightly, appalled by the child-mortality rate in 19th-century London (of 50,000 deaths recorded annually in the city, 21,000 were children under 10). The hospital was set up to remedy the situation and still receives an important part of its income from the legacy of Sir James Barrie, the author of *Peter Pan*. In 1929 Barrie made a gift of the copyright to the hospital, which benefits from royalties every time the book is sold or the play performed on film, stage, television, and radio. Although the royalties expired in 1987, 50 years after Barrie's death, a special Act of Parliament was passed in the following year to ensure that the hospital would continue to benefit from them in perpetuity. Of the original Victorian hospital buildings, the chapel survives, decorated with mosaics and touching memorials.

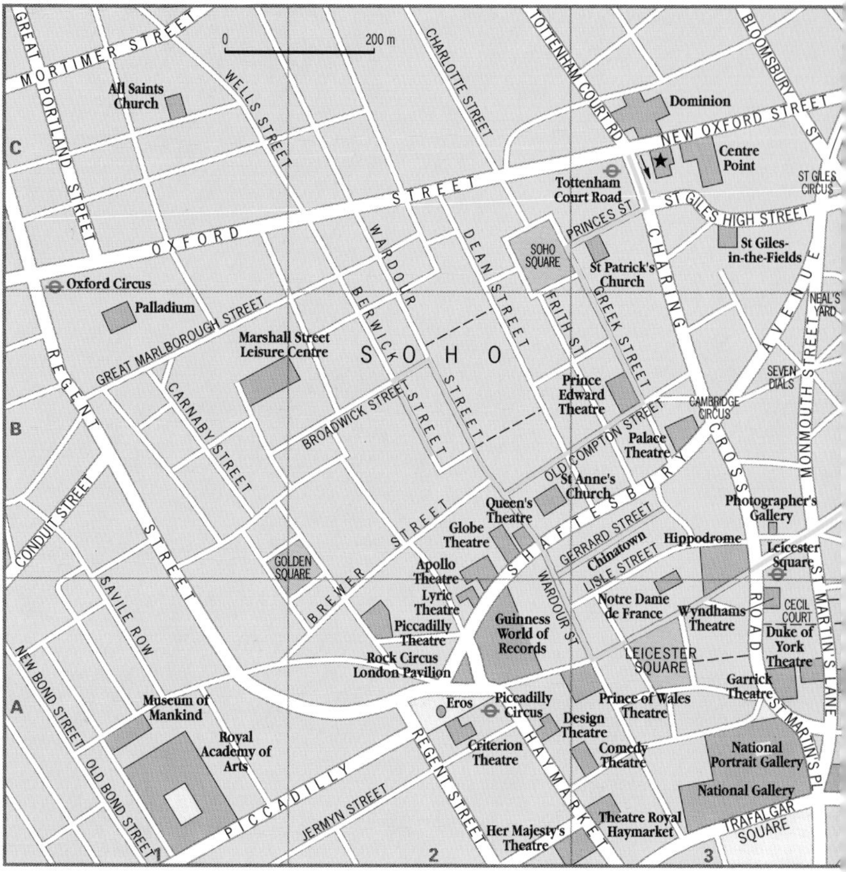

A corner of London's Chinatown

Soho and Covent Garden A mere two decades ago, Soho was a byword for sex clubs and sleaze, and Covent Garden was the run-down haunt of vegetable and flower traders. When the wholesale market moved to modern premises at Nine Elms in 1974, the whole future of Covent Garden looked uncertain. Eventually, the market halls were converted into small shops and stalls, and this became a largely traffic-free area where street performers entertain and visitors can relax in pavement cafes. Soho blossomed, too, as a determined effort was made to clean the area up, and the large Chinatown quarter at its heart was turned into a pedestrian precinct.

Soho and Covent Garden walk From Tottenham Court Road tube station, walk south down Charing Cross Road. Off to the right is pretty **Soho Square**, where office workers from the film, advertising, and design companies of nearby Dean Street and Wardour Street come to eat lunchtime sandwiches. Executives are more likely to be consuming expense-account lunches in the restaurants of **Greek Street**, which leads southwards out of the square.

Follow Greek Street to **Old Compton Street**, another gourmets' haven. Turn right at the end of Old Compton Street into Wardour Street, then take the third left into

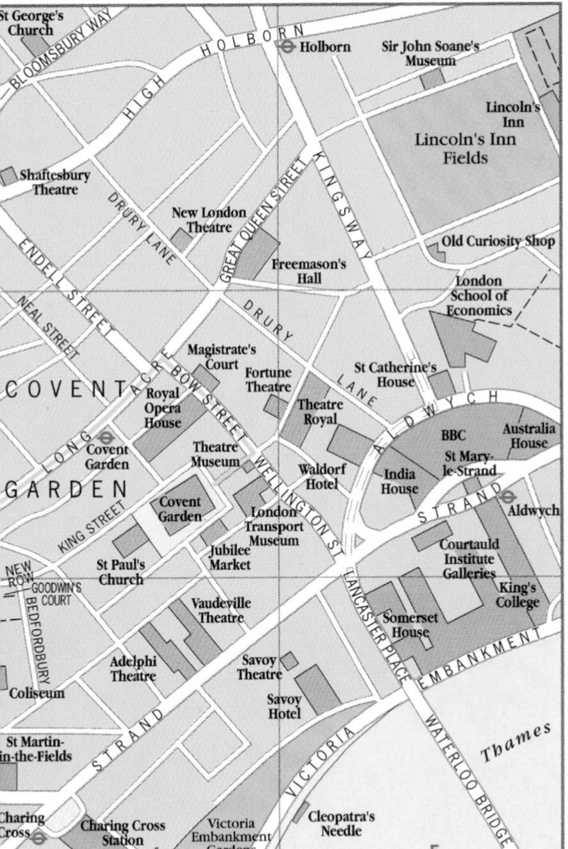

Broadwick Street for **Berwick Street market**, the best in London for fresh fruit and vegetables.

To the left at the end of Old Compton Street, Wardour Street continues south of Shaftesbury Avenue and leads to **Gerrard Street**, the heart of London's Chinatown. Top-quality Chinese restaurants line Wardour Street, which leads to the movie theaters of **Leicester Square**. The mechanical clock on the façade of the **Swiss Centre** is a popular attraction when it performs on the hour.

The northeastern exit from Leicester Square, Cranbourn Street, will take you across Charing Cross Road and into Long Acre, Covent Garden's main thoroughfare. The first right turn leads to the covered market, but it is worth continuing to the second right, **Bow Street**. It was from here that the Bow Street Runners, a prototype police force, operated in the early 19th century. Across the street is the **Royal Opera House**, home to both the Royal Opera and the Royal Ballet. Here prestigious productions are mounted in conditions that have improved little since 1858, when the stage, dressing rooms, and scenery stores were built. Controversial plans have been drawn up to modernize the Opera House and extend it into the plaza behind, substantially altering the appearance of the main Covent Garden Market.

■ Covent Garden is the spirited heart of central London, a mini-community within the city but with important differences. One is the freedom to roam many of its streets without the constant noise, pollution, and danger of traffic. Another is the fact that the shops are small, personal, and sell a wide range of interesting products, from buttons and bows to books and works of art. ...■

Seven Dials
Seven Dials stands at the junction of seven streets in a corner of Covent Garden that was once the haunt of prostitutes and thieves. A Doric pillar erected here in 1694, topped by seven sundials, was knocked down in 1773 because of a rumor that a large sum of money was buried at its base. It was later rebuilt on the green at Weybridge in Surrey. A replica, paid for by local residents and carved by trainee masons, was unveiled in 1989. It actually has only six sundials; the seventh is the column itself, which casts its shadow onto the pavement below, where the hours are marked by iron bollards.

The focal point of Covent Garden is the Central Market. This elegant building, designed by Charles Fowler, was completed in the 1830s, although the iron-and-glass roof over the central arcade was added in the 1870s. The wholesale fruit and vegetable market that operated here closed in 1974 and moved to Nine Elms, in south London. The market building was then converted to provide space for the scores of small specialist shops and cafes that now line the arcade, itself filled with market stalls selling antiques, crafts, toys, jewelry, and clothing. The **Punch and Judy** pub, on the southwestern corner of the market, opened in 1980, but its name is a reminder that the first Punch and Judy puppet show was performed in the square below on May 9, 1662—Samuel Pepys was one of those who came to watch the antics of Pietro Gimonde's marionettes. Mr. Punch's birthday is still celebrated on the second Sunday in May, as part of the Covent Garden May Fayre festival.

Entertainment takes place here all week from 10a.m. to dusk. The space in front of St. Paul's Church is used by street performers—clowns, fire-eaters, musicians, acrobats—and the day's program, organized by Alternative Arts, is posted on the church railings. These railings also frame the entrance to the Victorian public restrooms built below the square, an attraction in their own right.

St. Paul's Church is the oldest surviving building on the square. It was built by Inigo Jones in the 1630s, inspired by the cathedral in Livorno, Tuscany, which Jones had helped to design as an apprentice to the Renaissance architect Buontalenti. His client, the Earl of Bedford, who owned the Covent Garden lands, was a low churchman who disliked Gothic frills, and he told Jones to make the church as simple as a barn. Jones is said to have replied: "You shall have the handsomest barn in England," and that is what the building most resembles. St. Paul's is known as "the actors' church" because, being located near the Theatre Royal, Drury Lane, and the Royal Opera House, it is much used by playwrights, performers, and impresarios. Ellen Terry, Charlie Chaplin, Vivien Leigh, and Noel Coward are among the theatrical personalities buried here or commemorated on the wall plaques.

To the north of Long Acre, Covent Garden's main thoroughfare, lies a maze of little streets. Some are lined with warehouses once used to store fruit and vegetables, now converted to dance studios (such as the **Pineapple Dance Studios** 7 Langley Street), art galleries (such as **Contemporary Applied Arts**, 43 Earlham Street), and specialty

shops (such as **Neal Street East**, 5 Neal Street, packed with goods from China, Japan, and Korea). Some of the best shops line Neal Street, while the old warehouses surrounding Neal's Yard are a gourmet's paradise, especially for vegetarians. Excellent takeout natural food is to be had at the **Neal's Yard Bakery** (6 Neal's Yard), but beware of the sculpture on the opposite side of the yard, made of several wooden figures in a line. This is animated by putting a coin in a slot, and the surprise comes when the man at the end of the line spits a powerful jet of water at unwary onlookers. Just around the corner, in Shorts Gardens, is an animated water clock on the wall above the Neal's Yard food shop. Immediately to the left, at 17 Shorts Gardens, is the Neal's Yard Dairy, one of England's best cheese shops, selling cheeses made by small producers all over Britain and Ireland.

Taking tea in the plaza

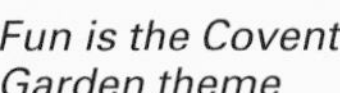
Fun is the Covent Garden theme

Pubs and cafes
Covent Garden has scores of pubs and sidewalk cafes, offering a cosmopolitan range. Nothing could be more English than the Lamb and Flag (33 Rose Street), a 300-year-old pub serving homemade food, where you are in constant danger of banging your head on the low ceiling beams. That is not why the pub was once known as the Bucket of Blood; bare-knuckle boxing bouts once took place in the upstairs rooms. The Rock Garden, on the plaza, serves American-style burgers and ribs, and there is live music in the converted banana warehouse every night. The Calabash, 38 King Street, is an informal restaurant, one of a handful in London specializing in African food.

■ **Book lovers should have little trouble keeping themselves occupied in the West End of London. For a feast of good bookstores—eccentric, specialist, antiquarian—head straight for Charing Cross Road. But beware of wasting too much time in a fruitless search for No. 84. Helene Hanff's book *84 Charing Cross Road* was based on her correspondence with the owners and staff of Mark's and Co.'s secondhand bookstore—but the original shop is no more. ...■**

Other specialist bookstores Books for Cooks, 4 Blenheim Crescent, Notting Hill, claims to be the largest shop in the world devoted exclusively to the culinary arts of every nation. You may also find rare or out-of-print editions among its range of secondhand stock. A short step away is the Travel Bookshop (13 Blenheim Crescent), which has the edge on Stanfords in one respect: It sells antiquarian and secondhand titles, as well as all the latest travel literature and practical guides. For books and magazines in European languages other than English, Grant & Cutler, 55–7 Great Marlborough Street, is the place to go; if they don't have what you want, try the European Bookstore, 5 Warwick Street: Both stock titles from the main French, Italian, Spanish, German, and Portuguese publishing houses. Forbidden Planet (71 New Oxford Street) doesn't sound like a bookstore, and some would dispute whether it sells books at all—but you will find plenty to choose from in the way of horror, fantasy, and science fiction.

A few absorbing hours can easily be spent in **Foyles** (Nos. 113–19) getting utterly lost and confused by the apparent lack of any system for displaying the books (some are shelved by subject, some by publisher). Even though this claims to be the world's largest bookstore, stocking over 6 million titles, you may not be able to find the book you came in for. If you have time, pay a visit to the exhibition gallery on the third floor, which frequently has good pictures for sale, including the work of well-known book illustrators.

At **Waterstones,** on the opposite corner of Manette Street, you may well have to negotiate piles of books stacked all over the floor, but the staff is very knowledgeable and can locate any title in stock. The store has a good range of travel books on the ground floor, poetry in the basement, and art books upstairs.

Heading south down Charing Cross Road you will find stores with specific themes. **Murder One** (No. 71), as its name suggests, has a huge stock of crime and detective stories. **Zwemmers** (Nos. 7 and 80) sells books on art, architecture, film, advertising, and design. There is scarcely an art book published that they do not stock, although the prices can be as staggering as the sheer weight of some of the beautifully bound and printed volumes. **Books for a Change** (No. 52) specializes in books on ecology, the environment, and green politics.

Secondhand book bargains on sale in Cecil Court

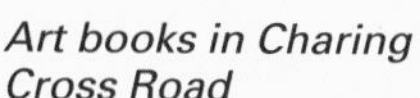
Art books in Charing Cross Road

The battle of the bookstores The once cozy world of bookselling has seen a radical change recently, as big bookstore chains fight for a larger and larger slice of the market. One of the leading players is Dillons bookstore, on Gower Street, which in the 1970s was a sleepy store patronized by students from London University. Being off the beaten track for many visitors, it decided to attract business with an aggressive advertising campaign. With slogans like "Foyled again? Come to Dillons" it tried to win trade from its arch rival, Foyles—and succeeded. It has also attracted much publicity by selling certain books at a discount—a good thing for the consumer, though smaller bookstores, who cannot afford to do the same, say that this will drive them out of business. Most book-lovers would hate to see this happening, for the quirky, friendly atmosphere and specialist knowledge of London's many small booksellers are far preferable to the faceless impersonality of the big chains.

While nearly all the stores mentioned so far specialize in new books, there are lots of little stores in between selling secondhand and antiquarian volumes. A word of warning, though: Pickpockets operate here, and with good reason—they know how easy it is to relieve preoccupied browsers of their wallets or purses.

There is one particularly good enclave of antiquarian bookstores on Cecil Court (the narrow alley next to 24 Charing Cross Road). From here you can continue up to New Row and the entrance to another branch of Waterstones, this one with a very large and well-organized stock, as well as a good children's section. From here you can emerge on Garrick Street and cross the road to Floral Street and the back door of **Stanfords**. In this store, the best in Britain for travel books, maps, and navigational charts, you are quite likely to stumble across well-known explorers and travelers either signing copies of their latest books or buying maps for the next trip. Almost next door, on Long Acre, the clientele at **Dillons** is made up of artists, architects, and designers who come here for books on the visual arts. Dillons has a much bigger store with a vast stock at 82 Gower Street—a long walk from here (the nearest tube station is Goodge Street) but worth seeking out just in case you have not yet found the right book.

The courts of Covent Garden
Although called "courts," the little lanes that run down from Covent Garden to Charing Cross Road are no more than narrow alleyways, with many a twist and bend where you would have risked a mugging in 18th- and 19th-century London. One example is Goodwin's Court, linking Bedfordbury to St. Martin's Lane, with a row of restored 17th-century houses on one side. Attractive as they look now, this and other courts were known as rookeries because of the sheer number of people who lived in their squalid ghettos. Straight across St. Martin's Lane is Cecil Court, now a smart enclave of excellent secondhand bookshops where you can buy rare first editions, maps, prints, and illustrated children's books. Cecil Court runs parallel to St. Martin's Court, the home of Sheekey's Restaurant and Oyster Bar, where wealthy diners come to enjoy pre-theater fish suppers in a setting that has scarcely changed since 1892, when the restaurant opened.

London buses as they used to be

►► London Transport Museum *141B4*

The Piazza, Covent Garden
Underground: Covent Garden
Housed in the old Flower Market (built in 1870), this is a far more enthralling museum than its title suggests. Children can enjoy climbing aboard the buses and trams or pretending to drive Underground trains, while adults contemplate the sheer immensity and complexity of London's public transit system: Over 6 million passengers a day are carried on bus, train, and underground journeys that add up to more 500,000 miles (800,000km). The development of that system is illustrated by replicas of early horse-drawn transportation, such as Mr Shillibeer's omnibus of 1829, which brought a whole new era of mobility to Londoners. Bus users may be surprised to learn that the idea was not invented in Britain: Shillibeer copied the idea from the French town of Nantes, where a Monsieur Omnès had been operating passenger vehicles under his company's Latin slogan (also a pun on his own name) of *Omnes Omnibus* ("all for everyone"). You can also see one of the first motorized buses, the Type B (known as Old Bill), which came into operation as early as 1897; it did not entirely supplant horse-drawn vehicles until the demand for horses on the battlefields of World War I led to their disappearance from London's streets. Another vintage vehicle on display is the railway locomotive built in 1866 to operate on the Metropolitan Line, fitted with a device to enable it to consume its own smoke. The first service, which opened in 1904, was operated by electric trains and opened up a whole new era: Londoners began to move to garden cities and suburban subdivisions on the city's fringes, commuting in to the center for work. To promote these services, London Transport hired some of the best graphic artists of the day to design posters, many of which are on display in the museum and available, as cards or reproductions, from the shop.

►► Theatre Museum 141B4

Russell Street
Underground: Covent Garden
This splendid museum really works hard to involve visitors (especially children) in the magic of the theater, with a program of activities and special exhibitions covering everything from make-up demonstrations to dressing up in theatrical costumes. Permanent displays trace the history of the stage since the 16th century using models, props, and costumes, bringing the subject right up to date with a look at the glamorous world of rock music—Mick Jagger's jumpsuit is a popular exhibit. The collection is arranged chronologically and is so varied that, like the theater itself, the scene constantly shifts to present new surprises. Here you come face to face with Hamlet, the great actors who have starred in the role, their costumes and historic set designs; and there, for a little light relief, is a display on the perennially popular farce *Charley's Aunt*, written by Brandon Thomas in 1892 and still regularly performed all over the country. You can see the dressing table where the great 18th-century actress, Sarah Siddons, used to apply her make-up before entrancing audiences in the role of Lady Macbeth, or admire Noel Coward's crimson monogrammed dressing gown and slippers. Other striking exhibits include the costumes worn by dancers in the innovative ballets choreographed by Diaghilev and the wheelbarrow that was used by the famous acrobat Blondin in his daring tightrope acts. The museum also has a well-stocked shop. You can buy tickets for shows at all the main London theaters from the booking (reservations) office in the entrance hall. Closed Monday.

Eliza Doolittle and Nell Gwyn
Two of the best-known names associated with Covent Garden both began as street traders. The Cockney heroine of Shaw's play *Pygmalion* (and of the musical based on it, *My Fair Lady*, by Alan Jay Lerner and Frederick Loewe) was Eliza Dolittle, a flower trader. The play opens with Eliza selling violets to pedestrians sheltering from the rain under the portico of St. Paul's Church. Eliza was, of course, a fictional creation, whereas Nell Gwyn really did exist, even if the events of her rags-to-riches life sound like a fairy story. She started out selling oranges to the patrons of the Theatre Royal in Drury Lane, then became an actress herself, making her stage debut in the same theater in Dryden's play *The Indian Queen* in 1665. Although, by some accounts, not a greatly gifted actress, she succeeded in charming Charles II, becoming his mistress and bearing several of his children, one of whom was made Duke of St. Albans by the king. Her portrait can be seen in the National Portrait Gallery.

Behind the scenes at the Theatre Museum

■ Some 40 theaters are packed into the area of London known as Theaterland, consisting of the Haymarket, St. Martin's Lane, Shaftesbury Avenue, and Charing Cross Road. This area comes to life after dark, as the audiences arrive to enjoy the illuminated façades, glittering interiors, and intimate atmospheres of its Victorian and Edwardian theaters. ...■

Opera houses
Opera has suddenly become a fashionable entertainment, after languishing as a minority or elitist art for many years. Part of the reason is that catchy arias, sung by the likes of Pavarotti, Carreras, and Domingo, have been used to promote everything from football to the Olympic Games. The great temple to the opera in London is the Royal Opera House, Covent Garden, fronted by E.M. Barry's sumptuous Corinthian façade and John Flaxman's Grecian frieze. Purists pay very large sums of money to come here and see opera performed "as it should be." They look down on those who go to the Coliseum, on St. Martin's Lane, to hear the English National Opera: To make opera more accessible, the ENO sings in English, to the dismay of those who think Mozart only sounds right in German or Italian. Even the Royal Opera is becoming a little less snobbish, however. In 1987, Placido Domingo's performance in *La Bohème* was relayed by huge screen and loudspeakers to crowds of appreciative but impoverished opera-lovers, gathered in the open air plaza alongside the theater—an experiment surely worth repeating more often.

Theaterland's range of entertainment is revealed in the pages of the listings magazine *Time Out*; to reserve seats, you can go to one of the hundreds of ticket agencies that operate in the West End—but you will pay a reservation fee for this service. Among the more reliable agencies offering a credit-card telephone reservation service are First Call (tel. 071 240 7200) and Ticketmaster (tel. 071 379 4444). A cheaper option, if you are fairly flexible about what you want to see, is to use the SWET (Society of West End Theatres) ticket booth on Leicester Square; this sells half-price tickets for that day's performances at any theater with spare seats. You can also reserve direct with the theater: *Time Out* gives the box office number and credit-card reservations are accepted. You stand a better chance of seeing one of the big hit shows during the week—Friday and Saturday are always the busiest nights. Even if a show is sold out, you can often get a ticket by lining up to wait for returns. It is unwise to buy from scalpers (ticket touts). Apart from the high price they charge, there is no guarantee that the ticket is not a forgery.

Historic theaters One of the oldest West End theaters is the **Theatre Royal, Drury Lane**, founded in 1663, when London's appetite for theater was all the more keen after 20 years of Oliver Cromwell's puritanical rule, when play-going had been forbidden. It was here that Charles II first saw Nell Gwyn, who was to become his mistress; and it was here that, during the 1740s, David Garrick revived Shakespeare's plays, scarcely performed

since the bard's death. The theater was rebuilt in 1811–12 after a fire and the auditorium, remodeled in 1921, is now used for big musical productions. The foyer and staircases are worth seeing for the impressive collection of statues and paintings of famous actors and managers.

The **London Palladium**, on Argyll Street, is the work of the prolific theater designer Frank ("Matchless") Matcham. He built 80 theaters during his 40-year career and was renowned for his lavish, outrageous style (this can be seen at the recently restored Hackney Empire theater, Mare Street, in the northeastern suburb of Hackney). The Palladium interior is still a frothy confection of gold, white, and scarlet but now lacks the box-to-box telephones that enabled amorous members of the audience to arrange post-theater assignations. The ever-popular *Peter Pan* had its first Christmas performance here in 1930, and the theater is famous for its pantomimes and for hosting the annual Royal Command Performance. Previous command performances took place at the **Theatre Royal, Haymarket**, and such a huge crowd gathered to see the first, in 1794, that 15 people were crushed to death. The present theater was built by John Nash in 1820 and specializes in "quality" plays; Ibsen's then highly controversial play, *Ghosts*, was first performed here in 1914. The theater has a resident ghost—that of Queen Victoria's favorite actor-manager, Mr Buckstone.

Across the street is **Her Majesty's Theatre**, rebuilt in 1897 in French Renaissance style, but originally built in 1704 by Sir John Vanbrugh, who was both a playwright and a successful architect. Many renowned operas received their first English performances here, including Wagner's *Ring*. It now hosts less highbrow entertainment—some recent successes include *West Side Story*, *Fiddler on the Roof*, and *Amadeus*.

Andrew Lloyd Webber

Andrew Lloyd Webber, the composer of several hit musicals, has been called one of Britain's most important economic assets. His productions attract so many visitors to Britain, who in turn spend money on hotels and restaurants, that he is single-handedly responsible for a large chunk of Britain's foreign currency earnings. *Cats*, which opened in 1981, is the longest running musical in West End theater history, and other hits, such as *The Phantom of the Opera*, *Aspects of Love*, and *Jesus Christ Superstar* are rarely off the stage. The secret of Lloyd Webber's success is to write tunes that, instead of sounding new, are instantly familiar. The dividing line between what is and is not genuinely original music is very thin: When Lloyd Webber composed the theme tune for the 1992 Barcelona Olympics he hired lawyers and researchers to ensure that it did not infringe any existing copyright—in other words, to check that he had not "subconsciously" copied someone's work.

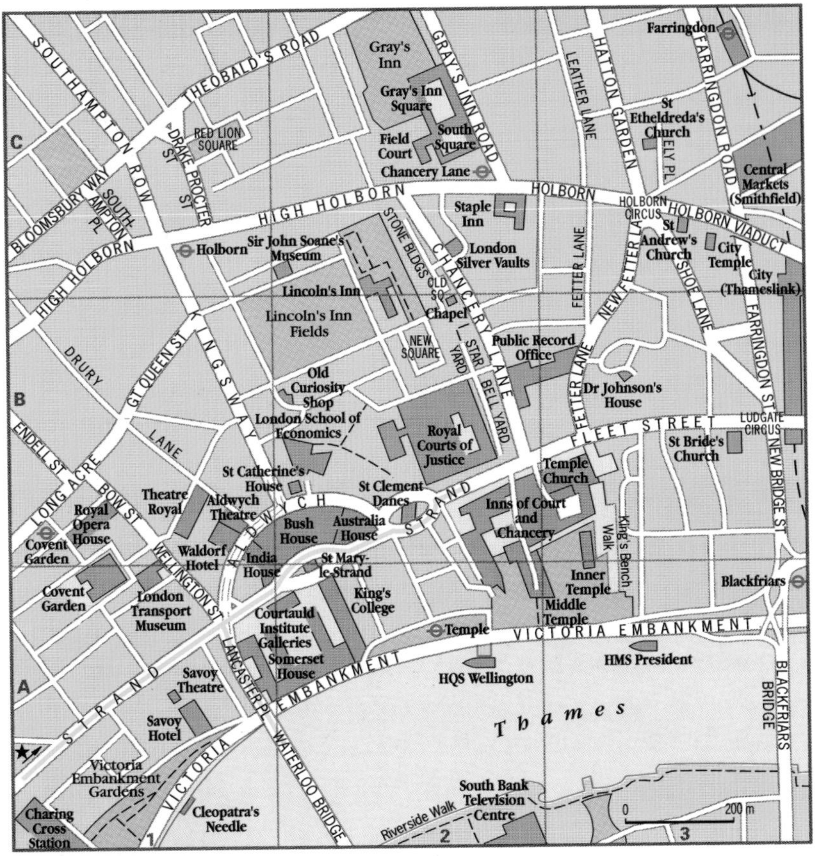

HOLBORN AND THE STRAND

Silver griffins on the City of London's coat of arms

Holborn and the Strand Holborn, to the north, and the Strand, to the south, form the two main east/west routes linking the City to the West End. The character of this district is heavily influenced by the presence of the medieval Inns of Court, with their collegiate-style buildings and noble open spaces providing a haven of tranquillity a short step away from some of London's busiest thoroughfares. The western end of the Strand, which was transformed by the arrival of the railway, is dominated by Charing Cross station. Dr. Johnson once commented to his friend and biographer, James Boswell, that "the full tide of human existence is at Charing Cross." That remains true today, for the station is one of London's busiest, bringing well over 100,000 commuters into the city every day.

Holborn and the Strand walk This route starts at **Charing Cross station**, which was opened in 1864 and is fronted by the Renaissance-style **Charing Cross Hotel**. Behind it, all is new, however: The station building, with its shopping malls and offices, was rebuilt in postmodernist style in 1990–91.

Turn right outside the station and walk along **the Strand**. With the coming of the railway, many of the Strand's older riverside mansions were demolished to make way for palatial hotels. One of these is the **Savoy**, halfway down the Strand on the right—the epitome of luxury, built in 1889 by Richard D'Oyly Carte, the impresario who produced the operettas of Gilbert and Sullivan. A striking feature is the hotel's stainless steel Art Deco frontage; many of its rooms are decorated in the same style.

Just beyond, on the right, Lancaster Place leads to **Waterloo Bridge**. The original bridge, built to commemorate Napoleon's defeat at Waterloo in 1815, was replaced in 1945 with a utilitarian concrete structure. Even so, the views to St. Paul's Cathedral and the Houses of Parliament are among the best in London.

Return down Lancaster Place and continue along the Strand. Opposite the main entrance to Somerset House is an island bounded by the Strand and the great arc of the **Aldwych**. On it are three notable buildings: **India House** (1928–30), **Bush House** (1923–35)—headquarters of the BBC World Service, and **Australia House** (1912–18). These huge buildings dwarf the tiny church of **St. Mary-le-Strand**, stuck in the middle of the road, but an exquisite early 18th-century building, designed by James Gibbs. Its counterpart, a little further along, is **St. Clement Danes**, built by Christopher Wren in 1680, with a steeple added by Gibbs in 1720. It was bombed in 1941 but beautifully restored and is dedicated to the Royal Air Force. Its floor is covered in crests carved in Welsh slate, one for each RAF unit. Within the spired and turreted **Royal Courts of Justice** (1874–82), the last major building on the Strand, judges hear some of the most important civil cases in the land; the public is admitted to the viewing galleries and to the Central Hall (courts closed August and September).

St-Mary-le-Strand

Staple Inn

Staple Inn, on High Holborn (to the right as you emerge from the Underground station), is one of London's oldest surviving timber-framed buildings. Built in 1545 as a hostel for wool merchants, the gabled building has projecting upper storys with oriel windows, while the shop fronts below date from the 19th century. As you walk through the archway, note the sign on the left saying that the porters have orders to prevent "Old Clothes Men" and "Rude Children" from entering. Beyond is a peaceful brick courtyard and a rose garden, a favorite place for office workers to eat their lunchtime sandwiches.

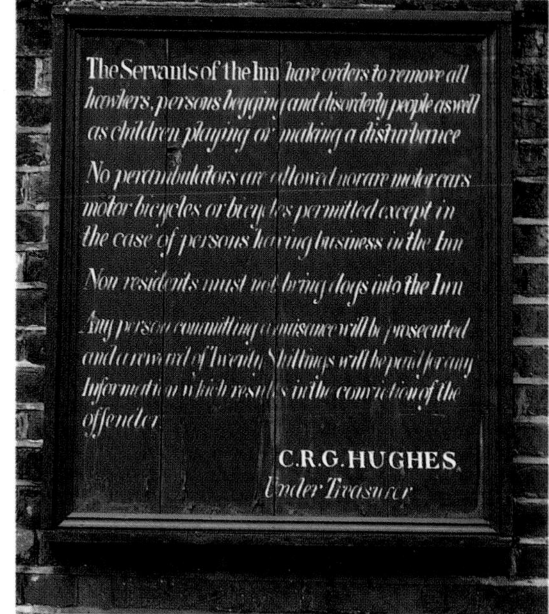

The Servants of the Inn have orders to remove all hawkers, persons begging and disorderly people as well as children playing or making a disturbance
No perambulators are allowed nor are motor cars motor bicycles or bicycles permitted except in the case of persons having business in the Inn
Non residents must not bring dogs into the Inn
Any person committing a nuisance will be prosecuted and a reward of Twenty Shillings will be paid for any information which results in the conviction of the offender
C.R.G. HUGHES
Under Treasurer

► **Gray's Inn** *150C2*

High Holborn

Underground: Chancery Lane

Gray's Inn is one of four Inns of Court established in the 14th century to provide accommodation for lawyers and their students. The layout of the Inns resembles that of an Oxford or Cambridge college: each has a dining hall, chapel, and library, and the buildings that house the lawyers' chambers are grouped around courtyards and gardens. Of all the Inns, Gray's Inn suffered most from wartime bombing, but the most important buildings have been well restored. These include the 17th-century entrance gateway, on the north side of High Holborn (at No. 21 and near to the Cittie of York pub, a favorite lawyers' haunt). This leads into South Square, with its statue of Sir Francis Bacon (by F. W. Pomeroy, 1912), the philosopher and statesman, who was a member of Gray's Inn from 1576 until his death in 1626. The Hall, on the north side of the square, is where Shakespeare's *The Comedy of Errors* was first performed in 1594. Passing through Gray's Inn Square and Field Court, you will reach the extensive gardens. These were laid out by Sir Francis Bacon in 1606, and the catalpa trees are said to have been planted from cuttings brought back from America by Sir Walter Ralegh. The raised terrace was a favorite place to walk during the 17th century and, as Samuel Pepys recorded in his diary, a good place in which to "espy fine ladies."

▶▶ Lincoln's Inn 150B2

Chancery Lane

Underground: Chancery Lane

To explore Lincoln's Inn, which has the finest gardens of any of the 14th-century Inns of Court, it is best to start at the brick gatehouse, on Chancery Lane. This dates from 1518 and bears the coat of arms of Henry VIII above the original doorways of stout oak.

The narrow pedestrian entrance leads to Old Buildings. To the right is the **chapel** and its stone vaulted undercroft, paved with 18th-century tombstones. Steps lead up from here to the chapel itself, completed in 1623; John Donne, the poet, preached "a right rare and learned sermon" at its consecration. The east window contains 228 coats of arms of former Treasurers of Lincoln's Inn. To the right is Old Square, leading to **Stone Buildings**, built of crisp, white Portland stone in Palladian style. A low gate to the left leads to **Lincoln's Inn Fields**, a large green area of manicured lawns and statuesque trees. Straight ahead are the **hall** and **library**: They look perfectly medieval but were built by Philip Hardwick as recently as 1845. To the left is New Square, where fig trees and wisteria climb over the late-17th-century buildings. If you walk down the left-hand side of New Square you will reach Lincoln's Inn Archway, sandwiched between the windows of Wildy & Sons, booksellers specializing in legal texts. The windows exhibit fascinating Victorian cartoons, engravings, and cigarette-card views of the Inns of Court.

The archway leads into Carey Street, once the site of the bankruptcy courts—hence the expression "heading for Queer Street" (Queer being a corruption of Carey) to describe someone who is in deep financial trouble. To the right is a lawyer's pub, the Seven Stars. From here you can reach Temple (see pages 158–9) by turning left into Carey Street and taking the first right into Bell Yard, which leads to Fleet Street, with the Temple entrance on the south side of the road.

Around Holborn Circus
Holborn Circus marks the busy meeting point of several roads leading into the City of London. To the north, Hatton Garden and its side streets are the traditional haunt of jewelers and diamond merchants, many of the shops here having been founded by Jewish refugees from persecution elsewhere in Europe. Leather Lane, running parallel to the west, has an entertaining street market on weekdays where stallholders call out their wares and perform all sorts of antics to attract trade. To the east, in Ely Place, is St. Etheldreda's Church, built around 1290 and well worth a visit for its tracery and stained glass.

Chancery Lane
If you are interested in antiques you should pay a call to the London Silver Vaults, 53–65 Chancery Lane. Originally this was set up in 1885 as a place where valuables could be stored in stout underground vaults, secure from the threat of fire or theft. Today the subterranean premises contain London's biggest concentration of antiques dealers specializing in silverplate and jewelry. Not far away is a curious sight that only male visitors get to see In Star Yard, up against the high walls of Lincoln's Inn, is an ornate cast-iron urinal—a pick-up point for gay men—which looks as if it has been transported here from Paris. There are several good secondhand bookshops nearby in the alleys linking Star Yard to Chancery Lane.

► Public Record Office *150B2*

Chancery Lane
Underground: Chancery Lane
The Public Record Office was set up in 1838 as the national repository for all documents relating to government and the law—such things as State Papers, Cabinet Meeting minutes, official government correspondence, census returns, and legal records. To house them, Sir James Pennethorne designed this splendid Perpendicular Gothic building, best viewed from Carey Street or Fetter Lane. The exterior has recently been cleaned to reveal all its crisp detailing. Magnificent as it is, the building is now far too small to hold all the records that have accumulated since the Norman Conquest of 1066 (they fill more than 81 miles of shelving), so most are stored in new archive buildings at Kew. In theory they are all accessible to the public, though the most recent government records are kept under lock and key until 30 years have elapsed (for documents that are considered especially sensitive, this rule is extended to 50 years or more).

The small museum of the Record Office displays a fascinating range of documents. Its star exhibit is the Domesday Book, two fat volumes detailing every property in England, compiled on the orders of William the Conqueror in 1085. In the cases around the walls you can read Shakespeare's will, in which he bequeathed to his wife, Anne Hathaway, the second-best bed, suggesting that not all had been well with their marriage. There are minutes of various trials, such as those of Guy Fawkes, Sir Walter Ralegh, and the Tolpuddle Martyrs, and early maps of America and Africa. Another case displays patent applications for cat's-eyes and Arkwright's Spinning Jenny. Finally, there is a display explaining how to set about tracing your ancestors and compiling a family tree. Closed Saturday and Sunday.

►► Sir John Soane's Museum *150C2*

13 Lincoln's Inn Fields
Underground: Chancery Lane
Sir John Soane (1753–1837) was one of those brilliant architects which Britain produces from time to time, whose buildings are so quirky and original that they defy classification. Examples of his work in London include the Bank of England (see pages 162–3), the Dulwich College Picture Gallery (see page 214), and this remarkable house. The house is actually two—he bought No. 13 in 1812 and its neighbor No. 14 in 1824 and remodeled the interiors to serve as his home and as a museum for his paintings, sculpture, architectural models, and drawings. The remodeling was brave and experimental: Split-level flooring creates a strange and disorienting experience and anticipates,by 100 years or more, one of the favorite devices of modernist architects. The rooms are crammed with objects and made more bewildering still by the use of mirrors. It's fun just to explore the labyrinthine house and make chance discoveries, but you can also join a lecture tour given every Saturday at 2:30 (tel. 071 405 2107 for details). Not to be missed is the Picture Room, where two of Hogarth's series of paintings are displayed. *A Rake's Progress* (1732–3) traces the career of Tom Rakewell in eight canvases, from his life as a gay young man about town to his imprisonment for debt

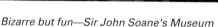

Bizarre but fun—Sir John Soane's Museum

The Old Curiosity Shop
On the opposite side of Lincoln's Inn Fields to Sir John Soane's Museum is another rambling old building, the Old Curiosity Shop (13–14 Portsmouth Street). Whether it really is the building that Dickens immortalized in his novel of the same name doesn't really matter—it certainly looks the part. The timber-framed building, with its overhanging upper floor, dates from 1567, and until its recent closure could fairly claim to be London's oldest surviving shop. Its neighbor is another colorful shop selling all sorts of junk, from old books and comics and antique teddy bears to colonial pith helmets and dress uniforms.

and final home in the Bedlam insane asylum (see page 200). *The Election* (*c.*1754) presents an equally cynical view of bribery and corruption in British politics illustrated in a series of four pictures.

The fascinating basement is a little like a horror-movie set, with views through the windows to the Monk's Cloister, built in the garden from architectural fragments that Soane rescued when the Houses of Parliament were being rebuilt. Another star exhibit is the Sepulchral Chamber containing the Sarcophagus of Seti I (who died around 1300B.C.). This was discovered at Thebes in 1817 and offered to the British Museum. When they declined it, Soane bought it and held a three-day-long party to celebrate his acquisition. Morbid as all this sounds, you cannot help feeling that Soane had a great sense of humor and that this collection is meant to bring a smile to your face. Closed Sunday and Monday.

Manet's Bar at the Folies-Bergère *(1882)*

Somerset House
Somerset House still houses an odd mix of government departments. One of them is the Inland Revenue, responsible for collecting income tax, as well as inheritance tax, home purchase tax, and land duty fees—an organization that everyone in the country loves to hate. Here too is the Principal Probate Registry, which holds copies of every will registered since 1858. The public is entitled to see any they choose—but you have to pay a fee. Immediately to the east of Somerset House is King's College, founded in 1828 by the Duke of Wellington, then Prime Minister, and the Archbishop of Canterbury. It was set up as a reaction to the founding of University College in 1826, called "the godless institution" because divinity was not on the syllabus; in contrast, King's put religion at the core of its teaching.

▶▶▶ Somerset House (Courtauld Institute Galleries) *150A2*

The Strand
Underground: Temple or Aldwych
Some of the world's most famous Impressionist paintings can be seen in the treasure-filled Courtauld Institute Galleries. The core of this collection was put together by the textile magnate Samuel Courtauld (1876–1947). He gave the pictures to the Institute that bears his name in 1931, aiming to provide students of art history with outstanding works that they could study in close detail. His gift was expanded when the art critic Roger Fry and other major patrons donated their private collections as well. In 1990 the whole collection was moved to the rooms of the Strand Block at Somerset House,

where they are hung to advantage beneath the ornate plaster ceilings.

You enter Somerset House through a triple-arched gateway facing onto the Strand. Façade sculptures symbolizing oceans and rivers, the Cardinal Virtues, and the Genius of Britain reinforce the building's monumental stature. Within is a courtyard and more façade sculptures of the Arms of Britain, the tritons and the Continents, and George III with the River Thames at his feet. The key to all this grandiloquence is the fact that Somerset House was built from 1776 to house important offices of state—among them the Navy Office, the Exchequer, and the Audit Office, the forerunners of today's government ministries. The Strand Block, home of the Courtauld Galleries, originally housed the Royal Academy, the Royal Society, and the Society of Antiquaries, and their classically inspired fittings have remained, including the elegant staircase and the ceiling decorations (it is intended that these will be restored to their original coloring when funds permit). The ceiling of the first gallery has the initials RA (for Royal Academy) worked into it, along with pairs of paintbrushes in the corner. Among the 15th- and 16th-century paintings here are Renaissance masterpieces such as Botticelli's *Holy Trinity with Saint John and Mary Magdalen* (1490–94). Parmigianino's *Virgin and Child* (1524–27) is an example of the High Renaissance or Mannerist style, characterized by brilliant coloring and contorted figures.

Gallery 2, the former Royal Academy Council Room, has the finest ceiling and several masterpieces. Rubens' *Descent from the Cross* (1611) is a *modello,* or trial piece, for his most famous work, the great altarpiece in Antwerp Cathedral known as the *Antwerp Descent*.

Gallery 3 has the initials of the Society of

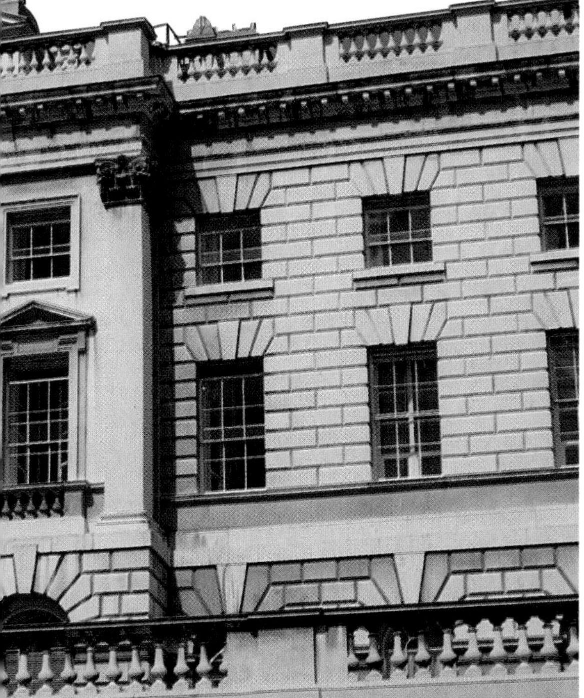

The Roman bath of Strand Lane

Strand Lane runs down the east side of King's College and halfway down, at No. 5, you can peer through a window at a curious plunge bath, built of red brick, with a rounded end and measuring about 13 ft. by 6 ½ft.. The bath is fed by a spring that delivers 2,000 gallons of icy water every day, then drains into the Thames. David Copperfield used to come here for a dip in what Dickens referred to as "the old Roman bath." The name has stuck, though nobody is quite sure whether it really is Roman; its first recorded mention was in 1784, and the best that archaeologists can say at this stage is that though it might be Roman in origin, much of the brickwork dates from around 1588.

Antiquaries worked into the ceiling and features more paintings by Rubens, notably the mysteriously poetic *Moonlit Landscape* (1635–40).

Gallery 4 is devoted to 18th-century Italian art—most of it missable—but then comes Gallery 5, the Royal Society Meeting Room, where plaster portraits of the Society's founder, Charles II, and of George III look down on the gorgeously colored works of Manet, Degas, Renoir, and Pissarro. Manet's *Bar at the Folies-Bergère* (1882) is the most eye-catching, and his *Déjeuner sur l'Herbe* (1863) is a smaller version of the painting in the Musée d'Orsay in Paris. Here too is Van Gogh's *Self-portrait with Bandaged Ear*, a reminder of the quarrel that the artist had with Gauguin (Van Gogh threatened his friend with a knife, then cut off part of his own ear in remorse).

The next gallery covers Post Impressionism, and the rooms on the floors above are used to display more Post Impressionist works, as well as changing exhibitions, as well as works by 20th-century British artists, such as Roger Fry, Duncan Grant, Graham Sutherland, and Ben Nicolson. The largest of these rooms, Gallery 8, the Great Room, was used for Royal Academy summer exhibitions until 1836 (for today's exhibitions see page 82). The "RA Line" runs around the room, a molding set 6½ ft. or so above the floor. Works favored by the RA Hanging Committee, to give them more prominence, were hung below the line; less favored works were "skied" above it. The term refers to the fact that the ceiling was originally painted to resemble the sky.

Middle Temple Hall
When exploring the Temple it is well worth checking whether Middle Temple Hall can be visited. This noble building is said to have been opened by Queen Elizabeth I in 1576 and has one of the finest hammerbeam roofs in England. Just as spectacular is the original Elizabethan oak screen at the east end, carved with big bold figures and statues in niches. The serving table, according to legend, is made from the timbers of Sir Francis Drake's ship, the *Golden Hind*. In this room William Shakespeare took part in a performance of his own *Twelfth Night* on February 2, 1601.

▶▶ Temple *150B3*

Fleet Street
Underground: Temple or Aldwych

The Temple takes its name from the Knights Templar, the crusading order whose 12th-century round church survives at the heart of this network of alleys and courtyards.

The Temple actually consists of two Inns of Court (the Inner Temple and the Middle Temple), but they are so physically intertwined that they seem like one large collegiate campus, where lawyers in black gowns stroll between their chambers and the Royal Court of Justice, on the opposite side of Fleet Street. Between the Temple and the Royal Court, in the middle of Fleet Street itself, is the **Temple Bar Memorial**, marking the boundary between Westminster and the City. Erected in 1880, it is topped by a bronze griffin (the symbol of the city) and is far less imposing than Sir Christopher Wren's gateway, which originally stood here. The gateway was built in 1672 but became an impediment to traffic and was taken down in 1878.

Temple Bar Memorial

Just west of the Memorial is a timber-framed gatehouse that leads from busy Fleet Street into the calm of Inner Temple Lane. This leads down to the **Temple Church**, past the elaborately carved Romanesque west door, which is no longer used; the entrance is now from the south. The Temple Church's circular nave, to the left, is known as "the Round". It was completed in 1185 and, in common with all the churches built by the Knights Templar,

Middle Temple Lane

the shape is modeled on the Church of the Holy Sepulchre in Jerusalem. A remarkable series of effigies is set into the floor of the Round: These three-dimensional figures of sleeping knights, dressed in crusading armor, all date from the late 12th and early 13th centuries. The Round was built at the point of transition between Romanesque and Gothic architecture. Looking up, you will see that the triforium has Romanesque intersecting arches, but the arches themselves are pointed, in the Gothic style, rather than rounded. The chancel, known as "the Oblong," has the same slender Purbeck marble shafts as the Round, but the style is full-fledged Early English. Added in 1240, the Oblong has been described as "one of the most perfectly and classically proportioned buildings of the 13th century in England."

Leaving the church and turning left past the pretty **Master's House**, you enter **King's Bench Walk**, an open space that has unfortunately been spoiled by its use as a parking lot. To the right, in Crown Office Row, is another leafy garden, but this one is strictly for the use of members of the Temple. An archway links Crown Office Row to the cobblestone alley of Middle Temple Lane.

Turn right, then left, to arrive in **Fountain Court**, where a huge plane tree and ancient mulberry dwarf the tiny circular fountain itself. Steps lead up on the right to **New Court**, flanked by ornate gas lamps that are topped by the lamb and flag symbol of the Middle Temple. Turn right beyond the steps to pass through an arch into Essex Court, then left into Middle Temple Lane. This brings you back into Fleet Street, passing a row of 17th-century timber-framed (but plastered) buildings on the right, whose jettied-out upper story forms a covered arcade at sidewalk level.

Lawyers' haunts
The Wig and Pen (Dining) Club, No. 229 Strand, is a favorite haunt for off-duty barristers. With its political and legal cartoons in the window, it is set in a tiny timber-framed building of 1625, the only one on the Strand to have survived the Great Fire of London. Nearby, at Nos. 222–5, the Law Courts" Branch of Lloyd's Bank has a surprisingly ornate interior: Egyptian-style tiles cover the entrance lobby, and the banking hall is decorated with Doulton-tile pictures of flowers, cherubs, and historic figures under stucco-work ceilings. All this dates from around 1883 when the building, originally a restaurant, first opened.

Effigy of a crusading knight in the Temple Church

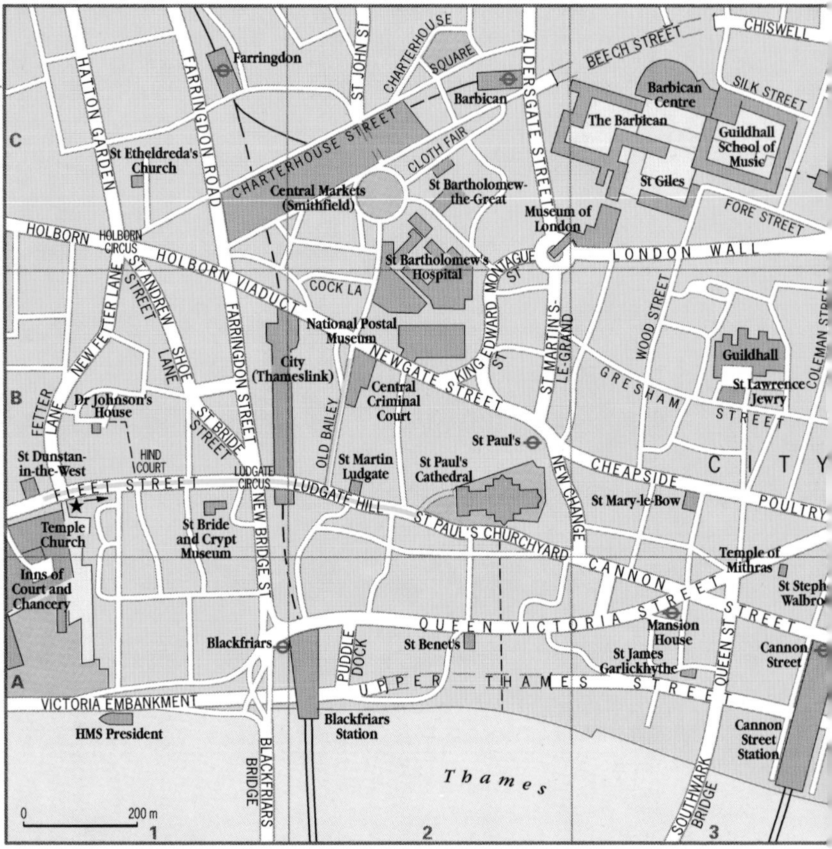

The City's new face

Dr. Johnson's House
Hind Court, off Fleet Street, leads to Gough Square, where Dr. Samuel Johnson lived in the 1750s, compiling his English dictionary in the attic. Saved from demolition in 1911 and lovingly restored, the house is open to visitors.

The City Londoners often refer to the City as "the Square Mile," a name that emphasizes how small it is in area, in contrast with its enormous role in the nation's affairs. It was here that London began, founded by the Romans as the administrative capital of Britannia. London has since grown to many times its original size, but the City, at its heart, has retained a distinctive identity, with its own police force and its own local authority, the Corporation of London, presided over by the Lord Mayor.

The City walk Starting at the Strand end, walk east along **Fleet Street**, where some of England's earliest printed books were produced in the 1490s. Five centuries later, Fleet Street was still synonymous with the publishing industry—but all that ceased in the 1980s when the big newspaper companies moved from their cramped premises to new high-tech offices all over London. There are, however, many reminders of the street's history. Near the junction of Fetter Lane and Fleet Street, **St. Dunstan-in-the-West** has both a bust of Lord Northcliffe, founder of the *Daily Mail* newspaper, and a 1586 statue of Queen Elizabeth I, as well as a clock dating from 1671. A little further on to the right, at No. 47, is **El Vino's**, a traditional wine bar that used to be packed with boozy journalists swapping gossip. On the left is another ex-haunt of

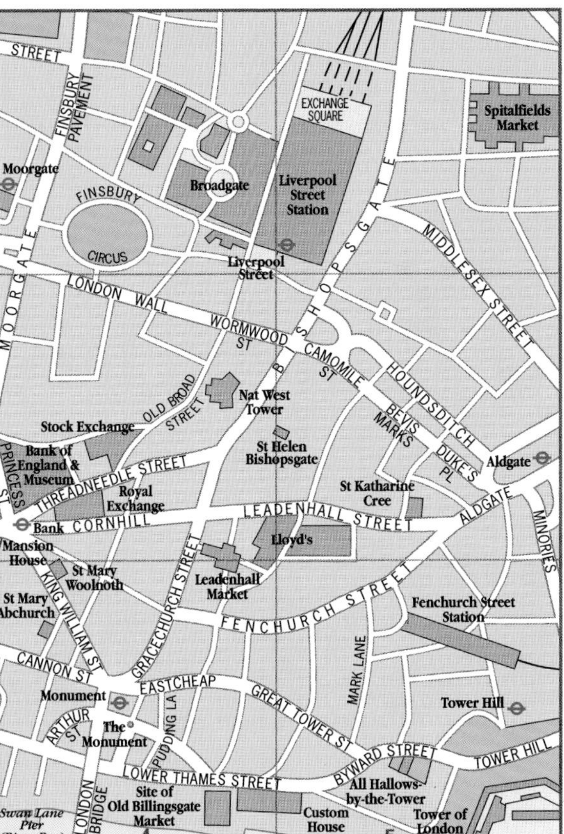

journalists, **Ye Olde Cheshire Cheese** pub, scarcely changed since it was rebuilt just after the Great Fire of London in 1666. Further down on the left are the striking façades of the *Daily Telegraph* building (1928) and the *Daily Express* (1931), the latter a daring modernist building of black glass and chrome. Just before the end of Fleet Street, on the right, a narrow lane leads to **St. Bride**, the journalists' church, with its "wedding cake" spire. Rebuilt by Christopher Wren after the Great Fire of 1666, this is one of the most fascinating churches in London, not least for its unusual crypt museum. Here, foundations revealed by excavation in 1952 show how the church is built over the remains of its three predecessors—15th-century, Norman, and Saxon—all overlying a Roman building. Various displays in the crypt cover the history of printing in Fleet Street.

Cross busy Ludgate Circus and climb Ludgate Hill towards St. Paul's. The second left-hand turn is the **Old Bailey**, synonymous with the **Central Criminal Court**, which stands here. Built in 1900–07 with a dome inspired by the nearby cathedral, it is topped by the figure of Justice, holding a pair of scales. The public is admitted to the viewing galleries of the tiny courtrooms (18 in all), and the guards at the doors will eagerly tell you which trials are likely to prove the most salacious or entertaining.

■ Bank is to the City what Trafalgar Square is to the West End: a chaotic junction of several roads, surrounded by magnificent public buildings. At the weekend the streets are deserted, but during the week you can stand on any corner at Bank and feel the pulse of this frenetic world of high finance and commerce as dealers, messengers, and brokers rush between their offices and the main financial markets. .....■

Weekend ghost town
The best time to explore the architectural riches of the City is on the weekend, when the streets of London's financial center are as still and quiet as those of a ghost town. The resident population of the City can be numbered in the hundreds. Most City residents live in the Barbican complex (see page 178) and are wealthy enough to afford second homes in the country—their number includes business tycoons and company chairmen, as well as TV and radio announcers who have to be up at the crack of dawn to prepare early morning news programs. When they disappear on the weekend, just about the only people left living in the City are the staff of St. Bartholomew's hospital, who have lodgings in the Charterhouse Square area. This is the time to see some of the City's poignant contrasts, such as the horse-drawn brewers' carts delivering barrels of beer to City pubs against a backdrop of modernistic skyscrapers: Whitbread's brewery is on Chiswell Street, and the company still keeps a team of 16 draft horses (stabled in Garrett Street) for their deliveries to several pubs in the vicinity.

A good spot for people-watching and admiring the architecture is the triangular space in front of the Royal Exchange, in the angle formed by Threadneedle Street and Cornhill, where there is a statue of the Duke of Wellington (1844). The **Royal Exchange** itself (built 1843–44) is a true temple to commerce, approached by a broad flight of steps and a Corinthian portico. The figures carved in the pediment depict Commerce, attended by merchants of all nations, holding the charter granted by Elizabeth I in 1570. This was when the exchange was first set up, in rivalry with that of Antwerp. Until recently this was where traders in the largest futures market outside the USA would operate, dressed in colored waistcoats and using an extraordinary system of hand signals and coded shouts. Dealing has now moved to nearby Cannon Bridge Station; Cousin's Lane (no public access) and the Royal Exchange is no longer open to the public.

With your back to the Royal Exchange, the building on the left is the **Mansion House**, the official residence of the Lord Mayor of London. This is another classical monument (built 1739–52), whose pediment carvings show London trampling on the figure of Envy (in other words, commercial competitors) and leading in the figure of Plenty. By contrast, the Flemish Gothic **Mappin & Webb** building (1870), between Poultry and Queen Victoria Street, seems out of place, but Londoners are fond of its quirkiness. The site's owner, Peter Palumbo, wants to replace the former jewelers' shop with something more modern, but a new design by James Stirling was dismissed by that influential architectural critic, the Prince of Wales, who said it resembled "a 1930s wireless set." The plans have now gone back to the drawing board.

On the right-hand (north) side of Bank is the vast bulk of the **Bank of England**, after which this whole area is named. The building resembles nothing so much as a fortress: At street level there are no doors or windows in the massive stone walls (except for the main entrance). Sir John Soane designed it to reinforce the idea of rock-solid security, for the Bank's role has always been central to the British economy. The Bank is responsible for issuing paper money, raising funds for the government, managing the nation's foreign exchange reserves, setting interest rates, and regulating the banking system of the country as a whole. The story of its work is told in an excellent museum (entrance in Bartholomew Lane, closed weekends October to Easter) with high-tech

displays that keep track, minute by minute, of all the international money markets.

Further down Threadneedle Street, Old Broad Street leads left to the **Stock Exchange**. Little did anyone suspect, when this building was opened in 1972, that 20 years later it would have become virtually obsolete. The dealing floor, where jobbers once traded shares in an atmosphere of tense excitement, is empty, since buying and selling is now done by telephone and computer in the offices of brokerage firms.

For a complete contrast, cross Threadneedle Street to explore the alley behind the Royal Exchange leading to **Cornhill**, **Birchin Lane,** and **George Yard**. These little lanes preserve the City's medieval street pattern and are lined with pubs and wine bars. They are a reminder of the days when traders used to do deals in the crowded and congenial coffee houses, before the markets were institutionalized. Something of the original atmosphere can still be savored in the oak-paneled upstairs bar of the **Jamaica Wine House**, St. Michael's Alley, Cornhill; this stands on the site of the coffeehouse where traders specializing in West Indian goods, such as rum and sugar, used to meet.

The Lord Mayor

The City of London has its own local government, headed by the Lord Mayor since 1192, when Henry Fitzailwyn was installed. Today the mayor is elected to serve for just one year. The election takes place on Michaelmas Day, September 29th, and the mayor is installed in the Guildhall on the Friday preceding the second Saturday in November. The next day the mayor drives through the streets leading the Lord Mayor's Show, a colorful pageant with lavish floats. At the Lord Mayor's Banquet, on the following Monday, the Prime Minister makes an important speech on government policy. Much of the rest of the year is spent attending ceremonial events to raise funds for charity.

The Bank of England

Skyscrapers

The City does not have many skyscrapers. This is a pity; London needs some tall buildings to provide a focus above the city's dull skyline. One of the few examples is the Nat West Tower (Old Broad Street). At 604 ft., it was Britain's tallest building when it was completed in 1981. Now it is second to the central tower of the 1990 Canary Wharf development (858 ft.). These buildings are too far apart to make a brave statement, but the English are deeply suspicious of tall buildings. Many rejoiced when the developers of Canary Wharf went bankrupt, as if this were just punishment for building on such a scale.

Guildhall

160B3

Underground: Bank

The Guildhall was built in 1411 and, despite severe damage during the 1666 Great Fire of London and during the Blitz of 1940, its stout medieval walls and impressive undercroft have survived intact. The roof was carefully reconstructed with stone arches by Sir Giles Gilbert Scott in the 1950s. The stained-glass windows incorporate the names of more than 600 past Lord Mayors, and the walls and roof are decorated with the coats of arms and embroidered banners of the City Livery Companies. These are the modern equivalent of the medieval trade guilds, who built the Guildhall for their meetings and ceremonies. The guilds were a powerful force in medieval London, responsible for fixing prices and wages and guaranteeing themselves a monopoly over trade by preventing nonmembers from setting up shops. Today the Livery Companies support the industries they represent (from brewers to weavers) by funding research and educational activities. From their ranks, the Sheriffs and Lord Mayors are chosen to run the City's affairs, and the Guildhall is where they are installed, amid great ceremony. Looking down from the Guildhall's west gallery are two strange figures: Gog and Magog. These giants, carved in limewood, were made in 1953 by David Evans to replace earlier statues that were destroyed in the Blitz. Figures of Gog and Magog, mythical founders of ancient Albion (Britain), used to be carried in city pageants and processions. Closed Sunday October to April.

Lloyd's of London

Broadgate's hanging gardens

▶ Leadenhall Market 161A4

Gracechurch Street
Underground: Bank or Monument
Amid all the markets dealing in stocks, shares, gold, insurance, and currencies, Leadenhall Market is a charming oddity that has nothing to do with finance but sells top quality food. Traders here sell meat, fish, and poultry from market stalls ranged either side of a graceful Victorian arcade built in 1881, with highly ornamented façades and roof in iron and glass. Stallholders mount impressive displays, which could have come straight out of a picture of Victorian or Edwardian London. Closed weekends.

▶ Lloyd's of London 161B5

Lime Street
Underground: Monument
The Lloyd's building, completed in 1986, is one of London's most exciting and controversial modern buildings. Designed by Richard Rogers (who also designed the Pompidou Centre in Paris), it is a daring building all of glass entwined in steel ventilation shafts, cranes, gantries, service pods, and staircases. The building is especially thrilling to see at night, when it glows a strange green and purple from concealed colored spotlights, creating a space-age effect. Ironically, this futuristic building houses one of London's most traditional institutions. Lloyd's evolved in the 1680s as a marine insurance market based at Edward Lloyd's Coffee House in Tower Street.

▶ Monument 161A4

Monument Street
Underground: Monument
Monument commemorates the 1666 Great Fire of London and was designed by Christopher Wren. The column, completed in 1677, is 203 ft. high; as the inscription at the base of the column explains, the fire broke out in Pudding Lane, 202 feet away. The gilded bronze urn at the summit symbolizes the flames of the fire. Below the bronze urn is a viewing platform, reached by a spiral staircase of 311 steps. The platform is enclosed by an iron cage because of the number of people who committed suicide in the 18th century by jumping from it. On a clear day, views stretch to the chalk downlands of Kent and Sussex. Closed Sunday October to end of March.

The Broadgate Centre
The Broadgate Centre, which wraps around Liverpool Street station at the top of Old Broad Street, is more than just a good example of modern office development. It is (or was) a political *cause célèbre*. Begun in July 1985, the first phase of the massive 4-hectare development was officially opened just two years later. The speed of construction was highly unusual for Britain, whose construction industry was dogged by strikes and industrial relations disputes that constantly interrupted work. To political supporters of the then Prime Minister, Margaret Thatcher, the building symbolized the new dynamism of the Thatcher era. To detractors, it was equally symbolic—a sham of façadism, all marble cladding hung on a rusty steel frame. The complex is, in fact, far better than this suggests and well worth exploring for its elevated walkways, outdoor sculptures, gardens, and the theatrical space used as an ice rink in winter and for open-air entertainment in summer.

London Wall
The road called London Wall is so named because of the surviving slab of the city's 2nd- to 4th-century Roman wall that runs along its northern edge, visible below pavement level. There is a particularly well preserved stretch alongside the Museum of London and another in St. Alphege Garden. The site of the wall can still be traced just by looking at a map of the city—to the east of London Wall, Houndsditch, the Minories, and Tower Bridge Approach perfectly preserve the course of its curving route down to the river. The stretch along London Wall was uncovered after World War II bombing flattened the area, leading to its wholesale redevelopment in the late 1950s. Six different architects were involved in the project, each given responsibility for one of the huge office buildings that line the route. Instead of exciting variety, what London Wall got was six of the dreariest blocks imaginable, featureless lumps of concrete and glass—so bad, in fact, that some of them were pulled down again in the late 1980s to be replaced by Terry Farrell's post-modern buildings that now span London Wall like a great monumental arch.

▶▶▶ Museum of London 160C3

150 London Wall
Underground: St Paul's

This entertaining museum traces the history of London through a series of imaginative displays. The first gallery, devoted to the archaeology of London, sets the tone with its reconstructions. One display shows a cross section of a London street. Evidence for the Great Fire of 1666 is plain to see: a thick layer of charred wood and black ash that still lies below the ground in many parts of London, providing archaeologists with an important benchmark for dating even earlier features. Another reconstruction uses fragments of masonry to show what the Roman city's monumental arch would have looked like. These fragments reveal the happy accidents that can occur when ancient remains are investigated. They were found during excavations in 1974–75, which uncovered a substantial length of the Roman wall. On close examination, some of the stones used in building the ramparts were discovered to have carving on their underside, depicting Mars and Mercury. By piecing them together it became apparent that they had come from a late 2nd- or 3rd-century arch, demolished in the 4th century, in the face of crisis, and used to heighten the walls. A section of that 4th-century wall is cleverly revealed as you follow the museum route: Just beyond the reconstructed arch is a great glass window that overlooks the remains of the wall in the garden outside. Life in Roman London is brought home in a series of displays—do not miss the little leather bikini trunks found at the bottom of a 1st-century London well.

Typical 1970s architecture—the Museum of London

Vintage fire engine, as used in London in 1862

The displays covering the medieval and later periods do not quite set the imagination on fire in the same way, but there are one or two striking exhibits: One of the earliest known examples of a swinging cradle, the features of Oliver Cromwell preserved in his death mask, relics of the Great Plague, and a good audiovisual on the Great Fire.

For many visitors, however, the best of the museum's displays are in the basement and cover more recent London history—shop interiors, kitchen furnishings, and toys. Children will enjoy exploring the dank depths of a 1940s air-raid shelter or the reconstructions of dismal Georgian prison cells, complete with the graffiti scratched by inmates. Less chilling are the 18th- and 19th-century costumes, dolls' houses, and Valentine's Day cards.

The growth of the London suburbs is illustrated by 1930s posters and advertisements extolling the delights of newly built housing subdivisions in the rural-sounding retreats of Golders Green and Hampstead Garden City.

Finally (near the exit, where it can be taken out for ceremonial occasions) there is the Lord Mayor's state coach, made in 1757 and still used for the Lord Mayor's Show every November (see page 163). The painted sides of the coach show allegorical scenes set against the background of old London.

Before leaving the museum it is worth visiting the well-stocked bookshop, which also sells models and toys, and checking on the program of special events and lectures. The museum also has a regular film season, screening films that were made on location in London, from classic Ealing comedies to more recent thrillers, such as *Mona Lisa* and *Buster* (on the life and haunts of the Great Train Robber). Closed Monday.

The Temple of Mithras
One of the Museum of London's most popular exhibits is a group of sculptures depicting Mithras, the god of heavenly light, whose worshippers subscribed to the highest standards of chastity, honesty, and courage. Mithraism was the main rival religion to Christianity in the 3rd and 4th centuries A.D. and the Temple of Mithras was mistaken for an early Christian church when it was discovered in 1954. The remains (still open to public view in Temple Court, Queen Victoria Street) consist of the foundations of a central nave with side aisles. The true nature of the building was realized when diggers came across the sculptures now displayed in the museum, deliberately hidden to save them from desecration at the hands of members of the rival cult, the Christians.

Monuments
Wren did not want his masterpiece cluttered with memorials, but its symbolic importance made this inevitable. One of the most imposing memorials is to Wellington, on the north side of the nave—a huge "four poster" topped by an equestrian statue. On the opposite side hangs *The Light of the World*, a much-loved painting by Holman Hunt. The tomb of the poet John Donne, on the south side of the choir, shows Donne wrapped in his shroud and was the only monument to survive the fire that destroyed the medieval cathedral.

▶▶▶ St. Paul's Cathedral 160B2

Ludgate Hill
Underground: St. Paul's
St. Paul's Cathedral is one of London's most awe-inspiring sights. Its dome is the third largest in the world and its graceful bulk is an important feature of the City skyline. The building also manages to communicate a sense of serenity, most notably in the famous (and fabricated) image of 1941 of the dome untouched but wreathed in the smoke and flames of the Blitz. This montage symbolized the undaunted spirit of Londoners during the darkest moments of the war and carried echoes of the cathedral's origins—born out of the flames of the Great Fire of London in 1666.

Wren's original design for rebuilding St. Paul's was based on High Renaissance ideas, but it was considered too Italianate and too modern—the clergy of St. Paul's wanted a traditional processional nave and sanctuary, rather than Wren's Greek Cross design. Wren adapted his plans but kept the dome that gives the cathedral such a wonderfully uplifting atmosphere.

On entering the church it is natural to head for the crossing beneath the dome, with its windows filtering down a strangely ambiguous golden light. On the sidewalk below

Gibbons' choir stalls

its very center is a memorial to Wren, composed by his son, which reads *Si monumentum requiris, circumspice* (If you are seeking his monument, look around you). The marvelous choir stalls and organ case near John Donne's tomb (see panel) were carved by Grinling Gibbons as part of Wren's original decorative scheme. Next it is best to visit the crypt, where you can see Wren's actual tomb, a simple black slab, and an audiovisual program explaining the history and construction of the building, from the laying of the foundation stone in 1675 to the placing of the last stone on the lantern above the dome in 1708. The crypt itself is massive, extending beneath nearly the whole of the church. In

St. Paul's Cathedral: the choir and high altar

Painters' Corner, for example, the monuments read like a roll call of great artists of the past, from Van Dyck to Constable. George Frampton's memorial is particularly charming: It features a small replica of the Peter Pan statue he made for Kensington Gardens (see page 111). In the center of the crypt are the ponderous tomb of Wellington and the Renaissance sarcophagus of Nelson. This last was actually made by Benedetto da Rovezzano for Cardinal Wolsey, then confiscated by Henry VIII but never used by him. Instead it remained empty until 1805, when Nelson's body was laid to rest within it, having been brought back from the Battle of Trafalgar pickled in spirits in a barrel. His coffin was made from the wood of the French flagship at the Battle of the Nile, *L'Orient*.

After the descent into the crypt the next and most exciting part is the ascent to the dome. There are 259 steps to the Whispering Gallery: by the time you get there you will be so out of breath that whispering is all you can do. The circular gallery carries sound around so that someone standing on the opposite side will hear your whispers quite clearly after several seconds' delay—though with so many visitors testing the acoustics it may be someone else's voice altogether. Views take in the nave below and the frescoes of the dome above, depicting scenes from the *Life of St. Paul* painted by Sir James Thornhill in 1716–19. If you have the energy you can now continue upwards to the Stone Gallery, which runs around the exterior of the base of the dome. Climbing higher still you pass through the timberwork that rests on the inner dome, supporting the wooden skin of the outer, lead-covered dome. Between these two domes is a third: the brick cone supporting the elegant lantern crowning the whole structure. This can be viewed from the Golden Gallery. There is one last spiral staircase (not accessible to the public) up to the ball, added in 1721, surmounted by a golden cross and looking over the city from more than 366 ft. above the cathedral floor.

Crypt, Whispering Gallery, and Dome closed Sunday.

Around St. Paul's

Although St. Paul's itself miraculously escaped major damage in the Blitz, the surrounding area was flattened and then redeveloped in the 1960s with a series of dreary, windswept buildings. These are due to be taken down and replaced, but there are several competing and equally controversial designs. They range from the highly modernistic (accused of being out of sympathy with Wren's masterpiece) to the more traditional (accused of being backward looking), based on Wren's own plan to surround his church with a series of Italianate piazzas and boulevards. Most Londoners favor the latter approach, which will give St. Paul's the setting it deserves and open up views of the façades, now rather hemmed in by busy roads or bad buildings and difficult to view properly. The south façade would benefit especially if the road in front of it were closed: Here Wren had the word *Resurgam* (I shall rise again) carved above the door and a phoenix rising from the fire carved in the pediment to symbolize the birth of the new church from the ashes of the old. The main (west) façade is the most richly decorated. The baroque twin towers, flanking rows of gigantic columns, are a quirky but successful piece of design to which Wren's gifted pupil Nicholas Hawksmoor may well have contributed.

City churches

■ The Great Fire of London broke out at a bakery on Pudding Lane on September 2, 1666. Four days later, when the fire's rage was finally quenched, nearly every building in the City had been destroyed, including more than 13,000 houses and over 50 churches. The great rebuilding that took place after the fire provided the architects of the day with a wonderful opportunity to create a new city. The churches built by Christopher Wren and his assistants remain one of the great lasting legacies of that age, their spires, towers, and domes as much a symbol of the City as the skyscrapers of today's financial institutions. .....■

Mighty bells

The Great Bells of Bow
The bells of St. Mary-le-Bow (Cheapside) are of great symbolic importance to Londoners: Only those born within the sound of the "Great Bells of Bow" qualify as true Cockneys. When the church was hit by a bomb in 1941, sending the bells crashing to the ground, the pieces were saved; in 1962 they were rehung, having been recast, and the church was restored to its former glory. Of the original Wren church (built 1670–80), the tower and splendid steeple survive, and below, in the crypt, restorers found remains of an 11th-century staircase.

St. Martin Ludgate (Ludgate Hill). Built in 1677–87, this church stands within a short step of Wren's masterpiece, St. Paul's Cathedral. The spire and portico of St. Martin seem designed to echo the twin towers fronting St. Paul's. Notable features of the interior are the galleries, reached through richly carved doors, and the pulpit.

St. James Garlickhythe (Garlick Hill). Wren was continually adding spires and towers to his churches in order to improve the London skyline. This church is an example: It was built between 1676 and 1683, but Wren decided to add the graceful spire in the early 18th century. In fact, some architectural historians think the spire may have been the work not of Wren himself but of his assistant, Nicholas Hawksmoor.

St. Stephen Walbrook (Walbrook). Some consider this to be the most majestic of all Wren's parish churches; it is one in which the architect experimented with ideas later used for St. Paul's, notably the large central dome. Henry Moore's stone central altar was placed below the dome in 1987. Critics of its abstract form refer to it, scathingly, as "the lump of Camembert."

St. Mary Woolnoth (King William Street). This astonishing building is the work of Nicholas Hawksmoor and was built between 1716 and 1724. Fronted by the powerful west tower, it is a strange and daring building that looks more like a pagan temple than a Christian church. Inside, do not miss the monument to a former rector of the church, John Newton, who died in 1807 having devoted many years of his life to campaigning for the abolition of the slave trade. He also wrote the perennially popular hymn *Amazing Grace*.

St. Mary Abchurch (Abchurch Lane). This is one of the few Wren churches to have remained virtually unaltered, complete with its woodwork. The chief glory is the huge reredos behind the altar, carved by Grinling Gibbons—all the more remarkable when you consider that it was carefully pieced together by restorers in 1948–53, having been shattered into over 2,000 pieces by a bomb that fell during the Blitz.

St. Helen Bishopsgate (Great St. Helen's). St. Helen is one of the few City churches not to have been destroyed by the Great Fire, and it preserves a remarkable series of 15th-century tomb effigies, including the fine recumbent figures of John and Mary de Oteswich and the wool merchant, Sir John Crosby. A later monument (1636) by Nicholas Stone commemorates the grandly named Sir Julius Caesar Adelmare, a judge in the Court of Admiralty.

St. Katharine Cree (Leadenhall Street). This is another church that escaped the Great Fire, and it is a very rare example of the transition from Gothic to classical, having been built around 1628. The nave arcades are supported on splendid Corinthian columns, but the vaulting is Gothic, as is the splendid rose window, symbolizing the wheel on which St. Katharine was martyred.

Sir Christopher Wren

Sir Christopher Wren (1632–1723) was an extraordinary man. In his youth he was regarded as a brilliant mathematician and appointed Professor of Astronomy at Oxford at the age of 29. With little formal architectural training he launched himself on a glorious career by designing the Sheldonian Theatre in Oxford; he was appointed surveyor general and principal architect for rebuilding the City after the Great Fire, on the strength of a comprehensive plan he drew up. Apart from St. Paul's Cathedral, Wren personally designed 52 churches for the City, of which 23 survived the bombs of the Blitz. He also inspired a whole generation of artists and architects, including Grinling Gibbons, the great woodcarver, and Nicholas Hawksmoor, creator of the English Baroque style.

St Mary-le-Bow

■ **Vegetarians and the squeamish should be warned that Smithfield is a raw, rough, and bloody place—London's main market for meat and poultry. Even the strong of stomach have been known to blanch at the sight of porters in bloodied aprons running around with great sides of beef or whole pig carcasses slung across their backs. You will also be sworn at in resounding terms if you get in the way—this is a no-nonsense place, to which visitors are welcome so long as they do not hold up the proceedings. .....■**

Above: Rahere's tomb, church of St. Bartholomew-the-Great

Cloth Fair
Cloth Fair is a quiet little street lined with timber buildings, antiques shops, and pubs running down the north side of St. Bartholomew-the-Great. It preserves something of the appearance of pre-Fire London, because the Great Fire died out finally at nearby Cock Lane. No. 43 Cloth Fair was for a long time the home of Sir John Betjeman, Poet Laureate and campaigner for the conservation of Victorian monuments. The house now belongs to the Landmark Trust, an organization that restores historic buildings and rents them as holiday homes (details from The Landmark Trust, Shottesbrooke, Maidenhead, Berkshire SL6 3SW. Tel. 0628 825925). The wine bar below and the adjacent pub have walls decorated with Betjeman memorabilia and old photographs of Smithfield. Another excellent pub further down the lane is the tiny Hand and Shears, on the corner of Middle Street, whose wood-paneled rooms, some no bigger than corridors, are usually packed with doctors from St. Bartholomew's.

Smithfield is the last remaining wholesale market operating in Central London, and it offers a unique example of a sight that was commonplace to Londoners until the 1970s, when cramped working conditions and the difficulties of truck access to London's narrow and congested streets drove long-established markets (such as Billingsgate for fish and Covent Garden for fruit, vegetables, and flowers) to new purpose-built sites on the edges of London. Smithfield (from "Smooth Field") was a livestock market at least as early as 1173, but the sale (and slaughter) of live animals was banned in the 1850s because of the squalor of the streets full of filth and entrails and because the drovers who brought their sheep, cows, and horses to the market delighted in terrorizing Londoners by making their charges stampede down the narrow streets. Smithfield has survived on this site because the meat market has declined in recent years, so there is space enough for the traders. This may yet change as a result of European Community regulations on the sale of meat or else because of development pressures—the market occupies a prime site, and the glorious cast-iron and glass hall that houses the market (built 1857–66 and modeled on Joseph Paxton's Crystal Palace) would make a good shopping center.

Smithfield's decline is due to the large number of butchers' chains that now buy direct from producers, but the market still supplies many top restaurants and specialist butchers, whose hyper-critical buyers come here at the crack of dawn. The market is all but finished by 9:30a.m., so you have to be an early riser to see it in full swing. As a concession to its hours, pubs in the vicinity open at 6:30a.m. and serve gargantuan breakfasts to the hungry and exhausted porters.

Alongside the market is St. Bartholomew's Hospital, one of the City's four great teaching hospitals. It was founded in 1123 by Rahere, Henry I's court jester, in gratitude for his recovery from malaria, contracted while on a pilgrimage to Rome. The older buildings, including the baroque Great Hall and staircase (decorated with paintings by William Hogarth of *The Good Samaritan* and *The Pool of Bethesda*) can only be seen on a guided tour Fridays 2p.m. from the main gateway, mid-April to end November). Without joining a tour, you can admire the

Smithfield porters still use traditional barrows

Charterhouse Square
Charterhouse Square was originally a burial ground for victims of the Black Death, the bubonic plague that carried off half of London's population in the 1340s. A Carthusian monastery was set up where the monks prayed for the souls of plague victims. The name of the square is an anglicization of Chartreuse, where the Carthusian order was founded in 1084. Though heavily restored, the buildings are worth visiting for the tranquil cloistered atmosphere (tours every Wednesday from April to July at 2p.m. from the main gateway). In 1611 the buildings were purchased by Thomas Sutton, who founded the Charterhouse School, where pupils included John Wesley, founder of Methodism, and the novelist William Thackeray. The educational tradition lives on: The buildings behind the Charterhouse now house St. Bartholomew's Hospital Medical School.

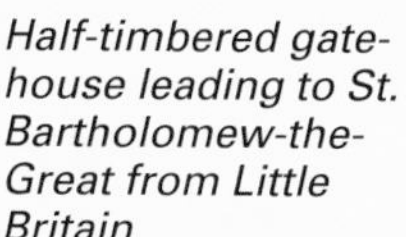

Half-timbered gatehouse leading to St. Bartholomew-the-Great from Little Britain

figure of Henry VIII over the gateway, the inner courtyard laid out by James Gibbs (1730–59), and the hospital church of St Bartholomew-the-Less.

Just to the east of the hospital entrance is a 13th-century stone archway topped by a timber-framed gatehouse dated 1559. This leads to the quiet, flower-filled churchyard surrounding London's oldest surviving church, St. Batholomew-the-Great, also founded by Rahere, for the Augustinian canons who maintained the hospital. At the Dissolution of the Monasteries, under Henry VIII, the nave was torn down, but the lovely Romanesque choir was allowed to survive, serving as the district's parish church. Rahere himself, who died in 1143, is buried here beneath the canopied tomb on the north side. On the opposite side, high up on the nave wall above the massive Norman pillars, is an oriel window, installed by Prior Bolton at the beginning of the 16th century so that he could observe the monks who were in his charge. The window is carved with a rebus (a pictorial pun) on Bolton's name, consisting of a crossbow bolt and a tun (barrel).

■ **London has an extraordinary range of pubs. Some offer live music or theater, some offer top quality food at a fraction of the price of a restaurant meal, some have waterside gardens, and many have historical associations and the decor to match. .....■**

The pub where Dr. Johnson drank

One of the oldest pubs in London is the **George Inn** in Southwark (77 Borough High Street), so venerable that it is maintained by the National Trust, the historic preservation body associated with stately homes. The rambling timber-framed coaching inn dates from 1676 and is unique in preserving its external galleries. For warm days there is outdoor seating in the courtyard and in summer this is turned into a stage, where extracts from Shakespeare's plays are performed. The **Black Friar** (174 Queen Victoria Street), on the other side of the river, is worth a visit for its entertaining Arts and Crafts decorations (best in the early evening, when not too crowded). The church-like interior is a riot of marble, mosaic, and woodwork, the walls covered in reliefs of monks at work and play above beautifully lettered mottos exhorting the oblivious drinkers below to reform and improve their dissolute lives. The whole pub is a charming joke.

Another wonderful piece of fun is **Jack Straw's Castle** (North End Way) in Hampstead. The name commemorates one of the leaders of the 1381 Peasant's Revolt, an uprising that was sparked off by the imposition of a poll tax that everyone in the country was expected to pay, no matter how poor. The pub is built on the site of an encampment set up by Straw's followers and looks every inch an 18th-century coaching inn (in some guides you will find it described as just that!). In reality it was designed by Raymond Erith in 1962–64 and is therefore the exact contemporary of skyscrapers such as Centrepoint.

A pub that does not require such an effort to reach is the tiny **Olde Mitre** (1 Ely Court, Ely Place), which was founded in 1546. It proudly displays the trunk of a cherry tree around which Queen Elizabeth I is supposed to have danced with one of her favorites, Sir Christopher Hatton, in nearby Hatton Garden.

No historic pub crawl would be complete without a visit to the **Olde Cheshire Cheese,** just south of here at 145 Fleet Street. Built in 1667, just after the Great Fire, it is the least altered pub in London, a rambling building of low beams, intimate rooms, and sawdust-covered floors. Not all of its original decorations are on display, however. Archaeologists researching the fabric of the pub in the 1970s discovered a blocked fireplace in an upper room, decorated with a series of highly imaginative 17th-century pornographic tiles (the details were then published in a respectable academic journal, which must have raised a few vicars' eyebrows). Perhaps the tiles help explain the appeal of the pub to a host of famous literary regulars, including Dr. Johnson, Pope, Voltaire, and Dickens.

Music pubs
Many pubs have music nights when live bands provide entertainment. The listings magazine *Time Out* provides a comprehensive guide, but the following pubs have well-established reputations for the quality of their acts. The **Half Moon** (93 Lower Richmond Road) in Putney has entertainment every night and is especially renowned for folk music. **Minogues** (80 Liverpool Road) in Islington is the place to hear traditional Irish folk, while the **Pied Bull** nearby (1 Liverpool Road) specializes in blues and African-influenced jazz. Jazz lovers in general are very well served but rarely is good music and good food combined so well as at the **Bull's Head** (373 Lonsdale Road) in Barnes, a huge Victorian pub by the Thames; it is wise to reserve in advance: tel. 081 876 5241).

Moving closer in to the West End, the **Cittie of York** (22 High Holborn) has several times been voted "Pub of the Year" by readers of London's *Evening Standard* newspaper. The pub is both huge and intimate, but the drinking area is divided into lots of small, cozy cubicles, designed, it is said, so that lawyers from the nearby Inns of Court can hold confidential discussions with their clients. The large open fireplace intrigues most visitors because it has no chimney (the smoke is carried away by means of a vent in the floor).

A short walk away from the Cittie of York is the **Museum Tavern** (49 Great Russell Street), yet another pub in which you never quite know whose famous bottom once occupied the seat you have chosen. Being so close to the Reading Room of the British Museum, it was (and still is) a convenient place for scholars to seek a spot of light relief from their mental labors; even Karl Marx used to slip in here for the odd drink from time to time while writing *Das Kapital*.

Firkin pubs
Some of the most entertaining pubs in London are run by an entrepreneur called David Bruce, who set out to revive the tradition of brewing beer on the premises. Pubs in the chain are instantly recognizable by the use of the word Firkin (a small barrel or cask) in their name (hence the Pheasant and Firkin, 166 Goswell Road, or the Goose and Firkin, 47 Borough High Street). In each pub you can watch the beer being brewed through glass observation windows and sample the result knowing that you are drinking a unique beer, rather than one produced by factory methods in quantities in excess of several million gallons a day.

Liquid lunch

Angel
Islington High St
Grand Union Canal (Regent's Canal)
City Road Basin
Wharf Road
Shepherdess Walk
New North Road
St Leonard's Hospital
Geffrye Museum
Kingsland Road
City Road
Sadler's Wells Theatre
Rosebery Ave
St John Street
Goswell Road
The City University
Shoreditch
East Road
Pitfield St
Lever Street
Bath Street
Moorfields Eye Hospital
Old Street
Curtain Rd
Calvert Ave
Great Eastern Street
Skinner St
Percival St
Finsbury Leisure Complex
Clerkenwell
Old Street
Bunhill Row
City Road
Wesley's House & Chapel
Shoreditch High Street
Pear Tree Ct
Clerkenwell Close
St James
Farringdon La
Clerkenwell Green
St John
Clerkenwell Road
Clerkenwell Heritage Centre
Museum of the Order of St John
Charterhouse
Britton St
Turnmill St
St John's Lane
St John St
Aldersgate Street
Bunhill Fields
Worship Street
Farringdon Road
Farringdon
Beech Street
Chiswell Street
Barbican
Barbican Centre
The Barbican
Guildhall School of Music & Drama
Finsbury Pavement
Spitalfields Market
Hatton Gdn
Central Markets (Smithfield)
St Giles
Moorgate
Broadgate
Liverpool Street Station
St Bartholomew's Hospital
Finsbury Circus
London Wall
Middlesex Petticoat Lane
Holborn Viaduct
Museum of London
London Wall
Houndsditch
National Postal Museum
Guildhall
Moorgate
Bishopsgate
City Thameslink
Newgate St
Nat West Tower
Central Criminal Courts
City
Stock Exchange
St Paul's Cathedral
St Paul's
Bank of England & Museum
Threadneedle St
Fleet Street
Cheapside

Clerkenwell, Islington, and the East End Wrapped around the City to the north and the east are scores of small communities such as Clerkenwell, Islington, Spitalfields, Whitechapel, and Bethnal Green. Each began as a small village with a parish church, a manor house, and cottages around a green. Rapid population growth in the 19th century turned them into one vast metropolitan sprawl. Even so, they each have a strong identity and are worth exploring for a different view of London.

Clerkenwell walk Start at **Farringdon tube station**, the first Underground station to open in London, on January 10, 1863. Soon it will be developed as an ultra-modern terminus feeding into the Channel Tunnel rail link. Near by, on Farringdon Road, a Dickensian street market specializes in old books and newspapers.

Walking straight ahead, up Benjamin Street, you will see one of the most controversial buildings of recent years, on the corner of Britton Street and Albion Place. Designed by Piers Gough in 1987 for the flamboyant head of Youth and Entertainment Features at the BBC, Janet Street-Porter, the house has received rave reviews from architects but has excited strong reactions from the public. The post-

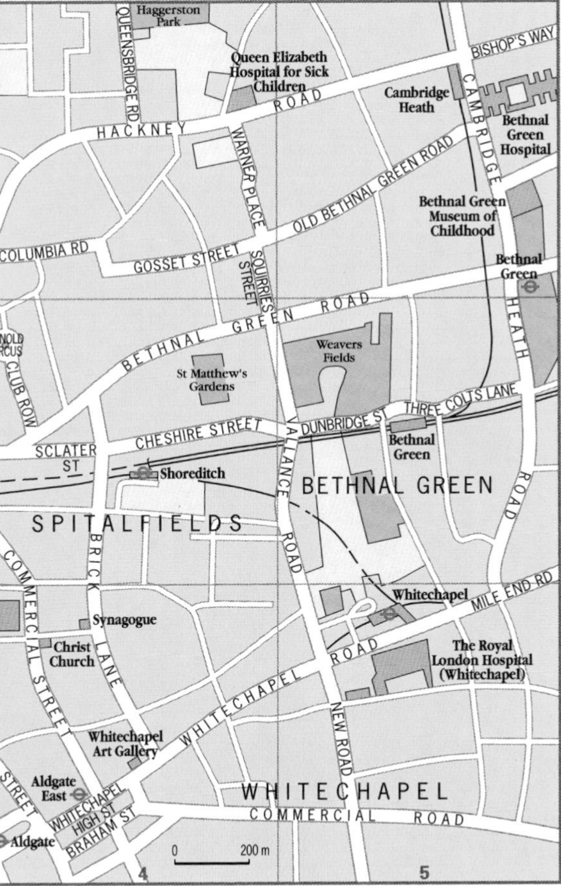

modern house was intended to stand out from its surroundings—and it has succeeded, using blue pantiles, brown brick, and steel lattice grilles thrusting up from the roof. Love it or hate it, you certainly won't miss it.

Continue up Albion Place, turning left in St. John's Lane to see **St. John's Gate** (1504), the gatehouse of the Priory of St. John of Jerusalem, the English base of the Knights Hospitallers, which evolved into the St. John's Ambulance Brigade. Across Clerkenwell Road is a small **museum** about the Order (closed Sunday and Monday).

Jerusalem Passage, a narrow alley, links St. John's Lane to Aylesbury Street; turn left to reach **Clerkenwell Green**, where the Palladian-style **Middlesex Sessions House** was built as a court of law in 1779–82.

Clerkenwell Close winds northwards from the green and leads past another splendid Palladian building: the church of **St. James**, built in 1788–92.

Take the first left, into Pear Tree Court, and left again, to **Farringdon Lane**. Between Nos. 14 and 16, a window reveals the remains of the medieval **Clerk's Well**, after which Clerkenwell is named. The quality of its water accounts for the presence of Booth's gin distillery further down on Turnmill Street, established in the 18th century.

The Barbican

Barbican Centre

176A2

Aldersgate Street (theater entrance on Silk Street)
Underground: Barbican

The Barbican Centre is one of London's most important arts locations. It is home to the Royal Shakespeare Company and the London Symphony Orchestra, and it mounts exhibitions and film seasons. Quite apart from all this there is a full program of free lobby exhibitions and musical entertainment, weekend activities especially for children, and an excellent bookshop specializing in the arts. The Centre stands on the northern edge of a massive housing complex that is an important example of postwar planning in its own right. In 1956, the government proposed that the 14-hectare area, left a wasteland as a result of the Blitz, should be developed for housing rather than office buildings. The architects, Chamberlain, Powell, and Bon, produced a plan that was very forward looking in its use of textured concrete. Some 6,500 people now live in the Barbican (which was not finally completed until 1981), many in high-rises over 402 ft. high. The buildings are beginning to show their age, the concrete facing having become stained and dirty. It is difficult now to realize how enchanting and futuristic the complex looked when it first opened, with tier upon tier of cascading plants and bright crimson trailing geraniums spilling over every balcony, softening the brutal outlines of the concrete. Most residents have simply given up gardening because of the winds and because so many of them are temporary residents—highly paid media personalities and business executives, for whom this may be only one of many homes. This gives a certain forlorn, unloved atmosphere to the complex, though the area right around the arts center is enlivened by sculptures, water gardens, fountains, and trees. The best spots to view the Barbican are from the Waterside Cafe (level 5) or the plant-filled conservatory (levels 8 and 9).

The Barbican maze
It is a standing joke among Londoners that once you penetrate the Barbican complex you may never get out. The various buildings are linked by a confusing maze of tunnels, elevated walkways, and staircases in which it is all too easy to get lost. To improve the situation, yellow markers have been placed on the pavements, leading eventually to the Barbican Centre arts complex. Alternatively you can use the church of St. Giles, Cripplegate, for orientation. This Tudor church was left a roofless ruin by the bombing that flattened the surrounding district but was rebuilt in 1952–60. Surrounded by water, it appears to float on its own island, detached from the massive concrete structures all around. Inside are memorials to people associated with the church: A bust of John Milton, author of *Paradise Lost*, marks the approximate position of his grave. South of the church are remains of the Roman and medieval city walls.

Bethnal Green toys

▶▶ Bethnal Green Museum of Childhood *177C5*

Cambridge Heath Road
Underground: Bethnal Green

This museum of childhood and social history holds the largest collection of toys in the world, so there is plenty to justify the trip out to a rather desolate area of London's East End. An outpost of the Victoria and Albert Museum, this collection is housed in an interesting iron-and-glass building that originally stood on the V & A's South Kensington site, but was re-erected here in 1875 and clad in brick with *sgraffito* (scratched) designs illustrating the Arts, Sciences, and Agriculture.

A wonderful collection of 50 doll's houses is displayed in the museum's Central Hall. You can peer into the tiny world of a grand late-19th-century country house, stuffed with heavy furniture, or envy the lifestyle of the tiny inhabitants of Whiteladies, a stylish 1930s modernist house complete with tennis court, swimming pool, and veranda for cocktails.

The lower galleries are used to display a huge toy collection, grouped by type (dolls, trains, teddy bears, optical and musical toys, for example). The earliest exhibits are 17th-century, and there are toys from every corner of the world, including puppets from India, China, and Japan.

The upstairs galleries, still in the process of development, are intended to illustrate the social history of childhood. Exhibits include children's clothing from the 1830s to the present day and reconstructed nurseries. Here, too, are books from the museum's vast Renier Collection, covering the way in which subjects as diverse as sex and religion have been presented to children during the past 400 years (viewing by special arrangment).

On Saturdays and during school holidays the museum mounts a program of free activities for children (tel. 071 980 3204 for details), and the shop is a good source of gifts for everyone. Closed Friday.

East End philanthropists
Bethnal Green, along with neighboring Shoreditch and Whitechapel, was notorious in the 19th century for its overcrowded slums and for the poverty of its working-class population. Many attempts were made to improve the quality of life in the East End, not all of them successful or even appropriate. One of them was the setting up of the Bethnal Green Museum in 1875, in an attempt to bring art and culture to the masses. Another was the model housing built at great expense by Miss (later Baroness) Burdett-Coutts, whom Charles Dickens nicknamed Lady Bountiful, after the character in Farquhar's comedy *The Beaux' Stratagem.* These dwellings of the 1860s were themselves condemned as slums a century later and demolished. Model houses of a later era can, however, still be seen in the western part of Bethnal Green. The Boundary Estate, centered on Arnold Circus (just off Shoreditch High Street), was built in Arts and Crafts style and completed in 1900. The buildings were of such high quality that they inspired urban planners to build similar complexes to house the poor in Paris, Amsterdam, Berlin, and Vienna. A good day to see them is Sunday; the trip can be combined with a visit to the Columbia Road flower market, just to the north, definitely one of London's most colorful street markets and a place where you can buy top quality house plants and flowers at rock-bottom prices (open Sunday only, 7a.m.–2p.m.).

Major arts sites

■ Apart from hit musicals and popular dramas staged in the commercial theaters of the West End, London offers a wealth of more serious entertainment for lovers of music, theater, and dance. The city's two principal sites for the performing arts are the Barbican Centre and the South Bank Centre; both have resident companies whose work is of the highest international standard. .....■

The Coliseum, in St. Martin's Lane, home of the English National Opera

The Barbican Center is the London home of the **Royal Shakespeare Company**. Plays by Shakespeare are usually performed in the larger Barbican Theatre, while new productions by other dramatists are staged in the smaller theater called the Pit. Cynics say the Pit is well named: The subterranean concrete does not provide a very appealing environment for an evening's entertainment, but the RSC overcomes this handicap with the sheer energy, wit, and imagination of its productions.

Sharing the Barbican Centre with the RSC is the **London Symphony Orchestra**—not only London's oldest orchestra but also the first to be run by its members. The LSO was formed in 1904 by 50 musicians from Henry Wood's Queen's Hall Orchestra, who walked out after a dispute and formed their own self-governing body. Guest conductors are chosen by the orchestra members and the LSO tries to include new works or those that are not often performed, in its Barbican concerts, along with the more popular works that are considered essential for attracting large audiences.

For really big orchestral and choral works, the Royal Festival Hall, the largest concert hall in the South Bank complex, is the place to go. Top orchestras such as the **Royal Philharmonic** and the **London Philharmonic** perform here regularly, but perhaps the most exciting productions to be seen are those mounted in the Queen Elizabeth Hall by the **Opera Factory**, a deliberately iconoclastic company that mounts premieres of new operas and startling reinterpretations of the classics by Mozart, Rossini, and many others.

The **Royal National Theatre**, also part of the South Bank complex, is another concrete monstrosity (although the backstage facilities are superb, as you will soon discover if you join a guided tour of the building: Book at the Lyttleton Theatre Information Desk, tel. 071 633 0880).

The building was planned to allow a great variety of production styles, ranging from experimental drama staged in the intimate Cottesloe Theatre to well-known classics presented with polished professionalism in the Lyttleton and Olivier.

For ballet lovers the **Royal Ballet**, based at the Royal Opera House, Covent Garden, may be the best known London company with the most glittering stage (and audience), but it faces healthy competition. The **English National Ballet** (once called the London Festival Ballet) sometimes performs at the London Coliseum, St. Martin's Lane, during the summer months and at the Royal Festival Hall, where its *Nutcracker* (staged every January) is perennially popular. The **Sadler's Wells Theatre** (Rosebery Avenue) lost its resident company in 1990 when the Sadler's Wells Royal Ballet was enticed to move to the city of Birmingham and change its name to the Birmingham Royal Ballet. The theater remains the favorite performance hall for major dance companies, from the Bolshoi and Kirov Ballets and the Dance Theatre of Harlem to the Ballet Rambert and the London Contemporary Dance Theatre.

The **London Contemporary Dance Theatre** also has its own site, The Place (17 Duke's Road), where you can see well-established favorites from the company's repertoire performed by some of the country's most promising young dancers. This company has helped to put London in the forefront of modern dance, and the annual Dance Umbrella season, which runs for six weeks every October and November, now has a worldwide reputation as the place to see exciting new works. The event is run by Riverside Studios (Crisp Road, Hammersmith), which is itself a busy and youthful arts center specializing in new work in all media and occupying a series of Thames-side buildings originally set up as TV studios for the BBC.

Despite being awash with arts events, London also has scores of festivals. Many London "villages" use them to reinforce their community spirit (see panel). Other events indulge fans of a particular medium: Among the best are the London Film Festival, hosted by the National Film Theatre in November (South Bank, tel. 071 928 3232) and Capital Radio's Music Festival (jazz, rock, and folk), held in June and July at locations all over London (see *Time Out* magazine).

See also **Nightlife**, pages 244–45.

Arts festivals

One of the most enjoyable arts festivals is the Kenwood Lakeside Concert season of classical music, performed in the open air on Saturday evenings in June, July, and August (tel. 071 413 1443); some gala evenings end with fireworks. Camden has a number of local summer festivals (tel. 071 911 1650), Covent Garden has its May Fayre (same number as for Camden), Greenwich has two weeks of music, theater and outdoor events in June (tel. 081 317 8687) and Richmond's July festival includes opera, drama, street entertainment and a Teddy Bear's Picnic (tel. 081 940 9125).

Musical treats

■ Islington has become a chic address for young Londoners. For those who can afford them, its terraces of late-18th- and early 19th-century houses offer elegant living in spacious well-proportioned rooms relatively close to the City and central London. As a result, Islington has a lively atmosphere, with its street markets, theaters, restaurants, and pubs. .....■

Islington Theatres
The King's Head, 115 Upper Street is one of London's oldest pub theaters, a Victorian gem, whose owners charge for drinks in pre-decimal money. The **Almeida Theatre**, Almeida Street, covers a wide range of drama, and puppets star at the **Little Angel Marionette Theatre**, 14 Dagmar Terrace, on Saturday and Sunday. At the **Tower Theatre**, Canonbury Place, Shakespeare and other classics are the speciality.

King's Cross Road provides a commercial introduction to the area, but walking up Vernon Rise soon brings you to the elegant stucco-fronted houses of Percy Circus, developed from 1819, where Karl Marx lived for a time. More genteel houses in the same mold line the streets and squares to the south, such as Prideaux Place and Lloyd Square. Across Amwell Street, Myddelton Square, with its gardens surrounding St. Mark's Church, stands at the heart of the New River Estate. This was developed in the 1820s from the profits generated by the New River Company, founded in the late 16th century to bring fresh water to London from the River Lea in Hertfordshire, over 40 miles away. The same channel, completed in 1613, still supplies this part of London with drinking water to this day.

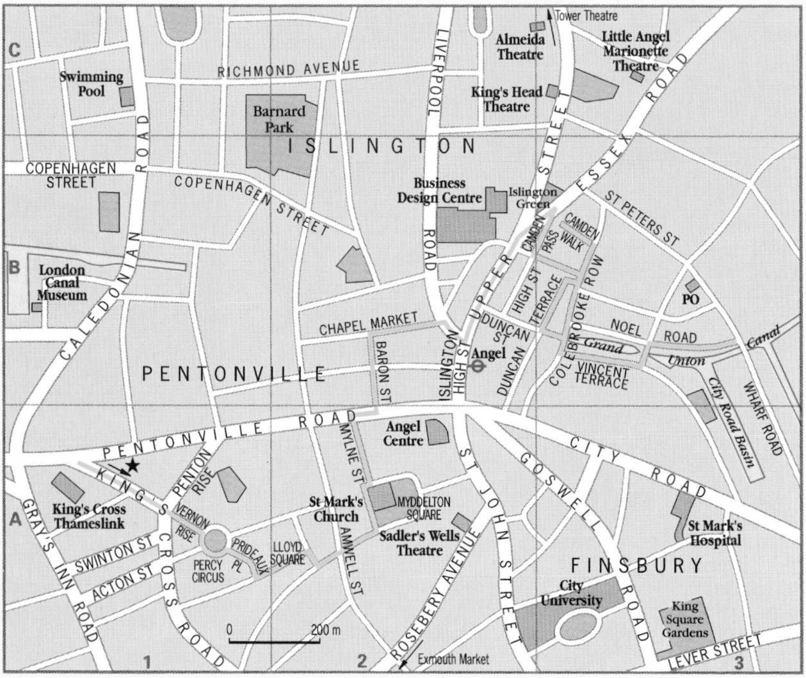

From Myddelton Square, Mylne Street leads north to busy Pentonville Road; on the other side, up Baron Street, you will find Chapel Market. Here, stallholders sell

top quality fruit, vegetables, flowers, and fish to Islington residents. Upper Street, with its raised sidewalks, leads northwards to the tiny triangular patch of grass that marks Islington Green.

On the left is the huge cast-iron and glass structure built in 1861–62 as the Royal Agricultural Hall, known simply as the "Aggie" to local residents. Originally this was built as a wholesale market for cattle, sheep, pigs, and poultry, when the sale of live animals was banned at Smithfield, the City's main meat market. It later came to be used for all sorts of events, from circuses and gala balls to Cruft's dog show. Today it houses the Business Design Centre, a permanent showcase for British design, and some idea of the building's splendor can be gained by visiting one of the Centre's many cafes and restaurants.

Across the street, on a more intimate scale, is Camden Passage, with its antiques shops appropriately located in handsome houses dating from the 18th century. On Saturdays and Wednesdays, street stalls also set up here, selling a mix of antiques and collectables, including jewelry, toys, clothing, books, and records. Nearby is the Camden Head (2 Camden Walk), a busy, friendly Victorian pub with a flower-filled patio for outdoor drinking in summer.

Camden Walk leads to Colebrooke Row and the parallel Duncan Terrace, two long rows of town houses, built from 1768 onwards and now among the most sought-after properties in Islington. Halfway down Colebrooke Row, on the left, Vincent Terrace is another pretty spot. It sits alongside the Grand Union Canal at the point where it emerges from the Islington Tunnel. The tree-filled gardens of Noel Road, backing onto the opposite bank of the canal, gives this attractive residential district an almost rural feel, and there are several good pubs serving food nearby, including the Narrow Boat, near Wharf Road Bridge, and the Island Queen, 87 Noel Road.

Little Italy
Rosebery Avenue, leading south from Islington, cuts through the district once known as Little Italy because of the large community of Italians that lived here in the 19th century, many making their living as entertainers and ice cream manufacturers. Exmouth Market, with its Italianate Church of the Holy Redeemer, its delicatessens and its market, still has a Little Italy flavor. It was here, at No. 8, that Joseph Grimaldi, one of the most famous pantomime clowns of the 19th century, once lived; he first appeared on stage as a child dancer at the Sadler's Wells Theatre on Rosebery Avenue.

Bunhill Fields
Bunhill Fields, on City Road across from Wesley's House, is the burial place of several Nonconformists, such as the author of *Robinson Crusoe*, Daniel Defoe, the poet William Blake, the hymn-writer Isaac Watts, and the author of *The Pilgrim's Progress*, John Bunyan. Originally the cemetery was a plague pit, opened up during the Great Plague that hit London in 1665, when people were dying in such numbers that their remains were simply dumped into one huge mass grave. Because it was never consecrated, the burial ground was later favored by Quakers, Methodists, and other Nonconformists, who could be buried according to their own rites rather than those of the established church. Today the cemetery is a delightful tree-shaded spot full of wildflowers. The offices of the *Independent* newspaper stand alongside—the newspaper's founder and editor claims he chose the site so that he could look out over the graves of great truth seekers from the past and be inspired by their example.

▶▶ **Geffrye Museum** *176C3*

Kingsland Road
Underground: Liverpool Street then bus: 22, 22A, 148, 149 or 243
Despite its out-of-the-way location, this treasure of a museum is well worth seeking out. It is like the Victoria and Albert Museum on a very much smaller scale, containing a series of rooms decorated in period style, using genuine furnishings rescued from demolished buildings. The museum is housed in a row of handsome brick almshouses grouped around a courtyard, built in 1715 with money bequeathed by Sir Robert Geffrye. From the entrance you enter a Georgian Street, made up of salvaged 18th-century shopfronts, and a re-creation of a carpenter's workshop—a reminder that the museum was created in 1914 to inspire crafts students in an area that had long been associated with furniture making. Beyond lies the Elizabethan Room, with its rush-strewn floor and handsome paneling, beginning a chronological sequence that covers every major period in English history. The later rooms are the most fascinating, especially if you are looking for ideas for decorating your own home. The Mid-Victorian Room, with its William Morris wallpapers and textiles, may be a little too stuffy and cluttered for modern living. By contrast the Voysey Room, named after C. F. A. Voysey, the Arts and Crafts architect and designer, is furnished with simple and honest pieces whose style has had a major influence on the current generation of furniture designers.

Having toured the period rooms, it is worth returning to the Reading Room, with its adjoining cafe. Unlike many museum reference libraries, this is an admirably informal room where you can browse through all the latest magazines covering the fields of applied arts and crafts. Closed Monday.

 **Wesley's House** *176B2*

47 City Road
Underground: Old Street
John Wesley, the founder of Methodism, lived in this Georgian house from 1779 until his death in 1791, along with several fellow preachers. Methodists from all over

the world come here to see the relics of their founder, but the museum is also of interest as a monument to nonconformity: It is interesting to note, for example, that former Prime Minister Margaret Thatcher was married in the chapel attached to the house—as many commentators have noted, the "enterprise culture," which she espoused during her premiership is a direct product of nonconformist values and the "Puritan" work ethic. This chapel was designed by Wesley himself and completed in 1778 in a style that he summed up as "perfectly neat, but not fine." In the crypt you can watch an audiovisual presentation on the history of Methodism, before touring the house. Here you can see portraits of Wesley, his clothes, furniture, pens, annotated books, and the prayer room in which he used to kneel at 4 every morning awaiting his daily orders from God. You can also see the electrical shock machine that Wesley used in an attempt to cure bouts of melancholia. Closed Saturday.

► Whitechapel Art Gallery *177A4*

80–2 Whitechapel High Street
Underground: Aldgate East
This gallery in the East End has acquired an international reputation for its provocative exhibitions of modern art. The material on display changes regularly but usually features the work of big-name artists from all over the world, working in all media. Check *Time Out* magazine to see what is on. If modern art doesn't interest you, you might still stop by to look at the building itself. It was built in 1901 in art nouveau style by the social reformer and ardent missionary, Canon Samuel Augustus Barnett, whose avowed aim was to "decrease not suffering but sin." He mounted exhibitions of paintings here that were extremely popular with East Enders. One can only guess what he would think of the work that is now shown in his gallery, but he would probably approve of the fact that the cafe is a popular place for local people to meet. Closed Monday.

Whitechapel
Whitechapel was named after its whitewashed parish church and was the place where church bells were cast for parish churches up and down the land. The Whitechapel Bell Foundry, 32 Whitechapel Road, moved here in 1738 and made such notable bells as Big Ben and the original Liberty Bell. The firm now repairs historic bells. In the 19th century Whitechapel was flooded with Jewish refugees from Eastern Europe. Some of their children went on to make a fortune (including Alfred Marks, co-founder of the Marks and Spencer chain). Most moved on to less crowded suburbs, such as Golders Green, but many still have the occasional meal at Blooms (90 Whitechapel High Street), London's best-known kosher restaurant, renowned for the wit (and brusqueness) of its waiters and its hefty portions of bortsch and salt beef.

Art nouveau

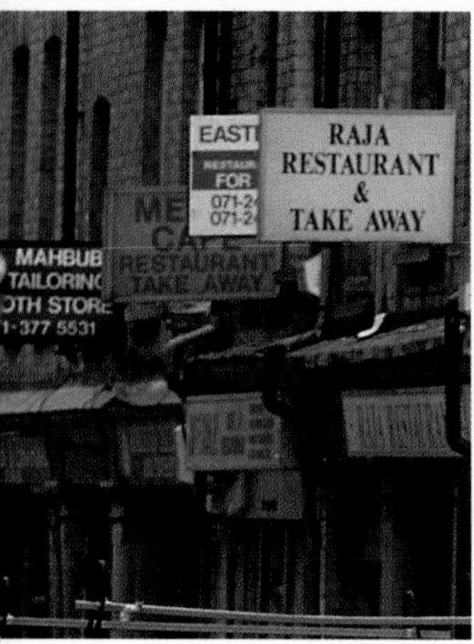

■ A visit to Spitalfields lets you sample the surprising contrasts of London's East End. This working class neighborhood has long been a home to the poorest of refugees. Its character was first formed by Huguenot weavers; their houses, many of them still standing, had skylit attics where hand-loom weavers worked all the hours of daylight to produce fine silk clothing. After the Huguenots came Jewish refugees from Russia and Poland, specializing in furs and leather, followed more recently by Bengali immigrants, who now toil in the same 18th-century buildings over sewing machines and steam irons, producing garments for sale in London's clothes shops and street markets. .....■

Jack the Ripper
In modern parlance, Jack the Ripper would be called a serial killer. His six victims were murdered over an eight-week period beginning on August 7, 1888, when the first horribly mutilated body was found by a Spitalfields Market porter in nearby Gunthorpe Street. The Jack the Ripper pub, near Christ Church on Commercial Street, has a window engraved with the full list of his victims. The police's failure to find the notorious murderer led to the resignation of the London Police Commissioner. The celebrated case stimulated the public's appetite for crime and detective stories, such as *The Adventures of Sherlock Holmes*, which Sir Arthur Conan Doyle began to pen in 1891.

The Spitalfields area begins at Liverpool Street Station, recently restored to its full Victorian splendor. Cross Bishopsgate to Artillery Lane, a narrow alley where No. 56 preserves a rare example of an 18th-century shop front. By turning left off Artillery Lane you will reach Brushfield Street, running along the south side of Spitalfields Market, where fruit, flowers, and vegetables were sold from the 1680s until 1991, when the market moved to Leyton, a suburb of East London.

The area is now earmarked as the "Covent Garden of the east," although there is still much work to be done on

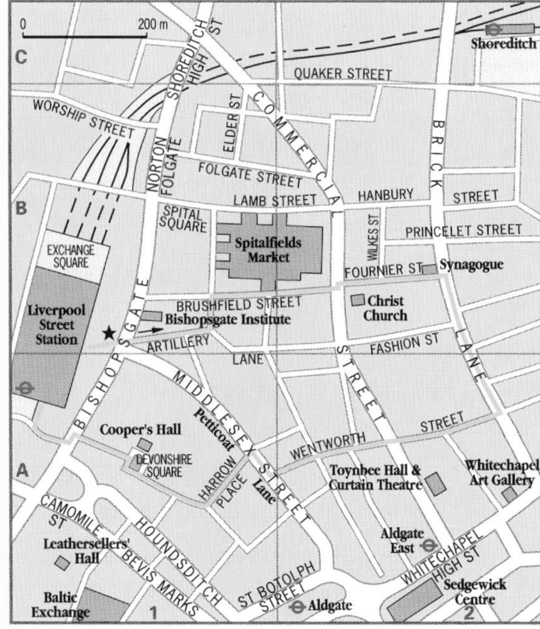

building and development. It currently houses a crafts market (open daily except Saturdays), a food market, and a Sunday market. Christ Church, towering above the eastern end of the market, may eventually become the focal point of the development. The huge church, built in 1714, is Nicholas Hawksmoor's masterpiece, and it provokes much debate among architectural historians because of its mixture of classical Renaissance and baroque elements. Long neglected, and even threatened with demolition, it is now used both as a church and as a concert hall. Some of the gravestones in the churchyard have epitaphs in French, marking the graves of Huguenot refugees who found a haven here after 1685 when the Edict of Nantes, which had guaranteed their right to religious freedom, was revoked. Some grew wealthy as master weavers in the manufacture of silks, damasks, and velvets. Their houses can be seen in Fournier Street, to the north of Christ Church. Built between 1718 and 1728, several have been restored by their owners with an almost exaggerated respect for authenticity, rescuing what were regarded as slum properties in the 1970s, faced with the threat of demolition.

Brick Lane, at the heart of a large community of Bangladeshis, Pakistanis, and Indians, is lined with shops selling exotic groceries, brightly printed fabrics, and saris, and the simple restaurants here serve some of the cheapest and most authentic curries to be found in London. At certain times of the week, this whole area of London seems like one huge street market. At the northern end of Brick Lane, stalls are set up at dawn on Sunday and further south and west, Commercial Street, Wentworth Street, and Middlesex Street are crammed with the stalls of Asian, Cockney, and Jewish traders at the weekend.

On the way back to Liverpool Street, it is worth seeking out Devonshire Square where, cheek by jowl with the bustling markets, is an office development sited within a group of warehouses dating from the late 18th century and originally built for the East India Company.

The New Georgians
The battle to save the Georgian houses of Spitalfields began in the late 1960s, when young Londoners took up residence in the buildings to save them from demolition. The Spitalfields Trust was then formed to buy run-down properties and make repairs before selling them on. New owners had to sign agreements to preserve their historic integrity. Some researched Georgian life in minute detail and attempted to live in 18th-century style, without electricity or modern plumbing. One such is Dennis Severs who, for a fee, gives candle-lit tours of his home, 18 Folgate Street (tel. 071 247 4013).

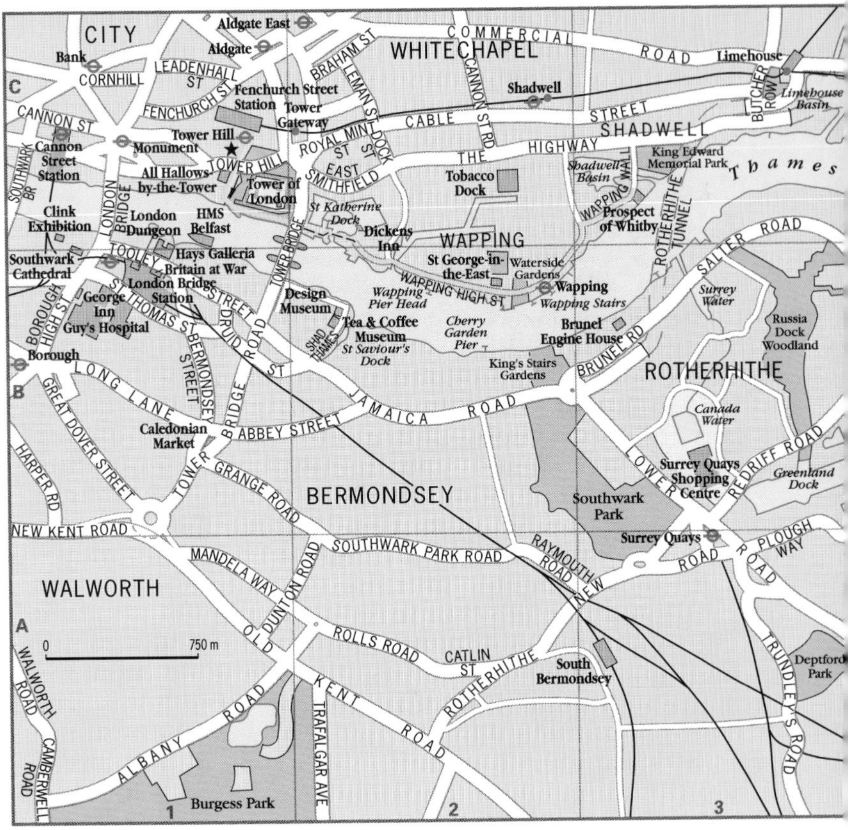

Docklands London's former docklands lie to the east of the City, covering a vast area, equal in size to the whole of central London. London's postwar decline as a port made great tracts of land available for development and, in the 1980s, Docklands was seen by some as a solution to inner-city decline. New apartments, offices, and leisure facilities would persuade people to live in London instead of commuting. The docks themselves represented the potential for marinas and water sports. In actuality, this transformation has proved much slower than was envisaged, and several developers have ended up bankrupt; there has also been fierce opposition to the policy as a whole. Nevertheless, the area is fascinating, with converted warehouses and historic buildings juxtaposed with post-modernist buildings.

Docklands walk This walk takes in old Docklands, as well as the revamped and the brand-new.

From Tower Hill tube station exit to your left towards Tower Gateway DLR station. Turn right to face Tower Bridge. Just before the bridge, steps lead down to the Tower Thistle Hotel. Beyond the hotel is **St. Katharine Dock**, first opened in 1825 and closed down in 1968. The warehouses were then converted to conference rooms, shops, and luxury apartments. Modern yachts and historic craft are moored in the three boat basins. The

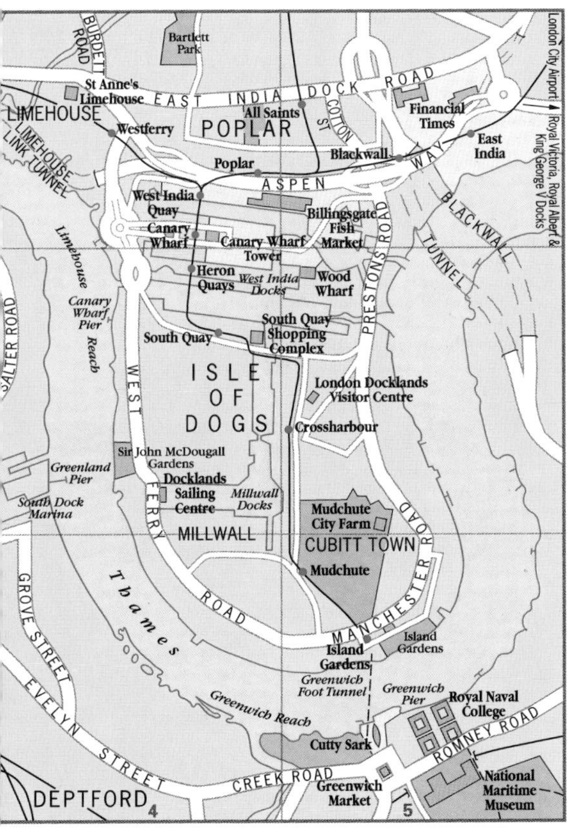

Dickens Inn, converted from an 18th-century brewery, stands alongside the Central Basin in an atmospheric old warehouse.

St. Katharine's Way leads south from the Dock, providing a link to Wapping High Street. This stretch of the route is lined with warehouses built to store tropical spices and valuable hardwoods. Now they have been made into expensive apartments, although prices have fallen since the 1980s, when a Docklands flat was the ultimate "yuppie" possession. Further on, **Wapping Pierhead** is lined with Georgian houses, once the homes of wealthy wharfowners. Beyond this, **Waterside Gardens** has views towards Hawksmoor's baroque church, **St. George-in-the-East**. Continue down Wapping High Street, past the Wapping tube station, and turn right into Wapping Wall for the **Prospect of Whitby** pub, once a haunt of Samuel Pepys and artists such as Turner and Whistler, who came to paint the river views.

The Docklands Light Railway runs from Tower Gateway Station (across from Tower Hill tube station) down to Island Gardens Station, at the tip of the Isle of Dogs. There are 15 trains an hour, and the system is driven by computers (no drivers!). The elevated railway passes through the heart of the docklands. From Island Gardens you can walk under the Thames through the Greenwich Foot Tunnel to Greenwich village (see page 217).

Tug in retirement

Shipyards and opium dens Limehouse was one of London's main shipbuilding centers in the 18th and 19th centuries. In the 1890s, Chinese sailors from Hong Kong and Canton also set up London's first Chinatown here, notorious for its opium dens and gambling parlors. Names such as Canton Street, Pekin Street, and Nankin Street, all to the north of East India Dock Road, are a reminder of that time, and there is still a sizeable Chinese population, as well as one of London's best and most authentic Chinese restaurants (The Good Friends at 139 Salmon Lane). Nearby, at the junction of Commercial, East India, and West India Dock Roads, stands the baroque church of St. Anne's Limehouse, built by Nicholas Hawksmoor in 1712–30. Somewhat forlorn, with its graffiti-scarred walls, the church is often locked because of repeated vandalism—such an important architectural monument deserves better.

► Canary Wharf *189C4*

Docklands Light Railway: Canary Wharf station

Canary Wharf is a staggering monument to the optimism of the 1980s, when there seemed to be no end to the demand for new office space, equipped with all the latest high-tech systems for computers and telecommunications networks. Existing buildings in the City of London were difficult to remodel into the huge open spaces demanded by modern financial trading companies, so developers looked east, to Docklands, a huge green site where zoning laws were deliberately relaxed to encourage ambitious building projects. Canary Wharf certainly was ambitious. The developers, Olympia & York, spent £1.7 billion in constructing a self-contained minicity covering 28 hectares, with over 3 million square feet of office space—enough to present a serious challenge to City landlords, who feared that older buildings in the "square mile" would be left empty as financial institutions migrated east. Canary Wharf was to have had four floors of shops, two hotels, exhibition and conference centers, swimming pools, tennis courts and gyms, and the principal buildings were to be lined by a series of plazas complete with statues, gardens, fountains, waterside walks, and historic ships moored in the adjacent West India Docks basin. Transportion was to be provided by extending the Jubilee tube line into Docklands. The whole project foundered in 1992 when the developers went into liquidation but not before the huge 805 ft. central tower had been completed.

This massive structure dominates the east and south London skyline; some people love its bold, thrusting outline, while others dismiss it as a giant stubby pencil. Most of the building is empty, although various potential tenants have expressed an interest, including government departments. Parts of it were open to the public until the discovery of an IRA-planted bomb was discovered inside; since then it has been closed.

► HMS *Belfast* 188C1

Morgan's Lane, Tooley Street
Underground: London Bridge
HMS *Belfast* is one of the largest warships ever built for the British Navy. Saved from the scrapyard in 1971, the ship is now moored on the Thames and run as an outpost of the Imperial War Museum. She was built in the Belfast shipyards of Harland and Wolff and launched by Mrs. Neville Chamberlain, wife of the then Prime Minister, just before World War II. On November 21,1939, just after going into service with her 850-man crew, the ship was almost destroyed by a German magnetic mine and had to be substantially rebuilt. She then played an important part in the D-Day landings of June 1944, as one of the ship's several small exhibitions reveals. Other exhibits include a collection of 60 paintings by the war artist John Hamilton.

► Limehouse 189C4

Docklands Light Railway: Limehouse station
Limehouse still retains its original historic character, and for that reason it was one of the first parts of the Docklands to be colonized in the 1980s, when apartments in converted warehouses were the height of fashion. The most attractive buildings are found in Narrow Street, where the locks at Limehouse Basin link a branch of the Grand Union Canal with the Thames. The Grapes pub, at No. 76 Narrow Street, was immortalized by Dickens in *Our Mutual Friend;* its restaurant is renowned for fresh fish.

Canary Wharf, a monument to market optimism

Rotherhithe
The docklands on the southern side of the Thames, across from Limehouse, have none of the glamour and cachet associated with the redeveloped areas of Wapping or the Isle of Dogs, but they have seen their fair share of history. You can get to Rotherhithe by train from Wapping station, passing beneath the river in a tunnel that was first opened in 1843 as a footpath to enable dockers living on the south bank to walk to their places of work in the north. The engineer was Marc Brunel (father of Isambard Kingdom). The Brunel Engine House, a short walk north of Rotherhithe station on Tunnel Road, was built to pump water out of the tunnel during its construction. Now it is a small museum of local history (open Sundays 11– 3, June to September).
Immediately to the west is the historic Mayflower pub (117 Rotherhithe Street). It stands close to the site from which the Pilgrim Fathers set sail in the *Mayflower* bound for Plymouth, Massachusetts, in 1620. The pub has a restaurant and is licensed to sell American postage stamps for the benefit of the many U.S. visitors who come here. The captain of the *Mayflower*, Captain Jones, is buried in the nearby church of St. Mary the Virgin, which has several other fine monuments to local merchants, shipbuilders, and sailors.

London Bridge City

■ London Bridge City is the rather unimaginative name dreamed up by marketing consultants for the redeveloped waterfront on the south bank of the Thames, stretching from London Bridge eastwards to Tower Bridge and beyond, into Shad Thames. Londoners are more familiar with the district's old name of Bermondsey, but since this was (and remains in parts) a very poor area of the East End, a new name was chosen that did not have quite the same humble connotations. .....■

New Caledonian Market
Something of the shadowy world of Dickensian London lives on in the New Caledonian Market (confusingly, this is also known as the Bermondsey Antiques Market—it is located at the junction of Long Lane, Bermondsey Street, and Tower Bridge Road). The market, which claims to be the biggest of its kind in Europe, opens to the public at 7a.m. every Friday, but long before the ordinary buyers arrive, a huge amount of trading will already have taken place between the stallholders themselves and the professional dealers who swoop at the crack of dawn to snap up the prize pieces. Everyone involved in the market denies that this is where thieves and burglars dispose of their stolen goods, but the suspicion lingers. This should not stop anyone interested in antiques and bric-à-brac from visiting, if only to savor the atmosphere and see the vast array of *objets d'art* on sale. The terms are strictly cash and persistent haggling is essential if you do not want to pay an exaggerated price. By 11a.m. most of the serious business wil be over for the day.

The more modern buildings in the London Bridge City development consist of dull towers of glass and are best ignored. In between, however, there are some excellent examples of warehouse conversion.

Starting at London Bridge (see map on pages 188–9) and following the riverside path, called St. Martin's Walk, you will come to Hay's Galleria, one of London's newest and most stylish shopping centers. The original Hay's Wharf has been filled in to create a courtyard for sidewalk cafes and gift stalls, sheltered from the elements by a glass atrium supported on iron columns. The blend of old and new works extremely well. Passing through the Galleria to Tooley Street you will find the Art Deco façade of St. Olaf's House, built in 1931 as the Hay's Wharf Company Offices by the architect H. S. Goodhart-Rendel. This extraordinary building, covered in jazzy stripes, has been superbly restored and looks exotic among the dark alleys and utilitarian architecture of the surrounding warehouses.

Tooley Street leads westward through a wasteland of industrial buildings awaiting redevelopment. On the opposite side of Tower Bridge along the riverbank, at Shad Thames, warehouse walls rise sheer as cliffs, linked, high above, by a network of metal gangway bridges; this is where the brutal Bill Sikes meets his end, falling from the gangways at the end of Dickens's *Oliver Twist.* Despite the dark and gloomy alleys, and the all-pervading smell of

Hay's Galleria

cloves and other spices once stored in these warehouses, the apartments they now contain are highly prized because of their proximity to the City.

An award-winning development lies just beyond, in St. Saviour's Dock. Here, in converting New Concordia Wharf to apartments and workshops, the developer, Andrew Wadsworth, retained as much of the original character and appearance as possible, including the wall cranes that once lifted goods out of the wharf basin and in through the great brick openings in the façade. Plans are afoot to allow cruise ships to moor near here in the future, thereby restoring the link between these buildings and the river.

Right on the bend, where Shad Thames curves round St. Saviour's Dock, is the new Design Museum, brainchild of Sir Terence Conran, style guru and founder of the Habitat chain, whose furnishings were all the rage in the 1960s and 1970s. The museum (closed Monday) started life in 1981 at the Victoria and Albert Museum and subsequently moved to its present site, a converted 1950s warehouse. The core of the museum consists of some 400 or so everyday objects, from typewriters and kettles to motor cars, selected as classics of modern design and permanently displayed as a study collection. This is augmented by temporary exhibitions that address themes such as Scandinavian design or look at new products and inventions, often chosen to be deliberately provocative. The museum has a very good bookshop and reference library, and the Blueprint Cafe serves excellent food.

Sculptural fantasy on the theme of the sea in Hay's Galleria

Bermondsey old and new
Plans to rejuvenate the Bermondsey embankment of the Thames, from Tower Bridge eastwards, include an effort to create an uninterrupted riverside walkway all the way to Cherry Garden Pier. This pier is traditionally the point at which ships passing upstream would sound their horns if they needed the central span of Tower Bridge lifted to let them pass through. Near the pier is one of the area's best-kept secrets, the Angel pub (101 Bermondsey Wall East), a 15th-century inn with a balcony built out on timber piles enjoying views of the City and the river. Past customers included Samuel Pepys and Captain Cook, while prints on the walls recall the appearance of old Bermondsey. The pub was once a notorious haunt of smugglers and thieves—before the River Police were founded to patrol the river in 1769, it is estimated that nearly half of all the cargo landed on these shores simply disappeared; many port workers and stevedores were involved in the racket.

▶▶ London Dungeon 188B1

34 Tooley Street
Underground: London Bridge
Horrific sights that would send a chill up the spines of most sensitive adults seem to have the opposite effect on children, as you will discover if your offspring demand to be taken to the gruesome London Dungeon. They will shriek with delight at the realistic portrayals of executions and torture, while adults squirm uncomfortably. The most appalling feature of this hugely successful attraction is that nearly every display is based on reality—the working models of instruments of torture, the painful scenes of martyrdom (particularly St. George), of hanging, flogging, boiling alive, burning at the stake, and disemboweling simply reflect the extraordinarily cruel punishments that human beings have devised and inflicted upon each other. Perhaps children can derive pleasure from the spectacle because they know (or think they know) "it is not real," whereas adults know only too well that it is.

One of the less grisly displays in the London Dungeon

▶ St. Katharine Dock 188C2

St. Katharine's Way
Underground: Tower Hill
St. Katharine Dock was built in 1824–28 by Thomas Telford and is the closest of all London's docks to the City of London, nestling up against the Tower of London. This proximity to the financial center made the dock a prime target for redevelopment when it became redundant in 1968, and the 19th-century warehouses have been converted to luxury flats for boat lovers, whose yachts are moored in one of the two main basins. Mingled in among them are historic vessels, including Thames sailing barges that are available to rent (with crew) and the lightship *Norse*, which once operated in the Thames estuary. The dock is a peaceful spot, popular for pub food served at the Dickens Inn, artfully restored from an 18th-century timber-framed brewery that was discovered incorporated into a warehouse of later date.

► Southwark Cathedral *188B1*

Borough High Street
Underground: London Bridge
Poor little Southwark Cathedral is so hemmed in by railway viaducts and thundering traffic that few people know it is there. The building is small for a cathedral, having only been elevated to this status in 1905. Before that it was called St. Mary Overie (a corruption of St. Mary Over the Water, so called because of its position on the south bank of the Thames). It therefore has little grandeur, but it does host an excellent series of lunchtime concerts (1:10p.m., featuring organ music on Mondays, classical recitals on Tuesdays, and jazz on Thursdays). It is also very rich in monuments, and some have, controversially, been painted and gilded to gaudy splendor in recent years. One of them commemorates John Harvard, who emigrated to Massachusetts in 1637 and died there within a year, leaving his wealth and his library for the founding of Harvard University. Shakespeare is also buried here—not William, but his younger brother Edmund. John Gower, the poet and friend of Chaucer, has a splendidly painted effigy, as has the great Jacobean preacher, Lancelot Andrewes, whose life was celebrated in T. S. Eliot's essay *For Lancelot Andrewes*. The best monument, in the north transept, is to one Joyce Austin; carved by Nicholas Stone in 1633, it uses the harvest as a metaphor for death—flanking the central figure are two girls sleeping in straw hats and flowing robes after a hard day's toil in the fields.

Historic vessels moored in the St. Katharine Dock

John Gower's tomb

The inns of Southwark
Talbot Yard, on Borough High Street, a short way south of Southwark Cathedral, marks the spot where the Tabard Inn once stood. This actual inn was immortalized in the 14th century by Geoffrey Chaucer in *The Canterbury Tales*, for it was here that the poet set out in the company of "nyne and twenty...sondry folk" on a pilgrimage to Canterbury. The Tabard Inn did exist in the 14th century when Chaucer wrote his tales of medieval life, one of a cluster of inns positioned at the main entry point to London from the south. Another nearby inn was the White Hart, mentioned by Shakespeare in *Henry VI* and by Dickens in the *The Pickwick Papers*. Another was the Queen's Head, which John Harvard sold in 1637 to emigrate to Massachusetts; when he died in 1638 he bequeathed half the proceeds from its sale to found Harvard University. Only one of Southwark's coaching inns has survived in its original form: the George Inn (1677), which has a galleried courtyard (see page 174).

Tower traditions
The Tower has many ancient traditions. One is the nightly Ceremony of the Keys, when the Chief Yeoman Warder locks the main gates of the Tower at 10p.m., after which a bugler sounds the Last Post. This ceremony has scarcely changed in 700 years, except that it now takes place under floodlight with an audience (book well in advance with The Resident Governor and Keeper of the Jewel House, Queen's House, H. M. Tower of London, EC3, enclosing a stamped addressed envelope). Six ravens live in the gardens; legend has it that the Tower will collapse if they fly away. Their wings are clipped, but they are well cared for by the Yeoman Ravenmaster. On May 21 members of Eton College and King's College Cambridge put white roses and lilies in Wakefield Tower in memory of Henry VI, who founded the institutions, and who was murdered here in 1471.

▶▶ Tower Bridge *188B1*

Underground: Tower Hill

Tower Bridge is a fanciful structure designed in Gothic style to complement its neighbor, the Tower of London. It was opened with great ceremony in 1894, and the only major change since then has been the installment of electrical motors in 1976 to lift the two massive central spans of the drawbridge so that ships can pass through. From the north tower elevators carry visitors up to the footbridge that links the two towers high above the river. The footbridge was built so that pedestrians could continue to use the bridge while the drawbridge was raised below. Now glassed in because of its reputation as a suicide spot, it offers sweeping views over London. The south tower leads to the main part of the museum, where you can see the steam-driven hydraulics of the Victorian era along with working models and videos showing how the lifting mechanism works.

▶▶▶ Tower of London *188C1*

Tower Hill

Underground: Tower Hill

The Tower of London can be one of the most crowded spots in London from Easter to October, so be prepared to get there early (it opens at 9:30a.m.). The appeal of the Tower is its long and bloody history; many famous and beautiful heads were parted from their pampered bodies in the confines of the castle. Henry VIII's second and fifth wives, Anne Boleyn and Catherine Howard, and Lady Jane Grey, who was proclaimed Queen of England in 1553 but deposed after nine days, were all executed

The style of Tower Bridge echoes that of the Tower of London

here, while Sir Thomas More and Sir Walter Ralegh were held here as prisoners before their journeys to the scaffold. Prisoners were brought in and out of the Tower by boat through the Traitor's Gate, still a watergate in the outer wall of the Tower, visible from the embankment. Many brutal deeds were done in this elegant prison, so it is no surprise that the Tower is the most haunted building in London: The headless body of Anne Boleyn has been seen gliding across Tower Green, and Sir Walter Ralegh's ghost supposedly walks the ramparts on moonlit nights.

Of course, the Tower was not just a place of torture and execution: It also served as a royal palace. William the Conqueror began its construction in 1078, building the central keep, known as the White Tower because it was whitewashed during the reign of Henry III (1216–72). Henry kept his menagerie here, including three leopards, given to him by the Holy Roman Emperor, and a polar bear, the gift of the King of Norway. The White Tower now houses a museum of arms and armor (although there are plans to reorganize the displays and possibly move the armor to a new museum). Here a series of armored suits made for Henry VIII reveal his evolution from slim youth to massive middle age. Although dark deeds had already been committed in the tower (the "Little Princes," Edward V, and his brother Richard were murdered in the Bloody Tower, possibly by their uncle, Richard III, in 1483) it was under Henry VIII that the pace of execution really stepped up. The site of the block was on Tower Green, in front of the Chapel of St. Peter ad Vincula, whose floor was raised in 1870 to reveal a pile of beheaded skeletons, including those of Henry VIII's discarded wives, Anne Boleyn and Catherine Howard.

The Crown Jewels are kept in the 19th-century Waterloo Barracks, beside the chapel. Most of the jewels date from the period after 1660; earlier regalia were melted down after Charles I's execution in 1649. Queen Victoria's Imperial State Crown has many famous jewels, but none so well known as the Koh-i-Noor (Mountain of Light) diamond on the Queen Mother's crown.

The 42 Yeoman Warders (nicknamed "Beefeaters" either because they once attended the king's table as "buffetiers" or because of the meat allowance they received from the Crown) have looked after the tower since their appointment by Henry VII in 1485. Dressed in Tudor-style uniforms, they conduct tours and are a mine of information about the Tower's history.

Beefeaters have been guarding the Tower since 1485

All-Hallows-by-the-Tower
The church that stands a short way west of the Tower, on busy Byward Street, is one of the oldest and most interesting in London. Its undercroft contains a small museum tracing the church's history from its foundation in the 7th century, along with a Roman floor. Pepys watched the Great Fire of London from the tower of this church in 1666. A more benign flame is maintained in the sanctuary used by Toc H, the movement founded by Tubby Clayton to foster the same spirit of Christian comradeship that he encountered in the trenches during World War I. Priests from this church have traditionally tended prisoners condemned to death in the Tower. Today, choirboys from the church join with Beefeaters to perform the ancient Beating of the Bounds ceremony every third year on Ascension Day. Originally it was the boys who were beaten at parish boundaries, to ensure that they never forgot where they were. Today the boys beat the 31 boundary markers with willow rods, urged on by the Chief Warder of the Tower with shouts of "Whack it boys, whack it!"

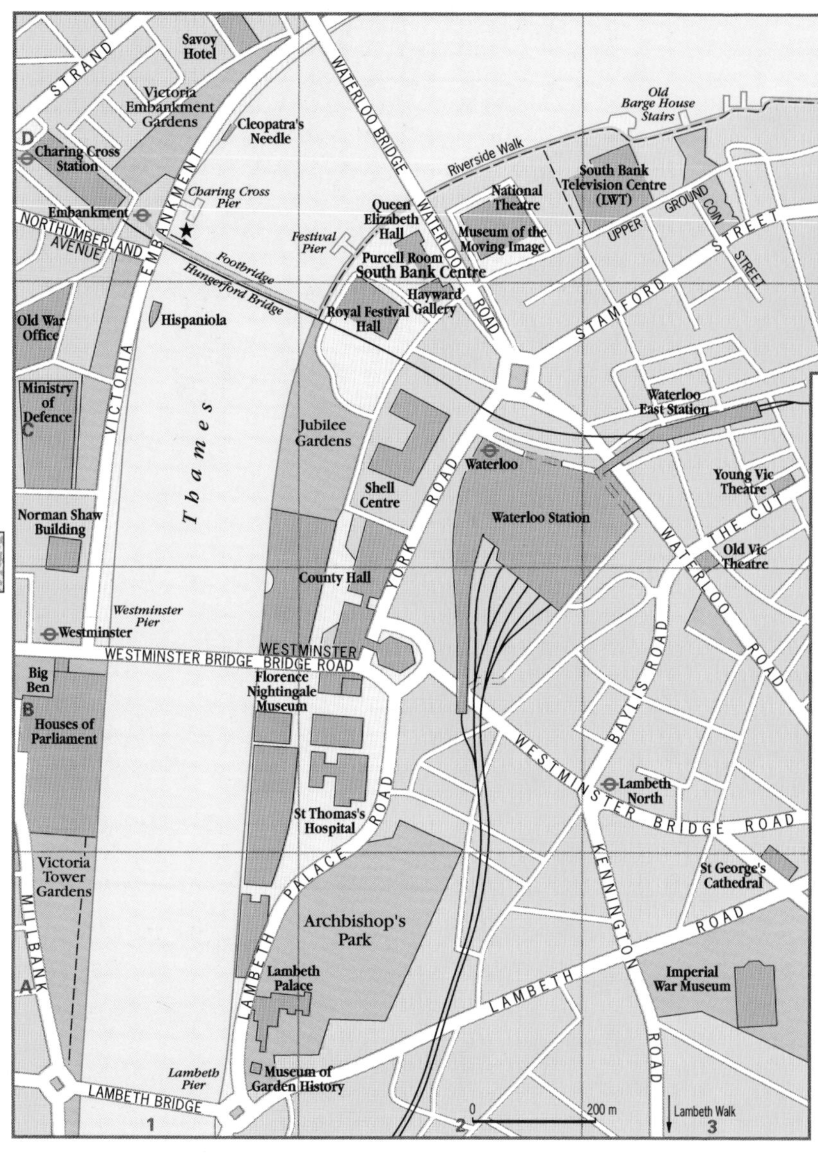

Bankside London's south bank has a long association with the theater. Theaters, bearpits, and brothels were banned from the City because authorities felt that apprentices spent too much time playgoing, so the actors moved to the south bank, out of the City's jurisdiction. Today, several developments are taking place in the area: In due course, it should be possible to stroll along the riverside, from Westminster Bridge to London Bridge, along a traffic-free boulevard, past theaters, restaurants and shops.

Bankside walk From Charing Cross or Embankment tube stations, on the north side of the river, an elevated walkway leads across Hungerford Bridge, with good views of

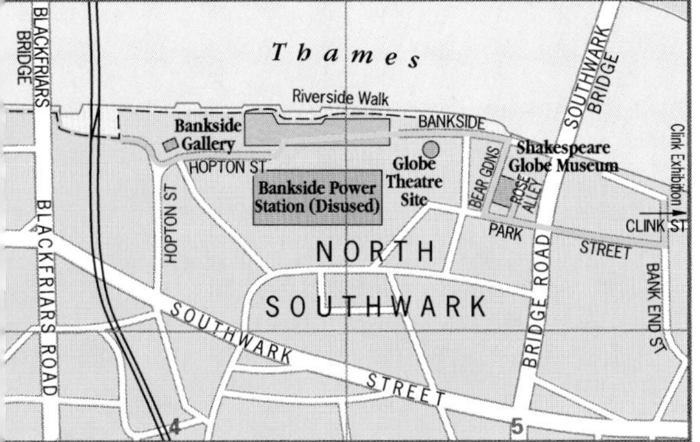

Somerset House and the City beyond. Steps descend from the bridge on the south bank to pass in front of the **Royal Festival Hall** and the **South Bank complex** (see pages 204–5). Here you will find street musicians, exhibitions, and a crafts market or you can slip into the Festival Hall for free foyer exhibitions and musical recitals.

The Riverside Walk continues under Waterloo Bridge, past the **National Theatre**, the **Museum of the Moving Image** (see pages 202–3), and the headquarters of **London Weekend Television**. It then runs under Blackfriars Bridge to join Hopton Street. The **Bankside Gallery**, on Hopton Street, shows watercolors, prints, and engravings by living artists. Further along, the walk passes the disused **Bankside Power Station**, which might be converted to an opera house. Next comes Bankside, where a replica of Shakespeare's **Globe Theatre**, originally erected in 1599, is being built by the American actor and entrepreneur Sam Wannamaker.

Bear Gardens leads off Bankside on the right. Here the **Shakespeare Globe Museum**, housed in a 19th-century warehouse, uses models to explain the history of Elizabethan and Jacobean theater. In the adjacent Rose Alley, the foundations of the **Rose Theatre** of 1587, which once hosted the plays of Shakespeare and Marlowe, were discovered in 1989. Its remains will be preserved in a gallery beneath a new office development.

Walk down Park Street, on the eastern side of Southwark Bridge Road, where Shakespeare's original Globe Theatre stood. Turn left in Bank End. Here you will find a recently restored pub dating back to the 15th century, the **Anchor Inn**. Its rambling rooms are decorated with a model of the Globe Theatre and other interesting memorabilia.

Set midway between Southwark and London Bridges, **Clink Street** was the site of a notorious prison, used from the 16th century on to detain heretics, and later thieves, vagabonds, and ruffians. The name is said to derive from the "clinch" irons that were used to pin prisoners to the wall or floor, and "the clink" has become a slang term for any prison. The Clink Exhibition, near by, reveals the gruesome nature of prison life. Close to it is the **Southwark Heritage Association's Visitor Centre** (closed Saturday) and a three-masted schooner, the *Kathleen & May*, which is moored in the St. Mary Overie Dock and maintained by the Maritime Trust.

Bedlam
The building that houses the Imperial War Museum was originally built to house the Bethlehem Royal Hospital, an asylum for the mentally ill, popularly known as Bedlam. The original hospital was founded in 1247 as the Priory of St. Mary Bethlehem, situated outside Bishopsgate. In the 17th century it moved to Moorfields and became a popular tourist attraction. Visitors were allowed in to watch the patients, who were placed in caged cells like animals in a zoo (the last of the paintings in the *Rake's Progress*, by Hogarth, depicts the scene—see page 155). The cruelty of such treatment was not appreciated until the late 18th century; the fact that George III suffered mental illness helped to bring about a more humane attitude. The asylum moved to this site in Lambeth in 1816 as part of an overall reform of the treatment of patients with serious pyschiatric problems. Criminal patients were then moved from here to Broadmoor in 1864, and in 1930 the remaining patients were moved to new premises in Surrey.

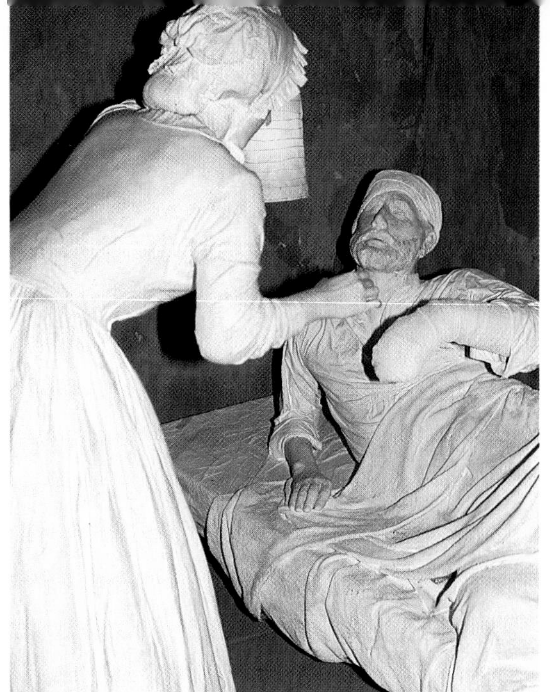

Florence Nightingale tends the wounded of Crimea

▶ Florence Nightingale Museum *198B2*

St. Thomas's Hospital, 2 Lambeth Palace Road
Underground: Westminster
St. Thomas's Hospital, founded in Southwark in 1213, moved to this site, directly across the river from the Houses of Parliament, in 1868. The move was partly inspired by reforms in the hospital design recommended by Florence Nightingale. She set up the first school of nursing at St. Thomas's and this museum traces the story of her life using audio visuals and a series of realistic reconstructions. One re-creates the barrack hospital at Scutari, in the Crimea, where Florence radically improved the conditions and standards of nursing care given to wounded soldiers. Another shows a typical Victorian slum cottage, as a reminder of the work she did in her later life in improving the lot of the poor in Liverpool and London's East End. Her famous lamp is on display; it earned her the nickname "the Lady with the Lamp," from grateful patients under her care in the Crimea—though her official title during that war was "the Lady-in-chief.".After meeting Florence in 1856, Queen Victoria is reported to have said "I wish we had her at the War Office!" Closed Monday.

▶▶▶ Imperial War Museum *198A3*

Lambeth Road
Underground: Lambeth North
Despite the title, suggestive of gung ho jingoism and militaristic pride, this is an enjoyable and thought-provoking museum. Some of the most recent displays, including *The Blitz Experience*, are immensely popular.

Several displays in the basement break away from dull historic narrative and take a thematic look at the horrors of

Machines of war

the two World Wars. They bring home what it actually felt like to live through the war from many different points of view: *The Blitz Experience*, for example, consists of a street scene littered with the rubble of collapsed and burned-out buildings, complete with the acrid smells of charred wood and the sound of air-raid sirens. The displays also cover war as experienced by concentration camp victims living under Nazi tyranny, RAF pilots (using flight simulators to convey the feel of a bombing raid), and members of the armed services fighting on various fronts, in Europe, Africa, and the Far East. Excellent use is made of audio visuals and documentary film footage, and the human side of war is also conveyed through the recorded words of war poets and the vivid pictures and sculptures of artists as diverse as David Bomberg, Carel Weight, Henry Moore, and John Piper.

On the ground floor the mechanical and technical aspects of war in the 20th century are explored, with huge exhibits of military hardware: tanks from Britain, America, and Russia; early submarines and aircraft, and missiles such as the German V2 rocket. The more insidious weapons of germ and chemical warfare are represented by John Singer Sargent's large and nightmarish picture of 1918–19, simply entitled *Gassed*.

Aerial warfare is the theme of the second floor gallery, which also includes a selection of weapons captured from the Argentinian forces during the Falklands Campaign of 1982.

The top floor is devoted to works of art by official war artists, including some of the most important painters and sculptors of our time. The theme of war and the re-creation of a brave new postwar world are conveyed in the fractured works of Wyndham Lewis, studies of the Clyde shipbuilding yards by Stanley Spencer, and by Sir Jacob Epstein's forceful head of Sir Winston Churchill.

Doing the Lambeth Walk
To the west of the Imperial War Museum, south of Lambeth Road, is the Lambeth Walk, a name immortalized by a popular song from the musical *Me and My Gal*, first performed in 1937 and recently revived in a hugely successful West End production. It was here that Cockneys would come for a Sunday afternoon stroll, a tradition that dates back to the 17th century when a spa, the Lambeth Wells, was opened, with a Great Room for music and dancing. There were several other popular diversions and pleasure gardens in the vicinity, including the famous Vauxhall Gardens, just south of the Lambeth Walk. Laid out just after 1660 with tree-lined avenues and arbors, and lit by lamps at night, the Vauxhall Gardens featured in countless novels, poems, and diaries as a fashionable gathering place with sideshows, foodstalls, dancing, and fancy-dress gala balls—a place of pleasure and of vice, for drinking, gambling, and prostitution were rife. The gardens finally closed down in 1859.

The Imperial War Museum

The Peddler's Window
A stained-glass window in the south chapel of St. Mary at Lambeth Church depicts a peddler and his dog and is inscribed with the prayer: "May God prosper the land as he hath prospered me." Designed by Francis Stephens, the window commemorates an impoverished 16th-century peddler who took shelter with his dog in the porch of the church one dark and stormy night. Many years later the peddler died a very rich merchant, and he remembered the church in his will, bequeathing an acre of land that he owned not far away to the parish on condition that they commemorate him and his dog in a window. Eventually that land was sold to the London County Council and on the site they built themselves a splendid new civic palace, the County Hall. This was the headquarters of London's local authority, a powerful elected body responsible for running everything in the city from public transport to education, until 1986, when the government decided to abolish the council. County Hall is now to be converted into a luxury hotel.

▶ Museum of Garden History *198A1*

St. Mary at Lambeth Church, Lambeth Palace Road
Underground: Lambeth North
John Tradescant is a name familiar to most plant lovers, if only because the Tradescantia (commonly called the spiderwort) genus was named in his honor. This was just one of the many plant families that this intrepid botanist introduced as a result of expeditions to America, Africa, and the Mediterranean. His aim was to seek out novelties for the aristocratic gardens that he managed, including those of Charles I, and he is credited with introducing the apricot, the Virginia creeper, the larch, the jasmine, the lilac, and many new varieties of bulb to Britain's shores. He was buried in 1638 in the graveyard of this church in Lambeth; when the church was closed down in 1977 a group of devoted horticulturalists set up the Tradescant Trust to convert it into a museum concerned with all aspects of garden history. The body of the church is used for temporary exhibitions, always interesting, featuring everything from botanical paintings to displays of antique gardening tools. Tradescant's son, also named John, followed in his father's footsteps and a stained-glass window, specially commissioned in 1981, shows them both alongside Adam and Eve in the Garden of Eden. The churchyard is a place of peaceful retreat, full of plants and flowers that the Tradescants brought to Britain from overseas. The tomb of John Tradescant the Elder is decorated with reliefs illustrating the dangers he encountered on his travels, including a crocodile and a multi-headed hydra. Nearby is the tomb of William Bligh, Captain of the *Bounty*, who was also a plant hunter; it was during his expedition to Tahiti to collect breadfruit in 1787 that the famous mutiny occurred.

Open daily except Saturday; closed from mid-December to early March.

▶▶▶ Museum of the Moving Image *198D2*

South Bank
Underground: Waterloo or Embankment
The Museum of the Moving Image (known as MOMI) is a must for everyone who loves film and television, and it's one of the best museums in London for keeping children entertained, especially on rainy days. It's full of hands-on exhibits, and the emphasis is firmly on participation. The staffers, who act as guides, are trained actors. Some dress as famous movie and TV stars, such as Charlie Chaplin, and bring the story of the silver screen to life through mime, narrative, and improvised theatricals. Others will put you through your paces as you audition for a place in the chorus of a Hollywood musical, help to make an animated cartoon, read the news on television, or star as the guest interviewee on a TV show.

If you don't like the sight of yourself on a TV monitor, you can always just wander among the maze of exhibits that cover the history of the moving image right back to the distant past of Javanese shadow theater, as popular 4,000 years ago as today. Wallow in nostalgia as you look at stills and clips from films and TV programs. The technical side of the subject is revealed through displays ranging from early cameras to modern satellite and micro-

Strange encounters await at MOMI

wave communications. Ethical issues are covered in sections devoted to censorship, the challenges involved in making objective documentary programmes, the contribution of the avant-garde or German Expressionism to modern cinematic ideas. Other displays look at the films of Hitchcock and Eisenstein, the Hollywood Dream Factory, and film-making in wartime. Most displays are enlivened by monitors that show newsreels, popular programs, commercials, and classic film clips. Other films are shown in the museum's own big-screen cinema, where the doorman and usherette, dressed in the costumes of the cinema's heyday, swap famous quips that were first heard on the lips of Mae West and Humphrey Bogart.

Closed Monday.

Film company symbol

Screen idol

Lambeth Palace
Right next door to the Museum of Garden History is Lambeth Palace, the official residence of the head of the Church of England, the Archbishop of Canterbury. It has been the archbishop's home since 1190, but the main building visible to the public—the brick gatehouse—was built in 1501. Frequently the palace has been at the center of stormy events. In 1534 Thomas More found himself facing a tribunal in the guard room; despite persuasion he refused to sign the Oath of Supremacy recognizing Henry VIII, rather than the Pope, as the head of the English church. For this he was hauled off to the Tower and from there to his execution for treason in 1535. From 1867 until recently the palace regularly hosted the Lambeth Conference, a meeting of all the bishops of the worldwide Anglican church, but the location has now moved as the palace is too small. Mrs. Rosalind Runcie, wife of former Archbishop Robert Runcie, transformed the palace gardens during the 1980s, and you can get a glimpse of her work by joining a guided tour (these are very popular and must be reserved in advance by writing to The Bursar, Lambeth Palace, London SE1).

Around Waterloo
Waterloo Bridge, named after the battlefield where Wellington defeated Napoleon, was opened on June 18, 1817. Described by the sculptor Canova as "the noblest bridge in the world," it suffered from structural defects and was demolished in 1936 to be replaced by today's rather dull structure (from which there are excellent river views). Waterloo Station, at the southern end of the bridge, was designed to be temporary, but the planned extension, taking trains across the river to the City, was never built. Instead an underground rail link, the Waterloo and City Line, was built in 1898 to link up with Bank Station. This still operates at peak rush hours and is known to commuters as "the Drain." The area south of Waterloo Bridge is now nicknamed Cardboard City because of the large number of homeless people who use the railway arches and pedestrian underpasses for shelter, building ramshackle structures from old boxes and junk. Immediately behind the station is the Old Vic, one of London's best-loved theaters. It was rescued from closing in the 1980s by the Canadian entrepreneur, Ed Mirvish, and has since been restored.

▶ Shakespeare Globe Museum 199D5

1 Bear Gardens, Bankside
Underground: London Bridge
In Shakespeare's time, playgoing was frowned upon by the City authorities because it encouraged apprentices to play hookey. In 1574 theaters were banned from the City, but the actors simply moved across the river, building playhouses such as the Rose (1587), the Swan (1596), the Globe (1599), the Hope (1613), and the Cockpit (1616).

The Shakespeare Globe Museum, set in a 19th-century warehouse, is at the heart of this once bustling theater district. It traces the area's history through maps, engravings, models, and displays. There is also a re-creation of the 1683 Frost Fair, held when the River Thames froze sufficiently to allow booths and stalls to be set up. Several such fairs took place between 1564 and 1814, though now the Thames flows too fast to freeze, as a result of the narrowing and deepening of the river channel. Shakespeare's original Globe Theatre stood a short distance from today's museum, on the corner of Southwark Bridge Road and Park Street. It was burned down in 1613 after two cannons, fired during a performance of *Henry VIII*, set the thatch alight. A new theater was built in 1614 but was demolished by the Puritans in 1642.

A third Globe Theatre is being built on Bankside by the Shakespeare Globe Trust, headed by Sam Wannamaker. Traditional timber construction methods are being used and the theater will stage works by Shakespeare in the style of his time. For information tel. 071 620 0202.

▶▶ South Bank Centre 198D2

Underground: Waterloo or Embankment
Grouped along the Thames embankment, on either side of Waterloo Bridge, are the buildings of London's most important arts complex. Apart from the concerts, plays, and exhibitions held in the main buildings, the traffic-free riverside terraces and lobby spaces are used for free exhibitions, street markets, and pass-the-hat musical performances.

The world of William Shakespeare

Bold but brutal—the South Bank arts complex

The first building on this site was the Royal Festival Hall, the centerpiece of the 1951 Festival of Britain, designed to cheer the nation after the years of rationing and austerity that followed World War II. The building itself is somber, but the acoustics are excellent, and the hall is often used for big choral works. Alongside are the Queen Elizabeth Hall and Purcell Room, both used for smaller concerts, and the Hayward Gallery, which stages major art exhibitions. These windowless buildings of weather-stained concrete were built in the Brutalist style of the 1960s, as was the Royal National Theatre, lying beyond Waterloo Bridge, which stages excellent drama productions. While architects admire their spacious and adaptable interiors and the unabashed use of modern materials, most people find the South Bank art buildings ugly, even sinister. A plan is in the works to reclad these buildings and make them more friendly. Tours behind the scenes are offered by the National Theatre (tel. 071 633 0880).

Far more modest in architectural terms is the National Film Theatre, built in 1956 and partly hidden beneath the arches of Waterloo Bridge. Its two auditoriums show a jam-packed schedule of interesting films. In order to buy tickets you have to become a member of the theater, but this is easy to do.

Coin Street and Gabriel's Wharf
A notable battle between planners, developers, and local people took place in the early 1980s over the future of the Coin Street site, adjacent to the South Bank Centre. Plans for a major office complex were eventually withdrawn, and the area has since been developed along friendlier community lines with a riverside park, housing, restaurants, and crafts workshops. One of the buildings saved from demolition was the Oxo tower of 1928—originally built as an eye-catcher displaying the Oxo brand name prominently to get around a ban then in force on outdoor advertising. Nearby Gabriel's Wharf (56 Upper Ground) is one of the area's main attractions; here you can visit crafts workshops specializing in jewelry, textiles, and leather, and shop in the weekend market. The wooden building on the wharf enjoys some of the best river views in London and houses several restaurants popular with those who are visiting the National Theatre.

Statue of Nelson Mandela on one of the South Bank Centre's walkways

■ **Despite childhood memories of long, boring afternoons spent on cold, wet playing fields, a great many British people are obsessively interested in sports, which is why even the serious newspapers devote a large number of pages to the subject. On Saturday afternoons, the climax of the sports week, a big segment of the population will be sitting in front of the television watching football, cricket, athletics, or horse racing. .....■**

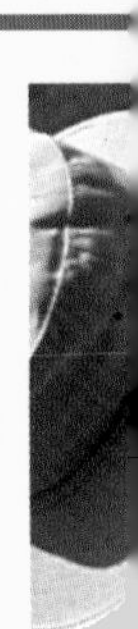

Oxford vs. Cambridge
Twice a year London plays host to sporting events for Britain's two most ancient universities, Oxford (the dark blues) and Cambridge (the light blues). One is the Varsity Rugby Match at Twickenham in December; the other is the Boat Race, held around Easter when teams race along the Thames from Putney to Mortlake. Most of the spectators have no connection with the universities; many are not even interested in sports. The appeal is in an amateur event with no big prizes or commercial sponsorship—even the result is forgotten as soon as the race or match is over.

When Britain does badly in international games (which these days is very often the case) the nation goes into a state of gloom, and questions are asked in parliament. It is assumed that Britain's rightful place is on top and that any defeat, especially at the hands of a country once ruled by the Empire, is seen as a sad reflection of the country's decline. The government, under the leadership of sports-loving John Major, decided in 1992 that the time had come to stop the rot. Substantial funds from the sale of National Lottery tickets are to be devoted to providing new sports facilities and better training. This is both so ignominious defeat does not occur quite so frequently and so Wimbledon might once again see a British tennis player get beyond the first round.

Visitors to London who want to watch sports should consult *Time Out* magazine for details or call Sportsline (tel. 071 222 8000) between 10 and 6 Monday to Friday for information on events in the area. It is very unlikely that you will get tickets for tournament finals, but if you have enough money and determination, you can try ticket agencies such as Keith Prowse, which has a special sports line (071 741 8989). Alternatively you can visit a number of sports museums where the record-breaking achievements of past players are immortalized.

London Marathon

One of the best is the lively Lawn Tennis Museum at Wimbledon, which recently won an award for its imaginative use of audio visuals to explain the history of the game. There is a display of tennis clothing and equipment that vividly shows that the speed and excitement of women's tennis in particular has improved as the players have discarded long skirts and hats (All England Lawn Tennis Club, Church Road, Wimbledon; closed Monday).

Equally worthwhile are the guided tours of Wembley Stadium (Empire Way; every hour on the hour 10–4; no reservation necessary), which take you behind the scenes at this vast, multi-purpose sports and entertainment complex. The stadium, with its capacity of 10,000, was completed in time to host the 1923 FA (Football Association) final, when Bolton beat the London team, West Ham. It was also the site of the 14th Olympic Games, held in London in 1948.

For cricket lovers, Lord's Cricket Ground (St. John's Wood Road) is almost a place of pilgrimage. The ground is named after the property developer Thomas Lord and not, as is often supposed, because so many early players were aristocrats. Lord set up the first cricket field in Dorset Square in 1787; when that was developed for housing, he moved the turf of the original ground first to North Bank and finally to the present site in 1811. This and other intriguing episodes in the history of cricket are covered by the Cricket Memorial Gallery at Lord's (open 10–5 when matches are being played and by guided tour starting at noon and 2p.m. on other days; tel. 071 289 1611 to reserve). The prize exhibit here is the tiny urn containing the Ashes, the trophy awarded to the winner of the England versus Australia test series (the trophy stays at Lord's even when Australia wins). The Ashes are those of a bail symbolically burned by Australian supporters after their defeat at the hands of the Marylebone Cricket Club (MCC) in 1883. Other exhibits include portraits of leading cricketers, such as W. G. Grace, and a stuffed sparrow killed by a fast ball bowled by Jehangir Khan on July 3, 1936. Lord's itself is particularly interesting from an architectural point of view: The tent-like structure which protects spectators who are seated in the Mound Stand is an innovative example of modern stadium design by Michael Hopkins and Partners (1986).

Wimbledon ball girl

The London Marathon
Another great annual event that perpetuates the spirit of amateurism is the London Marathon, held in April; the streets of the city are closed off for the day and thousands of spectators line the route to cheer on the 25,000 athletes taking part in the world's biggest event of its kind. First run in 1981, it has rapidly become one of the most atmospheric events in the city's seasonal calendar. Top international athletes cover the 26-mile (42.35km, 385-yard) course, from Blackheath to Westminster Bridge, in a little over two hours. It is the slower runners, however, who delight the crowds—celebrities, runners in outlandish costumes, children, senior citizens, disabled athletes. Most of them raise substantial sums of money for charity, from the friends, families and workmates who sponsor them.

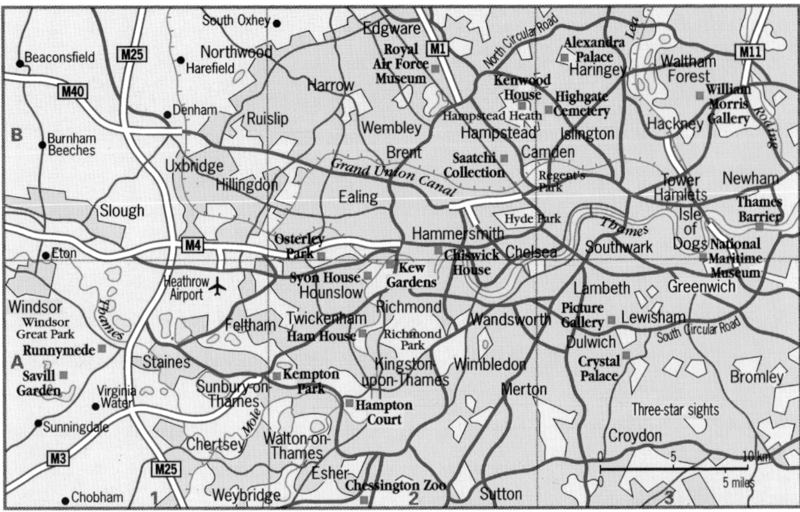

Travel information
Leaflets, tickets, and advice on a range of excursions and options can be obtained from the following information centers: **London Tourist Board Information Centre**, Victoria Station Forecourt (tel. 071 730 3488), for details of where to go in the London area, plus tour bookings, maps, and guidebooks; the **British Travel Centre**, 12 Regent Street (tel. 071 730 3400), for details of where to go throughout the British Isles, including rail, bus, plane, car rental, hotel, and theater ticket offices. Information and reservations for tours to Scotland or Wales can be obtained from the **Scottish Tourist Board**, 19 Cockspur Street (tel. 071 930 8661), and the **Wales Tourist Board**, 34 Piccadilly Street (tel. 071 409 0960).

Inter City trains link London to Britain's major cities

Excursions Inner London holds enough attractions to keep most visitors happy and entertained for weeks on end, but sometimes, when the city seems oppressive, it is worth escaping for a day to explore fresher delights, farther afield.

This section highlights the best of the villages, parks, river walks, museums, and stately homes within easy reach of central London, from the royal palaces of Hampton Court and Windsor to a display of the world's botanical riches at Kew Gardens, or the absorbing account of Britain's seafaring history at the Greenwich Maritime Museum. All these sites are well served by public transportation and if you buy a One Day Travelcard, from any Underground or British Rail station, you can enjoy unlimited travel by bus, tube, or rail in the London area.

London is also at the heart of the nation's rail and road network, which means that many other historic towns and cities are within easy reach of the capital. Scores of tour operators offer inexpensive day trips to Oxford, Stratford-upon-Avon, Canterbury, or Cambridge, and these can often be reserved through your hotel.

Alternatively, you may prefer to travel independently: Inter City Rail services will take you to towns as far away as Bath, York, or Edinburgh, or as near as Oxford and Cambridge.

Renting a car is perhaps the least attractive option because of England's congested road system and the difficulty of parking in London (or other major cities). On the other hand, a car is essential if you want to see some of England's gardens, stately homes, and rural back roads. In this case you should consider taking a train to the region that you want to explore and renting a car locally to avoid the traumatic experience of driving in London. In any event, remember that London's roads are busiest during the rush hours of 8 to 9a.m. and 5 to 6p.m., and long traffic jams are common on the roads that lead out of London on Friday evenings and on routes into the city on Monday mornings, as people travel to and from their homes in the country.

Inter City Rail Services
The following mainline stations in London serve the main cities and regions of Britain:
Paddington (tel. 071 262 6767) for Oxford, Bath, and the West Country.
Euston (tel. 071 387 7070) for Stratford-upon-Avon, the Midlands, and Glasgow.
King's Cross (tel. 071 278 2477) for Cambridge, York, and Edinburgh.
Liverpool Street (tel. 071 928 5100) for Cambridge, Colchester, Ipswich, and Norwich.
Waterloo (tel. 071 928 5100) for Winchester, Salisbury, Bournemouth, and Portsmouth.
Victoria (tel. 071 928 5100) for Gatwick, Brighton, Canterbury, and Dover.

Morning mist enshrouds King's College, Cambridge

Bath Abbey and the ancient Roman baths

The National Trust
Many of England's stately homes, castles, gardens, and landscapes are owned by the National Trust – including such London properties as Ham House (see page 231), Osterley Park (see page 228), and Carlyle's House (see page 90). The National Trust was set up in 1895 and has rescued many buildings, beauty spots, and antiquities that might otherwise have suffered from neglect or destruction. By joining the National Trust you can make a considerable savings on entrance fees and receive a comprehensive directory of all the Trust's properties in England, with transport details and opening times. Details can be gained at any National Trust property, from its London Information Centre at Blewcoat School, 23 Caxton Street, or by writing to The National Trust, Membership Department, PO Box 39, Bromley, Kent BR1 1NH (tel. 081 464 1111 for credit-card membership by phone).

Days out from London
Here are a few suggestions for day trips out of town that could easily be extended with an overnight stop.

Bath▶▶ The train journey from Paddington station to Bath takes just under two hours. The spa town's elegant Regency buildings, crescents, and gardens evoke the age of Beau Nash and the high society gatherings that took place in the Pump Room, Theatre Royal, and Assembly Rooms in the early 19th century. Additional attractions are excellent shops and the Claverton Manor Museum, devoted to American history.

Brighton▶ An hour by train from Victoria station, Brighton was the favored seaside resort of aristocratic Londoners including the Prince Regent (later King George IV), who built the extraordinary Pavilion, with its Oriental domes and Chinese-style state rooms. Nearby, the shops of the Lanes are a great place to browse. Walk along the Victorian Palace Pier promenade to enjoy the sea air.

Cambridge▶▶▶ An hour's train journey from King's Cross or Liverpool Street takes you to Cambridge – a wonderful place to see in spring, when the college gardens backing on to the River Cam are a mass of daffodils, or in summer, when you can rent a boat along the river, enjoying views of Kings College chapel, the Bridge of Sighs, or the self-supporting Mathematical Bridge, built of wood, without the help of nails.

Canterbury▶ Chaucer's pilgrims, heading for the shrine of St. Thomas à Becket, expected to take several days to journey from London to Canterbury, but now the cathedral city is an hour away by train from Victoria. The cathedral, with its stained glass, sits within the city's surviving Roman walls and not far away from the ruins of St. Augustine's abbey, founded in A.D.598, when Augustine was sent from Rome to bring Christianity to the British Isles. If you rent a car, Canterbury also makes a good base for exploring Leeds Castle, set on an island surrounded by parkland, and the famous garden at Sissinghurst, created by Harold Nicolson and Vita Sackville-West.

Oxford▶▶▶ Just over an hour's journey from Paddington station, Oxford was immortalized by the poet Matthew Arnold as "that sweet city with her dreaming spires." The university town is crowded with ancient collegiate buildings of honey-colored Cotswold limestone, many of which have lovingly tended gardens. It is also famous for its many good bookstores, its river walks, and its lively student atmosphere. If you decide to stay overnight, you could take a bus tour of Stratford-upon-Avon, where popular tourist sites are Shakespeare's birthplace and the poet's grave in Holy Trinity Church, alongside the River Avon.

Salisbury▶ Salisbury's glorious 13th-century cathedral has changed remarkably little since John Constable painted its needle-sharp spire rising out of the surrounding water meadows. The cathedral has been well restored in recent years and offers intriguing tours of the roof. Salisbury is just over an hour from London, by train from Waterloo. The 5,000-year-old stone circle at Stonehenge is only 10 miles (16km) outside the city (there is a bus that passes the site and leaves from Salisbury railway station).

English Heritage
English Heritage is a similar body to the National Trust, funded by the government and responsible for properties such as Chiswick House (see pages 212–3), Kenwood (see page 225), and Marble Hill (see page 234). Membership benefits include free admission to all properties for a year and a guide to all historic buildings and properties under the organization's care. For details, ask at any property or write to English Heritage, Membership Department, PO Box 1BB, London W1A 1BB.

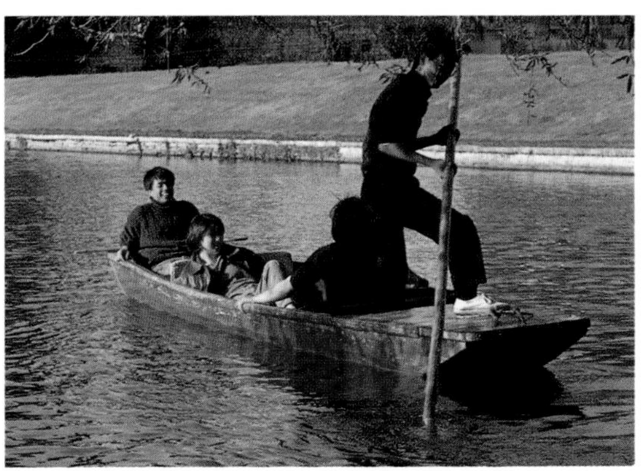

Gliding along the tranquil River Cam in Cambridge

Hogarth's House

The houses of Chiswick Mall
Chiswick Mall's houses betray the wealth of their original owners, able to afford that rare commodity in London, uninterrupted views of the River Thames and gardens that sweep down to the water's edge. One of the best buildings is Walpole House, a rare example of Restoration-period architecture, built around 1700 for Barbara Villiers, the Duchess of Cleveland, one of Charles II's mistresses. In the 19th century it served as a school, said to be the one on which Thackeray modeled Miss Pinkerton's Academy for Young Ladies in his novel *Vanity Fair*. Another building of note is Kelmscott House, on the Upper Mall, the home of William Morris from 1878 to 1896 and named after his country house in Oxfordshire. It was at the nearby Sussex House that Morris originally set up the Kelmscott Press to produce beautifully hand-illustrated books.

►► Chiswick *209B2*

In the 18th and 19th centuries, Chiswick was a favorite place of residence for artists such as William Hogarth, and it was here that Lord Burlington built Chiswick House, the most perfect example of a Palladian country villa in England. Unfortunately the village's charm has been spoiled by traffic thundering along the Great West Road to reach the M4 motorway, but to the south of the busy road network there is still much to see and enjoy.

The best way to get to Chiswick is by train from Waterloo. From Chiswick station, turn right and follow Burlington Lane for about 0.6 miles (1km) to reach the entrance to Chiswick House, with its fine Italianate gardens and the long, sweeping avenue that leads up to the house itself (closed Tuesday).

Chiswick House►►► This delightful villa was built in 1725–29 by Lord Burlington, a patron of the arts and an accomplished architect in his own right. His inspiration was Palladio's Villa Capra, near Vicenza in northern Italy, but the building is far from being a slavish copy. The main east front, for example, has an elaborate double staircase leading to the two-story portico, unlike any Palladian prototype. Flanking the staircase are fine statues carved by Rysbrack around 1730, representing Palladio and Inigo Jones, the English architect who did so much to introduce the ideals of classical architecture to England.

There is another homage to Inigo Jones in the obelisks on the roof that surround the central dome. These are, in fact, disguised chimneys and are copied from designs made by Jones for the Queen's House at Greenwich, as are some of the magnificent chimney pieces inside the villa. Lord Burlington intended the villa as a "Temple of the Arts," and the interior decoration reflects this fact. The ground-floor rooms, designed as private apartments, are relatively plain, but the upper floor is richly decorated with gilded cherubs, swags and scrolls, statues of classical deities, and ceiling paintings by William Kent.

The garden, also designed by Kent, makes a romantic setting for the villa. Although Italian in style, and dotted with temples, statues, and obelisks, it marks a departure from the strict geometric form of Renaissance gardens. Inspired by the landscape paintings of artists such as Claude and Salvator Rosa, the gardens are an idealized version of the Roman Campagna.

Chiswick Mall► An underpass leads from beneath the busy traffic circle called the Hogarth Roundabout to Church Street and St. Nicholas Church, the burial place of several famous artists and architects, including Hogarth himself, William Kent, Colen Campbell, and James McNeill Whistler. From the church you can walk for 1.2 miles (2km) along Chiswick Mall, the Upper Mall, and the Lower Mall, admiring some of London's finest 18th-century houses and perhaps stopping along the way at one of several riverside pubs. At the end of the Lower Mall, Hammersmith Bridge Road leads north to Hammersmith tube station for the journey back to central London.

Hogarth's House► Nowadays, Hogarth's House (closed Tuesday) stands to the north of Chiswick House on Hogarth Lane, close to a busy traffic circle. The scene was very different when the "little country box by the Thames" stood in open fields. Hogarth used it as his summer residence between 1749 and 1764, and the simple rooms are hung with copies of his satirical engravings, including the famous *Marriage à la Mode* of 1745 and *The Rake's Progress* of 1735. In the tiny garden, an ancient mulberry tree, under which Hogarth used to sit, survives and bears fruit despite having been hit by lightning and a World War II bomb, not to mention the traffic pollution.

Riverside pubs
As you stroll along the Mall you can choose from one of several historic pubs. The 16th-century **Dove Inn** (19 Upper Mall) is where Charles II and Nell Gwyn are said to have made secret rendezvous. A list of other famous customers (including Ernest Hemingway and Graham Greene) is displayed above the great fireplace. This pub earns an entry in the *Guinness Book of Records* for having the smallest public bar in England (a mere 5 ft. by 8 ft.). The **Old Ship** (25 Upper Mall) dates from the mid-17th century and is decorated with nautical relics, and the **Blue Anchor** (13 Lower Mall) is the popular wood-paneled haunt of members of the Amateur Rowing Association, whose headquarters are next door.

Chiswick House

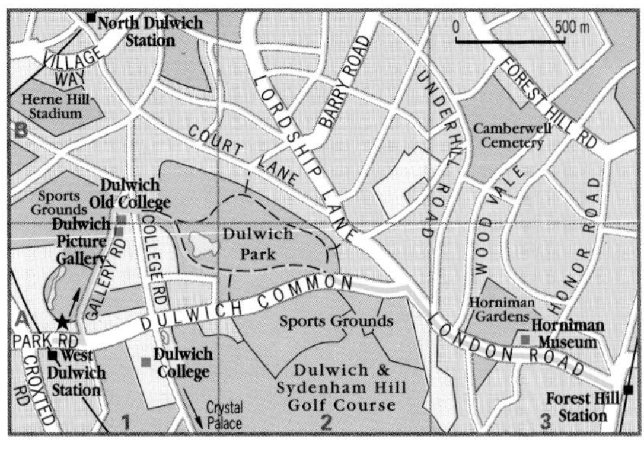

►► Dulwich

In 1605 Edward Alleyn, the actor manager who was friends with playwright, Christopher Marlowe, used his very considerable fortune (much of it amassed by running popular entertainments such as bull- and bear-baiting) to buy the manor of Dulwich. Here he built and endowed Dulwich College, a school for the poor, and ensured the survival of a large expanse of parkland in south London. The attractions here today include the Dulwich College Picture Gallery, with its collection of Old Masters, and the Horniman Museum, renowned for its ethnography collection.

To reach **Dulwich Gallery►►►** (closed Monday), take the train from Victoria station to West Dulwich and walk north along Gallery Road. The collection, consisting of some 300-plus masterpieces dating largely from the 17th century, is housed in the simple neoclassical domed building designed by Sir John Soane in 1811–14. This was the first purpose-built art gallery ever to be opened to the public in England, and its highlights include Rembrandt's portrait of *Jacob III de Gheyn* (stolen several times from the gallery but, fortunately, recovered each time), Van Dyck's *Madonna and Child*, and Poussin's *Return of the Holy Family from Egypt*. A rather morbid touch is the fact that the gallery also serves as a mausoleum. At the rear of the building is the tomb of Noel Desenfans, who was responsible for putting the collection together, and Sir Francis Bourgeois, who bequeathed it to Dulwich College in 1811 (see side panel).

Alongside the Picture Gallery, **Dulwich Old College►** dates from 1619 and now serves as offices. This was the original school founded by Edward Alleyn, but the buildings that now house the main school lie 0.6 miles (1km) to the south, housed in Renaissance-style buildings designed in 1866–70 by Charles Barry, the son of the architect who built the Houses of Parliament.

A path to the Horniman Museum leads through **Dulwich Park►** from the entrance just east of the Picture Gallery. The park is especially colorful in May, when the azaleas and rhododendrons are in full bloom, but there are fine trees to admire at all times of the year, including statuesque oaks, some of which are at least 200 years old, and a number of more exotic specimens, such as the Japanese pagoda tree.

The path takes you south of the boating lake, cafe, and

The history of Dulwich Gallery

The remarkable collection of paintings housed in the Dulwich College Picture Gallery was put together by the art dealer Noel Desenfans. He was commissioned in 1790 by the king of Poland to buy paintings for a National Gallery that was planned for Warsaw. When the king was deposed, Desenfans offered the collection to the British government, suggesting that it could form the basis of a new National Gallery. The government refused (it finally got round to founding today's National Gallery in 1824), so in 1807 Desenfans left the collection to his friend, Sir Francis Bourgeois, who in turn bequeathed it to Dulwich College in 1811. As a result, one of the best collections of art in the world, with major works by Rubens, Gainsborough, Van Dyck, Rembrandt, and Raphael, fit to grace any national museum, has ended up in a quiet (and sadly little visited) south London suburb.

aviary, and out by the lodge gates on Dulwich Common—once a royal hunting ground, now an exclusive golf course. Turn left, then right in Lordship Lane to reach the Horniman Museum on London Road.

Horniman Museum▶▶ is housed in an eccentric art nouveau building and is very popular with children, not least because surrounding park has animal and bird enclosures forming a mini zoo.

The entrance to the museum building, which was designed by C. Harrison Townsend in 1901, features a large mosaic by Robert Anning Bell: *The Course of Human Life*. Inside the museum, the exhibits reflect the quirky interests of Frederick John Horniman who, as head of his family's tea importing business, traveled widely in the 1870s and collected anything that appealed to his sense of curiosity: stuffed animals, fossils, musical instruments, puppets, masks, and tribal artifacts. Objects representing different cultures have been skillfully arranged to illuminate a number of topics, including initiation rites, the use of narcotics and stimulants, agriculture, crafts, fishing, and cooking.

For the return journey to central London follow London Road left to Forest Hill railway station, where frequent trains depart for London Bridge.

Crystal Palace
On a high hill just to the south of Dulwich, the Crystal Palace was re-erected in 1851, once it had served its purpose of housing the Great Exhibition in Hyde Park. The monumental glass-and-iron building, designed by Joseph Paxton, then became the centerpiece of a huge amusement park, opened by Queen Victoria in 1854. In 1936, the Crystal Palace went up in flames; 90 fire engines failed to quench the ferocious blaze. Today, all that remains of this vast Victorian Disneyland is the boating lake with some life-size models of prehistoric dinosaurs, made in 1854, set on a series of artificial islands. A small museum on Anerley Hill, near Crystal Palace station, covers the history of this fairy tale building and its sad demise (open weekends only). The site is still used for various entertainments, however, since the park now houses a major athletic stadium and concert bowl where pop and orchestral concerts take place in summer.

The art nouveau tower of the Horniman Museum

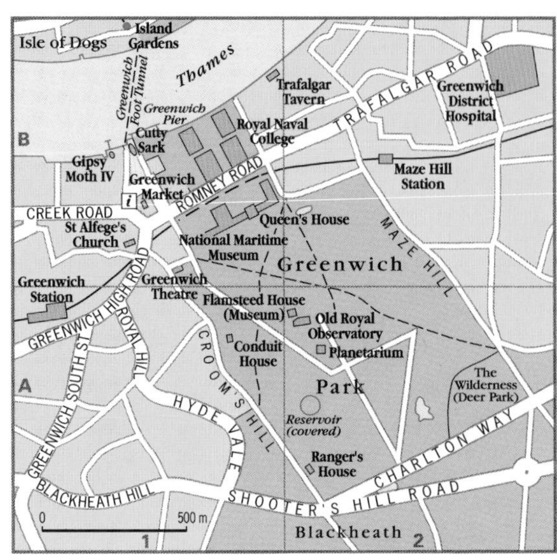

Greenwich pubs
In Greenwich you have plenty of choices when it comes to traditional pubs, many of which serve seafood and have outdoor terraces with river views. Perhaps the best is the **Trafalgar Tavern** (reservations advised for meals, tel. 081 858 2437) in Park Row, which Dickens immortalized in *Our Mutual Friend.* The interior is like a ship, with nautical relics on display and large windows overlooking the Thames. Another ship-like tavern, the **Cutty Sark**, is reached by following the riverside path, via Crane Street and Highbridge, to Ballast Quay; it's well worth the walk just for the view northwards up the vast expanse of the Thames to Blackwall. Within the center of Greenwich the choice includes the **Spanish Galleon Tavern** and the **Gipsy Moth**, both on Greenwich Church Street, or the **Coach and Horses**, built in 1730, in Turpin Lane alongside Greenwich Market.

Early telescope

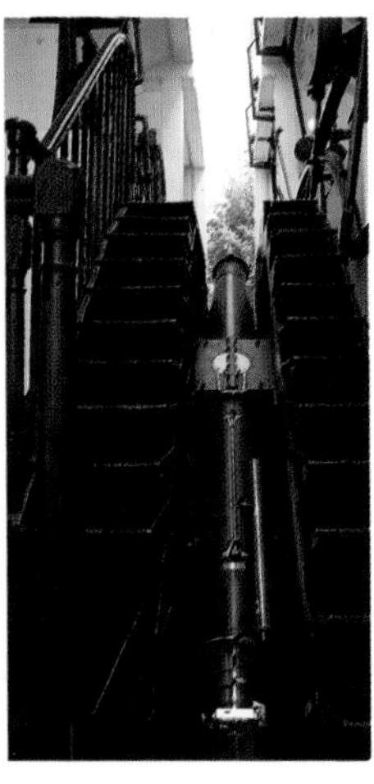

▶▶▶ Greenwich

Greenwich is every bit as beautiful as its name (a corruption of "green reach") suggests. Here, set in parkland that sweeps down to the river's edge, are some of London's most noble buildings: the Queen's House—built by Inigo Jones and nowadays used to house the National Maritime Museum, Wren's Royal Naval College alongside the Thames, and his Royal Observatory on the hill above. Add to this the attractions of the *Cutty Sark* and a delightful village, and you have the ingredients of a full and varied day out from central London.

There are several ways to get to Greenwich, including the train from London Bridge or the riverbus that leaves at regular intervals in summer from Westminster, Charing Cross, or Tower piers. Another option is to take the Docklands Light Railway from its western terminus at Tower Gateway, opposite the Tower of London, all the way to Island Gardens station at the southern tip of the Isle of Dogs. The advantage of this route is that you will enjoy superb views from Island Gardens across the river to the Royal Naval College, with the Queen's House beyond—a vista that Christopher Wren planned with great care. It is then a short walk, beneath the Thames, to Greenwich itself by means of the Greenwich Foot Tunnel.

The Cutty Sark

Both the foot tunnel and the riverbus bring visitors to Greenwich Pier, where the ***Cutty Sark*►►** lies moored in a dry dock, housing an exhibition of ships' figureheads below deck. This sleek and handsome ship, with its tall masts and intricate rigging, was built in 1869 as a tea clipper, carrying precious cargoes between Britain and the Orient. In 1871 she broke the world record for sailing between London and China, completing the trip in only 107 days, at her fastest covering 360 miles (580km) in a single day. Exploring the ship will give you some idea of the cramped living conditions that were endured by the 28-man crew.

Moored nearby, and dwarfed by the *Cutty Sark*, is ***Gipsy Moth IV*►,** the tiny yacht in which Sir Francis Chichester made the first single-handed circumnavigation of the globe in 1966–67. Nearly 400 years before that, Sir Francis Drake had been the first Englishman to sail round the world. The sword used by Queen Elizabeth II to knight Sir Francis Chichester was the same one used by Elizabeth I to knight Drake in the 16th century.

Immediately south of the pier is College Approach, the route into **Greenwich Village►,** lined with early 19th-century buildings, which flank the entrance to Greenwich Market. The covered market, built in 1831, is now only open on weekends and specializes in crafts. Another market, selling antiques, books, and period clothing, operates during weekends in the summer on Greenwich Church Street.

Splendid wrought-iron gates on King William Walk form the main entrance to the **Royal Naval College►►**, now used for officer training but originally built as a hospital for infirm and aged seamen. These monumental buildings, begun in 1664, stand around the open space of the Great Court. Christopher Wren, the architect, planned the symmetrical blocks, either side of the court, specifically to frame the impressive southward view of the Queen's House.

Two of the buildings are open to the public (every afternoon except Thursday). The Painted Hall features some of the finest baroque paintings in England, created by Sir James Thornhill in 1707–17 and featuring the monarchs, William and Mary, surrounded by allegorical figures symbolizing the triumph of virtue over vice. The Chapel, rebuilt after damage by a fire in 1779, is in neo-Grecian style, with statues of Faith, Hope, Charity, and Humility in the vestibule and a vast altar painting by Benjamin West, *St. Paul Shaking Off the Viper.*

St. Alfege with St. Peter
The parish church of Greenwich stands on the spot where St. Alfege, the Archbishop of Canterbury, was killed by invading Danes in 1012. The building is much more recent, having been rebuilt in 1711–14 by Nicholas Hawksmoor. The church has important musical associations. Thomas Tallis, the 16th-century composer whose settings for the Anglican liturgy are still performed in churches and cathedrals all over England, is buried in the churchyard. The keyboard of a 16th-century organ, which Tallis might have played, is preserved in the nave. The church is used for concerts and services, especially during the Greenwich Festival in June.

The domed entrance to the Greenwich Foot Tunnel, which leads beneath the River Thames to the Isle of Dogs

The Greenwich Meridian

Ranger's House
On the western edge of Greenwich Park stands Ranger's House, Chesterfield Walk, a grand 18th-century house that has had many aristocratic residents, including Princess Sophie Matilda, daughter of George III. She lived here from 1814, enjoying the title of Ranger of Greenwich Park. The house is now used to display the Dolmetsch Collection of historical musical instruments upstairs and the Suffolk Collection on the ground floor. The latter is a small but rich collection of English portraits of the 17th and 18th centuries. They include a remarkable series of paintings by William Larkin of ladies (mostly unidentified) dressed in gorgeous court costumes, probably commissioned in 1614 to commemorate the marriage of Elizabeth Cecil and Thomas Howard.

The principal attraction in Greenwich is the **National Maritime Museum▶▶▶**, entered from Romney Road, which occupies several buildings in Greenwich Park and tells the story of Britain and the sea.

The museum's central building, the **Queen's House▶▶▶**, is an architectural monument in its own right—the first building in England to be designed in the classical style, and the prototype for many subsequent public buildings and stately homes. Inigo Jones began the building in 1616 as a rural retreat for Anne of Denmark, James I's queen, but she died in 1619; it was Henrietta Maria, the French wife of Charles I, who presided over its completion in 1635. The finest feature of the interior is the "Tulip Stair," named after the pattern on its balustrade (probably intended to represent fleurs-de-lis, the symbol of France). This leads to the Great Hall, its dimensions forming a perfect cube, with ceiling paintings showing the Muses, the Virtues, and the Liberal Arts. The original paintings were moved to Marlborough House, Pall Mall, in the 18th century; these are a computer-enhanced replica.

To either side are the State Apartments (the king's to the east and the queen's to the west), furnished in 17th-century style. One of the most intriguing rooms is the Queen's Presence Chamber, where original painted decorations survive, showing the lilies of France impaling the British arms and symbolizing the marriage of Charles I to Henrietta Maria.

The long side wings, added to the Queen's House in 1807–16 to house the Royal Hospital School, now contain a huge collection of ships (real ones and models), paintings, navigational instruments, and the relics of naval heroes and explorers. The star attraction is the Neptune Hall, which explains the development of wooden boats from prehistoric times to the present day. In the adjacent

Barge House you can see the state barge made in 1732 for Frederick, Prince of Wales, a riot of carved and gilded decoration. Other displays tell the story of the explorers who charted the Arctic during the period 1818–76 and of early colonists who braved the Atlantic in search of a new life. In the Nelson Collection you can see the uniform jacket, with a bullet hole in the left shoulder, that Lord Nelson was wearing when he was fatally wounded at the Battle of Trafalgar in 1805.

The **Old Royal Observatory**►► is an annex to the Maritime Museum consisting of several historic buildings, high on the hill above Greenwich. The Greenwich Observatory was founded by Charles II in 1675; Flamsteed House was built in the same year by Christopher Wren for John Flamsteed, the first Astronomer Royal. Today the house deliberately gives the impression that Flamsteed and his wife still live there, with food on the table, clothes strewn around, and a chamberpot under the bed. Early telescopes and time-measuring instruments are displayed in the house and the large red ball on top of one of the towers still drops down its mast at 1p.m. each day, enabling Thames navigators to set their chronometers accurately.

From the start, the Observatory's job was to set standards of measurement for time, distance, latitude, and longitude—key components of navigation. The large Gate Clock measures Greenwich Mean Time, the standard by which time is set all round the world, and you can stand astride the Greenwich Meridian, marked by a brass strip crossing the Observatory courtyard: This marks the dividing line between the earth's eastern and western hemispheres (if you wish, you can buy a computer printout recording the precise time of your visit).

Setting the standard – Greenwich Mean Time

Macartney House
This is one of several elegant 17th- and 18th-century houses lining Croom's Hill, the winding road that links Greenwich village to the Ranger's House on Chesterfield Walk. General Edward Wolfe, who purchased the house in 1751, described it as "the prettiest situated house in England." General Edward was the father of the more famous General James Wolfe, who set off from this house in 1758 for North America, at the head of a force that captured Quebec from the French; Wolfe was fatally wounded in the process. A statue of Wolfe by Tait Mackenzie (1930), given by the Canadian nation, stands near by in Greenwich Park, not far from the Royal Observatory, and there is a memorial to him in St. Alfege's Church in Greenwich.

The National Maritime Museum houses a huge collection of ships

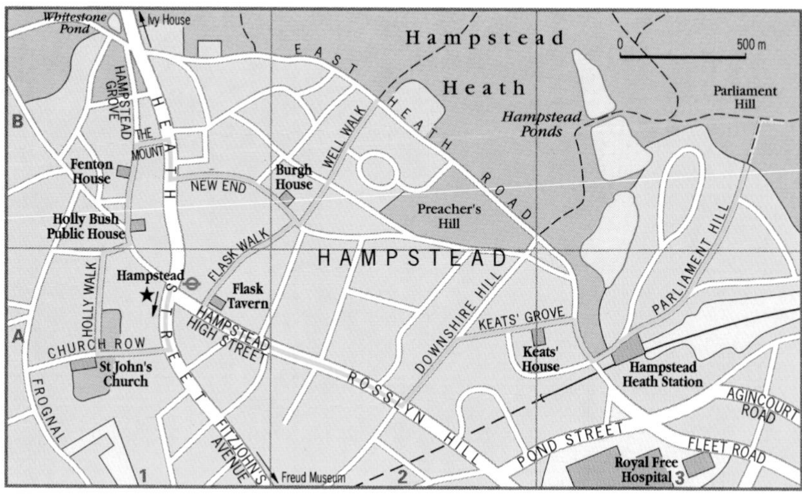

Hampstead Heath
In 1829, Hampstead's Lord of the Manor, Sir Thomas Wilson, wanting to capitalize on the popularity of the village, produced a plan to build new houses all over the vast 330-hectare expanse of sandy heath that he owned to the north of the village. This caused uproar, and opposition to the idea raged for 40 years until, at Wilson's death in 1869, conservationists finally won the battle to save the Heath for public enjoyment. The Heath is a vast nature reserve, as well as a public playground where Londoners come to walk, jog, ride their horses, enjoy picnics, fly their kites, and swim in the three ponds to the east of the Heath (Kenwood Pond for women, Highgate Pond for men, and Hampstead Pond for mixed swimming).

▶▶ Hampstead

Hampstead's pretty lanes and village atmosphere and its vast expanse of semi-rural heath have attracted many eminent writers, politicians, and intellectuals, past and present. Ballerina Anna Pavlova, Sigmund Freud—the father of pyschoanalysis, and the Romantic poet John Keats are among past residents whose homes have now been made into museums.

The tone of the area is intellectual, prosperous, and liberal. Several well-known left-wing writers and politicians live here—"champagne socialists," who live pampered lives while espousing egalitarianism. By day, Hampstead Heath is a fine place to walk and a popular place for families and children; by night, parts of the Heath are best avoided.

Hampstead tube station rises amid the intricate maze of attractive lanes that cluster around the High Street. From the station, Heath Street descends south to Church Row, with its Georgian houses fronted by iron railings. Halfway down the Row is the parish church of St. John, built in 1744–47, with its bold spire. Inside are memorials to many former Hampstead residents, including Keats, the architect Norman Shaw, the painter John Constable, and the novelist George du Maurier.

Holly Walk, off Church Row, leads north to Vernon Hill; by turning right here you come to Hampstead Grove, where the 17th-century **Fenton House▶** is open to the public (Saturday to Wednesday in summer, weekends only in winter). Built in William-and-Mary style in 1695, Fenton House contains beautiful period furnishings, English and European porcelain, and a collection of 17th- and 18th-century keyboard instruments (including a harpsichord of 1612, which may have belonged to Handel).

Many of the little lanes that run around Hampstead Grove are well worth exploring, and many of the houses display blue plaques recording the names of their eminent former residents.

Heading up Heath Street, you will come to New End, a street on your right. Here you will find **Burgh House**, a Queen Anne house which is open to the public

Wednesday to Sunday from noon. Built in 1703 by the physician Dr. Gibbons, its rooms are now used for art exhibitions and local history displays, and there is a good cafe in the basement.

Nearby, Flask Walk and Well Walk are reminders that Londoners once came here to take the waters at the Pump House, which has since disappeared. In Flask Walk, the Flask Tavern was the meeting place in the early 18th century of the Kit-Cat Club, a political and literary group whose members included Britain's first prime minister, Robert Walpole; the essayists, Addison and Steele; and Vanbrugh, the playwright and architect. Flask Walk leads to Hampstead High Street, with its good bookstores, boutiques, and restaurants.

Hampstead High Street leads down Rosslyn Hill where, on the left, Downshire Hill leads to Keats' Grove (formerly known as Wentworth Grove) and the Keats' House museum▶. John Keats came to live here in 1818, fell in love with his next door neighbor, Fanny Brawne, and became engaged to her in 1819. In 1820 he left for Italy for health reasons and died there in 1821. During the short time he lived in this house he wrote some of his best-loved poems, including *Ode to a Nightingale*; the plum tree under which he wrote this poem has gone, but a recent replacement in the garden marks the spot. The rest of the house displays letters, manuscripts, and furnishings in period style.

From Keats' Grove it is a short step to Hampstead Heath railway station, or you can walk up Parliament Hill for extensive views over central London—local legend claims that Queen Boudicca (Boadicea), the Iron-Age ruler who fought against the Roman conquest of Britain, lies buried beneath the hill.

Hampstead browsers

Nearby museums
To the south of Hampstead, at 20 Maresfield Gardens, is the house where Sigmund Freud lived from 1938, when he escaped from Vienna, until the following year, when he died. The house was kept as a shrine to Freud by his daughter, Anna, until she herself died in 1983, after which it opened as a museum (open Wednesday to Sunday from noon). Freud's famous couch, along with books, letters, and personal relics, are on display. To the north of Hampstead, on North End Road, is Ivy House, the home of the Russian ballerina, Anna Pavlova, from 1912 until her death in 1931. A small museum (open Saturday afternoon) displays memorabilia and overlooks the lake where Pavlova kept a flock of swans to remind her of her starring role in Fokine's ballet *The Dying Swan* (1907).

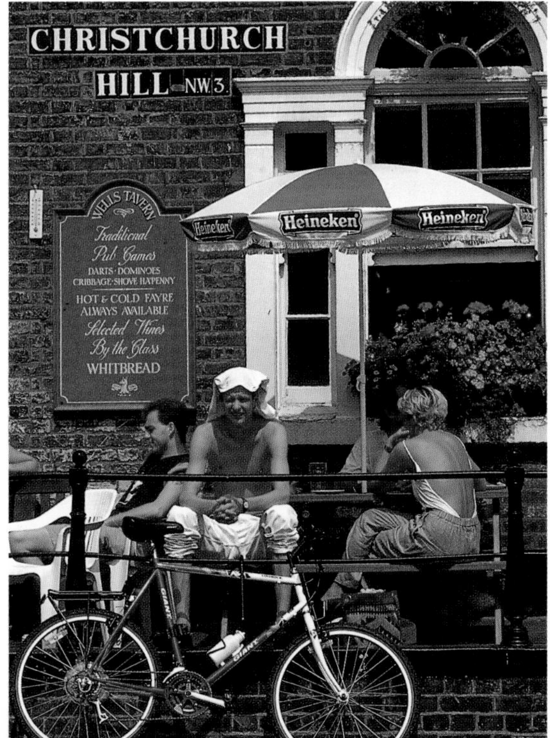

Hilly Hampstead offers plenty of places to rest

Hampton Court's vivid mix of styles

The Haunted Gallery
Ghosts are inevitable in a palace that has seen so much history, but one in particular is supposed to frequent the so-called Haunted Gallery. It was here that Catherine Howard, the fifth wife of Henry VIII, is said to have broken away from her guards after being arrested for adultery and rushed screaming to appeal to the king who, oblivious to her cries, attended mass in the nearby Chapel Royal. Howard, who continued to protest her innocence, was sentenced to death and beheaded in the Tower in 1542. A figure in white has been spotted in the gallery on several occasions since, uttering an unearthly and piercing scream.

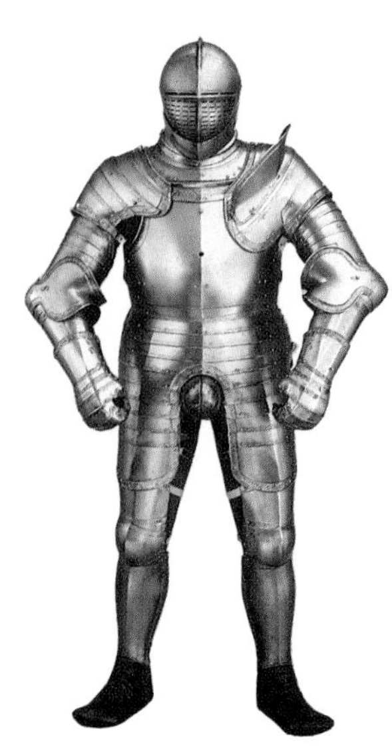

Henry VIII's armor

►►► Hampton Court *209A2*

Hampton Court is one of the oldest and most interesting of London's royal palaces. Wren's south wing, badly damaged by fire in 1986, has been superbly restored, and the palace, in typical Tudor style, looks like a miniature town which has grown in an organic, unplanned way, unity provided only by the warm reds and browns of the brickwork. The fastest way to reach Hampton Court is by rail from Waterloo station, but a more leisurely journey (of three to four hours) can be made by riverbus in summer, from Westminster Pier (tel. 071 930 2062 for details).

The palace Hampton Court is approached through the Trophy Gate, where its vast scale can be appreciated. The palace was not merely a royal residence: It also housed a huge retinue of courtiers and followers and does so to this day. The warren of courtyards and buildings to the left contains "grace and favor" apartments, where Crown officials, retirees, and dependants of the royal family live. The Landmark Trust also has two vacation homes here that can be rented by the week: Fish Court, which sleeps six, and the Georgian House, which sleeps eight. Details from the Landmark Trust, Shottesbrooke, Maidenhead, Berkshire SL6 3SW (tel. 0628 825925). Ahead is the Great Gatehouse, built by Cardinal Wolsey. Unfortunately, the gatehouse was cut down in the 1770s; it was originally two stories taller.

Set in the two side turrets are terra-cotta roundels depicting Roman emperors. These and Base Court, beyond, date from Wolsey's time. Anne Boleyn's gateway, opposite, is carved with the intertwined initials "H" and "A", for Henry and Anne, celebrating a marriage that lasted only four years before Boleyn was beheaded. Clock Court comes next, named after the astronomical clock on the gateway's inner side. On the left is Henry VIII's Great Hall, with its splendid oriel window and an impressive hammerbeam roof. Under the Great Hall are the Tudor Kitchens, with their vast fireplaces and ancient cooking utensils. Opposite is Christopher Wren's elegant colonnade, added when the State Apartments were remodeled during the reign of William III. Wren planned to demolish the whole palace and build a new one as grand as Versailles. Luckily, the royal purse could not afford this, and the Tudor buildings were left standing. But the State Apartments, which you enter here (they're on the second floor) are rich indeed, decorated with priceless paintings, furnishings, armor, and tapestries. Jean Tijou, the French blacksmith, made the ironwork balustrades of the staircases, Grinling Gibbons made the woodwork, and Verrio executed many of the ceiling paintings. Don't miss the views from the windows: The more intimate queen's apartments look into Wren's lavish Fountain Court, while the public rooms look over the gardens, with their leafy avenues, canals, and fountains.

Tudor chimneys

The gardens Like the palace, the gardens are a mixture of styles. To the south, between the Thames and the palace, is the Privy Garden, designed for the exclusive use of the royal family and separated from the river by Tijou's handsome wrought-iron screen. Here archaeologists have found formal beds and pathways buried beneath the top soil that were laid out as a Dutch garden during the reign of William III. The shrubbery that grew up here in the 19th century is now being cleared so that the late-17th-century garden can be re-created. Nearby is Henry VIII's Pond Garden and an Elizabethan Knot Garden of aromatic herbs. The Great Vine grows near the Banqueting House; planted in 1768, it still produces Black Hamburg grapes, on sale in season. To the north of the palace is the Wilderness, the Laburnum Walk, and the Maze, planted in 1714 in the reign of Queen Anne. Grab a snack at the cafe in the nearby Tilt Yard Gardens before entering the Maze—it may take you some time to get out!

Cardinal Wolsey and Hampton Court
Hampton Court started out in 1515 as an ecclesiastical palace, not a royal one, built by Cardinal Wolsey, the son of an Ipswich butcher who rose to fill the highest offices of church and state. As the confidant of Henry VIII he took a leading role in the king's complicated marriage affairs. He amassed great wealth and spent it extravagantly, intending Hampton Court to be the most splendid palace in the land. This spurred the King's envy, however, and Wolsey tactfully decided that it might be wise to present Hampton Court to Henry as a gift, which he did in 1525. This did not satisfy the king who, in 1529, had his former friend arrested on a charge of treason and then seized all of Wolsey's possessions, including the palace of Whitehall. Disgraced and rejected, the Cardinal soon fell ill, and within a year he was dead.

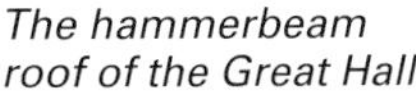

The hammerbeam roof of the Great Hall

Memorial to Karl Marx, Highgate Cemetery

Dick Whittington
On the left-hand side of Highgate Hill, about 275 yds. up from Archway tube station, look out for the Whittington Stone, set by the roadside. Here, according to legend, Dick Whittington rested with his cat on his way out of London, having failed to make his fortune in the city. Three times, as he rested, he thought he heard the Bow Bells chime "Turn again, Whittington, thrice Mayor of London," and the third time he decided to return. Thus goes the story; in reality, Richard Whittington was born the son of a Gloucestershire squire. He was, indeed, three times Mayor of London (in 1397, 1406, and 1419) but the fable of his rags-to-riches rise seems to have been invented in the 17th century, 200 years after Whittington's death.

►► Highgate *209B3*

Highgate still retains its village atmosphere, though since the early 19th century it has been swallowed up by London's northward expansion. The core of the village has many expensive 18th-century houses, which set the high-class tone of the whole area.

To reach Highgate, it is best to take the tube to Archway station and walk up **Highgate Hill**. The first bleak section, with its ugly hospital buildings, soon gives way to houses with elegant Georgian façades, on the right. On the left, a long wall separates the road from the peaceful oasis of **Waterlow Park**, a hillside garden with fine views toward Regent's Park and central London. At the top of the park, you can visit **Lauderdale House**, built in 1645 and briefly

Kenwood House and its paintings were bequeathed to the nation by the 1st Earl of Iveagh in 1927

the home of Nell Gwyn, Charles II's mistress.

Highgate village is grouped around **Pond Square**, which has a delightful mixture of Georgian cottages, grander houses, small shops, and restaurants. To one side is the **Flask** pub, so called because travelers used to stop here to fill their flasks with drink for the journey ahead. More Georgian houses can be found in The Grove, a little to the north (the poet Samuel Taylor Coleridge lived at No. 3).

Highgate Cemetery▶▶▶ You can reach Highgate Cemetery by walking south from Pond Square, down Swains Lane. The lane divides the cemetery in two: The western side can only be visited on a tour (summer Monday to Friday, noon–4; weekends, 11–4), but there is free access to the eastern half during the same hours.

A number of famous people are buried here, amidst the Victorian landscaping and the fascinating variety of funerary architecture. Among those buried in the Western Cemetery are the physicist Michael Faraday (died 1867), the poet Christina Rossetti (died 1894), and Elizabeth Siddal (died 1862), the beautiful wife of Dante Gabriel Rossetti. Rossetti buried a volume of unpublished poems with his wife but later had a change of heart, seeking permission to open the grave so that his work could be recovered and published.

In the Eastern Cemetery, the most famous grave is that of Karl Marx (who died in Hampstead in 1883), marked by a large head sculpted by Laurence Bradshaw (1956) and the inscription: "Workers of all lands unite."

Kenwood House (The Iveagh Bequest)▶▶▶ From the center of Highgate it is a 10-minute walk along Hampstead Lane to Kenwood House, gloriously situated in wooded grounds to the north of Hampstead Heath. This stately home, built in 1616 and remodeled by Robert Adam in 1764, was left to the nation in 1927 by the 1st Earl of Iveagh, along with its outstanding collection of paintings. Here you will find Rembrandt's brooding *Portrait of the Artist* (*c.*1665), Vermeer's *The Guitar Player* (*c.*1676), and Gainsborough's fine portrait of Lady Howe (*c.*1764), among many other important works by English and Dutch masters. Open-air concerts are given in the grounds, by the lake, on Saturday evenings in June, July, and August, with fireworks after some performances.

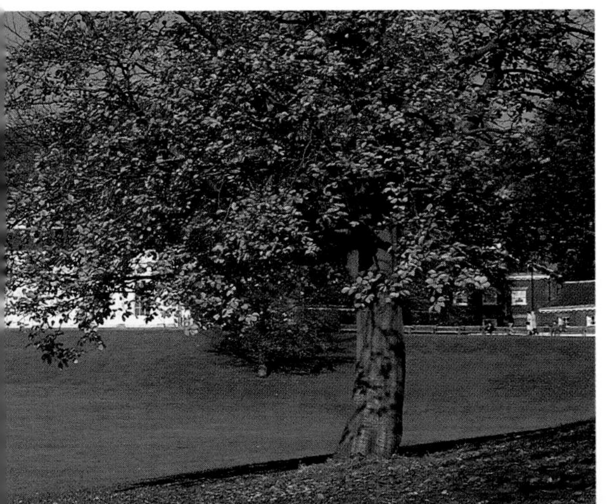

George Eliot's grave

Highgate Cemetery
Highgate Cemetery opened in 1839 as a commercial enterprise; burial plots could be purchased here as an alternative to overcrowded churchyards (where tomb robbing was a problem), and the London Cemetery Company guaranteed that the occupants of the graves would remain undisturbed, rather than (as was then common practice) the remains being dug up to make way for new burials. Highgate Cemetery was immensely popular but in time, with all the burial plots sold and no revenue for maintenance, it fell into neglect, and nature took control of the 20-hectare site. Today, managed by the Friends of Highgate Cemetery, the site has the added attraction of being an important nature reserve.

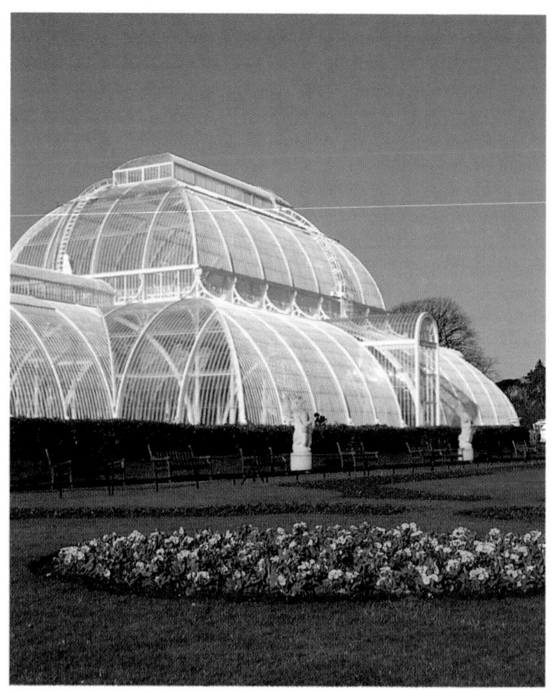

Decimus Burton's Palm House, guarded by the heraldic Queen's Beasts

Marianne North
Kew has a superb collection of botanical paintings representing the life's work of Marianne North (1830–90). These colorful pictures (mostly in oil) are crammed into a small gallery on the southeastern edge of the gardens. Marianne North traveled around the world to paint plants in their natural environment, before her forced retirement to Gloucestershire, caused by a tropical fever.

Kew and the rubber tree
Kew has sent seeds all over the world and was actively involved in the introduction of rubber to southeast Asia. The original rubber-tree seeds were smuggled from Brazil (who did not wish to share this profitable plant), propagated at Kew, and studied by Henry Ridley, who became the director of the botanic gardens in Singapore in the 1870s and persuaded many local landowners to develop new rubber plantations. Rubber is now a staple of the Malaysian and Indonesian economies.

▶▶▶ Kew 209A2

Whatever time of year it is, there is something to see at Kew's Royal Botanic Gardens. Even in the gray depths of winter, the Victorian glasshouses are full of luxuriant tropical growth, while spring and early summer bring massed bulbs, frothing groves of Japanese cherries and magnolias, or swathes of colorful azaleas and rhododendrons. There are plants here from every corner of the globe, and a trip on the District Line to Kew Gardens tube station can be a voyage through desert, swamp, and rainforest.

The gardens were created by combining two royal estates in 1772. Under the patronage of George III they developed into one of the world's foremost centers of horticultural research. The credit for this was largely due to Sir Joseph Banks, who became the king's adviser shortly after returning from a voyage round the world with Captain Cook on board the *Endeavour*. During this expedition Banks had recorded a huge number of hitherto unknown plants, which he now brought to Britain for the first time, growing them at Kew to assess their value, either as ornamental plants or as sources of food or medicines. The early botanic garden occupied a small part of the total area; the rest was landscaped by Capability Brown (his lake and Rhododendron Dell remain) and dotted with fanciful buildings for the amusement of courtly visitors: Of these, the oldest is the 10-story pagoda, towering at the southernmost end of the garden. It was built in 1761–62, to the designs of William Chambers.

The Palm House Kew began to change after 1841, when the gardens were handed over to the state, and several greenhouses were added. The earliest is the curving

Palm House, designed by Decimus Burton and built of wrought-iron and glass with techniques borrowed from shipbuilding. It opened in 1848 and was restored in the 1980s. In front of the Palm House are the Queen's Beasts, heraldic animals carved for the coronation of Elizabeth II in 1953. In the nearby Waterlily House (1852), the giant Amazonian lily sports leaves up to 6½ ft. across.

The Temperate House The next to be built was the Temperate House, also by Decimus Burton, beginning in 1859; by the time it was completed, 40 years later, it was the world's largest greenhouse. It has an elevated gallery from which to enjoy views of brightly colored plants, including the Chilean wine palm, planted in 1846 and now claimed to be the largest greenhouse plant in existence.

The Princess of Wales Conservatory Opened in 1987, much of this conservatory is below ground level (for insulation) and lit by a series of low, tent-like glass roofs. Computer controls simulate several different environments in the one building, so you pass from arid desert at one end to the orchid-filled tropics at the other. Each climate zone has its own weird and wonderful creations, from the stone-like lithops of the dry regions to the carnivorous pitcher plants of the Asian rainforests.

Queen Charlotte's Cottage Gardens British native wildflowers are the theme at this peaceful spot on the southwestern fringes of the site, where George III's queen had a rustic "cottage" built in the 1770s. This is now a woodland nature reserve, in accordance with the wishes of Queen Victoria; sheets of bluebells flower here in May.

Tropical profusion

Kew Village
The main gate to the Royal Botanical Gardens is on Kew Green, an immaculate triangle of green where long, lazy games of cricket are played on summer Sundays against a backdrop of late Georgian buildings, provided for members of George III's court. St. Anne's Church, built of yellow brick in 1714, stands on the southern edge of the green and is a quirky, attractive building with an octagonal cupola and Venetian-style windows. Thomas Gainsborough, the artist, is buried in the churchyard and two former directors, of Kew Gardens, William and Joseph Hooker (father and son), both have unusual memorials of porcelain decorated with ferns and flowers. Two museums stand nearby, on the opposite bank of the Thames. The Kew Bridge Steam Museum (Green Dragon Lane – open daily, but in steam on weekends only) houses several giant steam engines that once pumped millions of gallons of fresh water a day to supply the needs of West London. Steam-powered boats, trucks, and traction engines are also on display, as well as a Victorian machine shop and forge. Its near neighbor is the Musical Museum (368 High Street, Brentford – open weekends from April to October), housed in a converted Victorian church. There are 200 or so mechanical instruments crowded into the building, all in working order, as the guides demonstrate when they show you around, filling the church with magnificent sounds.

Adam-style finery

Osterley Station
Osterley Park can be reached by taking the Piccadilly tube line to Osterley station, then following the A4 Great West Road to the entrance on Thornbury Road. Take a glance at the station itself, a 1930s design by Charles Holden, modeled on the town hall in the Amsterdam suburb of Hilversum. Other tube stations by Holden have interesting architecture: He designed the circular concourse of Piccadilly Circus station in 1925–28, but his best work is on the Piccadilly line from Holloway Road, with its tilework, to Arnos Grove, frequently compared to a flying saucer.

▶ Osterley Park *209B2*

Osterley Park, on the western fringes of London, was built in the 1560s as a manor house for the wealthy City merchant Sir Thomas Gresham. After Gresham's death, ownership of the house changed many times, but the building remained untouched. In 1711 Sir Francis Child, founder of Child's Bank, acquired the property, using the capacious Elizabethan vaults to store large quantities of money but never actually living there himself. His grandsons, Francis and Robert Child, then decided to transform the house along neoclassical lines, hiring Robert Adam to do the work in 1761. Externally, the final result is a strange marriage of styles, for the Tudor brick corner turrets were retained but linked together by a grand open portico with a carved and painted pediment supported by Doric columns.

Inside the house, the sequence of remodeled rooms is exactly as Adam left them, beautifully restored during recent years and furnished with superb examples of 18th-century tapestries, chairs, and pictures. Even so, many visitors will find that the classical themes that give unity to the house and its decoration do become a little wearying and obsessive after a while. Horace Walpole, the writer, whose own home at Strawberry Hill introduced the neoGothic style, found some of the rooms "too theatric" and described the Etruscan Room as "painted all over like Wedgwood's vase." On the other hand, Walpole did take a liking to the rich pink, green, and gold ceilings of the Drawing Room, with its carpet of similar hues, describing the room as "worthy of Eve before the Fall"—a rather strange comment to make about such a sophisticated room, which is the exact antithesis of innocent naturalism. The description might perhaps have been more appropriately used for the tranquil garden, with its eye-catching bridge, its lakes, its stately trees, grazing cows, and long, meandering paths.

Tudor turrets, Adam interiors

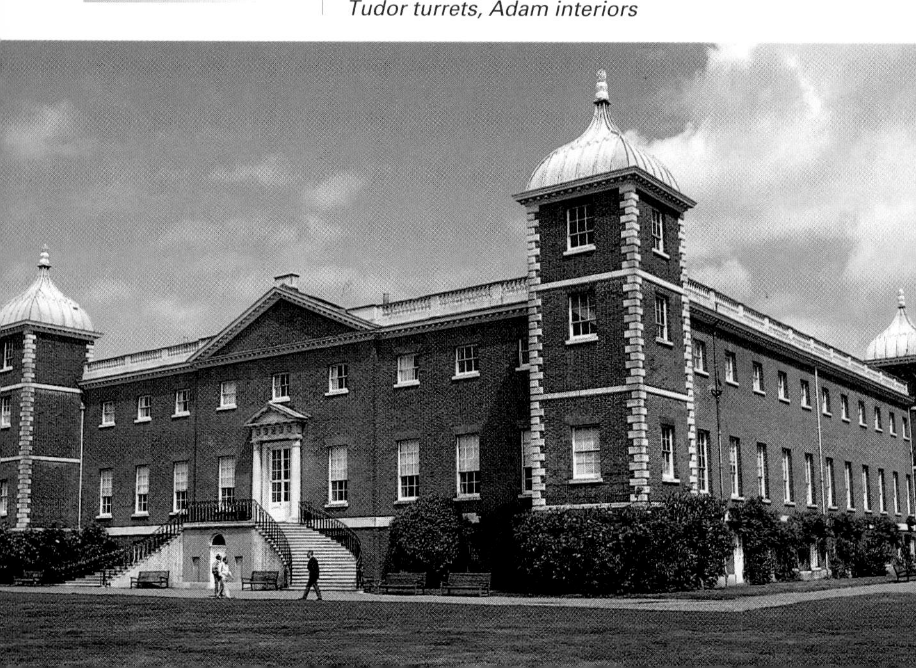

■ Dotted around the outer suburbs of London are several small museums that will appeal to visitors with special interests. Some are quite easily reached by tube; others require a little extra planning – but for those who like to wander away from the beaten tourist track, they provide an interesting alternative. .....■

The Saatchi Collection (98a Boundary Road; Swiss Cottage tube; open Friday and Saturday 12–6) was built up by the advertising mogul Charles Saatchi and his wife, Doris, and contains paintings by Lucian Freud, Howard Hodgkin, Frank Auerbach, and R. B. Kitaj. Only part of the collection is on display at any one time.

The William Morris Gallery (Water House, Lloyd Park, Forest Road, Walthamstow; Walthamstow Central tube then bus 269; closed Sunday and Monday) is worth the time and effort it takes to get there. The Georgian house was home to William Morris in 1848–58 and now displays a collection of textiles, ceramics, stained glass, and furniture designed by Morris and his contemporaries, as well as a collection of paintings bequeathed by the artist Sir Frank Brangwyn, which is rich in Pre-Raphaelite works.

The Royal Air Force Museum (Aerodrome Road, Hendon; Colindale tube) is housed in a series of hangars and loosely built around the history of the RAF. It starts with early experiments with flight (from balloons to man-lifting kites) and comes up to date with high-tech displays on modern fighter aircraft. A whole section is devoted to the Battle of Britain, and many historic aircraft are on display. An art gallery shows works by major sculptors and painters (Elizabeth Frink, Paul Nash, Graham Sutherland, and others), gathered together for temporary exhibitions on themes associated with flight.

Martinware
The late 19th century was an age of lively experimentation in the pottery industry, and no products of the period are more humorous and grotesque than the stoneware birds and face jugs produced by the Martin brothers (Charles, Edwin, Robert, and Walter) between 1873 and 1923. The firm moved to Southall in 1877, and the Southall Library has a small museum devoted to their wares (Osterley Park Road; Southall railway station; closed Sunday and Monday. Telephone for an appointment: 081 574 3412).

The RAF Museum in Hendon

Richmond Bridge
Richmond Bridge dates from 1777 and holds the distinction of being the oldest in London: All the other bridges were rebuilt at some stage in the 18th and 19th centuries to cope with an ever-growing traffic burden, but Richmond's elegant five-arch bridge survives in its original form. The design itself is even older—the architect, James Paine, used as his model a bridge designed by the great 16th-century architect Palladio for the northern Italian town of Vicenza.

Richmond

Richmond is a riverside village west of London, reached by Underground or by riverbus from Westminster Pier in summer. Its attractions include several good pubs, such as the White Cross in Water Lane or the Rose of York in Petersham Road, with good food and gardens overlooking the Thames. For the more energetic, there are walks along the leafy east bank of the river to Ham House, or up Richmond Hill to the 1,000-hectare Richmond Park.

If you arrive by train, the river lies to the left as you leave the station, walking down the shop-lined Quadrant to the Square. To the right, Duke Street leads to Richmond Green, an open space surrounded by 17th- and 18th-century houses. Northeast of the green is the Little Green, with its late Victorian Richmond Theatre and the Orange Tree theater pub, sites used for the Richmond Festival in June and July. South of the green, the four houses on Maids of Honour Row were built in 1724 for the ladies-in-waiting of the Princess of Wales. Behind this row, in Old Palace Yard, is the gatehouse of Richmond Palace, most of which was demolished by Parliamentarians after the execution of Charles I.

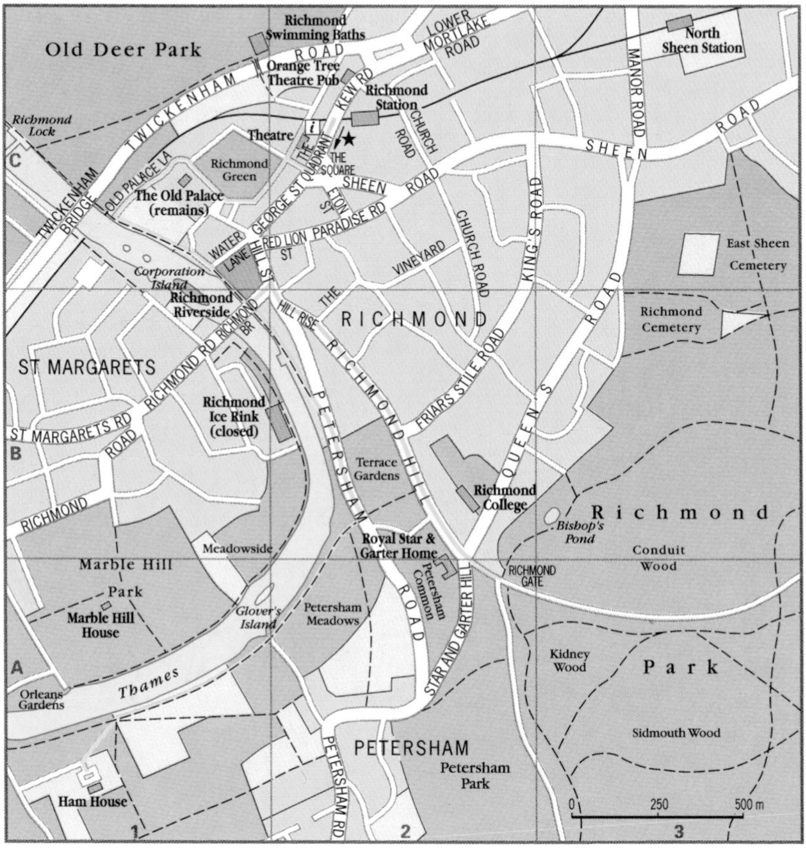

Little alleys full of antiques shops and boutiques lead south to the river itself, spanned by Richmond Bridge (see side panel). North of the bridge is the recently completed Richmond Riverside, a group of 20 buildings in classical style, arranged around four courtyards, with shops, a restaurant, and a tourist information center. The development is the work of Quinlan Terry, an architect who passionately believes in classical values.

A footpath leads south under Richmond Bridge (joining Petersham road for a short stretch), following the course of the Thames to **Ham House▶▶** and offering delightful views across the river and towards Marble Hill House (see page 234).

Ham House (temporarily closed; to reopen in April 1994) is a bold Jacobean building, dating from 1610, but remodeled in the 1670s, giving it a Restoration flavor. The rooms are particularly remarkable for their ostentatious woodwork, plaster ceilings, and furnishings, and the walls are hung with paintings by Lely, Reynolds, and Constable, contributing to the general air of sumptuous grandeur. In the gardens, which have been restored to their 17th-century formality, there is an orangery housing a cafe.

From Richmond Bridge, Hill Rise and Richmond Hill lead upwards for about 0.6 miles (1km) to **Richmond Park▶** ; turn around for views of the river as you climb the hill, which is lined by attractive 18th-century buildings, including Wick House, where the artist Joshua Reynolds lived. The park was enclosed by Charles I in 1637 as a royal hunting ground, and red and fallow deer still wander freely around the grassland, which is dotted with oak trees (some of which are over 600 years old) and man-made ponds. For garden lovers, the Isabella Plantation, towards the southern tip of the park, is spectacular in late spring when the azaleas and rhododendrons are in full bloom, and has many unusual and attractive flowering trees.

Bygone elegance in Richmond

Richmond Riverside
Quinlan Terry's classical design for the buildings of Richmond Riverside has proved surprisingly controversial. Many inhabitants of Richmond consider the buildings to be a pleasing addition to their handsome riverfront and a fine complement to the bridge. Architects, however, accuse Terry of being populist and backward-looking. They also claim the development is dishonest: Behind the classical porticos and façades there are ordinary, steel-framed offices. It is an argument that is likely to continue for some time. Competing designs submitted for the redevelopment of the area around St. Paul's Cathedral and Spitalfields, in the City of London, have produced a similar conflict between the classical and the post-modernist approach—with most of the public firmly ranged behind the former.

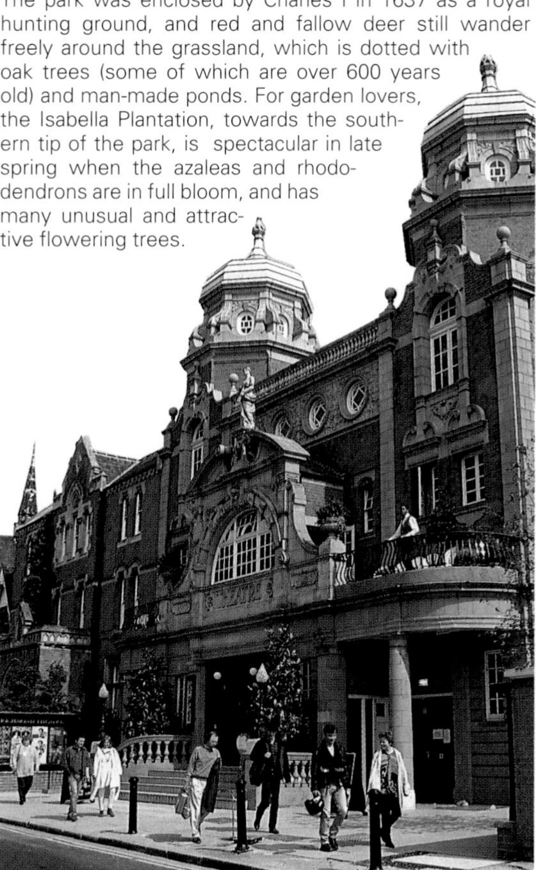

The Victorian Richmond Theatre

From Syon to the scaffold Several former inhabitants of Syon House ended up in the Tower of London or with their heads on a block. Before the house was built, it was the site of a convent, which Henry VIII seized at the Dissolution and gave to the Duke of Somerset. In 1541 Catherine Howard, the king's fifth wife, was imprisoned here, falsely accused of adultery, before her trial and execution. Next it was the turn of Somerset himself: He was appointed Protector to the boy king Edward VI at Henry VIII's death but was thought to exercise too much power; accused of conspiracy, he too was beheaded in 1552. Syon then became home to Lady Jane Grey, but only for a short while. Having been proclaimed queen in 1553 she was executed in 1554, the unfortunate victim of the political maneuverings of the age.

►► Syon House and Park 209A2

Syon House and Park offer an escape from the bustle of London and offer several attractions: a stately home by architect Robert Adam, grounds landscaped by Capability Brown, a butterfly house, and an art gallery (the house is open Wednesday to Sunday, 11–5, April to September, but the other attractions are open daily from 10a.m.). To reach Syon House take the tube to Gunnersbury, then bus 237 or 267; or go to Syon Lane station and walk down Syon Lane and Spur Road to the London Road entrance.

Syon House From the outside, this historic seat of the Dukes of Northumberland is grim and uninviting, but the battlemented mid-16th-century building contains some of the most magnificently decorated rooms in England. They are the work of Robert Adam, who remodeled the interior from 1761, employing costly marbles, gilded statues, and classical plasterwork to create a palace fit for one of the country's most powerful aristocratic families.

As you explore the house you'll discover that some rooms were exclusively for the males of the family and others for the females, a fact reflected in the decoration and furnishings. The immensely long but narrow Long Gallery, for example, was designed, according to Adam, to "afford variety and amusement for the ladies" and is finished in pastel mauve and green with highlights of gold. Around the cornice of the same room, portrait medallions illustrate the lineage of the Dukes of Northumberland, beginning with Charlemagne, the first Holy Roman Emperor, from whom the family claims descent. Several rooms are hung with important family portraits, including works by Gainsborough and Reynolds.

Syon Park The extensive grounds of Syon House (22 hectares) were landscaped between 1767 and 1773 by Capability Brown, a renowned exponent of the "naturalistic" style; his lakes, lawns and fine specimen trees all serve to create an idyllic version of the countryside.

In the distinguished company of the ancient gods at Syon

Family portraits of the Dukes of Northumberland

One of the most exciting features of the garden is the Great Conservatory, with a graceful central dome of glass and iron and two curving side wings. This was built between 1820 and 1827 by Charles Fowler (the architect of Covent Garden market) and is said to have been a major influence on Joseph Paxton's design for the Crystal Palace. The conservatory contains a variety of different gardens, ranging from the damp fernery to the hot dry cactus beds.

Also close to the house are formal flower-beds and a huge garden devoted entirely to roses is currently being planted. Ultimately it will contain more than 8,000 plants, including many older and more unusual varieties. Further away, a stroll around the lakes will show you many moisture-loving plants, flowering shrubs, and unusual trees.

Other attractions At Syon, visitors are always entertained. Within the grounds (housed in the former Riding School) is an excellent **garden center** with a wide range of plants for the house and garden.

The **London Butterfly House** has hundreds of large and colorful species flying freely in a jungle-like setting; there is also a display of giant spiders, scorpions, and other creatures that usually bring on a *frisson* of fear.

Syon also has a number of shops selling gifts and health foods, plus a cafe and a restaurant, although you can also take a picnic in the grounds.

Old Isleworth

Just outside the gates to Syon Park is the core of Old Isleworth, whose Georgian houses have recently been restored as part of a major redevelopment program transforming a formerly run-down area. All Saints Church, by Michael Blee, dates from 1969 and incorporates part of a 14th-century church destroyed by fire during World War II. Nearby is a famous riverside pub, The London Apprentice (62 Church Street), dating in its present form from the mid-18th century. Its Georgian interiors are decorated with original Hogarth prints. Apprentices from London would line up here for a drink in times past, which accounts for its name. The pub restaurant has good views over the river to Richmond Park and serves traditional English food.

Twickenham houses
York House, off York Street, is a late 17th-century mansion built by an Indian tea merchant, Sir Ratan Tata, with delightful gardens stretching toward the river. The building now houses local government offices, and the tourist information office in the adjacent Civic Centre provides details of tours that take place on Fridays. The villa built by the poet Alexander Pope, in which he lived from 1719 to 1744, has now been replaced by a school, St. Catherine's Convent, which lies south of Twickenham, on Crossdeep. But Pope's mineral-lined grotto survives from his garden, beneath the road, and can be visited by appointment (tel. 081 892 5633).

One of Twickenham's most famous houses is Strawberry Hill (on Waldegrave Road), now St. Mary's Training College. Horace Walpole (novelist and letter writer) bought a simple cottage here in 1747 and spent the next 30 years turning it into a neo-Gothic castle, extending it bit by bit and taking ideas from genuine medieval buildings. The building was enormously influential in reviving the Gothic style and led to many follies, churches, and even whole houses (such as Lacock Abbey in Wiltshire) being built in the same picturesque Strawberry Hill manner. The house can be visited by appointment (tel. 081 892 0051).

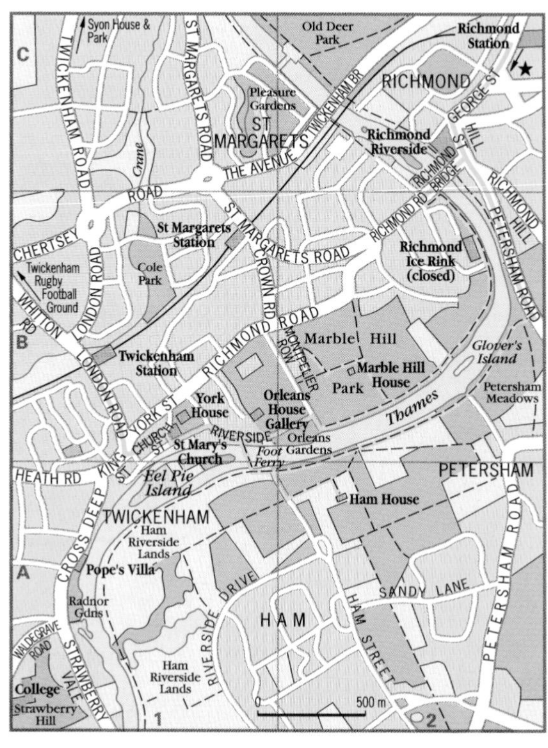

►► Twickenham

Twickenham, to sports fans, means the famous rugby ground where international matches are held, as well as the Varsity match between Oxford and Cambridge. The ground lies to the north of the village, on Whitton Road (with a museum open weekdays 10–2:30 on the history of the game). The village itself is best reached by taking the Underground to neighboring Richmond (see pages 230–1) or the riverbus, which sets off from Westminster Pier in summer.

From Richmond station, turn left and walk down the Quadrant, George Street and Hill Street to cross Richmond Bridge. On the opposite bank, take the riverside path south to Marble Hill House, set in its spacious and leafy park.

Marble Hill House► is an exemplary Palladian-style villa, built to make the most of the views over the river toward Richmond Hill. It was originally designed as a rural retreat for Henrietta Howard, mistress of the Prince of Wales (the future George II) in 1729; later it served as the abode of another royal consort, Mrs. Fitzherbert, secretly married to the future George IV in 1785, then rejected by him in favor of Caroline of Brunswick. As with all Palladian villas, the main rooms are on the second floor, the *piano nobile*. The Great Room is furnished as it would have been in the time of Henrietta Howard, when regular visitors included the writers John Gay, Horace Walpole, and Alexander Pope—the latter advised on the layout of the garden, with its groves of statuesque trees and manicured lawns.

From Marble Hill, visit Montpelier Row, to the northwest, to take a look at one of the best surviving examples of early rowhouse development in London, dating from 1720.

The riverside path continues upstream to the **Orleans House Gallery▶** , built by James Gibbs in 1720 and beautifully framed by woodland. The gallery is all that remains of Orleans House, which was demolished in 1927. The name derives from the fact that the Duc d'Orléans (later to become King Louis-Philippe of France) lived here from 1814 to 1817. Now the gallery displays art for sale and the Ionides Collection of Topographical Paintings of Richmond and Twickenham.

From the Orleans House Gallery, continue along Riverside towards **Twickenham Village▶**, passing two good waterside pubs that offer food and refreshment (the Riverside Inn and the White Swan). Beyond lie Church Lane, Bell Lane, and Water Lane, historic streets at the heart of Twickenham, lined with Georgian houses. The nearby church of St. Mary is an odd combination of medieval tower and classical nave, rebuilt in 1715. Inside are monuments to Alexander Pope, his parents, and his nurse: Mary Beach. Church Street, now pedestrianized, has good shops and is the site of a fair held in May during the Twickenham Week festival. London Road leads north towards the railway station for trains back to central London; otherwise, you might consider crossing the Thames by foot ferry from Riverside to visit Ham House (see page 231), and then walking back along the Thames to the tube station at Richmond.

Rugby at "Twickers"

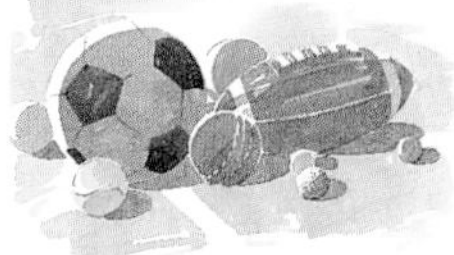

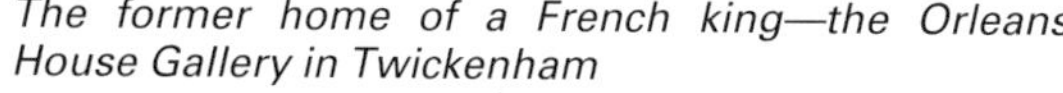

The former home of a French king—the Orleans House Gallery in Twickenham

Eton
Thames Street leads from Windsor Castle down to the river, where Windsor Bridge takes you to Windsor's twin town of Eton, on the northern bank. This is the home of exclusive Eton College, the private school that has produced no fewer than 20 prime ministers, and when school is in session you will see the students dressed in their distinctive tail coats and wing collars. The Tudor-style school buildings include a Museum of Eton Life, with displays on the school's history, and the chapel is worth visiting for its 15th-century wall paintings and stained-glass windows by the contemporary artists, John Piper and Evie Hone.

▶▶▶ Windsor *209A1*

In late November 1992 fire broke out at Windsor Castle, and by the time it was brought under control some of the State Apartments were reduced to charred ruins. Restoration work, costing upwards of £30 million, has now begun, while many parts of this historic castle remain open to the public (parts of the castle are closed when the royal family is in residence; tel. 0753 868286).

Windsor lies 21 miles (34km) west of London, and is easily reached by train from Paddington. Part of Windsor Central Station has now been converted to a waxworks museum run by Madame Tussaud's, recreating the scene in 1897 when a special train arrived here to celebrate Queen Victoria's Diamond Jubilee.

Windsor Castle The castle itself, reached by elevator and footbridge from the station, towers above the town on a chalk cliff. Its strategic site was first defended by William the Conqueror in 1070 and for the next 900 years the building was continually enlarged, growing from a medieval castle to a vast and complex royal palace. It took on its present appearance during the 1820s.

Most impressive of all the castle buildings is St. George's Chapel, a masterpiece of Perpendicular Gothic architecture, begun in 1478 and completed in 1511. Ten monarchs are buried here, but the best monument is that of Princess Charlotte (who died in 1817 in childbirth) in the northwest chapel. It shows the princess ascending to heaven with an angel carrying her stillborn child. The elaborate 15th-

Above: castle guard
Left: Windsor Castle gatehouse, built by Henry VIII

century choir stalls are covered in vignettes (animals, jesters, the Dance of Death, and Biblical stories) and surmounted by banners of the 26 Knights of the Garter, whose installation has taken place here since 1348.

The State Apartments are hung with works from the royal collections, but the star attraction is Queen Mary's Doll's House, designed by Sir Edwin Lutyens and given to the nation in 1923. The furnishings are designed at one-twelfth lifesize, the plumbing and lighting really work, and several authors and artists of the day contributed miniature paintings or handwritten books to the library.

Windsor town After visiting the castle, it is worth exploring Windsor's shops and public buildings. The Guildhall on the High Street was completed in 1707 by Sir Christopher Wren. Its Tuscan columns, on the ground floor, do not touch the ceiling; apparently, the town council insisted on having them, but Wren left the gap to prove that they were structurally superfluous. Continuing up the High Street you will pass the 19th-century parish church of St. John the Baptist; further on and to the left, St. Albans Street leads to the Royal Mews and an exhibition of the Queen's horses, carriages, and state coaches.

Windsor Great Park You can continue from here up Park Street to the Long Walk, which skirts Windsor Great Park. This 3-mile (4.8km-) avenue was laid out by Charles I and planted with elms, but the original trees died and had to be replaced in 1945 with chestnuts and plane trees.

Windsor Great Park
Windsor Great Park is a separate attraction in its own right, or rather several separate attractions. For the nature lover, there are long walks within the 800-hectare parkland, whose vast and ancient oaks are host to many rare butterflies (such as purple hairstreaks) and birds (including woodpeckers). On the southeastern fringes of the park, the Savill Garden (Englefield Green) consist of 14 hectares of woodland, along with formal rose gardens and perennial borders, named after Eric Savill, a former park ranger. There is also a well-stocked garden center. The Valley Gardens, 0.5 miles (0.8km) south near Egham, lie along the northern shores of Virginia Water, and are famous for massed flowering shrubs: viburnums, witch hazels, and mahonias in winter; camellias, azaleas, and rhododendrons in spring; and hydrangeas in summer.

Charges
When making a reservation, check what the quoted room rate includes: usually the price includes VAT (Value Added Tax) and a service charge, but it is best to be sure, because these can amount to nearly a third of the bill. Breakfast is often included in the cheaper hotels; the more upscale you go, the more likely it is that breakfast will be an extra.

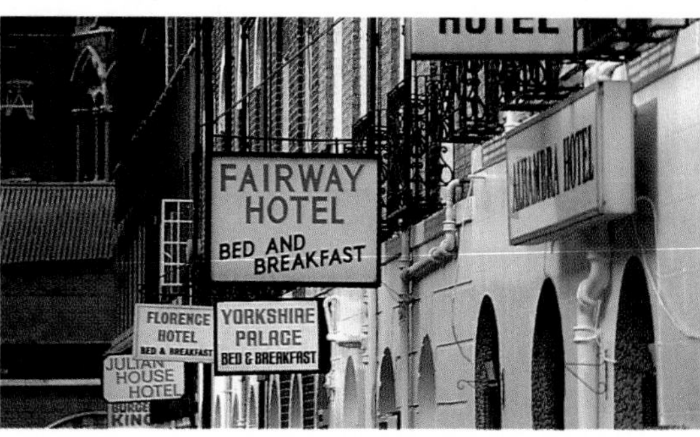

The cost of hotel accommodation in London is horrendously high. You can expect to pay £100 a night for a very ordinary room, and the rates begin to soar if you stay at one of London's grand old hotels such as the Connaught, Claridges, the Dorchester, or the Savoy. Good value hotels and guest houses do exist, of course (quite a number of them are listed in the Directory section at the back of this book). Rooms in these hotels are, however, very much in demand, and to get a room you must book well in advance—often two or three months prior to your visit. Many hotels will ask you to confirm your reservation in some way and will charge you a fee if you cancel at short notice or fail to turn up. In some cases you will lose any deposit you have paid and some hotels will charge the cost of the room to your credit card, so advise your hotel as soon as possible of any change of plans.

General tips Here are a few general points to bear in mind when staying in London:

• For cheaper hotels and guest houses within walking distance of central London, concentrate on the Bloomsbury area (for example, hotels in Gower Street or Cartwright Gardens, off Russell Square).

• Remember that many hotels geared primarily to business travelers offer much cheaper rates at the weekend. It is worth checking to see whether big chains such as the Forte group or Thistle Hotels are offering one of their regular weekend-break discount offers. Some hotels also offer lower rates to guests staying for a week or more.

• London is a popular year-round destination, but rates can be cheaper during February and March, and October and November. London is also generally quieter and less hectic during these months.

• Consider alternatives to hotels, such as renting apartments or staying with a London family. The **London Tourist Board** (tel. 071 730 3450) has leaflets on these plans and publishes a comprehensive guide to hotels, guest houses, apartments, and bed-and-breakfast establishments: This is called *Where to Stay in London* and is available from many bookshops or by visiting the LTB information center on the forecourt of Victoria station. There is also an Accommodation Booking Service here and at the LTB desk at Heathrow airport.

Hotel facilities The biggest problem with London hotels is noise: Many are located in busy streets, and the traffic seems to go on around the clock. Many hotels have

Promise of luxury

The Russell Hotel in Bloomsbury

double or triple glazing to keep out the sound but that can make rooms unbearably stuffy, especially since air conditioning is by no means a standard facility. You should bear this point in mind when choosing a hotel and, if you value peace and quiet, look for hotels on side streets in residential areas; or request a room at the rear of the hotel or higher up in the building.

Facilities you can pretty well take for granted in all but the cheapest hotels normally include a private bathroom, a television, and a direct dial IDD telephone—but beware the very high mark up that many hotels make on telephone calls. Increasingly even the cheapest hotels are supplying electric kettles and tea or coffee sachets so that guests can make their own hot drinks. For other facilities, such as car parking, 24-hour room service, gyms, and swimming pools, you can expect to pay a very high premium within central London.

Park Lane commands a high premium

Food and drink

London's cafes and restaurants compare with the world's best

Eating and drinking in London have undergone a revolution in the last 10 years. One major change was the reform of liquor licensing laws in 1988; pubs can now be open all day and many have turned themselves from rough and smoky "boozers" into pleasant all-purpose bars where you can go for breakfast, brunch, lunch, afternoon tea, pretheater snacks, or dinner.

Another change has been the huge increase in the range and choice of cuisines. Thai food was virtually unheard of in London in the early 1980s until the trail was blazed by **Bahn Thai** (21A Frith Street, 071 437 8504) and its near neighbor, **Chiang Mai** (48 Frith Street, 071 437 7444). The Big Bang, the liberalization of the London financial markets, also contributed to the culinary revolution. Suddenly, bankers and stockbrokers from every nation were heading for London and opening prestigious offices. Their desire to eat their own national foods led to the opening of scores of good Japanese and Korean restaurants, not to mention those specializing in good French and Italian food and even American styles, from Cajun to Californian.

Crazes in restaurants and foods have come and gone quite rapidly: Grilled goat cheese and deep-fried Camembert first appeared on menus around 1985, along with warm salads; Spanish-style *tapas* became all the rage in 1988, to be followed not long after by the saté craze; more recently a new wave of Italian food, from *linguini* to *ciabatta*, has become the passion of dedicated gourmets. The result of all this is a vast and bewildering array of restaurants where, whatever your taste, you can eat extremely well and at no great cost. Even the very top restaurants work hard to provide value for money (the recession has made sure of that). It is not difficult to spend £100 a head for a meal with wine at one of the great gourmet temples, such as the **Connaught Grill**; it is equally easy to find quality and variety at the quite reasonable price of £12 to £15 a head.

Snacking in Soho

Food for the budget-conscious visitor

Specialist guides
The restaurant section at the back of this guide lists a range of good restaurants but represents only a tiny sample. Real foodies should buy a full-fledged restaurant guide: *Time Out*, the London listings magazine, publishes one of the best and most comprehensive, compiled on the basis of recommendations received from ordinary Londoners.

Reservations For top restaurants, advance reservations are essential. It is also a good idea to reserve ahead at lunchtimes, because many restaurants in central London have a thriving business-lunch clientele. Many restaurants in the theater district are busiest before and after the shows, so you will stand more chance of getting a table between 7:30 and 9:30p.m. If you don't know the restaurant's telephone number or are having difficulty finding a restaurant with available tables, you can always use the free centralized Restaurant Services (tel: 081 888 8080); if you call this number you will get impartial and up-to-date information and a free reservation service.

Cheap and authentic Tips for eating well and cheaply:

• Choose a cafe or restaurant that does not have a liquor licence but allows you to bring along your own wine: some charge a small corkage fee, but you will save a lot, since restaurants mark wine up by 300 percent or more.

• Try fish and chips, the great British food. There is plenty of choice, even in central London. Award-winning chippies include the **North Sea Fish Restaurant**, 7–8 Leigh Street, in the Bloomsbury area, and the **Sea Shell Fish Restaurant and Takeaway**, 49–51 Lisson Grove, in St. John's Wood.

• Go for restaurants used by the local ethnic community – for example, go to Chinatown to see where the local Chinese eat, ordering the same food as they do; for authentic and cheap Indian food, go to Brick Lane.

• Go for vegetarian food, which is cheap because the ingredients cost less: **Neal's Yard**, in Covent Garden, has two of the best vegetarian restaurants in London and will prove that meat-free food can be tasty and varied.

Fresh fruit ice cream at Neal's Yard in Covent Garden

Shopping

Regent Street decked out for Christmas

Summer temptations on display in Berwick Street market

London offers shoppers a vast range, from mini-city department stores to wheelbarrow bargains and Dickensian specialist shops. A very large number of people come to London just to shop, and for that reason Oxford Street and Regent Street can be crammed to bursting point in summer and in the Christmas shopping season; police are brought in to control the tide of shoppers and particularly long lines can be expected at the most popular stores such as **Hamley's**, the world's largest toy source.

Opening hours The worst crowds can be avoided by shopping early. Shops and stores tend to open around 9a.m. (though some do not open until 10a.m.) and you will often find that service is more attentive during the slacker period before lunchtime shoppers begin to arrive. Shops have become increasingly flexible in their opening hours in recent years; it is now common to find them open until 9 or 10p.m. in the main tourist areas, though the big department stores have late-night opening on only one day a week (typically Wednesday or Thursday). Increasingly, too, there are plenty of small shops open on Sunday, but whether this will continue depends on a parliamentary review of Sunday trading laws.

Bargain time Twice a year, London shops slash their prices in order to sell off the previous season's remaining stock: The January sales start immediately after Christmas and are a popular event (determined bargain-hunters camp out in the streets for several days in advance to be first in the line when the sales open at Harrods, Debenhams, or Selfridges).

The summer sales begin in June or July and last to the end of August. Strict rules govern the way that sales operate in Britain, and the fact that you bought an item in a sale does not affect your statutory rights as a consumer;

Harrods – a celebrity among stores

you are, for example, entitled to a full refund if the goods prove faulty (unless they were sold as secondhand goods)—but it is essential that you retain your receipt as proof of purchase.

Tax-free shopping If the goods you buy are going to be exported to a non-European Community country you can claim relief from Value Added Tax; this can be a considerable saving (but you have to spend a minimum amount). Most leading stores have details of the tax-free shopping policy and can help with your claims.

Street vendors Beware of street vendors anywhere in London: The products they sell are often not what they claim to be, and while you are absorbed in watching their theatrical sales technique, they may well be picking your pockets.

Markets The same advice about pickpockets applies to crowded street markets, but otherwise, London's markets are enormous fun—the sales banter of stallholders is refreshingly direct and there are real bargains to be found. Here is a selection of the best:

- **Berwick Street** (Soho): top quality fruits and vegetables daily except Sunday.
- **Covent Garden**: antiques on Monday, crafts on Tuesday to Saturday, in and around the central arcade.
- **Camden Lock**: crafts, antiques, books, secondhand clothes, and food, Saturday and Sunday.
- **Portobello Road**: mainly fruit and vegetables during the week, but antiques on Friday and Saturday.
- **Camden Passage**: antiques on Wednesday and Saturday.
- **Petticoat Lane** and surrounding streets: a complete mixture serving City office workers and local East End residents—everything from silk saris to tacky ties, plus fruits and vegetables—daily except Saturday. There is more of the same nearby at **Leather Lane** (daily except Sunday) and at **Brick Lane** (Sunday morning only).

Bargain hunting

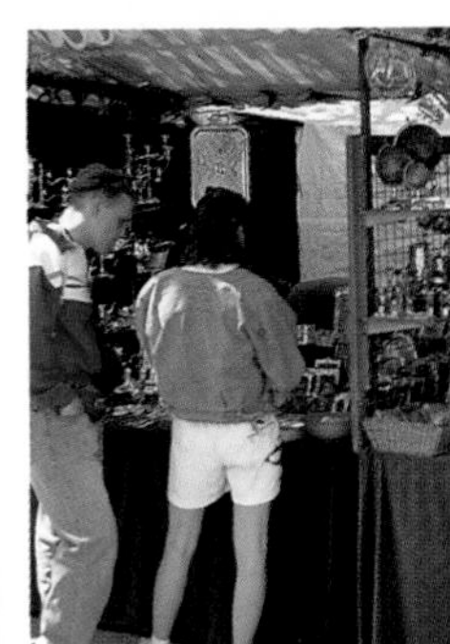

Partly housed in a converted church, Limelight is one of London's liveliest nightlife spots

London has rich and varied nightlife, a fact that is immediately apparent when you flick through the pages of *Time Out*—an indispensable guide if you want to know what is on where, and which clubs, nightspots, or discos are "in" that week. The magazine will also advise you on points of club "etiquette," such as dress codes, so that you look the part—most clubs frown on casual jeans, T-shirts, and athletic shoes. The preferred dress is "smart but casual," though for theme nights you will be expected to dress with flair. Clubs come and go with bewildering speed, but here are a few that have been around for a while:

Camden Palace, 1 Camden Road (tel. 071 387 0428); very popular with overseas visitors: vast and fun.
The Empire Ballroom, Leicester Square (tel. 071 437 1446); one of the biggest discos in Europe, with a famous light show.
The Hippodrome, Charing Cross Road (tel. 071 437 4311); another chic disco that uses all the latest technological effects.
Legends, 29 Old Burlington Street (tel. 071 437 9933); a very glossy club where new trends are seen first.
Limelight, 136 Shaftesbury Avenue (tel. 071 434 0572); set in a converted church, like its New York counterpart.
Samantha's, 3 New Burlington Street (tel. 071 734 6249); a well-established and comfortable disco club that appeals to the more mature crowd.

Stringfellows, 16 Upper St. Martin's Lane (tel. 071 240 5534); the glamorous haunt of the glitterati and of the paparazzi who make their living from following them.

Comedy, cabaret, and jazz
Bass Clef, 35 Coronet Street (tel. 071 729 2476); a dim and cramped basement but a very lively atmosphere, with live jazz Tuesday to Thursday, Latin jazz Friday, and African/Caribbean on Saturday.
The Comedy Store, 28A Leicester Square (tel. 071 839 6642); founded in 1979, and still going strong as the place to see both new and established comedians.
Dover Street Wine Bar, 8–9 Dover Street (tel. 071 629 9813); food and wine by candlelight with live jazz, blues, or soul (and dancing) every night (except Sunday) until 3a.m.
100 Club, 100 Oxford Street (tel. 071 636 0933); live jazz or R&B, depending on which night you go. Drinks at pub prices. Very hot and smoky.
Madame Jo Jo's, 8–10 Brewer Street (tel. 071 734 2473); often listed as part of the London gay scene, but it attracts a huge straight audience as well for scintillating cabaret performed by outrageously camp drag artists.
Ronnie Scott's, 47 Frith Street (tel. 071 439 0747); famous for top-quality jazz – so it gets very crowded, especially on Saturday, when reservations are essential.

Theater, music, and dance See pages 148–9 and 180–1 for details of main performance halls and ticket agencies.

Film Newspapers and listings magazines carry general movie information. A number of theaters show a changing schedule of art/classic/cult/kitsch or off-beat movies, usually with late-night screenings; try the following:
Lumière, 42–9 St. Martin's Lane (tel. 071 836 0691).
Screen on Baker Street, 96 Baker Street (tel. 071 935 2772).
Gate Cinema, 87 Notting Hill Gate (tel. 071 727 4043).
Ritzy Cinema Club, Brixton Oval (tel. 071 737 2121).

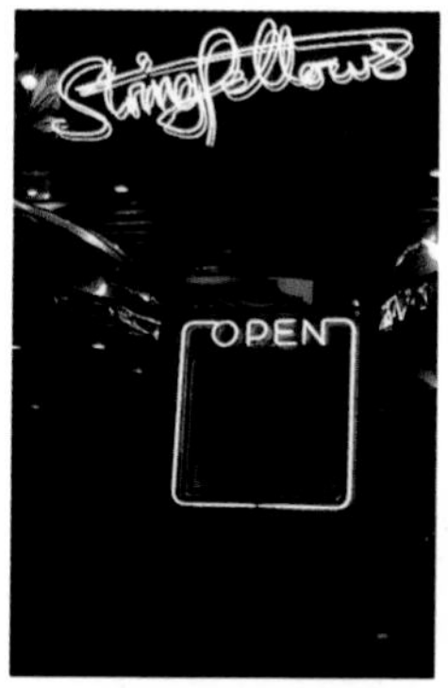

Haunt of the glitterati

Cinematic distractions in Leicester Square

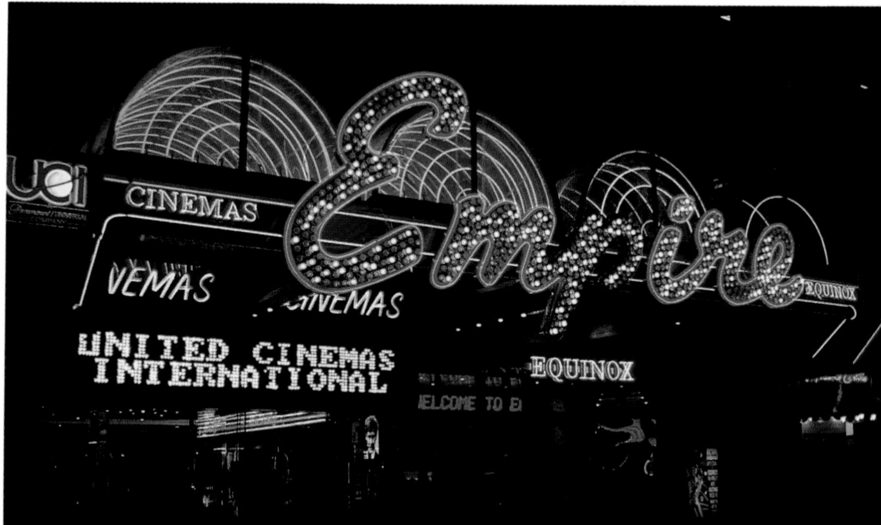

Itineraries

Victorian mail box

Here are some suggestions for making the most of your time in London.

A weekend in London

Since every minute is going to be precious, do as much advance planning and reserving as possible: Reserve hotels, theater tickets, and restaurants well ahead so you do not have to worry about practicalities on arrival; and forget the very popular attractions, such as the Tower of London or Madame Tussaud's, because you will waste too much time standing in line. Remember, too, that Westminster Abbey, St. Paul's, and other major churches will be holding services on Sunday, and visits are thus restricted—if you want to see them, plan to do this on Saturday. Saturday is also an excellent day for sampling markets, such as Camden Lock and Portobello Road. Museums open later on Sunday, so use your Sunday morning for a stroll around some intriguing part of London, such as the City, taking advantage of the relative quiet and lack of traffic to get a good look at the varied architecture.

A week in London

With a whole week at your disposal in London, you'll have a better chance of getting right under the skin of the city. You will probably have your own personal priorities, but consider following suggestions:

Day 1: take a guided tour by bus (see page 40) or a river trip (see page 55) to get your bearings.
Day 2: Explore Covent Garden, with its shops, stalls, street performers, museums, and restaurants, for a truly varied day.
Day 3: Visit one of London's big museums—there are plenty to choose from—in the morning, but plan something different for the afternoon, such as a stroll around St. James's Park and shopping in the Piccadilly/Regent Street area.
Day 4: Hit the popular sights of London, but be prepared to make an early start: You will not stand in line so long if

The National Gallery

you arrive early at the Tower of London or Madame Tussaud's; alternatively, skip Madame Tussaud's and pay a visit to the waxworks museum set out in the undercroft at Westminster Abbey instead—perhaps combining this with the Changing of the Guard at Horse Guards or St. James's.

Day 5: Get out of town altogether and take a trip to Greenwich or Hampton Court, both very rewarding full day trips with lots to see.

Day 6: Visit some more museums: If you have not seen the Victoria & Albert or the British Museum, now is the time to do so—you will find so much to see that you will promise yourself a return visit very soon.

Day 7: Your last day may well be spent shopping for presents in Liberty's or the huge department stores, such as Harrods and Selfridges; if you want something totally different, however, try the shops of Hay's Galleria and take a walk along Bankside for some last memorable views of London.

Best sights for children

1 Natural History Museum see pages 98–9
2 Madame Tussaud's see pages 120–1
3 London Zoo see page 125
4 Pollock's Toy Museum see page 138
5 Museum of London see pages 166–7
6 Bethnal Green Museum of Childhood see page 179
7 HMS *Belfast* see page 191
8 London Dungeon see page 194
9 Imperial War Museum see pages 200–1
10 Museum of the Moving Image see pages 202–3

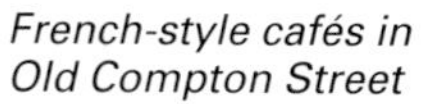

French-style cafés in Old Compton Street

Away from the hustle

1 Chelsea Physic Garden see page 91
2 Leighton House see page 109
3 Linley Sambourne House see page 114
4 The Wallace Collection see pages 126–7
5 Sir John Soane's Museum see pages 154–5
6 Somerset House (Courtauld Institute Galleries) see pages 156–8
7 Museum of Garden History see page 202
8 Dulwich Gallery see page 214
9 Highgate Cemetery see page 225
10 Kew (except on Sundays, when they can be crowded) see pages 226–7

London for free

London has the dubious honor of being one of the world's most expensive cities in matters such as hotel accommodation, but there are still some things that a visitor can do for free.

• Not all museums charge visitors. You can still get into the National Gallery, the British Museum, the Tate, and scores of other, smaller museums for free (even the V & A staff will let you in for nothing, waiving the so-called "voluntary" contribution if you can't afford it).

• It costs nothing to visit the Central Criminal Court (better known as the Old Bailey) or the Royal Courts of Justice, where you can watch the English legal system at work—ask the ushers who guard the entrance to the public galleries which of the trials is likely to prove the most entertaining.

• Both of the major arts locations—the Barbican and the South Bank—have free lobby exhibitions, children's events, musical performances, and other entertainment. With a little bit of nerve you may also be able to get in to listen to orchestral rehearsals and see some of the world's finest musicians and conductors at work.

• If people-watching, clowning, acrobatics, puppetry, and sidewalk musicians are more to your taste, Covent Garden market is the place to go, especially at lunchtime and weekends in summer. The quality of the street theater is very high—though you should, in all conscience, contribute a few coins, since the actors are probably as poor as you are!

• Go to Harrods or Liberty's or any other of London's bazaar-like department stores and dream of what you might buy if you could afford it.

• Go to an auction and watch others spend their fortunes —sales at Christie's, Sotheby's, Bonham's, or Phillips are fascinating to watch.

• Attend a lunchtime concert (many are free, but there is often a collection). There is usually a choice of several, and many take place in the appropriate setting of a Wren church (for details ask at the City of London Information Centre, across from St. Paul's Cathedral, for the leaflet called *Events in the City of London*).

Street entertainers

TRAVEL FACTS

Arriving

Entry formalities Since the new unified Europe came into existence on January 1, 1993, all European Community citizens have the right to enter the United Kingdom at will; in theory you need only to carry some evidence of identity, such as an I.D. card or driver's license. In practice the United Kingdom authorities are uncomfortable with the idea of open borders, arguing that checks are necessary to combat terrorism, smuggling, and illegal immigration. It is therefore advisable to bring your full passport—which, in any event, is usually required as proof of identity when cashing traveler's checks.

Visitors from outside the European Community must have a valid passport. Citizens of most Commonwealth countries, the U.S.A., Japan, and much of South America do not need a visa, but there are some exceptions (including Nigeria, Ghana, India, Bangladesh, Sri Lanka, and Pakistan). If in doubt, check with your travel agent or the British Embassy in your home country.

Airports Most visitors to the U.K. arrive at Heathrow or Gatwick airport. Both have excellent facilities, including tourist information, hotel reservations, and car rental services.

Gatwick From Gatwick, a train service operates from the airport railway station up to Victoria. The Gatwick Express leaves every 15 minutes between 5:30a.m. and 10p.m. and the journey takes just half an hour.

Heathrow The simplest way to reach central London from Heathrow is by Underground on the Piccadilly Line. Although there are some 20 stops before you reach Central London, the journey rarely takes more than 60 minutes. Buses are more expensive. The Airbus service picks passengers up from all terminals at every half-hour between 6:30a.m. and 10:15p.m. daily. Route A1 goes to Victoria train station with interim stops in Earl's Court and Kensington, while the A2 service goes via Marble Arch and Baker Street to Euston train station. Black taxicabs will take you from the airport direct to your hotel, but they are very expensive and best avoided unless you need help with your luggage.

London City This airport, mostly used by business travelers, is closest to the city center but not as well served by transportation, taxicabs, being the only foolproof option.

Stansted There is a good train service from London's third airport, Stansted, which departs every 30 minutes and takes 40 minutes to reach Liverpool Street station.

Liverpool Street Station, terminus for Stansted airport

London's distinctive black taxi cabs

❑ **Airport information:**
Gatwick 0293 535353
Heathrow 081 759 4321
London City 071 474 5555
Stansted 0279 680533 ❑

Other options Visitors from other European countries have a wealth of options for getting to the U.K., such as shuttle flights, which operate between smaller regional airports, trans-European train and bus services (including the Channel Tunnel), ferry, jetfoil, and hovercraft services. Competition for passengers is expected to become increasingly strong and it is well worth shopping around for the best deal. Inclusive packages, covering travel and hotel accommodation, often represent the best value.

Camping
As a way to beat the high cost of hotel rooms, camping does have its appeal, and an increasing number of visitors opt for this—staying in camper vans, rather than under canvas. Sites include **Hackney Camping**, Millfields Road, E5 (tel. 081 985 7656), and **Picketts Lock Centre**, Picketts Lock Lane, N9 (tel. 081 803 4756), but these are both in rather desolate east London locations. If you are an enthusiastic camper it would be better by far to look for a rural campsite outside London and travel in to the capital daily by train. There are many beautiful areas only 30 minutes away from the city by train, in Kent, Sussex, Essex, and Hertfordshire, for example.

Car breakdown
If you rent a car in London, the car rental company will usually give you the number of its 24-hour breakdown service. Otherwise, there are two main organizations offering breakdown services in the U.K.: the Automobile Association (A.A.) and the Royal Automobile Club (RAC). If you are a member of a similar organization in your own country, check before you travel to London whether you have the right to use the services of one of these organizations for free—and bring the necessary documentation.
Automobile Association: membership information tel. 081 891 1441. Emergency breakdown service: 0800 887766 (free phone).
Royal Automobile Club: membership information tel. 071 839 7050. Emergency breakdown service: 0800 828282 (free phone).

Car rental
It is not worth the expense and worry of renting a car in London if you only intend to travel within the city: Using public transit or taxis will cost you far less and save all the time spent looking for parking space and navigating unfamiliar roads. Even for trips out of London, it can be simpler to use train or bus services. If you do decide to rent a car, you will find a huge range of companies and options listed in the *Yellow Pages* telephone directory, and by phoning around you should get a competitive deal.

Some points to bear in mind:
- You must have a full driver's license (an international driver's license is not required).
- You must be over 18 years old to rent a car (and many companies have a higher age limit of 21); you must also have at least 12 months' driving experience.
- Reserving in advance is essential on weekends, especially for the cheaper end of the range (and at the very top end—Rolls Royces are much in demand at weekends for weddings).
- Car rental firms prefer you to pay by credit card so that they can check your address and identity—expect to encounter problems if you want to pay by cash or check (usually a very large deposit is demanded in this case).

❑ **Leading firms—central reservation numbers**
Avis 1 800 331 1212
Budget 1 800 527 0700
Eurodollar 1 800 800 6000
Eurocar 1 800 CAR EUROPE
Hertz 1 800 654 3131 ❑

Most Londoners travel by tube

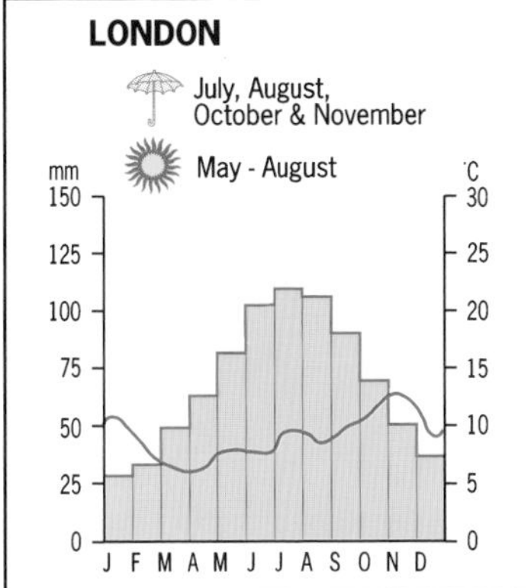

Climate

The British love to talk about the weather simply because it is so variable—changing hour by hour, if not minute by minute. All daily newspapers carry weather forecasts, as do all the TV and radio channels (usually just before or just after the main newscasts of the day) but as every Londoner will tell you, they are not always reliable. London has its own microclimate, because of the great number of heated buildings in the city, so frost and lingering snow are very rare. The temperature seldom falls below freezing point, though chilling northerly winds can make it feel cold in the winter. Rain is the biggest problem: Officially the wettest weeks are from late September to the end of November, but it can be just as wet in the middle of summer. As a rule of thumb, you can usually plan that if you carry full anti-rain gear—waterproof coat and hat, umbrella, boots—the day will probably be dry and sunny, but if you go out unprepared it will pour.

Fortunately, you are never very far away from shelter in London—unless, that is, you decide to go for a hike across Hyde Park!

A British policeman

Crime

A substantial amount of petty crime takes place on London's streets every hour of the day, and visitors are particularly at risk from pickpocketing and theft of property from parked cars (which is another good reason for not driving in London).

Here are some tips to make your vacation safer:

• Make photocopies of important documents such as your passport, and keep notes of traveler's check numbers and credit-card details. This record should be kept separately from the original documents and will help you obtain replacements quickly if the originals are lost or stolen.

• Lock all your valuables in a hotel safe: Most good hotels will allocate you a strongbox with its own key where you can put your money, jewelry, camera, and so on.

• If you must carry valuables, conceal them in a body bag or something similar and keep a tight hold on your camera at all times.

• Be especially wary in crowded situations, such as in street markets, on a bus or subway, or in crowds to cross busy roads, like Oxford Street. Be alert at all times and try not to become so absorbed in window shopping that you are oblivious to other people around you.

• Trust nobody and be wary of anyone who approaches you, no matter how innocently. Some people operate with accomplices who pick your pocket while you are distracted giving directions: Other thieves hang out wherever there are beggars or street musicians watching to see where you put your hand when asked for money—giving them a clue to where you keep your valuables.

If you are robbed you should do the following:

• Report the loss of credit cards and checks to the issuing company immediately.

• Report the loss of a passport to your embassy or consulate (see page 257).

• Make a report to the nearest police station and obtain a copy of your statement so that you can make an insurance claim.

Enjoying a rare spot of sunshine

• It is not sensible to be out in some parts of London late at night on your own. If you must be out, go as part of a group. Do not go to parks or commons after dark and keep to busy, well-lit streets. Buses, trains, and the tube are relatively safe at night, but it is a sensible rule stay with the crowds, rather than exposing yourself to the risk of attack by sitting in an empty carriage. After the public transit system closes down at night it is better to take a taxi, despite the expense, than risk being out on the streets alone—especially in the city suburbs.

Customs regulations
You will not normally have to pay duty on personal possessions brought into the U.K., but some goods, such as tobacco and alcohol, are liable to tax and duty. The amount that you are allowed to import without paying duty depends on where the goods were purchased. There are two different levels of duty-free allowance, as shown below, but you have to be over 17 years of age to qualify.

Goods purchased outside the European Community (E.C.):
• 200 cigarettes or 100 cigarillos or 50 cigars or 250 grams of tobacco.
• 2 liters of non-sparkling table wine.
• either 2 more liters of alcohol under 22% by volume (e.g., table wine, sparkling wine, fortified wines) or 1 liter of alcohol over 22% by volume (spirits and liqueurs).
• 60ml of perfume and 250ml of toilet water.
• other goods up to £36 in value.

Goods purchased in ordinary shops within the E.C. (i.e., where duty and VAT has been paid at the levels prevailing in that country):
Here, technically, there are no limits whatsoever on the amount of tobacco, alcohol, or other goods you

import, provided that you can prove they are for personal consumption and not for resale. H.M. Customs and Excise has issued guidelines covering what they consider to be reasonable quantities for personal consumption (amounts are per person):

- 800 cigarettes or 400 cigarillos or 200 cigars or 1kg of tobacco.
- 10 liters of spirits; 20 liters of fortified wines; 90 liters of wine (of which 60 liters may be sparkling); 110 litres of beer.

Disabled people
London is a better city than most for disabled people. As a general rule, it is a good idea to telephone in advance if you need special help or services so that the museum, restaurant, theater, or organization you are visiting can make arrangements. An organization called **Artsline** (tel. 071 388 2227) offers free information and advice for disabled people on all aspects of the London arts and entertainment scene, including museums, galleries, concert halls, theaters and cinemas. For accommodation contact the **Holiday Care Service** (tel. 0293 774 535), which offers a free advisory service; for specific transport advice, contact London Transport's office for disabled travelers (tel. 071 918 3312). The most comprehensive specialist guide to London for disabled people is *Access in London*, published by Nicholson, and researched and written by disabled people. If you are unable to obtain this from normal bookshops write to Access Project, 39 Bradley Gardens, London W13 8HE and enclose a cheque for £4, made payable to Access Project.

Clamping to deter illegal parking

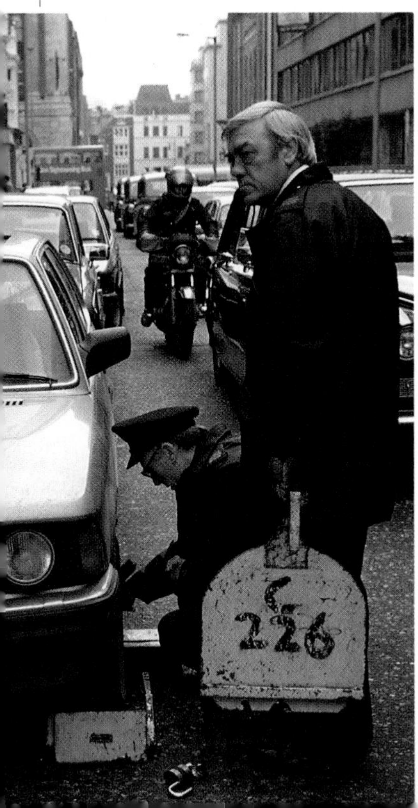

Domestic travel
For travel outside London, see pages 210–11. For travel within London see **Public transportation**, page 265.

Driving tips
The best tip for anyone contemplating driving in London is simple: Don't. London already has too many vehicles and it will take you much longer to get about by car than by public transit. Parking spaces are hard to find and your car will be clamped or towed away if you park illegally. Theft from cars is the biggest area of crime in the U.K. and is still on the increase. If you are foolhardy enough to ignore this advice, then:

- Carry lots of small change to feed parking meters. Do not outrun your allotted time, or return and insert more money once your time has run out; there are plenty of traffic police around to nab offenders, and the fines are expensive. Meter parking is usually free after 6:30p.m., after 1:30p.m. on Saturday and all day Sunday, but there are a few exceptions, so make sure you check what it actually says on the meter.

• Don't park on double yellow lines or in areas reserved for permit holders—to do so virtually guarantees that you will have your wheels clamped, meaning that the police will attach a locking device on your wheels so that your car can't move—a very expensive inconvenience.
• If you are leaving your car parked in London for any length of time, use a patrolled parking lot, staffed by attendants, despite the cost involved, rather than leaving your car on the streets, where it can be stolen.

❑ **24-hour parking garages in central London**
Park Lane (the biggest in central London, below Marble Arch traffic circle—there are usually spaces here even when all other car parks are full)
Brewer Street
Newport Place
Upper St. Martin's Lane

24-hour gas stations in central London
83 Park Lane
71 King's Cross Road
104 Bayswater Road ❑

Taking a rest from sightseeing

Car clamping If your car is clamped, the notice posted on your windshield will explain how to get it released. If you do not have the time to wait around, you can pay someone else a fee to do it for you: Try the **Car Recovery Club** (tel. 071 235 9901) or **Clamp Rescue** (tel. 071 837 7342).

Electricity
The electrical current in the U.K. is 240 volts, 50 cycle AC. Plugs are three-prong square. Most hotels also have two-pin 110 volt shaver sockets. To use most American or European appliances you will need an adapter.

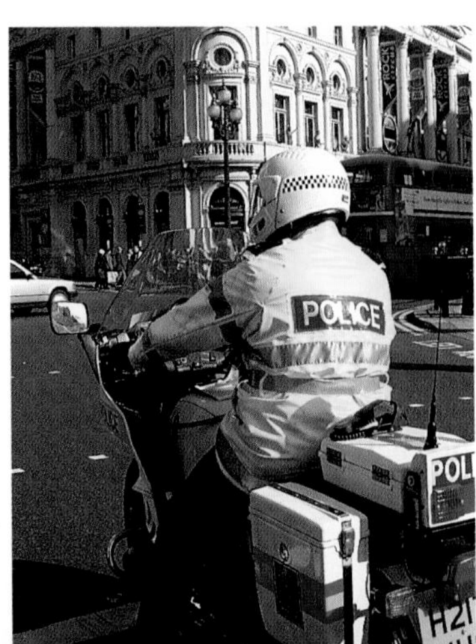

Embassies/consulates
Austria 18 Belgrave Mews West (tel. 071 235 3731)
Australia Australia House, Strand (tel. 071 379 4334)
Belgium 103 Eaton Square (tel. 071 235 5422)
Brazil 32 Green Street (tel. 071 499 0877)
Canada McDonald House, 1 Grosvenor Square (tel. 071 629 9492)
Chile 12 Devonshire Street (tel. 071 580 6392)
China 49 Portland Place (tel. 071 636 5726)
Denmark 55 Sloane Street (tel. 071 235 1255)
Egypt 26 South Street (tel. 071 499 2401)
Finland 32 Grosvenor Gardens (tel. 071 235 9531)
France 21 Cromwell Road (tel. 071 581 5292)
Germany 23 Belgrave Square (tel. 071 235 5033)
Ghana 104 Highgate Hill (tel. 071 342 8686)
Greece 1A Holland Park (tel. 071 727 8040)
India India House, Aldwych (tel. 071 836 8484)
Ireland 17 Grosvenor Place (tel. 071 235 2171)
Israel 2 Palace Green (tel. 071 937 8050)
Italy 14 Three Kings Yard (tel. 071 629 8200)
Jamaica 1–2 Prince Consort Road (tel. 071 823 9911)
Japan 101–4 Piccadilly (tel. 071 465 6500)
Kenya 45 Portland Place (tel. 071 636 2371)
Luxembourg 27 Wilton Crescent (tel. 071 235 6961)
Netherlands 38 Hyde Park Gate (tel. 071 584 5040)
New Zealand New Zealand House, 80 Haymarket (tel. 071 930 8422)
Norway 25 Belgrave Square (tel. 071 235 7151)
Pakistan 35 Lowndes Square (tel. 071 235 2044)
Portugal 11 Belgrave Square (tel. 071 235 5331)
Saudi Arabia 32 Charles Street (tel. 071 917 3000)
South Africa South Africa House, Trafalgar Square (tel. 071 930 4488)
Spain 20 Draycott Place (tel. 071 581 5921)
Sweden 11 Montague Place (tel. 071 724 2101)
Switzerland 16 Montague Place (tel. 071 723 0701)
Turkey 43 Belgrave Square (tel. 071 235 5252)
USA 24 Grosvenor Square (tel. 071 499 9000)
Zimbabwe 429 Strand (tel. 071 836 7755)

Home of the Prime Minister—No 10 Downing Street

CONVERSION CHARTS

FROM	TO	MULTIPLY BY
Inches	Centimeters	2.54
Centimeters	Inches	0.3937
Feet	Meters	0.3048
Meters	Feet	3.2810
Yards	Meters	0.9144
Meters	Yards	1.0940
Miles	Kilometers	1.6090
Kilometers	Miles	0.6214
Acres	Hectares	0.4047
Hectares	Acres	2.4710
U.S. Gallons	Liters	3.7854
Liters	U.S. Gallons	0.2642
Ounces	Grams	28.35
Grams	Ounces	0.0353
Pounds	Grams	453.6
Grams	Pounds	0.0022
Pounds	Kilograms	0.4536
Kilograms	Pounds	2.205
U.S. Tons	Tonnes	0.9072
Tonnes	U.S. Tons	1.1023

MEN'S SUITS

U.K.	36	38	40	42	44	46	48
Rest of Europe	46	48	50	52	54	56	58
U.S.	36	38	40	42	44	46	48

DRESS SIZES

U.K.	8	10	12	14	16	18
France	36	38	40	42	44	46
Italy	38	40	42	44	46	48
Rest of Europe	34	36	38	40	42	44
U.S.	6	8	10	12	14	16

MEN'S SHIRTS

U.K.	14	14.5	15	15.5	16	16.5	17
Rest of Europe	36	37	38	39/40	41	42	43
U.S.	14	14.5	15	15.5	16	16.5	17

MEN'S SHOES

U.K.	7	7.5	8.5	9.5	10.5	11
Rest of Europe	41	42	43	44	45	46
U.S.	8	8.5	9.5	10.5	11.5	12

WOMEN'S SHOES

U.K.	4.5	5	5.5	6	6.5	7
Rest of Europe	38	38	39	39	40	41
U.S.	6	6.5	7	7.5	8	8.5

Emergency telephone numbers
Dial 999 and state whether you need Fire, Police, or Ambulance. All calls are free and you can use any telephone—you can dial from a card phone without inserting a card or from a payphone without inserting any coins.

Health and insurance
In the event of serious illness or injury you can seek medical help at the emergency room (called casualty department) of any hospital that has one, and you can call up an ambulance by dialing 999. Most of the larger hotels have a doctor on call to deal with more routine problems, but a charge is often made for their services.

Free medical treatment is available to citizens of the European Community and some other countries with whom Britain has reciprocal arrangements. It is advisable to check the precise arrangements before you leave your own country because free treatment is usually only available to those who have completed all the necessary documentation in advance. All other foreign visitors (including those from the U.S.A. and Canada) are required to pay the full cost of the medical treatment they receive and you are strongly advised to arrange your health insurance before arriving in the U.K..

Lost property
Any property left on the bus or tube system will be taken to the **Lost Property Office** at 200 Baker Street (next door to the Baker Street tube station). This is open 9:30a.m.–2p.m. Monday to Friday. You must stop by in person (or write a letter) since they won't take inquiries over the phone. If you left something in a taxi cab contact the **Taxi Lost Property Office**, 15 Penton Street (tel. 071 833 0996). If you lose property on a train contact the station at which your train terminated (see telephone directories for station telephone numbers).

Insurance companies will expect you to report the loss of money or valuables to the nearest police station as soon as possible.

The world's news

Media

Overseas newspapers and magazines To keep in touch with events back home through your own favorite newspaper or magazine, the following newsstands (newsagents) pride themselves on having all the leading international papers in stock: **A. Maroni & Son**, 68 Old Compton Street (tel. 071 437 2847). Open Monday to Saturday 7a.m.–7:15p.m. and Sunday 7a.m.–1p.m. **Grays Inn News**, 50 Theobald Road (tel. 071 405 5431). Open Monday to Friday 4a.m.–5:30p.m.

Other good stores with an unusually large stock include **W. H. Smith's** Sloane Square branch, **John Menzies** at 104 Long Acre and **Capital Newsagents**, 48 Old Compton Street.

British magazines and newspapers The single most valuable publication you can buy while you are staying in London is the listings magazine *Time Out*. This packs in a huge amount of information about what is going on where in London, with all the relevant ticket information and telephone numbers. You may not

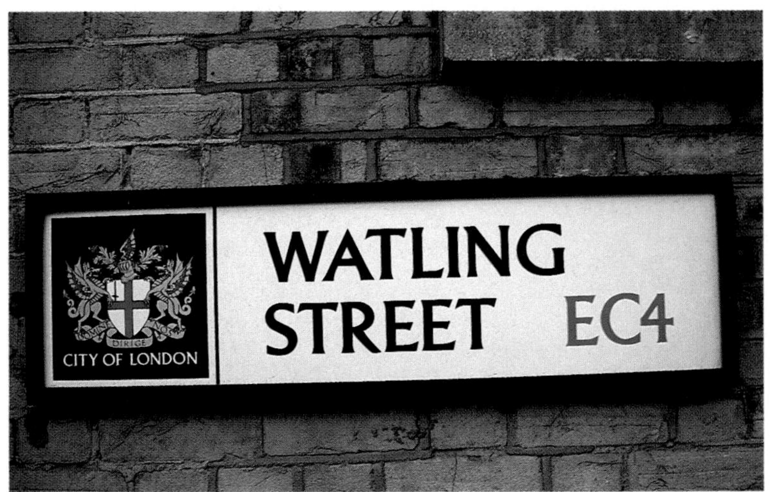

Signs to look out for

necessarily agree with what the reviewers have to say, of course. For a range of opinions on the merits of this or that play, musical, ballet, or opera production you can read the arts and the listings pages of the national daily newspapers. The *Independent,* the *Daily Telegraph,* the *Times,* and the *Guardian* are all serious newspapers with high standards of reporting on U.K. and international affairs, and good arts coverage. The *Financial Times*, printed distinctively on pink paper, covers world business news and market prices, but it publishes a good review section on Saturday—as, indeed, do all the above papers. In addition, the *Independent on Sunday,* the *Sunday Times,* and the *Observer* all bring out heavyweight Sunday editions with page after page devoted to cultural activities, restaurant reviews, travel, consumer affairs, shopping, and fashion, both in London and in the country as a whole.

London also has its own newspaper, the *Evening Standard*, which reviews restaurants and pubs as well as performing arts and exhibitions. Many of the "villages" of London, such as Islington, Hampstead, and Highgate, have their own weekly newspapers covering news and events of local interest.

Radio London has several radio stations that are good sources of music and of information about events in the capital. These include:
Capital Gold 1548AM: "golden-oldies" 24 hours a day, aimed at a broad range of listeners, but mainly those old enough to remember the Top 40 hits of the '60s and '70s.
Capital Radio 95.8FM: pop music and news 24 hours a day, aimed at younger listeners—the station you are likely to hear playing in many shops and taxis.
GLR (Greater London Radio) 94.9FM: a mixture of talk shows, reviews, interviews, and middle-of-the-road music.
LBC Newstalk (London News Radio from October 1994) 97.3FM: mainly news, interviews, and discussions.

In addition there are several national stations. Of these, **Classic FM** (100.99FM) is the most important commercial station. The output consists of popular classics; listen to the early morning program (between 7 and 8:30a.m.) for news of concerts in London where last-minute seats are still available, often at a discount. Otherwise the BBC still dominates the airwaves with its five channels:
Radio 1 98.8FM: mainly pop geared for young people.
Radio 2 89.2FM: middle-of-the-road and easy listening music.
Radio 3 91.3FM: serious music,

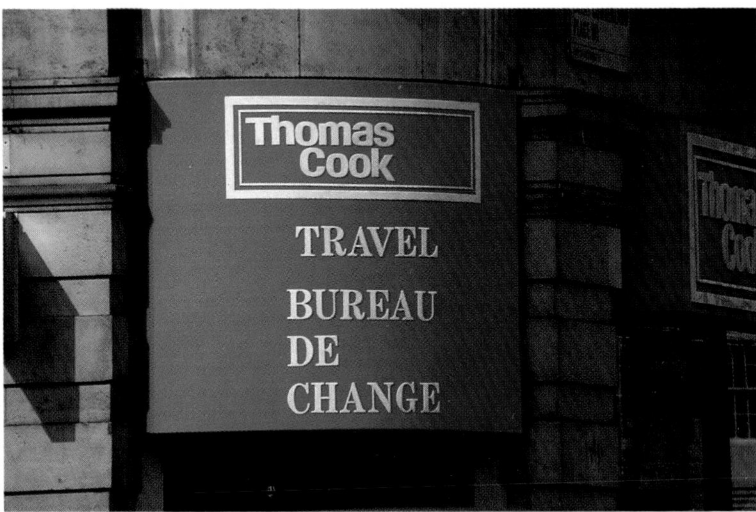

Currency dealers abound

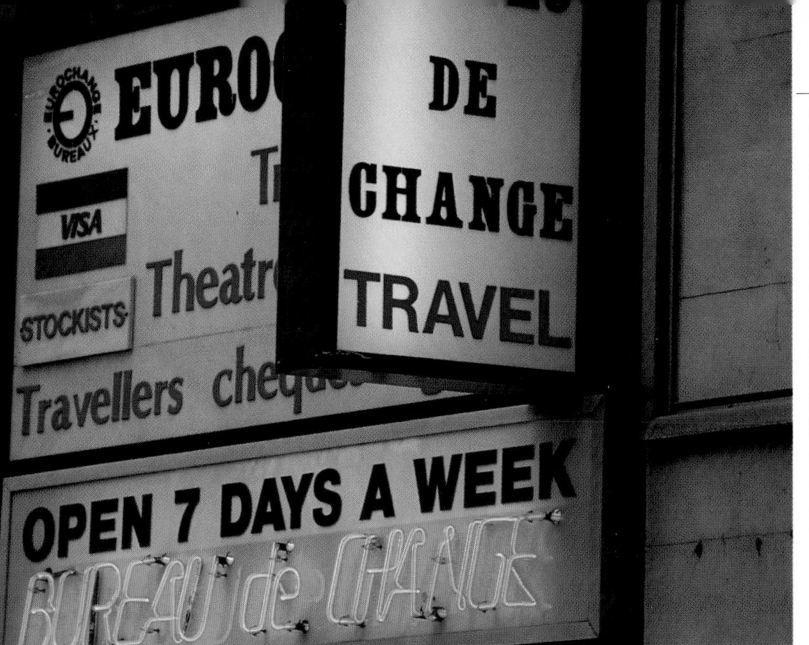

Shop around for the best rates

including live concerts.
Radio 4 93.5FM: news and current affairs plus talk shows and reviews (*Kaleidoscope* is the flagship arts program).
Radio 5 693 and 909MW: mainly sports plus children's shows and educational programs.

Television London has its own independent television networks—Carlton and LWT—which broadcast local news, while ITN provides national and international news programs for this and all other ITV areas. The other channels are BBC1, aimed at mainstream audiences, and BBC2 and Channel 4, both of which show a very broad range of cultural and special interest programs.

Money matters
Local currency Britain's currency is divided into pounds and pence (100p = £1). Notes are available in denominations of £50, £20, £10, and £5. Coins come in denominations of £1, 50p, 20p, 10p, 5p, 2p, and 1p.

Currency exchange Banks give by far the best rates of exchange, whether you are changing currency or traveler's checks, and only in an emergency should you consider using any other service. Hotels will change money and traveler's checks but give a very poor rate, as do those shops that accept U.S. dollars and other currencies. There are scores of *bureaux de change* in London's main tourist haunts, advertising rates that may look more attractive than those of the banks, but once you've paid their hefty commission fees you're actually getting less for your money. If, as a last resort, you decide to use a *bureau de change*, you should seek out a reputable organization like Thomas Cook or Chequepoint: their 24-hour branches can be found at or near Piccadilly Circus, Leicester Square, Marble Arch, and Victoria Underground stations.

Banks There are four main banks in the UK with branches all over London: They are the National Westminster, Barclays, Lloyds, and the Midland. Most of the major branches have a separate foreign currency window; if not, you can use any window that is open. All branches will allow you to draw cash against your credit card or cash Eurocheques (see below).

Credit cards You can use the four main credit cards (Visa, Mastercard, American Express, and Diners

Getting money the high-tech way

Club) just about anywhere in London, though retailers may not take kindly to your using them for small purchases—say, less than £10. One great advantage of using credit cards to pay for your purchases is the favorable exchange rate. Credit card companies use the Interbank rate, which can be several percentage points better than the tourist rate, for their exchange calculations. Moreover, by using a credit card, you avoid paying commission on exchange transactions. These advantages work only if you pay your credit card bill in full when you receive it and only use your card for purchases, not for cash advances. The very high rates of interest charged on cash withdrawals and credit card balances will more than wipe out any exchange rate gains.

Travelers' checks These are a safe and convenient method of carrying large amounts of money, since the checks can be canceled if they are lost or stolen and you can obtain replacement checks. Many stores, restaurants, and hotels will accept traveler's checks in payment for goods and services—but do make sure that you are being offered a favorable exchange rate. You can avoid the problem of exchange rates altogether by buying your checks in pounds sterling in the first place. It is also a good idea to buy some small-denomination checks so that you don't have to cash a big check if you find yourself short of cash towards the end of your trip.

Eurocheques, which are widely used in several other European countries, are not quite so easy to use in London, although all the major banks will allow you to exchange them for cash.

National holidays
Although banks and businesses close on public holidays, the trend in London is for tourist attractions and shops to remain open, except on Christmas, Boxing Day (the day after Christmas), and New Year, when almost everything shuts (and if any of these days falls on a Saturday or Sunday, the next weekday is taken as an additional holiday).

New Year's Day (January 1st)
Good Friday
Easter Monday
First Monday in May
Last Monday in May
Last Monday in August
Christmas Day (December 25th)
Boxing Day (December 26th)

Opening hours
In London the trend is increasingly for shops and sights to open later in the morning—at 10a.m. rather than 9a.m.—but to stay open later in the evenings—until 6p.m. or later in the major tourist haunts. Late-night shopping, when all stores remain open until 8p.m., is on Wednesday in the Knightsbridge and Kensington area and Thursday in the Oxford Street and Regent Street area.

Museums are as a rule open Monday to Saturday 10–6 and Sunday 2–6, but there are exceptions—check the listings magazines or daily newspapers first. Some government-run museums are closed all day Monday, and some commercial museums remain open until as late as 10p.m.

Pharmacies
Remember that many drugs that you can buy over the counter in other countries are only dispensed in Britain with a prescription from a doctor. If you are not eligible for National Health Service treatment you will have to go to a doctor with a private practice for a prescription: **Medical Express**, 117A Harley Street (tel. 071 499 1991), offers a private walk-in medical service; or you can ask your hotel to arrange for a doctor to attend to you if you need a prescription (it is also a good idea to know the generic name of any drugs you take regularly, since they may be sold under a different brand name in the U.K.).

If you have a simple ailment that can be treated with nonprescription drugs, go to a pharmacist and ask for advice. British pharmacists are highly trained and knowledgeable people who will do their best to help you. Pharmacies (Chemists) are to be found all over London. At night, these drugstores post a small sign on their doors telling you the address of the nearest drugstore that is open late. The following centrally located chemists open longer hours than others:

Bliss Chemist, 5 Marble Arch (tel. 071 723 6116). Open daily 9a.m. until midnight.

Boots the Chemist, 44–6 Regent Street (tel. 071 734 6126). Open Monday to Saturday 8:30–8 and Sunday noon–6.

Places of worship
For a full list of churches and their addresses, consult the "Places of Worship" section of the London *Yellow Pages* telephone directory.

Church of England **St. Martin-in-the-Fields**, on Trafalgar Square (tel. 071 930 1862), is a friendly and central church popular with overseas visitors. **Westminster Abbey**, Broad Sanctuary (tel. 071 222 5152), has a fine choir and **St. Paul's Cathedral** is a good place for organ music (tel. 071 248 4619).

Westminster Abbey

Islam **The Central Mosque**, 146 Park Road (tel. 071 724 3363), is the main religious center for London's Muslims. Further information is available from the **Council of Mosques** (tel. 071 636 7568).

Jewish There are Orthodox, Liberal, and Reformed synagogues all over London (200 in total); for further information contact the Central Enquiry Desk, **Board of Deputies of British Jews**, Upper Woburn Place (tel. 071 387 4044).

Roman Catholic **Westminster Cathedral**, Ashley Place (tel. 071 834 9452), is the main Catholic church in Britain. **Brompton Oratory**, Brompton Road (tel. 071 589 4811), has a wide reputation for its particularly good choral music and sung mass in Latin.

Police
The days of the friendly London bobby, ever willing to help tourists find their way, have unfortunately long gone. Today's police, overstretched by a rising tide of crime, are far too busy to patrol the streets (although that is what most law-abiding citizens want them to do), and the police today tend to be brusque and cynical rather than friendly and helpful. If you report a crime the chances of catching and prosecuting the perpetrators are very slim.
If you have your pockets picked or your bag snatched you will receive sympathy but little hope of getting your money back. Still, you should report the crime, if only because insurance companies insist upon it as a policy condition. Look up "Police" in the telephone directory to find the nearest police station. In an emergency, if you are in danger or under threat of any kind, dial 999 and ask for the police, who will usually respond rapidly.

Post offices
Many ordinary shops and newsstands sell postage stamps and phone cards. Post offices can also provide special services, such as parcel post, registered mail, or express deliveries. They normally are open Monday to Friday 9–5:30 and 9–noon on Saturday; many close on Wednesday afternoons. The branch near Trafalgar Square—24–8 William IV Street (tel. 071 930 9580)—is open Monday to Saturday 8–8. The branch at King Edward Street in the City (tel. 071 239 5420) houses the National Postal Museum and has a special sales kiosk for philatelists; it is open Monday to Thursday 9:30–4:30 and Friday 9:30–4.

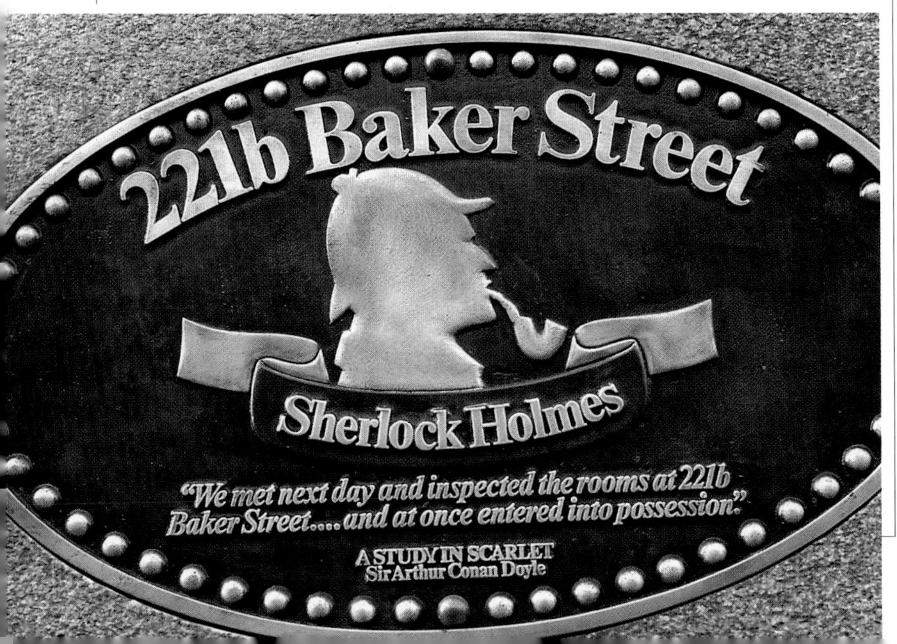

221b Baker Street
Sherlock Holmes
"We met next day and inspected the rooms at 221b Baker Street.... and at once entered into possession."
A STUDY IN SCARLET
Sir Arthur Conan Doyle

The unconventional detective

Royal Mail mailbox

Public transport
Londoners love to complain about the capital's public transit system, but it does work pretty well, considering how old the system is and how many people use it. The Underground, which dates back to the beginning of the century, is the biggest and busiest subway system in the world. The basic choice is between using the Underground system ("the tube") or taking a bus. The tube is usually faster but it can be extremely crowded during rush hours (8–9:30a.m. and 5–7p.m. on weekdays).

Travelcards If you buy a Travelcard, you can switch between the bus and tube system as you please, since the cards are valid on both systems, and on the Docklands Light Railway and certain rail services as well. One-day Travelcards are very economical if you think you are likely to make more than two or three journeys a day; the only drawback is that you cannot use them before 9:30a.m. on Monday to Friday and they are not valid on night buses. Weekly or monthly passes, on the other hand, can be used at any time of day, but to buy one you need a passport-size photograph. Further information on Travelcards can be obtained at any Underground station, and one-day Travelcards can be purchased at the self-service machines found in all stations.

An artistic view

Child fares Children under five travel free on the tube and buses. Children up to age 16 qualify for reduced fares but 14- and 15-year olds must carry a Child Rate Photocard as evidence of their age, available free from tube stations (they'll need to have a passport-size photograph and proof of age).

The Underground The Underground (or tube) runs daily (except Christmas Day). Trains start running at around 5:30a.m. Monday to Saturday and 7a.m. on Sunday, last trains run just after midnight on weekdays and 11:30p.m. on Sundays (the times of

Subway to the tube

the first and last trains out of each station are posted in the station entrances).The system is divided into five zones, and you pay more for trips that pass through one or more zones. A table of fares is usually posted close to the self-service ticket machines. These take coins and will normally give change (if not, a message saying "exact money only" will be lit). You can also buy tickets from the station ticket office, but expect long lines. Most stations now have automatic turnstiles, which will not let you through if you have the wrong ticket—for example, if you traveled further than you originally planned and have not paid the correct fare. In this case, you can present your ticket at the "Excess Fare" window and pay the difference.

Smoking is prohibited anywhere on the Underground. Technically, playing music and begging for handouts are illegal as well. If you feel you are being harrassed, report the incident to station staff or the transit police who patrol the Underground. Most platforms have strategically placed red panic buttons that you can press if you are in danger or feeling threatened—you can use them to speak to the transit police and get rapid help.

Buses Many people prefer to travel by bus in London, for a variety of reasons: Some people find the tube too hot and claustrophobic, while others can't deal with the long walks that are often involved between ticket office and platform (it's even longer when the escalators are not working, which happens fairly often). Above all, buses offer views and social contact. Visitors to London getting onto a bus will often ask for help and directions from the conductor or other passengers; conversations start and soon news, gossip, opinions, and family histories are being exchanged.

At main bus stops (signs show a red circle on a white background) you will find information on bus routes and times. The bus will stop here automatically. At request stops (white circle on a red background) you must wave your arm to stop the bus. Once on the bus, if you want to get off at a request stop, you must ring the bell, located on the hand rails well before reaching the stop.

Fares are set according to zones. Simply tell the driver where you want to go and he or she will tell you the fare (on old-fashioned buses with an open entrance at the back, a conductor will come and take your fare). Drivers and conductors prefer you to give them the precise amount of money but they will give change—although they'll probably grumble if you hand them a large-denomination

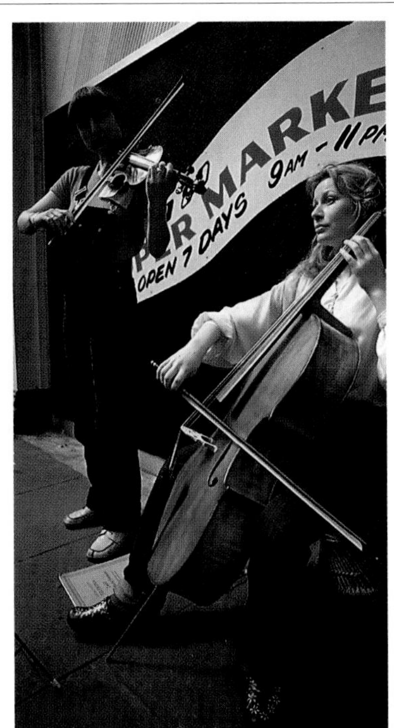

Performing for the fare

note. Hold on to your ticket until the end of the journey because inspectors regularly board the buses to check tickets and catch fare cheaters.

Daytime buses in London run from around 6a.m. to midnight on Monday to Saturday and from 7:30a.m. to 11:30p.m. on Sunday. In theory, buses run at least once every 10 to 15 minutes in each direction along the route, and much more frequently on heavily used routes. In practice, because of the traffic conditions, you can wait for 30 minutes for a bus to arrive, and then three will all come at the same time.

Night buses run between 11p.m. and 6a.m. on main routes through London; all of them pass through Trafalgar Square. A leaflet (called *Buses for Night Owls*) is available from London Transport information centers (see below) detailing the routes and times.

Docklands Light Railway The computerized and driverless trains of the Docklands Light Railway (DLR) serve

Working out the route

the newly developed Docklands area to the east of the City. The DLR is part of the Underground system, so Travelcards may be used. The system operates between Tower Gateway station (near Tower Hill Underground) and the tip of the Isle of Dogs. Mechanical and engineering faults have dogged the DLR, but it can usually be counted upon to run between 5:40a.m. and 9:30p.m. Monday to Friday with a more limited service at weekends (tel. 071 222 1234 for information).

River cruises London's river, the Thames, is an underutilized transport artery. A riverbus service used to operate between Chelsea and Greenwich, but this went into liquidation in August 1993 because there were too few regular passengers to make the service feasible.

At present the only way to travel on the Thames, enjoying London's skyline from a different perspective, is to use one of the tourist cruise services that operate from Westminster Pier (see page 55).

Travel information The main London Transport Information Centre, at 55 Broadway, is open during normal office hours and supplies free route maps and schedules as well as information brochures in several languages. You can also phone for information (tel. 071 222 1234). Travel information centers can also be found at Heathrow, Euston, King's Cross, Oxford Circus, and Piccadilly Circus tube stations and at Victoria train station.

Student and youth travel
If you have an International Student Identity Card you can get special deals on long-distance travel to the U.K., such as youth rail passes. Once in London, it is worth looking out for the theaters, movie houses, and exhibitions that offer reduced rates for students. The listings magazine *Time Out* has good information about student discounts and about getting the best out of the city's sights and entertainment at little cost generally.

Telephones
There are public telephone booths all over London—in the streets, in pubs and stores, in museums, and on station platforms. The once ubiquitous red telephone boxes have now virtually disappeared (a few remain in protected areas). They have been replaced with modern glass booths provided by one of the two main telephone companies: BT (British Telecom) phones are still the most numerous, but you will also see Mercury call boxes, which have marginally cheaper charges for long distance calls.

• **BT coin-operated phones**: These will only accept £1, 50p, 20p, and 10p coins.

• **BT card phones**: these accept BT phone cards, which can be bought from post offices and newsstands in various denominations. An increasing number will also accept credit cards.

You see more by bus

Near antiques in Islington

• **Mercury card phones**: these accept both credit cards (minimum charge 50p) and Mercury phone cards, which are sold at the same outlets as BT cards (Mercury cards are much better designed, with imaginative pictures on the upper face, and some early versions have now become collectors' items).

• **Dial tones**: when you lift the receiver you should hear a continuous dial tone. After you have dialed you will hear ring-ring-pause, ring-ring-pause to indicate that the number is ringing at the other end. A series of rapid bleeps means that the number is busy; a continuous note means the number is busy "unobtainable"—this is usually because you have misdialed, so try again.

• One way to keep the cost of calls down is to use public telephone services; hotel phones are horrendously expensive and calls are often charged at three or four times the

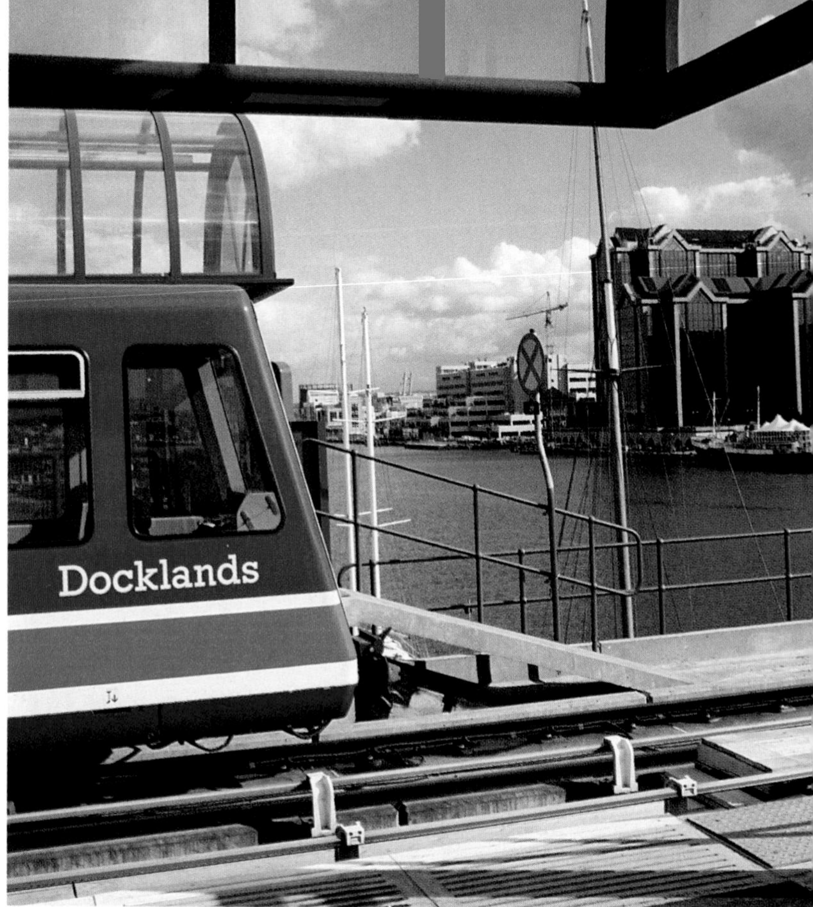

The Docklands Light Railway

official rate. The cost of a call from a public phone depends on when you make it. The cheapest times for calls within the U.K. are 6p.m.–8a.m. Monday to Friday and at weekends. The most expensive time is 9a.m.–1p.m. weekdays; it is slightly less expensive to call between 8a.m. and 9a.m. and 1p.m. and 6p.m.

❑ **Useful numbers**
International lines 010
Operator (for collect call/reverse charge/credit card calls within the U.K.) 100
International operator (for collect call/credit card calls outside the U.K.) 155
Directory assistance: London 142; rest of U.K. 192; overseas 153
International telegrams: 190 ❑

Time
Between October and March, Britain observes Greenwich Mean Time; during British Summer Time, from March to October, clocks are put forward by an hour.

Tipping
The British are ambivalent about the practice of tipping. Most people consider it an imposition if they are on the giving end, while those who are on the receiving (or non-receiving) end can react furiously to anyone who fails to give them what they consider a right. Taxi drivers are particularly touchy: if you don't give them at least 10 percent of the fare as a tip, you will hear yourself described in very unflattering terms. Waiters are equally demanding, the more so the higher up the price scale

you eat. Even if service is included in the price you may find that an additional gratuity is expected. Other people who expect tips are restroom attendants, hotel doormen, bell hops and room service waiters, red caps at train stations or airports, hairdressers and barbers, and sightseeing guides. At present bartenders do not expect tips—although you can, if you wish, offer to buy him or her a drink.

Toilets
Finding a toilet in London is not usually too difficult. Museums, pubs, restaurants, department stores, theaters and film cinemas all have them. They are also to be found on every major railroad station, but here you will need the right amount of change to insert into the entrance turnstile. Ugly aluminium "Loomatic" toilets are also springing up all over London: these, too, are coin operated. By contrast, London has some splendid "loos"—those at Harrods are decorated in Art Deco style, while those on the Embankment have glass cisterns (in which, it is said, a former attendant used to keep goldfish).

Tourist information
The London Tourist Information Board operates a number of information centers, where staff will be ready to help you with answers to specific queries and you can pick up brochures, books, maps, and other information. The main center is at Victoria station (see below), where there is a bookstore selling almost every available book on London. The other major centers are at:
Heathrow Terminals 1,2,3 Underground station and Heathrow Airport. Open daily 8:30–6.

Coin-operated "Loomatic"

One of the city's younger visitors takes a relaxing look at London

Liverpool Street Underground station. Open Monday 8:15–7, Tuesday to Saturday 8:15–6, Sunday 8:30–4:45
Selfridges department store (basement), Oxford Street. Open Monday to Saturday 9:30–6 (9:30–8p.m. on Thursday).
Victoria British Rail Station Forecourt. Open daily, Easter to October 8–7 (reduced winter opening hours).

Drinking in style at one of the city's pavement cafes

Women travelers
Quite a lot of useful information for women traveling alone can be gleaned from the advertisements in the monthly magazine *Spare Rib*, where you can, for example, find details of accommodation in London and the activities of local women's groups. There are two organizations providing 24-hour advice, counseling and support in the event of an emergency:
Women's Aid (tel. 071 251 6537); and
London Rape Crisis Centre (tel. 071 837 1600).

HOTELS AND RESTAURANTS

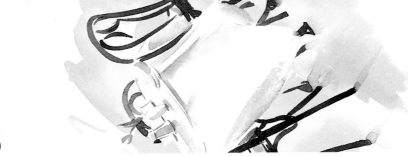

ACCOMMODATION

The following recommended hotels have been divided into three price categories:
- budget ($)
- moderate ($$)
- expensive ($$$)

WHITEHALL AND WESTMINSTER

Elizabeth ($) 37 Eccleston Square, SW1 (tel. 071 828 6812). Award-winning small hotel in Victoria overlooking fine private gardens (guests have access to these and the tennis courts). Reserve well in advance.
Windermere ($) 142–4 Warwick Avenue, W2 (tel. 071 834 5163). Another award-winning hotel in the Victoria area that has a great range of rooms and some excellent facilities.

ST. JAMES'S AND THE MALL

Dukes ($$$) 35 St. James's Place, SW1 (tel. 071 491 4840). Edwardian hotel near the exclusive St. James's area, where guests are made to feel like aristocrats.
Goring ($$$) 15 Beeston Place, SW1 (tel. 071 834 8211). Just beside Buckingham Palace and often used to accommodate royal guests, this is a fine hotel, which is full of old-world charm.
Stafford ($$) 16–18 St. James's Place, SW1 (tel. 071 493 0111). Masculine hotel with a club-like atmosphere and a restaurant serving traditional French food to a loyal clientele of regulars.

MAYFAIR AND PICCADILLY

Browns ($$$) Albemarle Street, W1 (tel. 071 493 6020). Distinguished Mayfair hotel founded by Lord Byron's manservant, James Brown, in 1837 and renowned for traditional service, with decor to match.
Claridge's ($$$) Brook Street, W1 (tel. 071 629 8860). This is the hotel where U.S. Presidents, guests of the Queen, monarchs, and public figures from around the world all stay; it's one of the country's most prestigious hotels.
Connaught ($$$) Carlos Place, W1 (tel. 071 499 7070). Renowned for having one of the best restaurants in the country, the hotel is equally distinguished, with rooms splendidly decorated with antiques and oil paintings. Reserve well in advance.
Edward Lear ($) 30 Seymour Street, W1 (tel. 071 402 5401). The former home of the nonsense-verse poet and artist is now a comfy 30-room hotel close to Marble Arch.
Forty-seven Park Street ($$$) 47 Park Street, W1 (tel. 071 491 7282). Le Gavroche, the Roux brothers' famous restaurant, is next door, and Albert Roux personally supervises this hotel's cuisine. All the rooms are suites, with sitting rooms and kitchens as well as elegant bedrooms and marble-lined bathrooms.
Inn on the Park ($$$) Hamilton Place, Park Lane, W1 (tel. 071 499 0888). Tastefully furnished rooms, superb views and one of London's top restaurants.
Le Meridien ($$) Piccadilly, W1 (tel. 071 734 8000). Popular Edwardian hotel run by Air France with top-quality restaurants and within easy walking distance of West End theaters and movie cinemas.
The Ritz ($$$) Piccadilly, W1 (tel. 071 493 8181). A byword for stylish opulence and high living, the Ritz has been comprehensively restored in recent years to the peak of mirrored and gilded splendor. Live cabaret, tea dances, and Palm Court afternoon teas provide ample opportunity for "putting on the Ritz."

CHELSEA AND KNIGHTSBRIDGE

Alexander ($$) 9 Sumner Place, SW7 (tel. 071 581 1591). Home-like hotel with garden, close to the Kensington museums.
Basil Street Hotel ($$) 8 Basil Street, SW3 (tel. 071 581 3311). Old-fashioned charm, not far from Harrods.
Berkeley ($$$) Wilton Place, SW1 (tel. 071 235 6000). Splendid hotel on Hyde Park Corner with a rooftop pool like a Roman bath and elegant period rooms.
Beaufort ($$$) 33 Beaufort Gardens, SW1 (tel. 071 584 52520. Top-class small hotel (28 rooms) with homey personal touches, located on a quiet square near Harrods.
Blakes ($$$) 33 Roland Gardens, SW7 (tel. 071 370 6701). Very fashionable haunt of media, music, and film stars, with glamorous decor; the creation of interior designer and actress Anouska Hempel.
Cadogan Thistle ($$) Sloane Street, SW1 (tel. 071 235 7141). Former home of Edwardian actress Lillie Langtry, and the place where Oscar Wilde was arrested, this is a classically elegant hotel.
Capital ($$$) 22 Basil Street, SW3 (tel. 071 589 5171). Very elegant hotel in the heart of Knightsbridge with award-winning restaurant and tasteful furnishings.
Claverly ($$) 13–14 Beaufort Gardens, SW3 (tel. 071 589 8541). Charm and traditional comfort in a quiet cul-de-sac

near Harrods.

Draycott ($$$) 24–6 Cadogan Gardens, SW3 (tel. 071 730 6466). Fashionably elegant hotel (regulars include Joan Collins) with impeccable service, working fireplaces, and a quiet garden, all a short step from Sloane Square.

Ebury Court ($$) 26 Ebury Street, SW1 (tel. 071 730 8147). Very much a family home rather than a designer creation, this hotel has won awards for its friendly, old-fashioned virtues and traditional English cooking.

Eden House ($) 111 Old Church Street, SW3 (tel. 071 352 3403). Very pleasant town house in a quiet Chelsea back street, with 14 rooms, some of which have private baths.

Five Sumner Place ($) 5 Sumner Place, SW7 (tel. 071 584 7586). Part of a pretty row of townhouses in a fine street in South Kensington, this recently won the British Tourist Authority award for London's best bed-and-breakfast hotel—perhaps because breakfast is served in the flower-filled conservatory.

L'Hôtel ($$) 28 Basil Street, SW3 (tel. 071 589 6286). As the name suggests, there is a French atmosphere to this Knightsbridge hotel that extends from the antique furnishings to the superb wines and food.

Hyde Park ($$$) 66 Knightsbridge, SW1 (tel. 071 235 2000). Palatial public rooms, luxurious decor, and extensive views across leafy Hyde Park are the hall marks of this stately hotel.

Magnolia Hotel ($) 104 Oakley Street, SW3 (tel. 071 352 0187). Good value rooms in a quiet area which is close to Chelsea and Sloane Square.

Number Sixteen ($$) 16 Sumner Place, SW7 (tel. 071 589 5232). Four Regency houses converted into a charming hotel with the atmosphere of a private town house and pretty, well tended gardens.

Stone House ($$) Sydney Street, SW3 (tel. 0435 830553). Stone House is the London "extension" of a well-loved Sussex hotel popular with visitors to the Glyndebourne opera festival. Though set in Chelsea, this hotel has a country-house atmosphere, and the excellent food is all home-produced, even down to the breakfast jams and honey.

Swiss House ($) 17 Old Brompton Road, SW5 (tel. 071 373 2769). Though more English-country-house than Swiss in atmosphere, this hotel in the Gloucester Road area has scarlet geraniums and ivy cascading from its window boxes. Very comfy and popular; reserve well ahead.

Willett ($) 32 Sloane Gardens, SW1 (tel. 071 824 8415). Large, bright rooms close to fashionable Chelsea, offering services such as a theater-booking agency.

KENSINGTON AND HYDE PARK

Abbey Court ($$$) 20 Pembridge Gardens, W2 (tel. 071 221 7518). Gracious Victorian mansion in Notting Hill, furnished with antiques in country-house style.

Abbey House ($) 11 Vicarage Gate, W8 (tel. 071 727 2594). Budget accommodation in desirable Kensington; 15 rooms, no credit cards.

Ann Elizabeth House ($) 30 Colingham Place, SW5 (tel. 071 370 4821). Basic and cheap hostel-type accommodation in Earl's Court.

Boka Hotel ($) 35 Eardley Crescent, SW5 (tel. 071 373 2844). Another basic but cheap hotel in Earl's Court, with discounts for those staying a week or longer.

Coburg ($$) Bayswater Road, W2 (tel. 071 221 2217). Luxuriously furnished Edwardian hotel with good views over Kensington Palace and gardens.

Curzon House ($) 58 Courtfield Gardens, SW5 (tel. 071 373 6745).

Dormitories, single and double rooms, use of kitchen, and weekly rates in the Gloucester Road area.
Garden Court ($) 30 Kensington Gardens Square, W2 (tel. 071 229 2553). Well-established, popular, and excellent-value small hotel on a leafy square in Bayswater.
Holland Park ($) 6 Ladbroke Terrace, W11 (tel. 071 792 0216). Quietly situated hotel with views over an immaculately tended garden and a blend of antique and modern furnishings, not far from Notting Hill.
Parkwood ($) 4 Stanhope Place, W2 (tel. 071 262 9484). This pretty hotel in a quiet street facing onto Hyde Park is popular with families, as the paintings by visiting children, hung in the "artists' gallery," demonstrate.
Portobello ($$) 22 Stanley Gardens, W11 (tel. 071 727 2777). This Notting Hill hotel is eccentrically furnished with Victorian and Edwardian antiques on the theme of travel and is very informal. Rooms range from tiny cabins to vast suites, priced accordingly.
Rushmore ($) 11 Trebovir Road, SW5 (tel. 071 370 6505). Arguably the best small hotel in Earl's Court, this is an interior designer's hotel par excellence, with *trompe l'œil* paintings on the walls, shutters and paneling, and themed rooms (blue awnings in the Ocean Room, rattan chairs in the Indonesian Room).
Vicarage ($) 10 Vicarage Gate, W8 (tel. 071 292 4030). A small hotel in the pretty Church Street area of High Street Kensington. Lives up to its name, having the solid, old-fashioned atmosphere of a rural vicarage.

MARYLEBONE AND REGENT'S PARK

Dorset Square Hotel ($$) 39–40 Dorset Square, NW1 (tel. 071 723 7874). Fine Regency house on a square where the MCC (Marylebone Cricket Club) once played, hence the cricketing allusions in the decor. Comfortable and very tastefully furnished.
Durrant's ($$) George Street, W1 (tel. 071 935 8131). Comfortable, family-run hotel just north of the shops of Oxford Street.
Gresham ($) 116 Sussex Gardens, W2 (tel. 071 402 2920). One of the best hotels in the Paddington area, with rooms far more luxurious than you normally get in this price category and friendly, efficient service.
Montcalm ($$) Great Cumberland Place, W1 (tel. 071 402 4288). Fine Georgian house restored with all modern conveniences. Beautifully maintained.

BLOOMSBURY AND FITZROVIA

Academy ($$) 17–21 Gower Street, WC1 (tel. 071 631 4115). Stylish conversion of Georgian town houses in the heart of Bloomsbury.
Arran House ($) 77–9 Gower Street, WC1 (tel. 071 636 2186). Small but welcoming hotel with a garden (used for barbecues in summer) and thoughtful extras, such as a coin-operated washing machine, microwave oven, and fridge.
Crescent ($) 49–50 Cartwright Gardens, WC1 (tel. 071 387 1515). Comfortable, clean, family-run hotel with access to nearby tennis courts; set in a quiet location in north Bloomsbury.
Garth Hotel ($) 69 Gower Street, WC1 (tel. 071 636 5761). Clean and comfortable rooms overlooking gardens, popular with Japanese students (hence the option of a traditional breakfast of miso soup, rice, and pickles).
George ($) 60 Cartwright Gardens, WC1 (tel. 071 387 6789). Like its neighbors, the Crescent and Harlingford hotels, guests at the George have use of the private gardens and tennis courts. Very cheap and central.
Harlingford Hotel ($) 61–3 Cartwright Gardens, WC1 (tel. 071 387 1551). The best of the hotels in this area of Bloomsbury, very friendly and comfortable, with unusually good furnishings for a hotel so cheap, plus use of nearby tennis courts.
Ibis ($$) 3 Cardington Street, NW1 (tel. 071 388 7777). French chain-hotel offering comfort and reasonable prices in the Euston area, with good facilities for people with disabilities.
Morgan ($) 24 Bloomsbury Street, WC1 (tel. 071 636 3735). Popular, friendly hotel with excellent rates for longer-stay guests; close to

the British Museum and Covent Garden.
Ruskin ($) 23–4 Montague Street, W1 (tel. 071 636 7388). Impeccably clean, small hotel next to the British Museum, with a splendid 19th-century mural in the lounge showing peacefully grazing cattle.
Thanet ($) 8 Bedford Place, Russell Square, WC1 (tel. 071 636 2869). A budget hotel, close to the British Museum, that stands out for its clean, fresh decor and for the excellent variety of its breakfast menu.

SOHO AND COVENT GARDEN

Fielding ($) 4 Broad Court, Bow Street, WC2 (tel. 071 836 8305). Very popular small hotel close to all the attractions of Covent Garden and Theaterland. The walls are decorated with theatrical prints, and the friendly staff will help with theater reservations. Reserving well ahead is essential.
Hazlitt's ($$) 6 Frith Street, W1 (tel. 071 434 1771). Once home of William Hazlitt, author and politician, this small Soho hotel retains many 18th-century features, and the rooms are charmingly decorated with antiques. Be sure to reserve well ahead.

HOLBORN AND THE STRAND

Savoy ($$$) The Strand, WC2 (tel. 071 836 4343). Founded by Richard D'Oyly Carte, with the profits from staging Gilbert and Sullivan operettas, the Savoy is a majestic hotel, a contender for the title "best in the world." Rooms overlooking the river, with vast marble tubs and huge shower heads in the bathrooms, are very much in demand.
Strand Palace ($$) 372 Strand, WC2 (tel. 071 836 8080). Across the street from the Savoy, the Strand Palace is vast (800 rooms) but efficient and offers relatively inexpensive rooms. Very convenient for Theaterland and Covent Garden.

CLERKENWELL, ISLINGTON, AND THE EAST END

New Barbican ($$) Central Street, EC1 (tel. 071 251 1565). Well situated for the Barbican arts complex and the City, this is a large and modern hotel with friendly and helpful staff.

DOCKLANDS

Tower Thistle ($$) St Katharine's Way, E1 (tel. 071 481 2575). Modern hotel enjoying spectacular views of the Tower of London, Tower Bridge, and St. Katharine Dock. Very convenient for the City.

OUTSIDE THE CENTER

Fifty-two Mount Park Road ($$) 52 Mount Park Road, W5 (tel. 071 997 2243). A little out of the way (in the west London suburb of Ealing), but the superb home cooking makes up for this, guests are treated like old family friends. Advisable to reserve well ahead.
Sandringham ($) 3 Holford Road, NW3 (tel. 071 435 1569). Small and friendly hotel with garden and all of rolling Hampstead Heath on the doorstep for early-morning walks or jogging.

YMCAs and YHAs

YMCA ($) National Council for YMCAs, 640 Forest Road, E17 (tel. 071 520 5599). You can write to the above address for details of all 18 YMCA hotels in London; they are extremely good value, and it is vital to reserve at least two months ahead. One of the best is the Barbican YMCA, 2 Fann Street, a purpose-built hotel with good sports facilities.
Youth Hostels (YHA) ($) 8 St Stephen's Hill, St Albans, Herts, AL1 2DY (tel. 0727 855215). Write to the above address for details of the seven youth hostels in London and reserve at least three months ahead for summer. The City of London Youth Hostel is excellent, located near St. Paul's, while the Holland Park Hostel is converted from the remains of a Jacobean mansion, set in gardens. The other hostels are at Oxford Street, Earls Court, Highgate, Hampstead, and Rotherhithe, the latter very new and purpose-built.

RESTAURANTS

The following recommended restaurants have been divided into three price categories:

- budget ($)
- moderate ($$)
- expensive ($$$)

See pages 88–9 for additional restaurant selections.

African

Calabash ($) The African Centre, 38 King Street (tel. 071 836 1976). Relaxed basement-restaurant just off the Covent Garden plaza, featuring dishes from all over Africa, explained by the helpful menu; washed down by Nigerian beer or wine from Zimbabwe.
Cottons Rhum Restaurant ($$) 55 Chalk Farm Road (tel. 071 482 1096). Caribbean restaurant with a sunny atmosphere, serving excellent fish dishes and delicious desserts. The reggae music can be very loud.

The Americas

Break for the Border ($) 8 Argyll Street (tel. 071 734 5776) and 5 Goslett Yard (tel. 071 437 8595). TexMex and Cajun food, huge burgers plus vegetarian dishes and Mexican beer. The music and the partying crowds make for a noisy atmosphere.
Café Pacifico ($) 5 Langley Street (tel. 071 379 7728). London's best Mexican restaurant, located in a cavernous Covent Garden warehouse. Superb range of beers and cocktails.
Ed's Easy Diner ($) 12 Moor Street (tel. 071 439 1955). More a place for a quick snack than a relaxed meal: authentic hot dogs, burgers, shakes, and fries and the sounds of the '50s and '60s.
Joe Allen ($$) 13 Exeter Street (tel. 071 836 0651). The Covent Garden haunt of journalists, publishers, and theatergoers, Joe Allen serves chic food (like salad of goat cheese with sun-dried tomatoes or lamb on wilted spinach) and is particularly renowned for its Bloody Marys.
Rock Island Diner ($) Plaza Centre, London Pavilion, Piccadilly (tel. 071 287 5500). Children love this place and get their own special menu. Good-value burgers, wets (fries in gravy), ribs, steaks, barbecue chicken, and the waitresses dance.
Smollensky's Balloon ($$) 1 Dover Street (tel. 071 491 1199). Another fun place for children, with Punch and Judy shows and magicians on Saturday and Sunday afternoons, non-alcoholic Kids' Koktails and filling food, from pasta to steaks.

British

The English House ($$$) 3 Milner Street (tel. 071 584 3002). Imaginative dishes based on game and seafood, served with flair in a pretty Chelsea town house. Reasonably priced set menu and good wines.
Fortnum and Mason ($$) 181 Piccadilly (tel. 071 734 8040). The renowned top people's department store has three restaurants serving everything from snacks (Welsh rarebit) to filling steak-and-kidney pie and top-quality roast beef. An excellent place to sample that British institution, the high tea (a massive meal of sandwiches, scones, and elaborate cakes).
Hotel Russell Carvery ($$) Russell Square (tel. 071 837 6470). Set lunches and dinners featuring a huge range of *hors d'œuvres* followed by roast beef, lamb, pork, turkey, or chicken. Sample the kind of food the English traditionally eat on Sundays, complete with all the trimmings, in a splendid Victorian dining room.
Tate Gallery ($$) Millbank (tel. 071 834 6754). Reservations essential, lunch only. Combine a visit to London's best modern art gallery with lunch in a restaurant renowned for selling top-quality wines at very reasonable prices. The food, such as poached salmon or beef in Madeira sauce, is simple but good.
Tiddy Dol's ($$) 55 Shepherd Market (tel. 071 499 2357).

This Mayfair restaurant set in a rambling 18th-century house caters unashamedly to tourists and does it very well: Wandering minstrels singing folk songs entertain, and the food—traditional English casseroles, pies, and roast meats—is excellent.
Veronica's ($$) 3 Hereford Road (tel. 071 229 5079). This Bayswater restaurant is worth seeking out for historically researched English food (the menu will explain what goes into delicious dishes such as salmagundy and watersouchy) plus a very good choice of British cheese and wines.
Wilson's ($$) 236 Blythe Road (tel. 071 603 7267). Despite an out-of-the-way location (in Shepherd's Bush), food lovers flock here (reservations essential) for consistently high quality food with a Scottish bias (try Athelbrose for dessert if it is included on the menu).
Wiltons ($$$) 55 Jermyn Street (tel. 071 629 9955). Very formal and sophisticated , with M.P.s, aristocrats, and royalty among the regular clients. Renowned for its outstanding fish dishes and traditional desserts, such as summer pudding.

Eclectic

Clarke's ($$) 124 Kensington Church Street (tel. 071 221 9225). Simple set menus (vegetarian dishes only by advance arrangement) that set gourmets alight—usually based around charcoal-grilled meat or fish and served with delicious homemade breads (which are also sold in the shop next door).

Le Caprice ($$) Arlington House, Arlington Street (tel. 071 629 2239). Reservations essential at this very chic restaurant favored by celebrities, where dishes range from traditional Lancashire hotpot to more exotic dishes such as bang bang chicken.

Ivy ($$) 1 West Street (tel. 071 836 4751). Very much a place to be seen, with stylish '30s decor and the work of well-known contemporary British artists on the walls. Popular dishes are eggs benedict and the Ivy mixed grill.

Kensington Place ($$) 201–5 Kensington Church Street (tel. 071 938 2458). Lively, young, and fashionable restaurant serving adventurous combinations (fish dishes are usually excellent). The place to be seen (and overheard—the tables are placed awfully close together.)

Langan's Brasserie ($$) Stratton House, Stratton Street (tel. 071 493 6437). Reservations essential. The notoriously drunk and abusive founder of Langan's Brasserie has passed on to another world, but the glitterati still flock here for live jazz in the bar and reliable food, from the famous bangers-and-mash to more delicate seafood dishes.

Leith's ($$$) 92 Kensington Park Road (tel. 071 229 4481). Pru Leith, famous for her cooking school, puts her principles into practice at this Notting Hill restaurant. Expect complicated and very rich concoctions and a wealthy, middle-aged clientele.

Noughts 'n' Crosses ($$) 77 The Grove (tel. 081 840 7568). Another gourmet temple, whose out-of-the-way location (near Ealing Broadway) is no barrier to success. The Hong Kong-born chef produces truly original dishes by combining the grand culinary traditions and the ingredients of Asia and France.

European/Middle Eastern

Adam's Café ($) 77 Askew Road (tel. 081 743 0572). Award-winning Tunisian restaurant in Shepherd's Bush, specialising in couscous served with tender grilled meats and chunky vegetable stew. Extremely good value.

L'Artiste Assoiffé ($$) 122 Kensington Park Road (tel. 071 727 4714). The name means "thirsty artist," and this highly entertaining restaurant, which is decorated with bric-à-brac from the nearby Portobello Road market, serves authentic and robust provincial French food.

Bertorelli's ($$) 44A Floral Street (tel. 071 836 1868). Bertorelli's is an institution, one of London's oldest and best Italian restaurants—the recent move from Soho to new Covent Garden premises has not made the slightest difference in its grand but friendly atmosphere or to the excellent quality of the food.

Bortsch 'n' Tears ($) 46 Beauchamp Place (tel. 071 584 9911). Hearty, noisy restaurant where you can fill up on Russian dishes—bortsch, of course, plus chicken Kiev or beef stroganoff—plus a wide range of different vodkas. Vegetarian dishes only by arrangement.

Boulestin ($$) 1A Henrietta Street (tel. 071 836 7061). Founded in 1925 by Michel Boulestin, the celebrated chef, this restaurant is still going strong and sticks faithfully to the classical French dishes of the master; equally renowned for the vast range of wines available.

Café des Amis du Vin ($) 11–14 Hanover Place (tel. 071 379 3444). Busy Covent Garden bistro, popular with theater- and operagoers, where you can have anything from a generous plateful of French cheese with bread, to French provincial classics such as casserole of Toulouse sausage and haricots.

Le Café du Marché ($$) 22 Charterhouse Square (tel. 071 608 1609). Reservations are essential at this restaurant on the fringes of the City in a converted warehouse. Expect an adventurous range of dishes on the daily set menu.

Café Grec ($) 18 Charlotte Street (tel. 071 436 7411). Charlotte Street is packed with Greek restaurants—this one is slightly more expensive but the food is more varied, while the decor and service are more sophisticated. Try the popular and reasonably priced *mezedes* for a real feast.

Café Italien ($) 19–23 Charlotte Street (tel. 071 636 4174). A great place for people watchers, who can eat outdoors on the sidewalk in warm weather. Excellent, authentic Italian dishes—such as grilled vegetables marinated in oil or pasta with hare stew.

Costa Dorada ($$) 47–55 Hanway Street (tel. 071 636 7139). The appeal of this Spanish restaurant is as much the live entertainment (flamenco shows twice a night) as the food. It is also popular with large groups so come here for a boisterous atmosphere (see Don Pepe below for a quieter alternative).

Don Pepe ($$) 99 Frampton Street (tel. 071 262 3834). This is the restaurant that members of the London Spanish community patronize. It offers the choice of a *tapas* bar (30 different dishes a night) or a formal restaurant specializing in rustic Galician dishes.

Elysée ($$) 13 Percy Street (tel. 071 636 4804). Despite the French name, this is a Greek restaurant, offering outdoor seating and an evening of live music, belly dancing, and plate smashing to accompany the grilled kebabs.

L'Escargot ($$) 48 Greek Street (tel. 071 437 2679). This recently revamped Soho institution features in a number of novels and counts well-known writers among its clientele. Classic French food (though the snails come from Surrey) and the choice of a lively brasserie downstairs or a formal restaurant above.

La Famiglia ($$) 5–7 Langton Street (tel. 071 351 0761). Boisterous Chelsea restaurant that specializes in hearty Tuscan dishes, such as *crostini, fagioli,* and wild boar.

Gavvers ($$) 61–3 Lower Sloane Street (tel. 071 730 5983). Those who cannot afford Le Gavroche, the Roux brothers' Mayfair restaurant (see page 88), can sample their style of cooking at this Chelsea restaurant staffed by Roux-trained chefs. Two set menus an evening and two at lunch. Reservations essential.

Maroush II ($$) 38 Beauchamp Place (tel. 071 581 5434). Very popular with Middle Eastern visitors, serving good Lebanese food. Other branches at 21 Edgware Road (tel. 071 723 0773) and 61 Seymour Street (tel. 071 724 5024).

Mulligans ($$) 13–14 Cork Street (tel. 071 409 1370). Mulligans is decorated like a Dublin bar (all brown walls

and woodwork), and the food is based on Irish home-cooking raised to gourmet standards. If the prices in the restaurant seem a bit high, try the upstairs bar with its cheaper menu.

Neal Street Restaurant ($$$) 26 Neal Street (tel. 071 836 8368). This temple dedicated to the finest Italian foods, with decor by David Hockney, attracts the seriously wealthy and those who share the owner's passion for mushrooms (which feature prominently on the menu and which are sought out from all over England). Fans of *grappa* will also have loads of choices.

Osteria Antica Bologna ($$) 23 Northcote Road (tel. 071 978 4771). This new-wave Italian restaurant in Clapham proved amazingly successful when it opened because of the huge range of novel dishes served at honest prices. Those who think it one of the best restaurants in London are also hoping that it will not be ruined by popularity.

Orso ($$) 27 Wellington Street (tel. 071 240 5269). If you do not fancy the trek to Clapham for the Osteria Antica Bologna (see above), try Orso instead, conveniently located in Covent Garden and popular (noisily so) for its modern Italian food.

Fish and Seafood

Green's Champagne and Oyster Bar and Restaurant ($) 36 Duke Street, St James's (tel. 071 930 4566). A stylish arrangement of eating and drinking areas (plus a famous oyster bar) where the fish and seafood dishes are always excellently prepared and are served in typically unfussy British fashion.

Lobster Pot ($$) 3 Kennington Lane (tel. 071 582 5556). One of the few Breton fish restaurants in England, specializing in *soupe des poissons, plateau des fruits de mers,* or *lobster à l'Armoricaine.*

Sweetings ($$) 39 Queen Victoria Street (tel. 071 248 3062). This City institution has been in business for more than 150 years, and it has a decidedly Edwardian atmosphere, with portly gents eating huge plates of excellently cooked and very fresh fish, followed by generous helpings of steamed puddings.

Indian

Bombay Brasserie ($$) Courtfield Close, Courtfield Road (tel. 071 370 4040). This restaurant in a palm-filled conservatory elevates Indian food to the heights of *haute cuisine.*

Chutney Mary ($$) 535 King's Road (tel. 071 351 3113). Imaginative cooking that draws on Anglo-Indian cuisine (salmon kedgeree, spicy crab cakes, and salads, for example) as well as more conventional Indian dishes.

India Club ($) 143 Strand (tel. 071 836 0650). The food here is very cheap and truly authentic, as you would expect from one of London's oldest Indian restaurants, which opened in 1950 to cater to the staff of the nearby Indian High Commission. Bring your own drinks (there is no corkage charge), and do not be deterred by the very basic decor.

Lahore Kebab House ($) 2 Umberston Street (tel. 071 481 9737). This is another very cheap place to eat with a frenetic atmosphere, brusque service, and no-frills decor, but the quality and authenticity of the food is outstanding.

Rani ($) 7 Long Lane (tel. 081 349 4386). This Finchley restaurant has won awards and high praise because everything is homemade (including the pickles and desserts), and because the vegetarian menu contains so many unusual dishes (all well explained). A connoisseurs' curry restaurant and very good value.
Star of India ($$) 154 Old Brompton Road (tel. 071 373 2901). A new-wave Indian restaurant with theatrical decor and live piano music most nights as the accompaniment to fresh appetizing dishes.

Jewish

Blooms ($$) 90 Whitechapel High Street (tel. 071 247 6001). A world-famous institution, renowned for the wit of the waiters as well as its huge portions of none-too-sophisticated dishes. There is not much for vegetarians.
Grahame's Seafare ($$) 38 Poland Street (tel. 071 437 3788). A comfy restaurant specializing in fish served in very generous portions: gefilte fish, smoked salmon, plaice mornay, and sole meunière are among the specialities.

Oriental

Ajimura ($) 51–3 Shelton Street (tel. 071 379 0626). Purists say this restaurant is far too westernized, but the customers return because, in comparison with other Japanese restaurants, the set-price meals are very good value.
Bahn Thai ($$) 21A Frith Street (tel. 071 437 8504). The first Thai restaurant to open in London still serves dishes you cannot get elsewhere, using authentic ingredients. The menu is very well explained, and if you have ever wanted to know what durian tastes like but have never dared try, go for the durian ice cream for dessert.
Chiang Mai ($$) 48 Frith Street (tel. 071 437 7444). Another long-established Thai restaurant, specializing in the food of the country's northern hill tribes—vegetarian dishes are especially good here.
Chueng Cheng Ku ($) 17 Wardour Street (tel. 071 437 1398). Authentic Cantonese and Shanghainese food and outstanding *dim sum* (served until 6p.m.).
Fung Shing ($$) 15 Lisle Street (tel. 071 437 1539). Elegant restaurant, highly regarded by local Chinatown residents.
Hong Kong ($) 6–7 Lisle Street (tel. 071 287 0324). Another restaurant popular with the local Chinese—the place to go for such authentic dishes as soft-shelled, crab, Chiu Chow duck, or surprisingly meat-like dishes made entirely of bean curd, vegetables, and soya.
Mekong ($) 46 Churton Street (tel. 071 834 6896). Despite the large number of Vietnamese living in Britain, London unfortunately has very few restaurants serving genuine Vietnamese food. This is one: The spring rolls are the real thing, and, if it is on the menu, you should go for the excellent beef soup.
Memories of China ($$) 67–9 Ebury Street (tel. 071 730 7734). The owner of this restaurant is the food writer and broadcaster Kenneth Lo, who was one of the first to make gourmet-quality Chinese cooking up-market when most people in Britain still associated it with cheap take-out joints. It still sets high standards, even if many Chinatown restaurants can now claim to be as good.
Now and Zen ($$) 4A Upper St. Martin's Lane (tel. 071 497 0376). The flagship restaurant of a chain specializing in food from all parts of southeast Asia—for a real feast, go for the evening set menu, which allows you to sample up to 50 different dishes.
Shilla ($$) 58–9 Great Marlborough Street (tel. 071 434 1650). One of the best Korean restaurants in London, popular with visiting businessmen who can-

not live without a fix of *kim chi* (here they serve it very spicy indeed).
Suntory ($$$) 72–3 St. James's Street (tel. 071 409 0201). This Japanese restaurant is one of only a small number of restaurants in Britain to have been awarded a prestigious Michelin star. In view of this you would expect the prices to be steep, but the quality is worth it (and the set lunch is not that expensive).

Vegetarian

All the restaurants listed in this directory have vegetarian dishes on the menu unless otherwise stated.

Mildred's ($) 58 Greek Street (tel. 071 494 1634). An imaginative range of dishes from all cuisines of the world, including fish dishes and several choices suitable for vegans. Bring your own bottle.
Neal's Yard Dining Room ($) First Floor, 14 Neal's Yard (tel. 071 379 0298). Another restaurant serving the best of the world's vegetarian cuisine (Mexican plates, Indian thalis, Egyptian pitas, and Turkish mezedes, for example). Communal tables. Bring your own bottle.
The Place Below ($) St. Mary-le-Bow, Cheapside (tel. 071 329 0789). Set in the crypt of Wren's church (whose tower houses the "great bells of Bow"), this outstanding restaurant produces vegetarian dishes of the highest standard—everthing is homemade and of superb quality. Bring your own bottle.

Index

287

INDEX

Picture credits

ALLSPORT (UK) LTD 206 London Marathon (S Bruty), 206–7 Lord's Cricket Ground (A Murrell), 207 Ball girl Wimbledon (B Martin). BANQUETING HOUSE 46 Int Banqueting House. BRITISH LIBRARY 133 Int British Library. BRITISH MUSEUM 131 Gold Alloy Torc, 132 Exhibit. COURTAULD INST. GALLERIES 156 Manet's *A Bar at the Folies-Bergère*. CROWN COPYRIGHT, HISTORIC ROYAL PALACES 197 Beefeater, 222 Henry VIII's Armour, 223 Great Hall Hampton Court. HARRODS LTD 87 Harrod's Food Hall. HULTON DEUTSCH COLLECTION LTD 38 Wearing Smog Masks, 38–9, 39 Festival of Britain. ILLUSTRATED LONDON NEWS 34 Queen Victoria, 87 Harrods Advertisment. IMPERIAL WAR MUSEUM 36–7 Aerial view of London, © JEWISH MUSEUM LONDON 135 Chanukah Lamp. KENSINGTON PALACE 112 Court Dress Collection. LONDON DUNGEONS 194 The London Dungeon. MADAME TUSSAUD'S 120 Chamber of Horrors. MAGNUM PHOTOS LTD 37 London at War (G Rodger). MARY EVANS PICTURE LIBRARY 69 Athenaeum Club. MUSEUM OF LONDON 24a Carving. NATIONAL GALLERY 51 Van Eyck's *Giovanni Arnolfini and his Wife*. NATIONAL TRUST 90 Carlyle's House. ORDE ELIASON/LINK PHOTOGRAPHY 108 Doll, Commonwealth Inst. PERFORMING ARTS LIBRARY 180–1 Ballet. PLANETARIUM 121 Planetarium. RADIO TIMES 1950's *Radio Times*. REX REATURES LTD 15 Queen Elizabeth II,16 Beatles, Punk,17 Mary Quant. JOHN ROGERS (COURTESY OF THE ROYAL BOROUGH OF KENSINGTON & CHELSEA 109 Leighton House. ROYAL GEOGRAPHICAL SOCIETY 22–3 Old Map, London. SCIENCE MUSEUM 100 Flight, 101 Exploring Space. SHAKESPEARE'S GLOBE 204 Globe Museum. SPECTRUM COLOUR LIBRARY Cover Big Ben, 12–13 Traffic, 74 Tessiers, 91 Chelsea Physic Garden, 93 Chelsea Flower Show, 156–7 Somerset House. TATE GALLERY 57 Mark Gertler 'Merry-go-round'. THE MANSELL COLLECTION LTD 25 Boudicca, 27 Chaucer, 28–9 16C Plan of London, 28 London Tower in Tudor times, 29 Henry VIII, 30 Plague, 32 Christopher Wren, 34–5 Great Exhibition. THE THEATRE MUSEUM 147 *Wind in the Willows*, 'Props' department. VICTORIA & ALBERT MUSEUM 104 Italian Cast Court, 105 'Acanthus' Wallpaper, 178–9 Engine, Carriage & Tank in Bethnal Green Museum of Childhood. WALLACE COLLECTION 126 Sèvres Tea Service, 127 *The Laughing Cavalier,* 224–5 Kenwood House. ZEFA PICTURE LIBRARY (UK) LTD Spine Beefeater, 3 Aerial view of London, 235 Rugby.
All remaining pictures are held in the AA's own photo library (AA PHOTO LIBRARY) with contributions from:
P BAKER 6,168a, 196. M BIRKITT 209, 211. P ENTICKNAP 18–19, 19. D FORSS 223a. R MORT 9, 12, 26b, 35, 72, 97,1 16, 136c, 137, 146, 162–3, 164, 165, 166, 171, 175, 176, 183a, b, 213, 216a, b, 240a, b, 241a, b, 242a, b, 247, 249, 254, 265b, 268, 272a, b, 275, 276, 278, 279. S & O MATHEWS 21a, 210, 219. B SMITH 34a, 64, 66, 78, 84, 96b, 143a, 144b, 182–3, 200b, 201, 217, 226, 227, 229a, 245a, 255, 263, 267, 269b, 270, 277. R STRANGE 4a, b, 5a, b, 7b, 10–11, 10, 11, 13, 21b, 22, 30–1, 31, 40–1, 40, 48, 49, 52, 53, 55a, 59, 60, 70, 74–5, 76–7, 76a, b, 77, 78–9, 79, 80–1, 80, 81a, b, 82, 83, 85, 86a, b, 88a, b, 89, 92, 93a, 95a, b, 98, 98–9, 102–3, 102, 104, 106, 107, 110–11, 111, 112–13, 113, 114, 115a, b, 117, 118a, b, 119b, 122a, b, 123, 124c, 125a, b, 126a, 128, 129, 130–1, 134a, b, 136a, b, 138, 139, 140, 148–9, 152–3, 155b, 158, 159a, 160, 162, 168b, 169, 172, 173b, 178a, 181, 184, 185, 186, 187, 191, 198, 224a, 225, 231a, b, 235b, 236, 236–7, 237, 238a, b, 239b, 244a, 245b, 246a, b, 250, 251, 252, 253, 256a, b, 259a, b, 261, 262, 265a, 266, 271, 274. M TRELAWNY 47, 63, 68–9, 130, 155a, 159b, 170a, 190, 195a, 202, 212, 228a, b, 232, 233, 269b. R VICTOR 18, 170b, 174–5, 195b, 218b, 243b, 248, 280. W VOYSEY 20–1, 45, 54, 66–7, 67, 124b, 142–3, 142, 143b, 144–5, 145, 180b, 188, 192, 192–3, 193, 197a, 203c, 205a, b, 238b. T WILES 7a, 14–15, 14, 65, 273. P WILSON 50–1, 56, 96a, 150, 151, 174, 200a, 203a, b, 264. T WOODCOCK 20, 24b, 26a, 33, 55b, 71, 124a, 166, 208, 214, 216a.

Contributors

Series advisor: Ingrid Morgan **Designer:** Design Directions Ltd
Joint series editor: Susi Bailey **Indexer:** Marie Lorimer
Copy editor: Nia Williams **Verifier:** Paul Murphy